"AT THE BARRICADES"

"AT THE BARRICADES"

 A MEMOIR

A. Alan Borovoy

"At the Barricades": A Memoir
© Irwin Law Inc., 2013 ·

Published in 2013 by

Irwin Law Inc.
Suite 206
14 Duncan Street
Toronto, ON
M5H 3G8

www.irwinlaw.com

ISBN: 978-1-55221-337-7
E-BOOK ISBN: 978-1-55221-338-4

Cataloguing in Publication available from Library and Archives Canada

The publisher acknowledges the financial support of the Government of Canada through the Canada Book Fund for its publishing activities.

We acknowledge the assistance of the OMDC Book Fund, an initiative of the Ontario Media Development Corporation.

Printed and bound in Canada.
1 2 3 4 5   17 16 15 14 13

To the memory of my dear childhood friend Louis Goldstein,
whose courage impressed me then and inspires me now.

Contents

Preface

On July 1 2009, after more than forty-one years, I retired from my position at the helm of the Canadian Civil Liberties Association (CCLA). In October of the same year, I received an honorary doctorate from the University of Waterloo. From the time that my retirement was announced (a few months before it actually occurred) until and even beyond the Waterloo doctorate, I was questioned many times, by the press and public, on the same subject: To what extent, if any, has Canada improved on its record of human rights and civil liberties? Having done so many interviews by the time the doctorate rolled around, I decided to make this subject the theme of my convocation speech.

While acknowledging periodic fluctuations (every few years and every few months) in the country's human rights performance, I concluded early on that the overall *trajectory* was in the direction of improvement. Consider this example: a few years ago, a friend of mine doing research at Queen's University came upon a revealing document—the minutes of the Queen's Senate for October 29 1943. Under the heading "Statistics on Jewish Registration," the document read as follows:

> At Toronto University . . . the percentage [of Jewish students] has been 6% but in medicine 25–30% on occasion. The University is much concerned about the situation in medicine. . . . At McGill University . . . Jewish students in Arts . . . are admitted only on an academic standing of 75% or

over; other students are admitted on standing of 60% or over. This regulation is publicly known and seems to operate without any friction.

I read this excerpt aloud at the Waterloo convocation. The audience reacted in stunned silence. The theme of those minutes appeared to emanate from a planet light years away. In the short span of history since that Queen's meeting occurred, the changes in our society have been nothing less than monumental.

Shortly before those minutes were written, a graduate of the Harvard Law School with a brilliant scholastic record returned to Toronto and found himself unable to obtain a job with a Toronto law firm. That graduate was Jewish. However, by the mid-1970s, that hapless Jewish graduate had become the chief justice of Canada: Bora Laskin.

At the end of the 1930s, a boatload of Jews fleeing the horrors of Hitler's Nazism was unceremoniously denied admission to Canada. The incident failed to provoke anything resembling a significant controversy. In the 1970s, boatloads of Vietnamese fleeing the horrors of Asian Communism were not only admitted to Canada but, in many cases, also subsidized to do so.

In the 1940s, racial, religious, and ethnic discrimination were both legally permissible and socially respectable. Today, such discrimination has become unlawful in the marketplace and disreputable in many social situations. Indeed, in today's Canada, there are anti-discrimination laws in virtually every jurisdiction and human rights commissions with full-time staff to enforce those laws.

In the 1940s as well, this country inflicted both capital and corporal punishment on certain convicted felons. Today, such punishment has been effectively abolished. Until as late as the 1980s, civilian complaints against the police were handled mostly by the police themselves. Today, a growing number of jurisdictions have involved more civilians in this process. Today, there are laws in virtually every Canadian jurisdiction protecting the personal privacy of citizen information and ensuring public access to government information. Such laws were largely absent in yesterday's Canada.

Another feature of yesteryear was the shortage of protective safeguards for people under arrest. There was little or no subsidized legal aid, and if the police failed to provide access to a lawyer, they were often able, nevertheless, to make use of any incriminating statements that were made. Today, the non-observance of such safeguards is more likely to preclude the admission into court of any evidence obtained in those circumstances. By now the national security activities of government have been subjected to an array of restraints and controls. The *War Measures Act* has been replaced with much narrower legislation and Canada has entrenched in its Constitution a *Charter of Rights and Freedoms*.

In my convocation speech I was careful to point out that I was not remotely suggesting that matters in our society were close to Utopian or even satisfactory. My purpose was to impress upon these graduates that it was possible to fight the many injustices that we continue to face.

However, in the course of reflecting on all these changes, I experienced an epiphany: I had not simply been a witness to these developments. On a number of occasions, I was also a participant. Either an organization with which I was affiliated or I personally had had an actual hand in helping to bring about these social reforms. It was at this stage that the idea of writing a memoir took a firm hold of me. The result of these ruminations is the ensuing book.

That epiphany did not initiate the idea of my writing a memoir. It reinforced an idea that was being urged upon me by friends and colleagues for several months. What follows was put together from a combination of materials in the office, old newspaper clippings, certain additional research, and sheer memory. Indeed, I surprised many colleagues and especially myself with what I was able to recall from my memory. And, as I delved into the past, additional experiences came back to me. I found myself remembering things that had never dawned on me when I began the exercise.

Anyone familiar with the other books I've written might observe that a number of incidents related on these pages have been recounted in earlier works of mine. Despite my discomfort in repeating them, I simply could not omit them from my memoir. They played too important a role in my personal history. Of course, they were used for different purposes in the various contexts where they appeared.

The idea for the title of the memoir came to me from a plaque (see picture in photo insert) presented to me by the Board of Directors of the Canadian Civil Liberties Association (CCLA), on the occasion of my

40th anniversary with the organization. The plaque expressed the organization's gratitude for my four decades "at the barricades." The quotation marks are designed to indicate that the words were not mine. I don't believe the word "barricades" was intended to portray my work as militaristic. Rather, I believe what my colleagues had in mind was the unremitting, interminable nature of the conflicts that have engaged us. Such conflicts rarely get completely resolved. But they often get modified or reformed so that what faces us tomorrow is less bad than what we had to address yesterday. In this sense, I could think of my work with the CCLA and earlier, as having been "at the barricades."

As usual, I have much gratitude to express. I thank the Broadbents (Alan and Judy), the Sheldon Chumir Foundation of Calgary, and my successors at the Canadian Civil Liberties Education Trust for the generous financial assistance they made available. I am particularly grateful to John McCamus, Owen Shime, Ken Swan, Sydney Goldenberg, and Cyril Levitt for reading the entire manuscript and commenting so helpfully on it. My thanks also go to Reverend Dawn Clark, Danielle McLaughlin, Noa Mendelson Aviv, Merrilees Muir, Andrea Baltman, and Myra Merkur for their helpful appraisals of certain sections of the memoir.

I was also the beneficiary of helpful knowledge, materials, and assistance from Eric Goldstein, Ron Biderman, as well as Abby Deshman, Cara Zwibel, Sukanya Pillay, and Dora Chan of the staff at the Canadian Civil Liberties Association (CCLA). I also acknowledge the indispensable assistance of former staff members: Steven McCammon, David Schneiderman, Alan Strader, Glen Bell, Erica Abner, Marie Molliner, Helen Cainer, Catherine Gilbert, and Eleanor Meslin. Moreover, my publisher Jeff Miller, editor Pam Erlichman, and production manager Heather Raven were helpful throughout the process. I was blessed with a cracker-jack researcher in Taryn McKenzie-Mohr. She found materials that I believed were impossible to uncover. I was also impressed with the supplementary research provided by Matt Benedict and Jackie Strandberg. Both Taryn and Matt also did some indispensable typing, as did Ann Lee and Donna Gilmour.

My successor at CCLA, Nathalie Des Rosiers, played a special role. Her hospitality helped a lot to ensure that I had a pleasant atmosphere within which to work. Nathalie also provided valuable advice in specific areas of the law upon which I felt the need to comment.

Last, but certainly not least, was the unremitting help provided by the Canadian Civil Liberties Association. This is a good point at which to express my congratulations to the organization. In 2014 it celebrates its 50th birthday.

Although I received much help from many people, I remained the one who made the decisions. Thus, whatever flak is forthcoming, belongs to me alone.

A. Alan Borovoy
Toronto
September 1, 2013

part one
The Formative Years

CHAPTER ONE

Hamilton, Grace Street, and Harbord Collegiate

I have never practised, studied, or received psychiatric treatment. But my profound lack of expertise does not inhibit me from attempting to explain critical aspects of human behaviour, particularly my own. I have often been asked for an explanation as to what impelled me to lead the kind of life I have and do the kind of work I have. It is possible, of course, that I was dropped on my head when I was a baby, but I have no conscious knowledge of such mishaps. I will draw on my memory, therefore, to come up with the best explanation that I can.

I believe that one of the most enduring influences on my life was the decision of my parents, Rae and Jack Borovoy, to move our little family from Hamilton to Toronto in the summer of 1938 when I was six and a half years old. My father's drugstore in Hamilton had just gone belly-up as a consequence of the Great Depression. Although both of my folks worked long and hard hours in the drugstore, I was growing up in an overprotected cocoon. My mother dressed me as a virtual Little Lord Fauntleroy and, bereft of regular playmates, I played days on end all by myself. To whatever extent I have been described as "imaginative," that faculty had its beginnings and a vigorous workout during my days in Hamilton.

Since my folks were so often busy in the store, I also spent great amounts of time in the company of a teenage babysitter named Gracie. By the time we left Hamilton, Gracie had filled my head with stories and even descriptions of Heaven, Hell, and Purgatory. These images interacted with my developing imagination in such a way that I became imbued with the pervasive presence of an all-knowing God. In later years, it occurred to me that Gracie must have been a Catholic. Paradoxically, her influence likely increased my susceptibility to my parents' efforts to envelop me in Judaism.

At six years old, of course, I was not aware of the financial devastation our family was experiencing. I was a relatively well-behaved, well-dressed, shy, overprotected, lonely, imaginative little boy. In the summer of 1938, my parents took me from this Hamilton sanctuary and we moved into the house owned and occupied by my grandparents on Grace Street in Toronto. The house was also occupied by an aunt and a number of uncles, my mother's siblings. I quickly became the centre of much attention.

The street, however, was another matter. It was working class and, compared to the situation in Hamilton, even somewhat tough. Immediately to the west and north of us were two parks — the Beatrice tennis courts and Bickford Park, respectively. These parks were the hub of much activity: tennis, skating, baseball, football. Less respectable activities also flourished there — mammoth crap games (where hundreds of dollars were won and lost) and, in the bushes, sex. I was soon to see it all. Incredibly, a number of the crap games were actually operated by a big guy in his early twenties; he took a rake-off from every participant, except his partner who also played. How could he get away with it? No one would have dared to set up a crap game in competition with him at that park. Not infrequently, however, those games were the target of police raids.

Although my parents had been wiped out financially, they enjoyed a certain amount of prestige that emanated from my father's status as a professional man. For these purposes, it didn't hurt that, unlike most of our neighbors of their generation, my folks spoke English without a European accent. My mother was born in Canada and my father came here at the age of three.

At the time, I was universally perceived on the street as the Little Lord Fauntleroy that Hamilton and my mother had made of me. It didn't take long for me to realize that, in my then incarnation, I would never make it on Grace Street. One by one, I began to shed the concomitants of my

Fauntleroy presentation. My breeches had to give way to long pants; windbreakers took over from coats; open shirts and sweaters replaced buttoned shirts with ties. My parents would no longer be "Mama and Daddy"; they had to become "Ma and Pa" just as my friends addressed their immigrant parents. In Hamilton, I had been called "Sonny." In Toronto, I insisted that name had to go. When I went anywhere with my elders, I did not want any of them to hold my hand. Indeed, I preferred the company of the gang on the street to that of my elders in the house. I was determined to become a full-fledged Grace Street boy.

Moreover, contrary to my reticent Hamilton behaviour, I became quite scrappy in Toronto. Perhaps by way of compensation for the fact that I was not physically the strongest kid in the group, I was ready to fight at the drop of a hat. During the time of my elementary school years, I got involved in a host of fist fights. Typically, I was the one who threw the first punch. And just as typically, I wound up the loser in most of these physical encounters. But they all stemmed from my adamant refusal to be pushed around in any way. This was one of the ways I hoped to make it on Grace Street.

Whenever I think of my pugilistic orientation of yesteryear, I can hardly believe it. The very idea of engaging in such activity today strikes me as repugnant and completely counter to my nature. I believe that the last fist fight I was in occurred around the age of fourteen. I don't now remember what started it but I do remember that my adversary kicked a lot of mud in my face and that the fight lasted at least a couple of hours. Being absolutely worn out from it, I was relieved when some of the boys made moves to put a stop to it. If they hadn't, I think I would have dropped, not from a blow, but from sheer exhaustion.

Only once about a year later did I come close to a physical fight. In Jackson's Point, Ontario, I was in the middle of a touch football game with a group of my friends. At one point, I missed a pass and the ball (which I happened to own) rolled onto the blanket of a few people who had been picnicking there. I was about fifteen; they were in their mid- to late twenties. I began to walk toward their blanket to retrieve the ball. One of the men seated there picked up the ball and asked whether I wanted it. When I replied in the affirmative, he threw the ball over the fence behind him. This enraged me; my elementary-school instincts returned with a vengeance. I was not going to let that bully get away with what he had done. I began to charge toward their blanket where a little tin of Planters peanuts was positioned in front of my antagonist. My aim was to kick the peanuts in his face.

As I charged toward their blanket, my antagonist started to stand up. Suddenly, I felt a hand on my back, grasping me firmly. It was Harold Nisker, one of my friends who had been playing with us. He was 6'2" and more than 200 pounds. As he restrained me with one hand, he motioned to the man on the blanket with his other hand. He called out, "Sit." The man shrank under this command, and the would-be fracas ended. I have often thought that if my friend had not intervened when he did, I might have had to be carried out on a blotter.

The most significant impact of my youthful scrappiness on my later behaviour was the willingness it created in me to *fight* for what I regarded as important. Although I abandoned physical fisticuffs as I entered adolescence, I retained a somewhat feisty disposition that proved valuable in other situations. As a result of other developments, which I shall try to explain, self-vindication gave way to less egocentric aims. I continued to fight, of course, but, in much different ways, for much different goals.

A no-less important outcome of my transition from Hamilton to Grace Street was my attitude to wealth and its symbols. To me, identification with Grace Street meant sharing in its economic privations. Psychologically and emotionally, I felt increasingly part of the working class, the dominant economic element on the street. That also meant sharing the responses of my neighbours to the rich people who, at the time, lived in the northern regions of the city—as we called it then, "up the hill." This consciousness accelerated my denigration of nice clothes and other elements of material comfort.

Toward the end of elementary school, my aversion to symbols of wealth almost precipitated an emotional upheaval. My parents began to muse about the possibility of our part of the family moving "up the hill." Since Hamilton they had lost a good deal of the privacy that they had once enjoyed. Although they had good relations with my grandparents and the others in the house, they always yearned for a more intimate living arrangement.

But the thought of moving away from Grace Street traumatized me to the core. And this reaction was exacerbated by the idea that I might actually wind up living among—and be identified with—the very rich people against whom I had developed such well-entrenched prejudices. I protested that the people on Grace Street were "my people"; there was no way I could ever harbour similar feelings about the patricians in the north end of the city. Besides, I had heard so much about life at Harbord Collegiate—I just had to attend there.

Fortunately, the idea of moving was short-lived. Talk of it soon stopped and, in fact, I did go to Harbord Collegiate. But I have long suspected that my Grace Street attitudes to the rich and to the workers contributed psychologically to my later need to champion the cause and needs of the disadvantaged.

In many ways the social milieu on Grace Street fuelled my developing orientation. I remember, for example, the mother of one of my friends a few doors away calling out to a butcher who had just delivered a package to her house. Between the time she received the package and he had returned to his car, she learned that his employees were on strike against him. She felt embarrassed to do business with a strike-bound operation, so she shouted out that he was to make no more deliveries to her house during the course of that strike. Such incidents and stories about them occurred with sufficient frequency to make a strong impact on me.

Another factor that must have helped to shape my attitudes was the special relationship I had with one of the boys on the street. Louis Goldstein was probably my oldest friend. When we met and for many years thereafter, he wore a brace on his leg that had resulted from an attack of polio when he was about three years old. A further complication in his life was the fact that he was an orphan who was being raised in a foster home on Grace Street.

For some reason, he began to confide in me at an early age. For long periods of time, therefore, I was seeing the world through his eyes. He keenly felt his differentness. And it hurt.

One aspect of Louis' painful differentness was the school's insistence on calling him by the name with which he had been born rather than that of the family with whom he lived. In view of the way I was identifying with him, I grew up angry at the school authorities. Indeed, during a television interview years later I ventilated my indignation over this treatment. On television, I called the educators of that era, "insensitive bastards." In talking about that period of our lives, I felt myself actually reliving much of the experience.

Louis was, however, no "cry-baby." Indeed, he was quite courageous. When we went to steal apples from a neighbour's tree, it was Louis—with his brace—who climbed the trees and actually took the apples. Despite his brace, he played baseball and learned to ride a bike. In many ways, he exercised leadership in my Grace Street gang. These admirable characteristics enhanced the credibility of whatever he told me. I grew up, therefore, taking it all very seriously.

Certain incidents involving Louis were particularly noteworthy. One of them has stuck in my mind for more than 70 years. We were then in Grade 3; the year was 1940. During a noon hour when we were climbing a fence, Louis developed a tear in the seat of his pants. Even though we went home for lunch, he returned to school for the afternoon, with his pants unmended. I began to suspect that he never told his foster mother what happened. Despite whatever efforts the Goldstein family had made to ensure that Louis felt accepted, he could well have felt too intimidated to ask for help. After all, his self-image at that point was not very strong.

Believe it or not, that very afternoon, the teacher called upon Louis to go to the front of the class and write something on the blackboard. As he was writing, he was holding the seat of his pants in order to conceal the hole as much as possible. Normally, this was the kind of situation that would have provoked derisive laughter from kids like me. On that occasion, however, I did not laugh. Since I was so aware of his alienated feelings, I could not laugh at the embarrassment he was then experiencing.

Notwithstanding these hardships, I did not generally treat Louis with kid gloves—he would not have tolerated it. Neither, of course, did he treat me that way. We were very much boys evolving as street kids. During our elementary schools years, we traded punches on many occasions. The exchange of intimacies coexisted with the normal aspects of our very boyish relationship.

It is simply not possible to witness so closely the impact caused by hardship without being deeply affected by it. Undoubtedly, I was. The plight of my dear friend Louis lodged in my psyche at an early age and would not be disgorged even with the passing of the years. It is not difficult to imagine how that experience contributed to my evolving concerns with social justice.

Another factor of lingering impact in the transition from Hamilton to Toronto was my attitude to mischief-making. In Hamilton I had been a veritable "goody two-shoes." On Grace Street in Toronto I learned and imbibed the joys of getting into trouble. Of course, I'm not talking about guns and drugs. The Grace Street gang specialized in a much less harmful form of mischief. We stole apples from the trees of our neighbours, sneaked into shows, and walked out of restaurants and bowling alleys without paying the bill. I hasten to point out that these activities had no financial motivation. We didn't do such things in order to save money; we did them because they were *fun*. The whole point of the exercise was simply to get away with it.

It may be of interest to know that I never engaged in shoplifting. To me, that represented theft, which I considered immoral. I do not suggest that the distinction was meritorious. At this point, I'm simply describing these activities, not attempting to justify them.

And, in school, we were delighted to make nuisances of ourselves. I remember how proud Louis and I were when our grade 6 teacher lamented aloud on the subject of troublemakers in class: "If it isn't Alan, it's Louis; if it isn't Louis, it's Alan." Louis and I were proud to be linked this way. What survived for me from this juvenile troublemaking was a willingness to defy authority. This may help to explain the delight I acquired in later years from embarrassing those who wield government power.

*T*here is no doubt that a highly sensitizing aspect of my younger years was my experience with anti-Semitism. Significantly, rejection has the capacity to evoke a multitude of responses: resentment, rage, hurt, shame, a desire for revenge, a need for vindication, and feelings of inferiority, to name just a few. At one time or another, I was probably subject to all of the foregoing and more.

Moreover, anti-Semitism has many manifestations, and I experienced a good number of them. Although I was only one year old and living in Hamilton at the time, the infamous 1933 riot at the Christie Pits was still part of the folklore on Grace Street when I grew up there in the 1940s. After all, Grace Street is one long block south of the Christie

Pits. In my day, enough remnants of the Pits gang had survived in order to make trouble for us Jews. From time to time, members of that notorious gang would descend upon our park (Bickford Park immediately south of the Pits) and randomly beat up any Jews they were able to find. Indeed, on a number of occasions, I fled from them myself. Moreover, it was a rare event that any of our gang members strayed into the Christie Pits. We regarded doing so as dangerous.

But the Pits gang had no monopoly on anti-Semitic violence. We encountered that from many quarters. Not infrequently, Jewish kids, myself included, would be accosted by tough-looking characters who would ask whether we were Jewish. Such situations created a dilemma for us. If we acknowledged being Jewish, we could look forward to getting the hell beat out of us. If we denied it, we felt like traitors to our people. At some point, I developed a compromise position: I would admit my ethnicity, as I took off. During those years, I developed a certain fleetness of foot.

But even when we were not being explicitly threatened, we often anticipated the prospect of it. And even when the anti-Semitism was not necessarily associated with the threat of violence, it was often accompanied by expressions of disapproval. These things happened sufficiently often that it became advisable to consider in advance our possible responses. Early on, I became persuaded that if anti-Semitic sentiments were expressed in any social situations where I found myself, I had a moral obligation to say something. It was simply wrong to let the impression be created that anti-Semitism was acceptable. In view of the amount of it that existed in Toronto during the 1940s, it will readily be appreciated what a challenge being Jewish could be.

Another problem faced by Jewish kids arose in the public schools we attended. The teachers had no qualms about including Christian hymns among the pieces we sang in music class and no inhibitions about focusing on the *New Testament* for moral inspiration in the morning. (Toward the end of my elementary school years (1944), the Legislative Assembly of Ontario actually prescribed regular Protestant instruction for all such schools.) One of our coping mechanisms involved a self-imposed taboo on uttering the name of "Jesus" when we sang or recited. On the basis of today's standards we can only marvel at the insensitivity afflicting the professional educators of that era.

An experience later in my life dramatized how all those coerced religious practices affected us Jewish kids. It arose in 1989 at the 100th birthday party for my elementary school, Clinton Street Public School. A few weeks before the event, the president of the home and school association telephoned me and asked whether I would deliver the toast to the school at the banquet. Of course, I immediately said that I would be honoured. She then rejoined that my toast would occur just after the grace. With all the diplomacy I could muster, I explained to her how inappropriate a religious grace would be at an event of this kind. She said she would relay my views to the principal and that ended our discussion.

At the event, the principal preceded his introduction of me by reciting a litany of things for which we are grateful, without ever mentioning to whom or to what we owed that gratitude. Upon taking the microphone, I simply said, "That was the classiest grace I ever heard." The audience broke into enthusiastic applause. Most of those in attendance had gone to the school at around the same time as I did and also had to suffer the indignity of involvement in Christian exercises. The applause spoke volumes about how they felt, as did the fact that those feelings had lingered for more than forty years.

Our ethnic identity also exerted a potential impact on our futures. There were restrictions, for example, on the number of Jews who would be admitted to professional schools, such as medicine. Jewish kids were also advised that, even if they could get into engineering, they should decline to do so because they would be unable to get employment afterwards. Even where summer jobs were concerned, Jewish kids faced such impediments.

On one occasion when I was seeking summer employment around the end of high school, I was confronted with an application form that asked for "religion." Of course, that suggested the likelihood that, upon acknowledging my origins, I would be denied the job I was seeking. I decided, however, to do something about the situation. I went in to see the personnel manager and asked him directly why the company needed to know what my religion was. His reply was that some religions tended to restrict a person's availability at certain times. He said, for example, that some religions tended to discourage working on Saturday. I found myself suggesting to him, that, instead of seeking our religious identity, the company could simply ask more direct questions relating to the candidates' willingness to work at particular times. He said that they would consider my suggestion and I left the premises without ever filling in that part of the application form.

To my surprise, I received a telephone call from the company a couple of days later, inviting me for a second interview. Since I had already secured another job, I declined the invitation. In many ways, I was sorry not to pursue the matter. The best outcome for that incident would have been for me to get the job and perform in it. Nevertheless, I felt that I had scored somewhat of a victory.

One weapon that Jewish kids like us learned to use in connection with anti-Semitism was humour. The ability to laugh at such disabilities—and at ourselves—proved to be a very effective coping mechanism. I remember fondly the comments of a Grace Street chum about one of his attempts to secure summer employment. In response to the question "religion" on the application form, he reportedly wrote, "Formerly a Jew but I need the money."

In later years when my friend, Louis Greenspan, was attempting to provide a medical history during a doctor's appointment, he was asked to name the leading causes of death in his family. He replied, "Hitler and Stalin." In yet another situation, a man we met told us that there was so much anti-Semitism in the neighbourhood where he grew up, it wasn't until he was twenty-one that he realized "Jew-bastard" were two separate words.

Our North American encounters with anti-Semitism, of course, could not be compared to what our fellow ethnics experienced in Europe. Throughout the centuries, the Jewish people of Europe were the victims of regular pogroms. In our era, the Nazis represented a special species of cruelty. Even though most of us on this side of the ocean never had to put up with anything like what was inflicted on our European counterparts, we were nevertheless affected by it. The realization that Jews are the targets of such venomous hatred is bound to provoke deep feelings of anxiety wherever such Jews happen to be. For these and other reasons, we followed eagerly the developments of the Second World War and experienced both relief and joy on that May morning in 1945 when our grade 8 teacher relayed to us the news that the Allies had finally prevailed in Europe.

Elsewhere, I have described the speech that my grandfather made at the reception for my bar mitzvah. It was the late winter of 1945 and the world was just beginning to learn about the magnitude of what the Nazis had done to the Jews. With tears streaming down his face, my grandfather urged upon me a lifelong vigilance for the welfare of the Jewish people.

The experience of anti-Semitism simply cannot be ignored. One way or another, Jewish people worked out responses to it. Some chose to "suck up" to the Gentile establishment. Others developed one species or other of nationalism. The nationalists focused their efforts almost entirely on Jewish-related causes. From the days of my earliest consciousness, I was attracted most to a more universalist response that identified the interests of Jews with those of all people, particularly victimized minority groups.

I'm not quite sure how I began to evolve in this way. Perhaps, at first, it grew out of the moral ideal that, in order to get justice, you must do justice. Perhaps, my experience with marginalization impelled me to identify with those whom life had treated similarly. I know, for example, that I was quite young when my sympathies were aroused for the suffering of the blacks in the Southern United States. At some point, I must have been influenced by a very pragmatic analysis: there were not enough Jews to take on anti-Semitism by themselves. It was clear that we needed allies. We could not expect potential allies to take up the cudgels only for Jews. We were much more likely to attract support by framing our position as one of opposition to all forms of unwarranted discrimination.

Accordingly, I embraced the universalist approach at a very early age. But, at some point I stopped thinking of universalism exclusively as the best way to defend Jews. Although I have always believed that it performs this objective better than any alternatives, I rarely think of it in such parochial terms. As far as I am concerned—and this has been the case for a very long time—I believe in the validity of secular, liberal universalism. I have never pulled my punches, or even considered doing so, just because my adversary may have happened to be Jewish. Jewish employers, proprietors, and landlords got the same treatment from me as did everyone else when they committed acts of unwarranted discrimination.

Despite my growing universalist orientation, I was nevertheless stirred by a nationalist development that occurred in the middle of my high school years—the creation of the state of Israel. Many of us sat glued to our radios when the UN voted on the partition of Palestine. To this day, I cannot watch the film of Israel's proclamation without having my eyes fill with tears. What always gets to me is the meeting at which David Ben-Gurion proclaimed the independence of the new country after two thousand years. The meeting culminated with the singing of the anthem *Hatikvah*. Years later, I was similarly moved when I saw Barack Obama's nomination being seconded by one white delegate after another. Both the creation of Israel and the election of Obama represented the triumph of victims over oppression. For universalists, both were truly causes for celebration.

Youthful experiences have a way of providing psychological support for philosophical convictions. So it was with my growing egalitarian orientation.

At around the age of fifteen or sixteen, my friends and I had organized a baseball league that played in Bickford Park. I was the manager of one of the teams. In that connection, I was approached by a black fellow whom I'd never met; he wanted an opportunity to play in the league, particularly for my team. But I was taken aback when he asked me point blank whether his race would be a problem. I assured him that our interest in him focused exclusively on his ability to play ball; his colour was of no consequence.

For the longest time, however, I was unable to purge this encounter from my psyche. What pain had led this young man to ask me whether his race would matter? What indignities had he suffered because of his colour? I wound up feeling not only bad for him but also mad at our society. Why, I asked myself again and again, should anyone have to endure discrimination because of something so unimportant as the colour of his skin? Although incidents like this deepened my egalitarian proclivities, I should also mention that he turned out to be a damn good ballplayer.

As for gender discrimination, there was always a group of girls close to the Grace Street gang. We played tennis together, and skated together, not to mention spending hours of hanging out and joking together. This experience created an atmosphere of easygoing comfort; it helped to fuel my developing egalitarian philosophy. In my case, my views in this regard were also bolstered by a negative factor. One of my grade 8 teachers could find nothing more imaginative to do on Friday afternoons than to read to us from the rules of etiquette by Emily Post. I used to come home from these classes angry over all the artificial rules that purported to keep the sexes in their place. In addition to reinforcing my evolving egalitarianism, these classes created in me a lifelong contempt for Emily Post.

During my teen years, I even became somewhat friendly with a gay man. Although he was not open about his orientation, it was also not a state secret. He had propositioned—but never assaulted—a number of my friends. I shared an interest with him in politics. And we frequently stood on the street corner arguing over our respective views. Although I would have been disquieted if he had ever invited me to have sex (which, fortunately, he never did), I was fully able and pleased at that tender age to have him as an intellectual companion.

Economic privation was another phenomenon that exerted an influence on me at an early age. I have often described Grace Street as essentially upper working class. But, although people in that category usually do better than those who have less, they nevertheless live in a state of constant insecurity about their future. My own home, while not strictly working class, experienced a similar state of financial insecurity. In some of the neighbourhoods nearby, however, there was much greater privation, indeed pockets of outright poverty. Even if I did not directly experience it, I couldn't help but be influenced by it. During the course of my personal evolution, I developed a need to right the economic wrongs that fate had imposed upon so many families, including my own. Very likely, such considerations propelled much of my politics in a leftward direction.

One of the most pivotal values I acquired during my youth was the need to question the conventional wisdom around me. Somewhere toward the end of elementary school, I developed the notion that no principle or value was so sacrosanct that it couldn't be questioned or even challenged. This value has stayed with me all of my life and has never let go.

How did it happen? Again, my lack of psychiatric involvement precludes a definitive answer to this question. But I do have some ideas.

I credit my parents with much of the attraction I have felt for my questioning disposition. When I was very young my father refused to tell me how he voted in elections. His explanation for this secrecy was that he did not want to exert an undue influence on me; he wanted me to think for myself. Both he and my mother established an atmosphere in our home that I used to describe as a "court of appeal." They were always prepared to listen to a reasonable complaint or argument from me. At times, they even reversed themselves on matters of discipline. And they did it with grace.

In mid–high school, I had a discussion with my folks about my ultimate choice of occupation. While they had some very helpful advice about it, they always insisted that the choice was mine. Although I shared much of their reverence for the Jewish religion during the course of my adolescence, I ultimately broke with it during my university years. Despite their continuing reverence and involvement, they were completely accepting of my heresies. When you are brought up in the way I was, it was not a surprise that I learned to think for myself and engage in the kind of questioning I did.

There were additional influences that strengthened this disposition. At some point during my adolescence, I learned that none of the four uncles (my mother's siblings) with whom we lived had had a bar mitzvah. In view of the fact that my maternal grandfather with whom we also lived was learned in—and reverent about—the Jewish religion, it was indeed surprising that he allowed that to happen. According to my mother, however, none of his sons wanted to have a bar mitzvah and my grandfather would not foist it upon them. In the crunch, he opted to respect their autonomy. Somehow, my grandfather was able to carry all this off. Despite the unique tolerance he practised, he remained a highly respected figure in the organizations and circles he inhabited. In any event, his example was a potent one; I'm sure it influenced my evolving orientation.

One of the maternal uncles with whom we lived also reinforced my propensity to question the conventional wisdom. He was a feminist before the word was coined. For that era, his attitudes were quite non-conformist. He rejected the sexual double standard between men and women and he rejected the then prevalent notion that unmarried men should have sex only with "disreputable" women. Indeed, he even seemed to reject such categories entirely. In later years, he provided more corroboration of his pro-feminist stance: he urged his two daughters to become professionally trained so that they would be truly independent. One became a lawyer and the other a doctor.

One of my grade 8 teachers also contributed to my developing attitudes. He was a great believer in phonetic spelling and, on many occasions, he harangued us students with his denunciations of the accepted English spelling. Despite the fact that I could never get my knickers in such a twist over an issue like spelling, I believe that this man nevertheless captured my imagination. Here was an authority figure criticizing authority. At my young age, he legitimated for me the exercise of questioning authority.

Another factor that reinforces the propensity to question is authority figures who behave with conspicuous foolishness. Unlike the other influences, this was a negative one but I'm sure it contributed. I can actually say that I was blessed in this regard to have two thoroughgoing paragons of idiocy as principals of the schools I attended.

As for the more contentious of my public school principals, one incident (there's no need for more) will suffice. On one occasion during my last few days at the school, I went into his office with my autograph book. Since the book contained so many messages from teachers and fellow students, I thought it would be appropriate to ask the principal for his autograph. When I asked him, he reached into his desk, pulled out a stamping device, and stamped my book with a replica of his signature. Even at the tender age of thirteen, I recognized this act as the behaviour of a monumental ignoramus.

The more contentious of my high school principals was, as they say, a "piece of work." At one point, he promulgated a rule that the male students may not walk on the front sidewalk within the school's perimeter. He announced that he was not about to impose a similar restriction on the female students because they, unlike the boys, did not walk on the grass adjacent to the sidewalk. Imagine how that rule would fly in the era of gender equality!

Another one of his rules provided that students were not allowed to smoke "within sight of the school." We heard that he suspended a student he saw smoking within several blocks from the school. The lesson that this incident conveyed is that students must not smoke anywhere within the *principal's* sight. This principal struck an impressive blow against intellectual freedom when he reportedly prohibited the student debating society from taking up the question of whether there would be a depression within five years. The explanation we got was that such a debate would encourage excessive pessimism among the students.

One of his more ludicrous rules was that there must be no comedy skits or singing at the campaign meetings for the student council. Even more ludicrous, however, was the way he enforced this rule. When one of the candidates began to sing a cute little song she had composed, the principal stood up, interrupted her, and declared that the singing must stop. At that point, numbers of students began to file out of the auditorium in anger over what he had done. His action reverberated throughout the school. The next day, large numbers of students gathered at the drugstore across the road from the school and refused to return even after the bell had rung. All of this produced a one-day strike and a grievance committee of students.

In the face of such authority figures, it was simply impossible for a rational being to avoid questioning authority. As a result of the multiple influences on me in this regard, I began to question almost every accepted truth, doctrine, value, and belief that I encountered. When you question so much, you need some reputable way of assessing your various positions. For me, the ultimate measure became whatever best satisfied the fruits of intelligent inquiry.

So, as I made my way through high school, I was questioning everything: social mores, sexual taboos, school practices, political doctrines, and even religious beliefs (including my own). The more I questioned, the more I believed that rationality must be the basis for what is accepted or rejected. Indeed, I formulated my position in the following terms: my most basic commitment must be to the possibility that I'm wrong. That has always managed to co-exist with an awful lot of conviction that I'm right. Nevertheless, by stating the proposition in this way, I hoped to guarantee that I would always be open to discussion and debate.

One of the great frustrations of my youth was my persistent inability to be a good baseball player. That inability was responsible for a lot of the hurt that I experienced during my elementary and high school years. It was exacerbated by the fact that my parents met when my father was the coach of my mother's softball team. Moreover, most of the Grace Street boys (myself included) were ardent baseball fans.

The only time I remember pulling off a good play, I credited my brains rather than my brawn for the achievement. During one game, I somehow managed to get on base. (For the life of me, I cannot remember how.) When I reached first base, there were less than two out and one of my teammates was on third base. After the pitcher delivered his next pitch, I walked in between first and second base and simply sat down on the field and started to taunt the pitcher. Predictably, he became angry and started to chase me with the ball. As I had anticipated, this distraction opened the way for my teammate on third base to head for home. The pitcher's final throw to home plate was too late to catch the runner from third and he was able to score. My opponents then attempted to nail me and predictably threw the ball over the head of the second baseman, enabling me to get to third base.

Of course, this is not the kind of play that could ever succeed in professional baseball. They're just too quick. Unfortunately, I don't believe I ever replicated that feat. I simply couldn't get to first base frequently enough to pull that off again.

Somewhere in late public school or early high school, I fell in love with football. Unlike the situation with baseball, I played a half-decent game of touch football. But, with my underweight and scrawny physique, it was clear that I would never be a tackle football player. Early on, therefore, I had to renounce my fantasy of becoming the quarterback for the Toronto Argonauts.

Show business, however, was another matter. In mid–high school, I developed a comedy team with two of my buddies. We were good enough to play in some big amateur reviews. Indeed, at one point, the director told my parents that he thought I had real natural talent to be a singing comic. I think that my interest in show business was largely inspired by the movie *The Jolson Story*. And, while I very much enjoyed my show-business activities, a New York nightclub singer who befriended me strongly advised me not even to consider such a career unless I was simply "burning" to do it. Upon confronting my deepest priorities in this way, I came to realize that such ambitions were simply unsustainable for me.

As long as I can remember, I always had an interest in writing. While I was engulfed in the sports world, I thought of trying to be a sportswriter. I soon realized, however, that this too was not really for me.

Round about the middle of high school, I started to become intensely interested in politics. I believe that this interest was a manifestation of all those early influences recounted above that pushed me in the direction of social justice. This all found its greatest expression for me in the 1948 US presidential elections. I started to read and listen to (no television back then) everything relevant that I could.

At the time, my main focus was the expanding Cold War between the United States and the Soviet Union. By then, the Americans had launched the Marshall Plan for the recovery of Western Europe, dispatched aid to resist Communist guerrillas in Greece, and were confronting the notorious Berlin blockade by which Soviet dictator Joseph Stalin had encircled and was attempting to suffocate West Berlin, a vital outpost of Western democracy in the middle of Communist East Germany.

My leftward leanings, however, created in me a deep skepticism about America's behaviour and intentions. Indeed, I became enthralled with the "peace candidate" of that campaign, Henry A. Wallace, who had served as US vice-president under Franklin D. Roosevelt between 1940 and 1944. After Wallace had been somewhat unceremoniously dumped as a result of Southern pressures at the 1944 Democratic Party convention, he had become secretary of commerce under Roosevelt and then under Truman. But, at the early stages when the Cold War began to heat up, Wallace made a controversial speech at Madison Square Garden that seriously questioned the foundations of the US position. In the result, he wound up resigning from the Truman cabinet and soon thereafter he began to launch an independent bid for the presidency of the United States.

Wallace's statements and indeed his entire career appealed to my developing interests. Here was an experienced government official whose outlook on the world so mirrored my own. During the spring, summer, and fall of 1948, I found a special reinforcement for my political views: my maternal grandfather, Chaim Honichman, with whom I talked about these issues ceaselessly and listened to the American political party conventions. In this regard, my grandfather was both ideal companion and, as always, an inspiration. All through the piece, Henry

Wallace was our shared hero. Although Wallace himself was not a Communist, there was evidence that his Progressive Party was effectively controlled by them. At the time, I remained supremely oblivious.

In early October of 1948, I lost my grandfather (to a fatal heart attack) and in early November of that year, Henry Wallace and I lost the American elections. But the small "l" liberalism that I had developed soldiered on. I soon discovered periodicals of the liberal left including the American magazines *The Nation* and *The New Republic*. In the aftermath of the American election, they continued to fuel my political instincts. Although I made a point of reading the *Communist Manifesto* shortly thereafter, I was never much taken with Communism even in its theoretical form. During the late 1940s, Grace Street, its surrounding neighbourhood, and Harbord Collegiate provided many opportunities for political debate and discussion. It was an atmosphere that I couldn't resist.

During this period, my occupational interests were also being honed. While I was still interested in writing, I had long abandoned the idea of being a sports reporter. But in keeping with my developing political interests, I fantasized about being a political newspaper columnist. My parents advised me that newspaper writing could be an unreliable way to guarantee a living. They suggested that I focus on something like law and, with that in my pocket, I could then look again at newspaper writing or even something else. But the idea, they counselled, was that I have something more substantial to fall back on. As always, however, they assured me that, as far as they were concerned, the choice had to be mine. I found their advice to be quite sensible and decided, therefore, that I would set my sights on law school.

In the midst of all my questioning and challenging, it was impossible that religion would escape my critical scrutiny. All during high school, I had remained reverent about Judaism, particularly in its Orthodox incarnation. Indeed, I had been prepared on many occasions to defy the prevailing ethic among my friends and I remained kosher, ordering nothing more than toasted fried egg sandwiches when I went out to restaurants. But, although I remained in the fold, I was questioning my faith, more and more.

CHAPTER TWO

At University in the 1950s

*I*n June of 1950 at the end of my high school career, I considered myself—in addition to being a full-fledged Grace Street boy—a small "l" liberal and an egalitarian. If *Commentary* magazine had then heard of me, it would likely have labelled me an "anti-anti-Communist." Having just gone through the Henry Wallace campaign, I thought that the United States was the prime culprit of the Cold War and the Soviet Union was its hapless victim. During the ensuing period, I was destined to undergo some profound changes.

Coincidentally, just as I finished writing my "matric" examinations (late June of 1950), the Korean War broke out. Communist parties all over the world denounced South Korea as the aggressor. And yet, as I remember the events, the North Korean army advanced rapidly inside South Korea. Here's how the Internet described it: "In the initial stages, North Korea's troops overwhelmed South Korea's forces and drove them to a small area in the far south."[1]

If the South Koreans were the aggressors, I found myself asking, how come they were in such retreat at the *beginning* of the war? As events developed, I considered the Communist explanations increasingly devoid of credibility. This marked the beginning of an important intellectual journey for me. I propose to deal with it here because, in my generation, the phenomenon of Communism was a very central issue.

How one related to it helped to determine one's position on a host of issues that were concerned with social justice and fair play.

As I entered the University of Toronto in the fall of 1950, I harboured growing suspicions of Communist behaviour. These suspicions were strengthened by another development at around this time: Henry Wallace resigned as leader of the US Progressive Party over differences relating to the Korean War. By then, the small "l" liberals in the Progressive Party had become virtually the only non-Communists in the United States who questioned the fundamental assumptions of their country's posture in the Cold War.

For years, much of the non-Communist left had managed to ignore or excuse the mounting allegations of Soviet repression. But, in light of Communist duplicity over Korea, these reactions no longer worked for me. I had to question—and I did—the forced collectivization of agriculture through the deliberate starvation of thousands upon thousands of people, the purge trials of the 1930s involving confessions of treason on the part of hundreds of Soviet officials and Communist Party activists, the slave labour camps of Siberia, the mysterious late 1940s' disappearance of the Soviet Yiddish writers together with the closing of the Yiddish publishing houses and Yiddish theatre. In view of the mountains of evidence, I was simply repelled by the Communist charge that these manifestations of Soviet repression were merely "fabrications of the bourgeois press."

Nor could I accept the rationalization that the impugned Soviet behaviour was needed to root out capitalist and right-wing influences. Despite my own left-wing orientation, I believed—early on—that my right-wing and capitalist adversaries were ethically entitled to elementary freedoms. In any event, however, the right-wing was not the only victim of Soviet persecution. From the days of Lenin (and it got worse under Stalin), the left-leaning Mensheviks and Jewish Labour Bund were high on the Soviet enemies' list. Even in the middle of the Second World War, Stalin found it necessary to execute two Polish Jewish *socialists*, Henryk Ehrlich and Victor Alter. Moreover, in 1948, the Communist Party of Czechoslovakia, with the backing of the Soviet Union, engineered a coup against the small "l" liberal regime of that country. The deposed government of Jan Masaryk was no practitioner of right-wing values. By the early 1950s, Communist governments in

Russia and Eastern Europe had done their best to ensure that the trade union movements of their respective countries would function devoid of independence. Indeed, most of these unions, were transformed into instruments of those Communist governments and controlling Communist parties.

In 1952, there was a major development in the Communist world and in my attitude toward it. I refer to the Prague trials in which more than a dozen leaders of the Czechoslovakian Communist Party were prosecuted for various shades of treason. Significantly, the overwhelming number of them were Jewish. The trials became hotbeds of anti-Semitic invective.

Consider, for example, the prosecutor's interrogation of the defendant Geminder. There were several questions relating to the defendant's ability to speak the language of the country. At one point, Geminder agreed with the prosecutor that he lacked adequate fluency in that language or any others. This disclosure prompted the prosecutor to conclude that the defendant was simply a "homeless, rootless cosmopolitan."[2]

When I read this exchange in a transcript of the trials, I was enraged. In a panel discussion at the university shortly thereafter, I read these excerpts aloud. When I finished reading them, I slapped the material down on the table in front of a Communist Party member who was participating in the discussion. And I rhetorically asked, "What has any of this got to do with a legitimate trial for treason?"

On the basis of such evidence, I concluded that Soviet Communism was indeed—to use the later words of Ronald Reagan—an "evil empire." By itself, however, this characterization would not suffice to brand the Soviet Union as the primary aggressor in the Cold War. I reached that conclusion largely from the fact that, at the end of the Second World War, the United States withdrew its troops from Europe and went home. It also substantially demobilized its fighting forces. Of course, the United States was a democracy and, by the end of that terrible war, the American soldiers and people were desperate to resume ordinary civilian life.

The Soviet Union, on the other hand, kept about 175 divisions of the Red Army and continued to occupy the countries of Eastern Europe that they had captured from the Nazis. Of course, the Soviet Union was a dictatorship and, therefore, less susceptible than was the United States, to the popular will. Under the pressure of that Soviet presence, one Eastern European country after another succumbed to Communist hegemony. And, in 1948, the Soviets imposed their blockade of West Berlin. By contrast, the United States did not begin to re-arm until the creation of NATO, some four years after the end of the war. As all of these developments insinuated themselves into my consciousness, I experienced considerable relief that Harry Truman, rather than Henry Wallace, had won the 1948 election.

An adequate appreciation of my political and intellectual adventures during the course of my university career requires this valid assessment of the Soviet Communist system. Indeed, one other factor should be added to the profile. Communist parties throughout the world simply could not tolerate opposition. This intolerance applied to both non-Communists and Communists. Indeed, the Communist parties purported to adopt a system they called "democratic centralism." Once a decision was reached, it became incumbent upon all Communist Party members to support it. This phenomenon will help to explain the instant flip-flops that characterized Communist Party positions over the years. Consider, for example, the efforts of Communist parties in the 1930s to promote a "popular front" against the Nazi regime of Adolf Hitler. But, as soon as the Nazi–Soviet non-aggression pact was signed in 1939, Communist parties across the world precipitously abandoned their anti-Nazi agitation. In the immediate wake of the June 1941 Nazi invasion of the Soviet Union, however, Communist parties flipped back again and called for an anti-Nazi front. In *Darkness at Noon* and *The God That Failed*, Arthur Koestler wrote insightfully about this authoritarian feature of Communist behaviour.

In this connection, an incident comes back to me. Shortly after Georgi Malenkov took over the reins of Soviet power on the death of Joseph Stalin, the Soviet politburo expelled Lavrenti Beria, the then head of the KGB, amid allegations that, for thirty-five years, Beria had been an American and Zionist spy. Fresh from this news, a friend and I ran into a U of T Communist Party member that we both knew. We were eager to hear how a live Communist dealt with this incredible story. The fellow looked directly at my friend and me and solemnly regurgitated the story: Yes, Beria had been working for the Americans and the Zionists for thirty-five years. Since we were seated only a few inches from each other, I kept feeling the need to pinch myself because I was engulfed in sheer disbelief. I couldn't resolve the dilemma: Was this guy a deliberate liar or did he really believe what he was saying? I finally decided that there was no need for me to resolve the problem. Either way, these Communist Party members were deeply untrustworthy. And that's all that really mattered.

A few years later—during the last third of my university career—I became involved in a fascinating meeting. The setting was a culture club we had organized at the time called "Tojo's Tigers," named after the instigator of these meetings, the enterprising Murray "Tojo" Rubin, a long-time friend of mine. Our guest for the evening was J.B. Salsberg, for many years a member of the Ontario legislature and activist in the Canadian Communist Party. The meeting occurred in the early winter of 1957 during the time of the twentieth congress of the Soviet Communist Party.

By some magic of cosmic coincidence, our meeting with J.B. Salsberg took place within a day or two after Soviet politburo member Anastas Mikoyan denounced the dead dictator, Joseph Stalin. But Soviet Communist Party chief Nikita Kruschev had not yet spoken on the matter. So, when we got Salsberg, it was obvious that something momentous appeared to be happening, but it was not yet clear exactly what.

On this topic, I led off the questioning. I simply asked Salsberg a forthright question: What did he think of Mikoyan's denunciation of Stalin? Salsberg replied that, in fact, he had been disturbed for some time over the behaviour of his Soviet colleagues. This reply galvanized me. Why, I asked him, had you not said anything publicly about these uneasy feelings? After all, I pressed him, when developments in the West bothered you, you didn't hesitate to speak out publicly—why was Soviet injustice entitled to more solicitous treatment? To this day, I can still remember the words that formed the guts of Salsberg's reply: "There's a time to speak up and a time to keep quiet."

Later at that same meeting, my friend Murray Chusid, another participant, spent some time denouncing the Jewish Communist newspaper, *The Vochenblatt*. At that point, Mr. Salsberg asked Murray why he never wrote a letter to the newspaper's editor. Chusid's keen sense of irony prompted the following reply: "You know, Mr. Salsberg, there's a time to speak up and a time to keep quiet."

As we all know by now, Nikita Khrushchev also denounced Stalin at that twentieth party congress. And he did so in particularly vitriolic terms: "the cult of the personality."[3] Within several months of that historic congress, J.B. Salsberg visited the Soviet Union and, upon his return, he announced his resignation from the Communist Party. Having spent the greatest part of his adult life serving that cause, he must have found it particularly painful, at long last, to sever his ties. To their credit, many of Salsberg's erstwhile foes in the Jewish community and the labour movement warmly welcomed his return from the political periphery he had inhabited so long. In any event, these incidents tell us a lot about the nature of the Communist Party and its members—authoritarian, dictatorial, tightly disciplined, and anti-democratic.

Significantly, my growing hostility to the Communist movement had managed all along to co-exist with a vehement rejection of the extremist form of anti-Communism that had unfolded in the United States. I was revolted, for example, by the US McCarran Act, Wisconsin senator Joseph McCarthy, the Hollywood "blacklist," the loyalty oaths, the hearings of the House Un-American Activities Committee, and the 1953 execution of Julius and Ethel Rosenberg. For me, the challenge had become how to achieve a responsible anti-Communism that avoided the pitfalls of the American hysteria. I shall relate how I began to deal with a number of the conflicts and pressures that, at the time, invariably confronted non-Communist liberals. As I began to learn, liberals also have dogmas and double standards. And it's often difficult to take them on.

*A*s I indicated earlier, in my late high school years I had become an avid reader of the American liberal magazines *The Nation* and *The New Republic*. This proclivity followed me into university. At some point near the inception of my university career, my attention was attracted to an issue that was being addressed in *The Nation*. A key article in that magazine called for US recognition of Communist China and the seating of that regime in the United Nations. So far, so good. I joined the liberals of *The Nation* in their wish to include Red China among the nations with which they sought to have diplomatic relations. But an editorial in the same issue of that magazine expressed opposition to the possibility of US diplomatic relations with Spain's fascist government of Francisco Franco.

Why, I asked myself, should the right-wing totalitarians of Spain be treated more harshly than the left-wing totalitarians of China? It couldn't be that the Spanish fascists were so much worse than the Chinese Communists. Indeed, there was some evidence that the Chinese regime was significantly worse. I remember scouring every page of that *Nation* magazine, but, despite my efforts, I was unable to find an explanation for the differential approach that had been adopted there.[4]

Somewhere around that time, I came upon another issue in *The Nation* magazine that troubled me. One of its editorials announced that *The Nation* had launched a lawsuit against *The New Leader* magazine. Apparently, *The New Leader* had published a letter rebuking the foreign editor of *The Nation* for his alleged "commitment to the service of the Soviet Union." According to *The Nation,* such an allegation was tantamount to an accusation of criminal behaviour. This is the factor that, in the opinion of the plaintiffs, lifted the conflict out of the realm of mere political polemics and made it suitable for action in court.[5]

Upon reading the letter that provoked this messy situation, I was far from convinced that it was fair to interpret the complaint as a manifestation of anything close to criminal behaviour. There were no allegations of an agency or conspiratorial relationship between *The Nation*'s foreign editor and the Soviet Union. Granted, the letter writer provided documentation of a remarkable similarity between the views of *The Nation*'s foreign editor and those of the Soviet Union. But this was evidence of parallel thinking, not necessarily institutional subservience. Thus, the "commitment" implied by the writer of the letter was primarily of an intellectual rather than a criminal character. The writer was accusing both the foreign editor and *The Nation* of an intellectual orientation that effectively betrayed the ideals of an independent liberal publication. On this basis, the issue should have been thrashed out in the market place of public opinion and not in a court of law.

The Nation had declared that one purpose of its lawsuit was to defend freedom. It warned that the magazine had no intention of conducting the lawsuit anywhere but in the courts. However, *The New Leader* argued that, if a central motive of *The Nation* here was the cause of freedom, it would not have closed its pages, in this way, to further commentary on the conflict. It would have done what *The New Leader* did: encourage commentary from many sources.[6] Despite my having been a long-time fan of *The Nation*, I thought that *The New Leader* had the more persuasive position. Thus, I had to face disillusionment by the liberal left on two scores: the double standards as between fascists and Communists and the basic hostility to free and open debate when left-leaning liberals were the ones under attack.

From the middle of high school until well into my university years, I was an executive member of the Toronto Jewish Youth Council. As the youth branch of the Canadian Jewish Congress, we were entitled to some level of participation in Jewish Congress deliberations. In the very early 1950s, I attended, in that capacity, the meeting at which the regional division of the Canadian Jewish Congress decided to expel its Communist-dominated affiliate, the United Jewish People's Order (UJPO). When I first heard of the proposed expulsion, my liberal reflexes were outraged. I viewed the congress plan as an unwarranted infringement on the civil liberties of its constituents. And so I began to consider how — not whether — to oppose what the congress was about.

Then, I attended the stormy meeting at which the congress made its fateful decision. While a number of the participants turned me off with their outright reactionary views, I was impressed with at least some of the others. During the weeks that this controversy raged, I had a few discussions with the late Ben Lappin, the then director of the congress's central region. He impressed upon me the distinction between how the state relates to its citizens and how voluntary organizations relate to their members. As for the latter, they must be entitled to regulate and restrict their membership according to their various objectives. These were distinctions that, in the utter naïveté of my youth, I had not really considered. Once I began to consider them, my analysis began to lead me in directions quite different from those upon which I had initially ventured.

As I began to apply this new analytical framework to the relationship between the Canadian Jewish Congress and the UJPO, I re-thought my position. Was it not, I asked myself, one of the purposes of the Canadian Jewish Congress to protect the welfare of the Jewish community at home and abroad? Since most assuredly this was one of the congress's animating objectives, how can it be squared with the UJPO's defence of what the Soviet government had done to that country's Yiddish writers, publishing houses, and theatre? Couldn't the UJPO position be seen as tacit support for a policy of official anti-Semitic discrimination? On that basis, there was a strong argument for the ethical propriety of the expulsion.

But I did not have a chance adequately to work through the implications of this position before I had to cast my vote in the Toronto Jewish Youth Council. Since I thought that there was a good argument in favour of the expulsion and since a negative vote on the part of the Jewish Youth Council could mean disaffiliation from the congress, I decided to support the expulsion. In such circumstances, opposition to the congress decision was simply not worth it.

In a somewhat different capacity, I had occasion, once again, to deal with the issue of that expulsion. In the early 1950s, I was the editor of *The Hillelite*, the publication of the B'nai Brith Hillel Foundation at the University of Toronto. I hit on the idea of publishing a debate about that issue and so I invited a senior student who was in favour of the expulsion and another senior student who was opposed to it, to publish their views. The writer who opposed the expulsion was not himself a Communist or fellow traveller; his opposition was based upon his view of civil liberties principles. As always, we invited other students to comment on the issue by way of letters to the editor. One day, I received a particularly vitriolic letter, condemning the expulsion. The letter was written by a Hillel member who also happened to be a member of the U of T Communist Party. The paid, full-time director of Hillel, a reform rabbi, told me that I should not publish the contentious letter. But I insisted on publishing it.

The rabbi said that the matter should be referred to my colleagues on the Hillel executive. Of course, I could not disagree with this. The issue split the executive wide open. The meeting was punctuated by lengthy, impassioned speeches. In the result, the executive resolved, by a very narrow margin, to back the position I had adopted.

This time, the rabbi said that, before publication occurred, he felt the need to consult the Hillel Commission, a special advisory committee that B'nai Brith had established to provide guidance. At the meeting of the commission, a new document was introduced to the debate: a directive from the international Hillel organization to all affiliates, instructing them not to allow their facilities to be used for the dissemination of "Communist propaganda." On the basis of this directive, Hillel Commission members expressed reservations about the publication of the letter in dispute.

But I argued that the directive did not contemplate the kind of material at issue. In my view, the directive was not intended to censor the opinions of Hillel members who were students at the university. At most, it was aimed at interventions from the outside. To interpret the directive as broadly as had been suggested, I believed that it would be necessary to explicitly bar Communists from membership in Hillel. Since this had never been done, I argued that it was wrong to withhold the normal concomitants of membership from any legitimate Hillel member.

I should point out that, despite the merit I saw in the Jewish Congress expulsion of the UJPO, I would have been opposed to denying Communists membership in Hillel. The Canadian Jewish Congress exists to promote and protect the welfare of the Jewish community. Public support for an official policy of anti-Semitism (like the one practised in the Soviet Union) can be seen as incompatible with that objective. Hillel, on the other hand, is designed to be a "home away from home" for Jewish students and a place for them to expand their knowledge of Jewish tradition. Such a psychological and educational mandate is not necessarily offended by being open to card-carrying student Communists.

Following the meeting of the Hillel Commission, the rabbi told my colleagues and me that he thought it was appropriate to ask the international Hillel organization itself whether the directive should be interpreted so as to apply to the letter in question. By then, it was becoming clear to me that the rabbi's strategy was to delay the issue out of existence. After all, he was the only lingering presence in the organization; students were there for a much shorter period. At this stage, I am unable to recall exactly how it happened, but I do know that the letter in question never appeared in a Hillel publication. I must say, however, that I acquired an important lesson in organizational tactics. Better to delay than to debate.

Within a few months, I got involved in another issue that was seen and debated as having civil liberties implications. The Toronto Symphony Orchestra (TSO) discharged six musicians because US immigration policy rendered them unable to play at concerts in that country. The policy in question reportedly arose from suspicions that these musicians had been involved in Communist front organizations. A number of us began to ask the obvious question: What the hell does Communist sympathy have to do with the ability to play classical music? But this incident occurred in the early 1950s when US Senator Joe McCarthy and the House Un-American Activities Committee were riding high. A number of Torontonians, in protest, cancelled their season's tickets to the TSO concerts. Editorials, media commentators, and others publicly denounced what the orchestra had done.

At the University of Toronto, a group of us students created a civil liberties club so that we could weigh in on the matter. But, almost from the beginning of our organizational efforts, we were confronted with an issue that often bedevilled reform efforts in those years. What to do about Communists who sought membership in our civil liberties club? It soon became clear that the overwhelming majority of those in the club believed that our membership should be open to Communists. In the view of the majority, excluding Communists would represent the very thing we were fighting against.

A minority of us (including me), however, took a different position. Since the purpose of the club was to fight for civil liberties, we saw no reason why it should have to contain people who were against civil liberties. We thought that those who endorsed or excused the atrocities perpetrated by the Soviet Union had demonstrated an obvious opposition to civil liberties. We argued by analogy: the Canadian Jewish Congress would not breach civil liberties if it denied membership to Nazis; the National Association for the Advancement of Colored People (NAACP) would commit no impropriety if it denied membership to adherents of the Ku Klux Klan. On the same basis, we contended, a viable civil liberties organization could exclude Communists. In our view, there was no contradiction between fighting for the rights of Communists in the general society and opposing the rights of Communists to join a voluntary organization that stood for the very freedoms the Communists are against.

At the showdown meeting of the civil liberties club, my side, of course, lost quite overwhelmingly. After the vote was taken, a few of us on our side got up to leave; we were in the process of resigning from the club. One of our group was the then president of the club, Stan Schiff. Upon seeing that they were about to lose their president, the remaining members of the club decided to open nominations for his replacement. Another member of our group that was resigning was my friend Murray Chusid, the guy with the keen sense of irony. As we were walking out, he raised his hand to nominate a replacement for Stan Schiff as president. The name he proposed was the then president of the U of T Communist Party. Needless to say, his proposed candidate did not accept. But Chusid's gesture proved to be a most colorful way for our group to terminate its involvement in the civil liberties club. Despite all the sound and fury of that battle, the club never did very much afterwards. Indeed, in a little while it simply faded from the landscape.

A growing influence on me during a lot of the time I was involved in the foregoing conflicts emerged on the pages of *The New Leader* magazine. When I looked up that magazine to learn about its version of the dispute with *The Nation*, I became very curious about its orientation and I began to look at other articles. One of them in particular caught my attention. It was an article by a philosophy professor at New York University; his name was Sidney Hook. That first article dealt with the rights of Communist teachers. After I read the piece, I was prepared to dismiss Sidney Hook as an irredeemable reactionary. He came down essentially against the right of Communists to teach.

But, despite my initial revulsion, I became somewhat mesmerized by the potency of Professor Hook's arguments. The more I thought about his article (and I thought about it plenty), the more logical I found it to be. His position was that Communist Party membership involved a commitment that contravened the canons of academic integrity. In their research, writing, and teaching, professors are supposed to employ the methods of intelligence and follow them wherever they lead. No less important, they must be truthful about the evidence: dig it all out and disclose what they find. Membership in the Communist Party, on the other hand, involves a willingness to use any subterfuge, any stratagem, or even distortion to advance the class struggle as the party sees it.

Hook was careful to enunciate certain distinctions. His argument applied, not to Communist sympathizers, but to party members who were subject to the organization's discipline. Nor was he arguing for the *automatic* exclusion of party members. He said that they should be regarded as *presumptively* unfit; the onus would then fall upon the impugned teachers to demonstrate they were less than subservient to the party line. Moreover, Hook also insisted that the issue must be handled by the faculty as a question of professional ethics, rather than by a Congressional committee as a question of national loyalty.

It wasn't necessary to agree with Sidney Hook in order to be thoroughly stimulated by his arguments. And so, I was. I began to seek and read all of his articles and books that I could get my hands on. Since he was quite prolific, I wound up with a lot to read. There were books such as *Heresy Yes; Conspiracy No* and *The Hero in History*. I began to follow *The New Leader* regularly so that I could read his latest pieces as they appeared. I even picked up books by Sidney Hook's mentor, John Dewey. I got interested in the philosophical foundations of Hook's polemical material. While I was not necessarily agreeing with all of his political pronouncements, I was becoming increasingly persuaded by his philosophical position. Within a few years, I began to think of myself as a philosophical pragmatist. That basic orientation has remained with me ever since.

To me, it is significant that these various manifestations of my growing anti-Communism were evolving alongside my developing views on a host of other subjects related to social justice. I was becoming increasingly interested in social democracy, the labour movement, civil liberties, and the fight against racial and ethnic discrimination. Paradoxically, as I found more common cause with the right-wing on the subject of Communism, I became more opposed to them on virtually every other subject. While I was still an undergraduate, I joined the social-democratic Cooperative Commonwealth Federation (CCF), the predecessor of today's New Democratic Party (NDP). In rather short order, I became one of the campus CCF's lead debaters. A frequent adversary in these debates was a spokesman for the campus Conservatives, the future broadcast mogul, Ted Rogers.

In one of those debates, we dealt with the issue of US foreign policy. Although I had moved quite some distance from the dovishness I embraced in the Henry Wallace campaign, I retained some significant disagreements with US foreign policy, particularly as it was practised in the early 1950s by John Foster Dulles, secretary of state to US president Dwight Eisenhower. Although I am unable, at this stage, to recall very much detail about those debates, a little bit of my favourite rhetoric has lingered with me. At the conclusion of one of my speeches, I made the following statement: "Teddy Roosevelt warned Americans that they should speak softly and carry a big stick. Today America is speaking loudly, swinging the stick aimlessly, and thus succeeding only in creating a noise and a gust of wind."

And, in one of the model parliaments, I led off for the CCF after the opening speech made by a representative of the Tories. He wound up his speech with a criticism of the Liberals for being concerned only with Quebec and Ontario to the exclusion of the Maritimes and the West. He accused the Liberals of being what he called "a middle-of-the-country" party. As the very next speaker, I began by saying, "While the Liberals may indeed be a middle-of-the-country party, the Tories are a middle-of-the-century party — the sixteenth century. They just can't get adjusted to the fact that Good Queen Bess is dead and talkies are a reality."

At an Osgoode Hall model parliament a few years later, I was again leading off for the CCF club. In my opening speech, I used the term "political harlot" to describe the incumbent Liberal government. In the midst of one of my rhetorical flourishes, a member of the student Liberal government got up on a point of personal privilege. He jokingly complained about my invective; he said that, after all, harlots are dubious women who do things for money. I stood up immediately and proclaimed: "The member is quite right, I apologize unreservedly. There is an important difference between harlots and the government. Harlots give you value for your money." The fellow who interrupted me turned out to be Ian Scott, in later years a brilliant lawyer and Ontario's Attorney General.

The subject matter of my debates during my university years included government Medicare, the nationalization of certain public utilities, government economic planning, American foreign policy, and whether labour unions were "too big for their boots." As for the labour movement, there was a particularly bitter strike during my years at the university. It was waged by the United Steelworkers Union against mining companies in Noranda, Quebec. I came up with an idea to translate our CCF club's trade union sympathies into some practical action. My suggestion was that we create a front organization to be called "Student Committee for Aid to Mining Communities." Under that rubric, we would attempt to secure the university's permission to hold a tag day, essentially for the strikers. Not surprisingly, we were unable to pull it off. But these examples will illustrate the multi-sided nature of my political agenda. There were many issues to be addressed by those concerned with social justice and I wanted to do my part.

During my University years, my interest in sports waned and changed. I continued to play touch football whenever I could but the opportunities for it began to dwindle. I played tennis with some frequency but I regret to acknowledge that my skill never quite matched my experience. Baseball almost disappeared from my agenda. I certainly stopped attempting to play it and I even stopped watching it.

Notwithstanding these developments, I had an adventure concerning baseball in my early university period. I believe the year was 1951. In the late summer, I was travelling with three friends down the East Coast of the United States. When we stopped over in New York, we became taken with the idea of going to Ebbets Field to see the legendary Brooklyn Dodgers. It wasn't necessary to have a topical interest in baseball to be fascinated with the famous Brooklyn Dodgers and their colourful fans.

So, off we went to Brooklyn and Ebbets Field. On that particular day, the Dodgers were playing against the Philadelphia Phillies. Being in a mischievous mood, we made a point of buying Philly pennants on our way into the stadium. During the course of the game, we would vigorously wave our pennants whenever the Phillies pulled off a meritorious play. Needless to say, our pro-Philly partisanship made us the object of considerable heckling from the Brooklyn fans in our sector of the stadium.

In one inning, Brooklyn got the bases loaded. At this point, our Dodger-fan neighbours began to inundate us with anti-Philly invective. This was followed by two quick outs of Brooklyn batters. We responded with appropriate amounts of flag waving and invective of our own. Then, the famous Gill Hodges came up to bat for Brooklyn, and, wouldn't you know it, he hit a Grand-Slam home run. The Brooklyn fans went wild. In the middle of the melee, I sneaked out. When I reached the outer periphery of the stadium, I bought a Brooklyn pennant. Upon returning to my section of the stadium, I held the Brooklyn pennant aloft.

The Brooklyn fans in my section responded by according me the first standing ovation of my life. With few exceptions, they seemed generally pleased by the speed with which I behaved like a Canadian Benedict Arnold.

*A*nother activity in which I became very involved during the course of my university life was working with kids at a summer camp (Camp Ogama near Huntsville in Muskoka, Ontario). As a result of co-incidence and historical accidents, a few friends and I acquired leadership positions at that middle-class Jewish camp (ages six to sixteen). Because of the seniority of our positions, we were able to make significantly more money than was available to ordinary counsellors. It became a major help in paying for my university tuition.

We became very interested in raising the consciousness of our campers to the world around them. Thus, a unit-wide or camp-wide program at our camp would not be a colour war; it would be "the Geneva Peace Conference" or the "Hungarian Revolution." We didn't only sing ordinary camp songs. We sang songs of work, justice, and freedom. We taught our kids songs from the Spanish Civil War, a hymn from the Warsaw Ghetto, ballads from the labour movement, and many songs of racial equality. Our special Friday night programs did not simply pay tribute to the kids' Jewish heritage; they also contained some critical issues. In one of those programs, there was a dramatization that addressed the seventeenth-century excommunication of the great philosopher Spinoza from the Netherlands Jewish community.

We encouraged discussion on a myriad of issues that were aimed at making the kids question, challenge, and think. The staff we assembled there included Mickey Cohen (later to become deputy finance minister for Canada), Owen Shime (who became one of Canada's leading labour arbitrators), Erna (Newman) Paris (who became an award-winning author), Gordie Wolfe (who became the director of the Jewish Family and Child Service), Stephen Lewis (who became leader of the Ontario New Democratic Party and Canada's ambassador to the United Nations), and Millie (Rotman) Shime (one of our most talented) whose early death at forty-six deprived Canada of a brilliant contribution. When you bring together a group of people like that, they are bound to do some very interesting things. And they did.

The combination of my CCF and camp involvements introduced another influence to my life: David Lewis. When I met David, he was the national president of the CCF, having served for many years as its full-time (poorly) paid secretary. David, of course, was also the father of my camp colleague, Stephen Lewis. The elder Lewis had arrived in Canada from his native Poland at the age of twelve. Despite the fact that he then spoke no English, he completed elementary school and high school in six years, and, after a period at McGill University, he applied for and won the coveted Rhodes Scholarship. When we met in the mid-1950s, David was in the process of becoming one of the top union lawyers in Canada.

Since I had to augment my legal studies by articling to a practising lawyer, I thought I could do no better than David Lewis. From him, I could hope to learn a lot of labour law, a field in which I had a growing interest. I would also be in a politically attractive atmosphere. Of course, I wanted no part of the commercial priorities of any Bay Street law firm. I got the job and spent the large part of two years at the law offices of Jolliffe, Lewis, and Osler.

In many ways, the experience was a disappointment. Although the partners were certainly nice to me, they left me on my own for long periods of time. Fortunately, they allowed me to take legal aid criminal cases in what was then magistrates' court. That involvement proved invaluable. On the few occasions when I did some work for the firm, I learned some helpful lessons. In this regard, David himself proved to be particularly interesting. He was a much more practical man than his newspaper clippings would have suggested. Invariably, he would begin his presentations with concessions to his adversaries. In that way, he circumscribed the area for the court's involvement, a tactic that had the effect of setting the judges at their ease. This enabled the judges to side more comfortably with David Lewis, and not infrequently they did.

In addition to his brilliance and dedication, David also had an abundant supply of self-appreciation. I should also point out, however, that he could be quite good-natured about acknowledging this proclivity. Indeed, in one telephone call with me, he actually described himself as "arrogant." When he said this, both of us laughed — knowingly.

Nevertheless, the one way in which David proved to be most helpful to me was in the example he set. Here was a brilliant man who could have done almost anything he had wanted. But he chose to make his considerable talents available to the less advantaged people in society. Although I had intended by then to live that kind of life anyway, the fact that he had chosen likewise gave a special respectability to my plans and ambitions.

While I am on the subject of lawyers whose work I had occasion to admire during the course of my university life, the name of Joseph Welch soars into my consciousness. He was the Boston aristocrat who almost singlehandedly brought down Senator Joe McCarthy. The scene was the Army–McCarthy hearings which I used to watch religiously on television. McCarthy's senate committee was purporting to investigate some alleged Communist activity in the American army. This time, the bully McCarthy picked on the wrong target. The well-entrenched conservatives in the army hierarchy would have none of the senator's smear tactics.

At one point in the hearings, McCarthy made some disparaging remarks about a young man who had worked in Joseph Welch's office. When McCarthy made this remark, Welch was acting as counsel to the army. As soon as McCarthy finished what he was saying, Welch laced into him. The memorable words with which the rebuke began were, "Senator, have you no shame?" When Welch completed his remarks, the audience broke into enthusiastic and sustained applause. It proved to be the high point in the increasingly well-watched hearings.

Not long after those hearings, the United States Senate passed a vote of censure on senator Joseph McCarthy. His career was effectively at an end. That couldn't have happened to a more deserving guy.

*W*hen I entered university in 1950, I was still somewhat reverent about the Jewish religion. Exposure to the liberal arts soon began to erode that involvement. But the decisive development occurred in 1955. I was travelling by car with two of my friends, (Berril Garshowitz and Louis Goldstein, the de facto leader of the Grace Street Gang,) through the United States. After spending most of the night travelling in Nevada, we reached Salt Lake City, Utah, in the early morning, rented a hotel room, and went to sleep.

Later in the day, we visited the world-famous Mormon Tabernacle. The guide was giving us a tour and explaining the Mormon faith to us. According to his explanation, the church is governed by twelve living apostles of Jesus Christ. And they govern the church by Divine revelation.

This triggered my curiosity. Since a revelation from God is necessarily an unusual communication, I asked whether these living apostles could possibly make a mistake as to whether it was really God at the other end of the communication? Moreover, I asked whether they could be so sure that they got the message straight. Was it not possible that there may have been a "not" that they didn't "hear"? Of course, the guide assured us, their religion does not accept human infallibility. In that case, I pressed him, you must acknowledge the possibility that they could be mistaken.

After this went on for several minutes, the guide finally agreed that there was a possibility that the apostles could be mistaken. But, he added, it was not likely. At this point, I realized that his position was based on intellectual quicksand. I should also point out that at no stage was I playing the role of smart alec. During the whole encounter, I was honestly and genuinely curious about their religion.

In later years, one of my companions at the tabernacle—Berril Garshowitz—reminded me that, upon leaving the place, I appeared very excited. I now realize why. That conversation had laid bare the basic flaw in the whole doctrine of revelation. And that flaw was not confined to the Mormon religion. It necessarily applied to all claims of communication between God and human beings. As I began to argue it, the doctrine of revelation required faith, not in God, but in the human recipient. We had to believe that, despite the recipient's finiteness, there could be no mistake either in the identification of God or in the accurate receipt of the message. Either way, fallible, finite human beings are not worthy of that much faith.

Since that time, I have discussed this issue with numbers of people, including theologians and philosophers. As I have explained, I don't necessarily deny the existence of God. I simply claim that God is not relevant for moral purposes. We cannot derive moral guidance from God because such guidance would require knowing God's will and that is the one thing that, without becoming mired in contradiction, we are unable to discern.

Since my analysis applied to all Divine-human communication, it had to include the beliefs in Judaism as well. Even the milder concepts of Divine inspiration, found in the more liberal Jewish denominations, had to be caught. After all, how does one determine which inspirations come from God and which come from other sources? The very exercise of attributing God to anything triggers the fallacy. The attributor, being human and finite—like the Mormon apostles—could be wrong, and thus, the rock of the faith turns to quicksand.

All the while that my challenges of religion were growing, I was becoming increasingly attracted to the more strictly cultural side of my heritage, particularly the Yiddish language. Perhaps it was the earthy sounds; perhaps it was the warmth generated by the memory of my grandparents; perhaps it was because Yiddish was so often spoken in Grace Street homes; and/or perhaps it was the way that language expressed the key experiences of love, pathos, and humour. I was learning not only to understand Yiddish, but also to speak it, at least in its very colloquial incarnation. Regrettably, I have never really become fluent. But I can often get by. There seemed to be a pervasive paradox with me—the more I questioned the Jewish religion, the more I embraced the Yiddish language.

Somewhere around 1958, I read a debate in *The New Leader* magazine between Bertrand Russell and Sidney Hook.[7] The issue concerned whether we should prefer to be Red or dead. Bertrand Russell had said that, in the final crunch, he would prefer to surrender to Soviet Communism rather than accept the annihilation of the human race. Sidney Hook responded by arguing that, in acknowledging that this was his crunch position, Bertrand Russell had *already* surrendered. After all, what incentive would the Soviets have to negotiate with the West if they knew in advance that the West would prefer capitulation to annihilation? Siding with Sidney Hook in that debate did not mean accepting, for example, the "massive retaliation" doctrine of John Foster Dulles. There was no inconsistency between the adoption of a more prudent and restrained foreign policy, on the one hand, and a recognition that surrender was out of the question, on the other hand.

Of course, the factor that made it possible for me to support Sidney Hook in that debate was that, by 1958, I had resolved that the preservation of democracy was the highest value of political life. This view had been heavily influenced by my growing revulsion over the barbarism produced by the twentieth century—Nazism, Fascism, Communism, genocide, and apartheid. If our species has learned anything from that century of horrors, it should be that the one hope there is for humanity is democracy. Democracy is the only system in this world that puts a premium on human dignity. For this reason, I also developed the conviction that, despite its many faults, the United States had to prevail in the Cold War.

All of this made me increasingly sensitive to a phenomenon that elsewhere I have called "equivalence mongering." Although I was involved in many fights against the injustices perpetrated by the Western democracies, I resolved not to treat them as the equivalent of the injustices that emanated from totalitarian dictatorships. Thus, for example, I would not use "holocaust" or "KGB" to describe Western injustices. I was prepared to be vigorous in my attacks on Western injustices but I did not want to be guilty of any obscene comparisons.

And so, with a BA, an LLB, and admission to the Ontario Bar, I completed my formal education at the end of the 1950s. But, although much of my formal education was very valuable, my informal education has proved to be more durable. In addition to all the foregoing influences, some of my close friendships fuelled my various convictions. Harbord Collegiate's 1950 valedictorian, Mel Finkelstein, was deeply involved with me in the fight against the rabbi at Hillel. Moreover, he and I spent long hours discussing the issues that were grabbing me. Very often after taking out young women on a Saturday night, we would ditch our dates at about 2 a.m. and walk the streets until dawn—deep in conversation about the problems of the world. At camp, I began exploring philosophical matters with Sydney Goldenberg who was initially a camper, but a brilliant one. My exchanges with him have continued to this day.

Upon law school graduation, I still considered myself a small "l" liberal and egalitarian, but a much more skeptical one. No longer an anti-anti-Communist, I had become an unequivocal anti-Communist and perhaps even a Cold War hawk. Moreover, I was a social democrat, a civil libertarian, a secular Jew, and a philosophical pragmatist. It is with this intellectual equipment that I set out to face the world.

ENDNOTES

1   "Korean War: Military History," in Brough's Books, available online at www. dropbears.com/h/history/korean_war.htm.

2   Vladimir Tismaneanu, *The Devil In History: Communism, Facism, and Some Lessons of the Twentieth Century* (Berkeley, California: University of California Press, 2012) p. 65.

3   Paul Halsall, Nikita S. Khrushchev, "The Secret Speech — On the Cult of Personality, 1956," *Modern History Sourcebook* (July, 1998). Available online at www.fordham.edu/halsall/mod/1956khrushchev-secret1.html.

4   See, for example, *The Nation*, November 25, 1950, 474. Note that, in this article advocating the recognition of Red China, the author made the case essentially on the strategic basis that such recognition was a prerequisite for ending that war in Korea. I would have thought, nevertheless, that if the Nation's writers had the kind of moral qualms about recognizing Red China's government that they harboured about the fascist government in Spain, the article at least would have expressed some element of regret that considerations of reality were driving its advocacy. No such disclaimers appear in this piece. I was satisfied, therefore, that *The Nation* had indeed succumbed to double standards See: J. Alvarez Del Vayo, "Making Time," *The Nation*, November 25, 1950, 474, and "The Shape of Things," *The Nation*, November 25, 1950, 269.

5   "Why the Nation Sued," *The Nation*, June 2, 1951, 504–5.

6   "The Nation Censors a Letter of Criticism," *New Leader*, March 19, 1951, 16–18.

7   Sidney Hook, *Political Power and Personal Freedom: Critical Studies in Democracy, Communism and Civil Rights* (New York: Criterion Books, 1959) p. 42.

part two

The Labour Committee Years

CHAPTER THREE

Transitions and Objectives

*O*n June 1 1959—a year after I was called to the bar—I began work at the Labour Committee for Human Rights. This was the culminating event of a transition year that proved to be both frustrating and fruitful: "frustrating" because my unremitting efforts to get a job in the labour movement were not producing results; "fruitful" because I managed to get involved in some interesting and meaningful activity.

Since at least my late high school years, I had become determined to marry my vocation with my avocation. I was simply not going to spend all those years of my vocational life doing boring, meaningless things so that at some distant point in my retirement, I could finally do what I really wanted to do. Not for me. My regular work must enable me to contribute to social betterment and it must provide an outlet for whatever creative, oratorical, and/or writing abilities I happened to have.

Shortly after graduation, I was approached by a small group of Reform rabbis. Their object was to interest me in the possibility of my becoming a Reform rabbi myself. And so, they invited me to lunch at which we might have a productive exchange of views.

Although the lunch was certainly pleasant and even interesting, it got nowhere. From the outset, I told them that I was far from convinced about the reality of God. This didn't seem to faze them. But, after I outlined some of the arguments that I had developed during my visit to the Mormon Tabernacle, my rabbinic friends began to appear conspicuously less eager about me. I believe that I actually persuaded them of my theological unfitness for life in the clergy, even their progressive clergy.

Shortly thereafter, I resumed what I had begun a little bit earlier—knocking on doors in the labour movement. It was my conviction that labour represented the pressure group in society whose self-interest coincided more than most, with a progressive view of the public interest. So I approached labour leaders that I knew from the Co-operative Commonwealth Federation (CCF) and those whom I hadn't before met. One after the other, however, simply did not have anything available for me by way of employment. In my frustration, I remember saying to one of these labour leaders that they were going to force me to become a millionaire, and that's not what I wanted.

As I continued with these efforts, I was able to find some part-time employment. Surprisingly, I was approached by my old friend, the rabbi who was the director at Hillel. He was intending to take a sabbatical leave for a few months and asked whether I would be available to serve as part-time acting director of the organization during his absence. Thus, it became apparent that, despite all the conflict I had had with this rabbi, he harboured some respect and even affection for me. I accepted his offer and served in that post for a few uneventful months thereafter. It is also remarkable that, years later after the rabbi's death, Mel Finkelstein and I—both student adversaries of his—were the only former students to show up at his unveiling.

At some point during this transition period, I became a columnist for an Anglo-Jewish magazine called the *Jewish Standard*. This provided me with a few dollars (very few) and a platform from which I could rail against the foibles of the Jewish community. The column titled "Pointed Paragraphs" engaged me on a monthly basis for about two to three years.

One of my targets was a recurring ritual practised by the brotherhood of a particular Conservative synagogue. Periodically, this synagogue presented an award for intergroup relations to certain members of the general community that it considered worthy. Apart from my skepticism about such awards, I became deeply suspicious when I noted that almost invariably the recipients of this award were very rich people. Moreover, a little research revealed that at least two of those recipients were members of an elite private social club with a long-standing reputation for excluding Jews from its ranks. I had a field day writing about that situation.

It soon appeared that my work struck a raw nerve. The synagogue brotherhood invited me to have dinner with its executive members. Of course, I was delighted to accept the invitation. Although civility was largely observed, it was obvious that a number of those people were quite upset with what I had written. All of which created in me a sense of importance way beyond my standing in the community. I was still under thirty and had only recently graduated.

Another column was devoted to the phenomenon of the Jewish Communist. This was written at a time of serious upheaval in the Canadian Communist Party, following as it did on the heels of the Soviet denunciation of Joseph Stalin. I poured over issues of the Canadian Communist Party newspaper and examined the conflicts between those who were called "left-wing sectarians" and those who were called "right-wing opportunists." I also interviewed former and remaining Communist Party members. In the case of a remaining Jewish Communist, I particularly questioned him about the Soviet accusation that Stalin had created a "personality cult." I pointed out that this allegation appeared incompatible with the Marxist analysis of society in which social and economic relationships essentially determined personal behaviour and not vice versa. I am unable now to remember the answer I got but I do recall that it was something less than coherent.

Another column resulted from a survey that I organized among Florida hotels most frequented by Toronto Jews. I arranged for a woman to write these hotels and ask about available accommodations, including their policy on whether she could bring a black person with her. I published the replies, with names and addresses, in a column soon afterwards.

Not one of those hotels indicated a willingness to accept black people on terms and conditions equal to those of whites. A number of the hotels simply said that they were unable to extend their accommodations that far. A couple of the hotels said that they had no pool facilities for "coloured people"; in another case, the hotel replied that persons of colour would have to eat alone in the kitchen because there were no dining facilities for them. Virtually all of the replies assumed that our question concerned "coloured maids."

Both in my column and in numbers of speeches to Jewish organizations thereafter, I lambasted those of my fellow Jews who were prepared to go to such hotels and subsidize the obscenity of racial segregation. As I argued it at the time, to us it was simply a matter of a vacation but to the blacks, it was a matter of their very dignity. At no time, of course, did I believe that only Jews were guilty of such misconceived priorities. Then and now, I believe that apathy about such matters is endemic to the human condition in general. I targeted the Jewish community at the time because I was writing to Jews in a Jewish publication.

At some point in the mid-spring of 1959, I learned of an exciting job opening at the Labour Committee for Human Rights. I had heard much about this organization over the years. It was the one that took on the racial discrimination practised against blacks in Dresden, Ontario, restaurants. The idea of working for the Labour Committee stirred my activist hormones.

Having first established that the organization was administered by the Jewish Labour Committee (JLC) in Montreal, I immediately telephoned long distance to the JLC director, Sid Blum. After I identified myself to him, he said to me, "I hear that you're a good lawyer, why would you want this job?" To which I replied, "You let me worry about that; just make sure that I am on your list of interview targets when you come to Toronto."

A few weeks later, I received word from Sid Blum's office that he was coming to Toronto on a designated weekend and that he would telephone me during the course of his stay. As it happens, I was supposed to go to the wedding of one of my favourite cousins in Detroit during that same weekend. But the prospect of working at the Labour Committee trumped anything and everything I might have considered doing on that weekend. I cancelled plans to go to Detroit and simply stayed home, waiting for the phone to ring. The call did come, I had the interview, and, not too long afterwards, I got the job. It was slated to begin on June 1, 1959.

For me, this was a dream job. I was to be paid for fighting racial, religious, and ethnic discrimination. And I would be doing it in the public marketplace at large as a representative of the trade union movement. Thus, the job combined two of my favourite causes: labour and equality.

A word about the structure of the organization. There were a number of "human rights" committees of trade unionists across the country affiliated with various labour bodies: municipal labour councils, provincial federations of labour, and the Canadian Labour Congress. The set-up was originally conceived by the late Kalmen Kaplansky when he was the director of the JLC of Canada.

Founded in the 1930s to mobilize trade union opinion against Hitler, the JLC, at first and during the war, focused its energies on rescuing Jewish trade unionists and socialists from both the Nazis and the Communists. In post-war North America, however, the organization turned its attention to the fight against domestic racism. In Canada, this objective found its most effective expression in the various labour committees for human rights whose existence Kaplansky promoted across the country. Thus, the operation was a partnership between the Jewish and general labour movements. Due to a high level of shared philosophies, that partnership functioned harmoniously.

In part to avoid competitive fundraising within the Jewish community, the Canadian Jewish Congress (CJC) provided financial assistance to the JLC's program. This arrangement also involved the JLC in another partnership of sorts. Unlike the partnership with the general labour movement, the partnership with the CJC did involve the JLC in some differences over philosophical objectives. Unlike the CJC and most other Jewish anti-discrimination organizations, anti-Semitism was not necessarily the JLC's highest priority; it was equally immersed in combatting discrimination against blacks, Asians, and aboriginals.

A further word then about the philosophy of the Labour Committee. In contrast to other organizations in the field then and since, it was not a goal of the Labour Committee to promote love, kisses, and/or harmony among the diverse groups in the community. The Labour Committee sought to generate, not goodwill, but fair play. Instead of asking employers, for example, to like blacks, Jews, or aboriginals, the Labour Committee admonished employers to *hire* the well-qualified members of these groups, whether they liked them or not.

Needless to say, the Labour Committee was not opposed to the creation of intergroup goodwill. It was simply not prepared to wait for a state of harmony to prevail before it insisted on fair play in the here and now. Consonant with this approach, the Labour Committee focused on pressure as the vehicle for furthering its objectives. Although it would hope to succeed with rational persuasion, it was prepared to create social disruption. And, in many public market transactions it was prepared even to apply legal coercion.

The job, the organization, and the philosophy enthused and excited me. After a year of knocking on doors without getting a rise, the world began to glimmer. I was very much looking forward to taking up the reins of my new job.

CHAPTER FOUR

Amending and Enforcing the Law

$\mathcal{W}$ithin a couple of years before I started at the Labour Committee, a Toronto landlord had refused to rent one of his many apartments to a black family. He explained that this was strictly a business decision; he did not want to alienate his other tenants. Perhaps the fact that I knew some members of the landlord's family made me particularly angry over this act of discrimination. Certain subsequent events exacerbated the situation: a board of inquiry headed by a judge actually ruled that housing was not then covered by our anti-discrimination laws. Moreover, Ontario's premier of the day, Leslie Frost, reportedly told a delegation from the Ontario Federation of Labour (OFL) that the province was not "ready" for a law against housing discrimination.

All of these circumstances collaborated to convince me that the quest for such legislation should enjoy high priority on my agenda for things to do. Fortunately, my national director, Sid Blum, and my local Labour Committee were enthusiastically supportive. With my arrival on the job, therefore, the campaign began.

The idea was to publicize real cases of discrimination and to set up test cases and conduct surveys to dramatize the breadth of the misconduct. But the campaign had hardly gotten under way when a real case arose. In September 1959, a bare couple of months after I started at the Labour Committee, the *Toronto Telegram* reported an incident in St. Catharines, Ontario. Soon after having rented an apartment to a black couple, a landlady served a notice of eviction on them. According to the landlady, certain neighbours complained about having blacks in the area.

On the day the matter was reported, *Telegram* reporter Gord Donaldson telephoned me to ensure that I was aware of the case. Shortly after that telephone call, I got into my car and headed for St. Catharines. During the course of the drive, my mind was working overtime. I felt the need to come up with an idea that would either persuade the landlady to recant or, at the very least, keep the issue boiling in the press.

The drive was just long enough for me to produce a bright idea. I would compose and circulate a petition among the neighbours; it would be addressed to the landlady and it would tell her that the undersigned neighbours had no objection to having a black family living that close to them. At the time, I didn't really know what response I would get. But I thought that the petition would enable our side to win a victory either way. If the neighbours signed, the landlady might change her mind; if the neighbours refused to sign, the press would likely carry a story about the need for remedial legislation.

To my delight, the neighbours overwhelmingly, and without hesitation, signed the petition as I had drafted it. Only one man refused to sign. Of course, I asked him for an explanation. The man looked around at what was a dilapidated area and said that he was opposed to having blacks live there because they would "ruin the neighbourhood."

At that point, I went to the landlady's place and showed her the petition. By then, the Tely reporter had also joined us. As I reviewed the matter with the woman, I detected some equivocation. On the spot, I drafted a revocation of eviction notice and asked her to consider signing it. With the press watching, I urged her to sign. Within a short while, she did. With that, the landlady, the reporter, and I went to the apartment of the black family, delivered the revocation to them, shook hands, and took pictures. The next day, the *Telegram* ran a story with pictures of the landlady, the black family, and the petition. The headline of the story was "Neighbours Rally Behind Negroes — Hate Monger Loses."[1]

Fortunately, the story also contained some quotes from me about the need for legislation to deal with housing discrimination. After all, I argued, victory in this case was not enough; how many others were being denied housing simply because of irrelevant factors such as race, creed, and colour?

My little petition also had an impact that survived this story. It helped to quell the fear that a fair rental policy would be bad for business. I replicated this experience on many occasions and was able to secure housing for people who had otherwise been denied. This tended to demonstrate that, despite whatever racial prejudices people have, they are often able to identify with the plight of those who are disadvantaged. For the greatest number of people, their sense of fairness trumped their prejudices.

The petition also produced political benefits. It helped to persuade the politicians that they could safely support the legislation. They would not lose any popularity; they might even win some.

While I was happy to exploit the petition phenomenon as much as possible, I was prepared nevertheless to face the possibility of what position I would adopt in the event that people refused to sign. This was a question that frequently arose at conferences where I was invited to speak and workshops that I was invited to conduct. I began to develop a proposition that business interest could not suffice to justify racial discrimination.

I often argued by analogy. Suppose it was discovered that certain equipment in a factory was dangerous to life and health. Who would be prepared to defend the refusal to replace such equipment simply because it was expensive to do so? Similarly, doctors, lawyers, and accountants would not be relieved of their professional ethical obligations simply because compliance would cost too much. Thus, if financial considerations would not outweigh considerations of life, health, and public confidence, why should they outweigh respect for human dignity? On this basis, I would insist on pursuing those landlords who invoked business interests to justify racial discrimination. As already indicated, however, the business interests at issue invariably hovered on the edge of triviality.

Situations continued to arise in which I uncovered discrimination and wound up winning without resorting to publicity or my petition. One example will suffice. Shortly after the St. Catharines case, a mixed couple (the husband was black and the wife was white) complained to us of their inability to rent in a suburban Toronto apartment building. Within a very few days following their submission of a signed application, they received a letter from the company that owned the building.

The letter stated that the couple would be ineligible for an apartment "due to the peculiarities of the economic structure of the building." The obfuscation here, of course, was nothing short of elegant. It demonstrated a capacity to be both impressive and meaningless at one and the same time.

Before pointing the public finger at the landlord corporation, I had to verify the facts. No more than a day elapsed before I sent a white couple into the impugned apartment building to pretend they were interested in renting. The male member of that test couple was my old friend Berril Garshowitz. He was able to look like innocence itself. Indeed, when we were at the blackjack tables in Reno, Nevada, years earlier, a number of people mistook him for the youthful Freddy Bartholomew, then a Hollywood actor of some repute. In this situation, however, he wanted to look like a snob. So, Garsh kept pressing the rental agent as to what class of people they had there. The rental agent replied that they had nothing but the best—businesspeople and professional people. After this continued for a bit, Garsh asked the rental agent in hushed tones whether the building rented to black people. The rental agent was quick to provide assurances, "Oh no, we take their deposit money and then return it a few days later on some pretext or other."

Of course, my test couple readily provided us with sworn affidavits that contained this incriminating admission. That's why we sent them there. (We almost always sent our testers in pairs so that we could corroborate everything we alleged.) I then delivered the affidavits to Gord Donaldson at the Tely. At that point, he telephoned the apartment house construction company to get their side of the story.

When they heard that the Tely was investigating the case, they sent a public relations man down to the *Telegram* to attempt to take the reporter and me out to lunch. Needless to say, we declined the invitation. The PR person also spent a considerable amount of time telling us how much he liked black people and that he had gone to school with them. While indicating our great delight with his personal history, we continued to ask whether this particular black person was going to get this particular apartment. With that story sitting on the press ready to roll at any time, our large corporate adversary surrendered, and admitted the mixed couple as tenants in their building, where I know they lived in harmony for many years thereafter.

Since this landlord did the right thing before there was any publicity, it would have been inappropriate to publicize the matter afterwards. While I was happy to win the case for the complainant couple, I was sorry that I could not use it in order to publicize the need for a change in the law. But there were numbers of others that I tested with my own test teams of blacks and whites in order to verify the suspicions of the victims. In those cases, I often publicized what happened and did get my licks in for fair housing legislation. In addition to St. Catharines, such cases occurred in Toronto, Hamilton, Windsor, and Newmarket. It seemed to me at the time that I was going virtually everywhere in order to build the case for the law we sought.

In the interests of ensuring that no victory in a particular case undermined my ability to publicize the misconduct involved, I conducted a survey. I chose a neighbourhood containing twenty-six apartment buildings in Toronto. (I don't remember how I happened to choose that particular neighbourhood.) I arranged for black testers to go in, pretend they were interested in renting, and report the results. If they were told that there were "no vacancies," our white testers would go in a few minutes later and repeat the test. In as many as 50 percent of the targeted buildings, accommodations miraculously appeared moments after our black testers had been told that none existed. I took the survey results to the press, and turned over the relevant names and addresses of the buildings and the participants. The publicity was considerable and, again, I was able to drive home the message of the need for a fair housing law.

Once I had collected a significant amount of evidence, from both surveys and "real" cases, I began the job of trying to line up support for a delegation and brief to the government at Queen's Park. The brief made the intellectual case for the desired legislation and, on the basis of pleading, cajoling, buttonholing, and arm-twisting, I set about to organize support. I would send draft copies of the brief to every reputable relevant organization I could think of, asking both for whatever comments they had on the brief and ultimately to participate in our proposed delegation and to allow us to use both their names and those of their various organizations. This recruitment effort involved me in travelling to the places where those organizations resided. In addition to Toronto, my travel agenda included Hamilton, St. Catharines, Windsor, etc.

During the course of this exercise, I hit upon what struck me as a rather novel idea. I would ask these organizations to join ours in a delegation to their respective municipal councils. We would ask the councils to both endorse our brief and agree to participate in the delegation. My thinking was that these local delegations would give our cause additional and recurring exposure in the press and, in the result, the considerable political clout accompanying municipal endorsement of our brief. In the case of Toronto, Hamilton, and Windsor, we were able to enlist municipal council support. In St. Catharines, we lost in a close vote. At the time of our ultimate delegation, however, a few of the dissenting councillors participated with us.

All the while, of course, I was setting my sights on the various organizations whose support we needed. The easiest to get were our brothers and sisters in the labour movement. We just sent letters out to them and they provided their endorsement and pledges of participation almost immediately.

Certain welfare agencies and church groups required more persuasion. In one case, the director of a social welfare agency complained that our survey of twenty-six apartment houses was far from adequate to make the case. She contended that we needed to do more research. My instincts told me that no amount of research was likely to satisfy the kind of bureaucrat she embodied.

My response to her was twofold. I asked her whether she would need to know how many murders would be committed before she would agree to outlaw murder. My second response relied on our labour representatives on her board of directors. We thought that, if they pressed hard enough, the business representatives on her board would likely provide their support because, on such matters, they would not want to alienate those from labour. According to the reports I subsequently received, it appears that that is exactly what happened.

In the case of certain conservative church leaders, they expressed concerns for the freedom of property owners. They questioned whether such property owners should not retain the right to choose their tenants as arbitrarily as they wished. I responded by arguing that the freedoms of both landlords and tenants were at issue. After all, the inability of people to obtain housing despite their qualifications diminishes their freedom. So, in my view, it wasn't a question of freedom vs. restrictions;

it was a question of freedom vs. freedom. There was no reason why tenant freedoms should so completely be trumped by landlord freedom.

Moreover, I also pointed out that the freedom to be lost by the landlords was a very small one and, in any event, the law would apply only to self-contained dwelling units and not to situations involving the landlord in more intimate living arrangements with the tenants. Fortunately, the mainstream churches began to come on board. I suspect that this development was partly attributable to the growing number of liberals occupying top positions in the churches and interdenominational competition among the churches themselves. As time went on, none of them wanted others to be seen as more concerned than they were for the interests of victimized minorities.

On January 11, 1961, our deputation assembled in a pre-selected room at Queen's Park. According to the press, some fifty organizations represented by more than a hundred individuals were in attendance. Labour, of course, was very well represented: the OFL, the labour councils of Metropolitan Toronto, Hamilton, St. Catharines, and Windsor; the United Auto Workers, the United Steelworkers, the Oil Workers, the Rubber Workers, the Amalgamated Clothing Workers, the International Ladies' Garment Workers' Union, and our co-sponsors, the Jewish Labour Committee. There were also delegates from the Anglican Church, United Church, Presbyterian Church, Catholic Church, Unitarian Church, Canadian Jewish Congress, and community welfare agencies such as the Ontario Welfare Council and the Social Planning Councils of Toronto, Hamilton, and Windsor. There were also delegates from black, Chinese, and Japanese organizations. The Toronto, Hamilton, and Windsor city councils appeared with us as well.

Before the chair of the Labour Committee, Eamon Park, read the brief, I made sure to introduce everyone in that room. I named all of the individuals, together with the organizations and communities from which they came. I thought that those to whom we were presenting the brief—the premier and minister of labour—should be made aware of the number and variety of people who thought this issue was important enough to elicit their personal attendance. Since the minister of labour represented St. Catharines, I made sure that we had a very large number of delegates from there. At one point while I was introducing them, he asked, "Didn't anyone stay home today?"

My labour colleagues informed me that the premier's demeanour was much more responsive this time than it had been when they last discussed the issue with him. Indeed, a bare few weeks later the government introduced a bill into the legislature, amending the Fair Accommodation Practices Act to include multiple housing.[2] On the day the bill was introduced, I got a phone call to come to the legislature. I did, of course, and watched with excitement as both government and opposition parties expressed their support for the legislation. At one point, a pageboy delivered a note to me. It was from Allan Grossman, a member of the Conservative cabinet. The note chastised me for sitting behind the CCF contingent in the House rather than the Tory contingent. He thought I should be more demonstratively respectful of the fact that it was the government that introduced the bill.

Not long after the bill was introduced, it became the law. Our campaign that carried on from June 1, 1959 until January 11, 1961 had finally produced victory.[3] It was a marvellous way for me to cut my teeth with the Labour Committee. And I was still under twenty-nine years old. Indeed, I would not turn twenty-nine until March 17th of that very year.

*A*t some point during those first couple of years of my tenure with the Labour Committee, we addressed the woefully inadequate way Ontario's anti-discrimination laws were being enforced. Those charged with administering and enforcing those laws were overworked officials of Ontario's Ministry of Labour who were already handling a number of other statutes. Thus, their human rights efforts could occupy only some of their time. While these officials were conscientious, their activity lacked initiative, imagination, and pizzazz.

Arguing that "part-time enforcement reflects half-hearted commitment," we started to campaign for the creation of a human rights commission with full-time staff. While we repeated the foregoing theme in a number of public forums, much of our effort was also behind the scenes. We goaded, prodded, and pushed and, of course, recruited some of the senior labour leaders to assist in the effort.

Two back-room functionaries were particularly helpful in this regard. One was Tom Eberlee, a native of Premier Frost's hometown of Lindsay. Eberlee knew Frost and had ready access to him. Eberlee was also highly intelligent and deeply supportive of strengthening the government's human rights efforts. The other effective functionary really took me by surprise. It was A.A. McLeod. For years, McLeod had been a Communist member of the Ontario legislature. Notwithstanding the miles that separated his ideology from that of the premier, there was considerable warmth and affection between the two men. Of course, by the time that we had started lobbying for a human rights commission, McLeod had already left both the legislature and the Communist Party. He too was very intelligent and supportive of what we were about.

Early in this effort, we also identified the man who we thought should become the first full-time director of the commission. It was Dr. Daniel G. Hill who was then working for the Social Planning Council of North Toronto.

I had met and consulted with Dan Hill during the period before I got the Labour Committee job. Dan, the great-grandson of a black American slave, came to Canada with his white wife in the early 1950s. They had expected that life in Canada for a racially mixed couple would be somewhat less onerous than it would have been in the United States at that time. In Canada, Dan earned a PhD degree in sociology from the University of Toronto. There was a close relationship between the Hills and the Labour Committee. Dan's wife Donna was one of my predecessors as Director of the Labour Committee and her successor was at this time my boss, Sid Blum, who also maintained a close friendship with both Dan and Donna.

In either late 1961 or early 1962, our campaign bore fruit. The Ontario government announced the creation of Canada's first Human Rights Commission and its first full-time director was going to be Dan Hill. I believe that the enabling legislation was enacted in June of 1962, along with the integration of Ontario's various anti-discrimination statutes into one law: the Ontario *Human Rights Code*.

When he started his new job, Dan was a veritable house on fire. He did something that, until then, was hardly ever done: he aggressively publicized the existence of the Ontario *Human Rights Code*, the Ontario Human Rights Commission, and his availability to enforce complaints. In short order, the number of complaints increased substantially.

Moreover, it didn't take long for Dan and me to develop a highly collaborative relationship that endured for many years. We often plotted together. I would set up test cases and publicize them. Then he would respond by invoking the machinery of the *Human Rights Code*: first, an attempt at conciliation and, if that didn't work, a public board of inquiry with its various instruments of coercion. Not infrequently, we would decide together what places the Labour Committee should test. On some occasions, he would come up with suggestions for me that were based upon reports he got at the commission.

Among the early targets of our activity were recreational facilities—golf clubs and bathing beaches—in and around Windsor, Ontario. In this regard, the Labour Committee responded to an invitation from a Windsor black leader, Professor Howard McCurdy of the university's department of biology. Shortly after my arrival in Windsor, I met with McCurdy and together we formulated a plan for testing local golf clubs and bathing beaches that he had reason to believe pursued policies of discrimination against blacks. He agreed to recruit black testers and a mutual friend of ours, local criminal lawyer Saul Nosanchuk, agreed to recruit white testers.

Before I relate the next moves that we took, I feel impelled to disclose something of the interactions among the plotters. I am unable now to remember the precise cause but I do recall that Howard McCurdy and I had quite an argument about tactics when we first started to work together. What bears re-telling is the fact that both of us were headstrong people who resolved to overcome their difficulties in the interests of the cause to which they were both committed.

At one point before these matters were settled, I telephoned my boss, Sid Blum, in Montreal. I frankly sought his advice on how to deal with McCurdy. Characteristically, Sid resorted to humour. Instead of advising me regarding the merits of my exchange with McCurdy, Sid scolded me for butting into other people's business. Much of my anxiety was dissolved by the laughter that Sid provoked. Howard and I went on to do a lot of good stuff together.

On an early summer weekend, two carloads of us began to drive around to local recreational facilities that we believed were generally open to the public. We were: four testers (two blacks and two whites), Saul Nosanchuk (the driver of one car), Howard McCurdy, and me. Saul's car happened to be a lovely convertible. For years, I was amused over the spectacle of us young rebels going out to cause trouble in a luxurious convertible.

There was one other person in our convoy who deserves special mention: *Globe and Mail* reporter Marv Schiff. In the past, we had found the local Windsor newspaper (the *Star*) to be somewhat reluctant about reporting such bad news as discrimination about the Windsor area. We reckoned that, if the *Globe and Mail* saw fit to publish such matters about Windsor, the local Windsor newspaper would feel obliged at least to follow suit.

In all, we tested about seven or eight places: about five or six golf clubs and about two or three bathing beaches. In the case of the golf clubs, our black testers were told that these were private clubs and that in order to play there, it was necessary to be a member. Then they were told that membership was closed for the season, even though the tests were carried out in June. Similar tests were conducted at the bathing beaches. In all of the cases we tested, the white testers were told a few minutes later that they would be admitted on payment of a couple of dollars admission fees. The white testers had never been there before in their lives. Thus, there was no way they could have been taken for members.

A few moments after the blacks were rejected and the whites were accepted, Marv Schiff went into each of the establishments with pad and pencil in hand in order to get their side of the story. While I am unable at this point to recall the responses in detail, it was clear at the time that the places we tested had committed discrimination.

In Monday morning's *Globe and Mail* (following the weekend), a prominent story appeared about racial discrimination in Windsor. Later in the day, similar stories appeared in the Windsor *Star*. One of the *Star*'s columnists subsequently revealed his parochialism when he wrote a column complaining about the *Globe*'s alleged impropriety in being involved in the way it was with us outside agitators. In fact, the columnist had the poor grace to make a point of the fact that the reporter's name was Schiff, a name he considered especially appropriate in one who went there to stick a "schiv" into the heart of Windsor.

Another element in our campaign involved the filing of anti-discrimination complaints under the relevant legislation. We believed that, if there were helpful laws then in existence, we should use them. And so, we set about to give the government machinery a good workout.

In the majority of the cases where we had found discrimination, the proprietors were responsive to the government's attempts to promote conciliation. In most such cases, a settlement was reached by an apology and an offer to accommodate blacks thereafter. Two cases require special mention: a bathing beach that adamantly refused to play ball and a golf club that, upon investigation, we learned was genuinely a private club.

In the case of the bathing beach, the government went to the next stage of enforcement: the establishment of a public board of inquiry to hear all the evidence. On the morning just before the board was slated to begin, the bathing beach proprietor appeared to be overcome by a panic attack. He urgently asked for an opportunity to discuss the matter in private before the public proceedings began. Apparently, the prospect of having to explain his policies before a live audience somehow had unnerved him. During the private discussions, however, he came up with a rather weird proposal: he said that he would rope off a special area just for blacks.

Of course, it didn't take long for the government, the Labour Committee, and the complainants to reject his "compromise" out of hand. After some additional reconsideration—with the board waiting in the wings—the bathing beach proprietor capitulated. He signed the same apology and offer of subsequent accommodation that the golf club owners had signed.

The case of the genuinely private golf club posed a different sort of problem. In my view, it would not have been proper to use the machinery of the law against it. I took the position that such clubs should be free to practise such discrimination but, if they so persisted, we should attempt to ostracize them.

In canvassing a number of community organizations in Windsor at the time, I learned that the secondary men's teachers' federation and the United Auto Workers Union (as they then were) were in the habit of renting the facilities of this golf club for their respective annual golf tournaments. This was the leverage I sought. Having recruited in advance the cooperation of these two organizations, I told the leaders of the golf club at a meeting we arranged that those groups would thereafter shift the locale of their respective tournaments unless the club agreed to a new membership policy.

We drew up a contract which provided that, as a condition of those organizations continuing to rent facilities there, the club would agree that thereafter it would avoid discrimination in its membership policy.

This very much appealed to my sense of equity. The club could practise discrimination if it wished but we were able to persuade two leading organizations that decent people should not go to indecent places. In the result and with some fanfare, a "fair practices agreement" was signed by all the key parties.

In view of all the settlements we secured—with the public golf courses, with the public bathing beach, and with the private golf club—we believed that we had significantly advanced the cause of equality in the Windsor region. And, while we were at it, we developed some strong links between the Labour Committee, on the one hand, and Windsor activists, on the other hand. Years later, I had occasion to be amused by the contrast between what became of my two key Windsor collaborators of that period and myself. Howard McCurdy was elected to Parliament and Saul Nosanchuk became a provincial court judge. I, of course, remained a professional agitator.

One of the Labour Committee's most helpful allies in the early 1960s was Pierre Berton who, at the time, was writing a daily column for the *Toronto Star*. One of his favourite targets was racial discrimination and he went after it with particular flair. Like the Labour Committee, he periodically conducted surveys and, when he found discrimination, his columns would wind up publishing the names and addresses of the wrongdoers. This tactic proved highly effective in smoking out and embarrassing those who practised discrimination.

One of Berton's early targets, at this time, was the Ontario tourist industry. At one point, he sent letters to a number of randomly selected summer resorts and, on behalf of a Jewish-sounding name, attempted to reserve accommodations. About two or three days later he wrote to the same places, on behalf of a Gentile-sounding name and requested identical accommodations. In about one-third of the places, his Jewish couple were told that there were no vacancies for the period they requested but the Gentiles were readily accommodated. It never worked the other way around.

In the aftermath of the sensation caused by this Berton column, my then boss, Sid Blum, wrote to me from Montreal and suggested a follow-up by our local Labour Committee. He wanted us to test these places. He expressed it to me in typical Blum style, "Take a nice Jewish girl, go up north, and get into trouble."

Sid's letter triggered a few forays into summer resort country. On one occasion, I took test teams of Jews and Gentiles (the Jews introduced themselves by name when they approached the resort for accommodations). At a later time, I took test teams of blacks and whites, and on another occasion I took one witness and drove around to a number of the summer resorts for personal conversations with people.

When we tested for discrimination, we not infrequently found it. We then blew it up in the press and filed complaints. Once more, there was a round of settlements in which the tourist operators promised thereafter to be scrupulous about obeying the law. On one occasion when we visited for a discussion, a couple of Jewish guests intercepted me and assured me that there was no discrimination at that resort. In the words of this Jewish guest, "We Jews know when we're not wanted." Remarkably, it never seemed to occur to him that I too was Jewish. On a later occasion, Pierre Berton invited me to join with him at a meeting of tourist resort operators. Both of us spent an extended period of time answering the questions of those proprietors. I thoroughly enjoyed the experience.

One of the new initiatives that Dan Hill adopted when he first became Human Rights Commission director was to pack the hearing room whenever there was a public board of inquiry. The idea, frankly, was to intimidate those who practised discrimination. This proved to be a critical factor in the case of the Windsor bathing beach. It was also helpful when a board of inquiry was convened in the case of a Chatham boathouse owner. He had refused to rent boats to blacks for fishing. As was his custom, Dan went through the community and recruited a large attendance of interested people. Invariably, when anti-black discrimination was involved, Dan made sure that a large number of blacks were in the audience.

In the Chatham case, something different happened. Until that time, those accused of discrimination often surrendered either at the end or the beginning of a hearing. In the Chatham case, the boathouse owner surrendered smack in the middle of the hearing. At the time, I was acting as counsel for the black complainant, and I was subjecting the boathouse owner to a scathing cross-examination. In the middle of it, he said, "Okay, I'll take them."

With that, the judge adjourned the hearing and the parties went into · his chambers and began to negotiate a settlement. On the spot, Dan Hill and I tried to facilitate a proper outcome: the black complainants would pay deposit money and reserve boats from that point until the end of the season. In one or two cases, the complainants said that they didn't particularly like fishing. Dan told them, however, that in the interests of the cause, they had to go fishing. In the result, parties of blacks wound up fishing at that place on a number of weekends between then and the end of the season. In short, our side won.

One of the ways in which Dan Hill and I worked in those days involved his steering me in the direction of situations where, on the basis of reports he received in his office, he had reason to believe discrimination was being practised. Perhaps one of the most noteworthy of these situations involved the Canada Manpower Centres. This was the federal government's employment service. According to what Dan was told, it appears that a number of these centres were prepared to process discriminatory job transactions.

I set about to test them. Using a handful of volunteers across the country, I arranged for telephone calls to some twenty-one offices. In all cases, our testers pretended to be representing an American firm that was planning to locate in that particular community, they said that they just wanted to get an advance indication of the kind of service they could expect from the Manpower centres. Among the questions our testers asked was whether that office of the Manpower centres would accept discriminatory job orders: would they screen out non-whites, for example? The results were disquieting. In only four of the twenty-one offices we tested, was there an indication that discrimination would not be accommodated. Seventeen of the twenty-one offices we called expressed a willingness — and not infrequently enthusiasm — about serving the interests of racial discrimination.

We arranged to release the results at a human rights conference that our organization was convening shortly thereafter. Of course, we tipped off the press in advance as to what they might expect. In front of television cameras and bright lights, I announced the results of the survey. After I spoke, Dan Hill got up and solemnly expressed his "concern" over what I had revealed. Each of us was playing his part: I was the outside agitator and he was the inside conciliator.

The story was the lead item on the television news that night and it appeared on the front pages of the *Globe and Mail* the next day.[4] On that day, the Members of Parliament were jumping all over the minister, demanding to know how all this could have happened. The minister promised to look into it. To the best of my knowledge, the Manpower offices were subsequently computerized so that it would be more difficult to accept discriminatory job orders. We tested them a few years later and found no evidence of such discrimination.

The very nature of the work spawned continuing challenges. At some point in the mid-1960s, I received a telephone call from a black woman who contended that, because of her colour, she was denied a job as a temporary stenographer at an international business fair in Toronto. By the time she called me, the fair had ended and the prospective employer was about to return to his home in the United States. The usual *modus operandi* under the *Human Rights Code* simply could not be invoked. No settlement with this employer was then possible. There was no job he could offer her and there was no point in extracting from him a promise to be a good boy thereafter.

When nothing else appears workable, there is always money. I placed a quick telephone call to Dan Hill and both of us readily agreed that, if we could still find this guy, we would try to pressure him to compensate the woman for the discrimination she had suffered. I cannot now recall exactly how we did it, but we were able to arrange a fast meeting with this exhibitor before he left town.

The meeting that ensued turned out to be a good illustration of the kind of role play in which Dan and I often engaged. I was the "bad cop" to his "good cop." I began by trying to impress this guy with how very much the members of my committee would like to stick it to him. Dan then stepped in as the great conciliator and suggested money as a way of resolving the dispute. Without hesitation, the exhibitor offered several dollars. I snarled and Dan solemnly shook his head. The exhibitor then offered more money. Again, Dan and I said it was unacceptable. The exercise continued with more and more money being offered by way of settlement. At one point, I almost burst out laughing at how easy it was to get money from that miserable son of a bitch. Fortunately, I was able to bite my tongue hard enough to keep from laughing and Dan remained beautifully poker faced.

At the end of the discussion, we went away, having obtained a significant amount of money for the complainant. To my knowledge, this was the first time that money had been used to resolve a human rights complaint. The press carried a story about it the next day. Not long after that, the *Human Rights Code* was amended in order to ensure the legality of such transactions.

*B*y the mid-1960s — partway through my tenure with the Labour Committee — the Ontario *Human Rights Code* dealt with the selection and treatment of employees by employers, the selection and treatment of customers by proprietors, and the selection and treatment of tenants by landlords. But there was nothing then that would apply the machinery of the Code to the relationship between public licensing bodies and those who needed such licences to practise their various occupations in Ontario. In the mid-60s, I became involved in just such an issue.

In its July 1965 report, the College of Physicians and Surgeons of Ontario promulgated a new restriction: medical graduates who obtained their primary training in India would no longer be eligible for a licence in the Province of Ontario. This ban was slated to apply not only prospectively but also retrospectively. In short, its impact was retroactive.

A number of Indian doctors who had come to Ontario before this ban was imposed, complained to the Labour Committee. We began to investigate. Early on, our committee called upon the Ontario Human Rights Commission to use its good offices in an attempt to promote a voluntary settlement of the dispute. In making this request, we candidly acknowledged that discrimination in such matters was not then covered by the Ontario *Human Rights Code*.

Within the next few months, the commission directed a number of questions to the college. The college's responses to these questions contained as comprehensive a statement as it was then possible to find, outlining its position on the issue. By then, the Labour Committee had focused on the case of one of the Indian doctors, Krishna Baichwal, a graduate of Grant College at the University of Bombay.

According to the Ontario college, "the deficiencies in [Dr. Baichwal's] undergraduate medical education are those common to Indian medical colleges" among which it identified "older schools depleted of staff to provide for the newly established institutions." This comment squares with an earlier description in which the Ontario college noted that India had recently undergone a substantial expansion of medical education facilities. According to the college, such material failed to show that Dr. Baichwal's medical education "had been equivalent to that in Canadian or American colleges."

But, in a letter dated May 2, 1966, the Labour Committee pointed out that, although the staff-student ratio at Dr. Baichwal's college was not as favourable as its counterparts in US and Canadian colleges, it was far more favourable than what could be found in many European institutions which were recognized by the college. According to the World Health Organization (WHO) directory of 1953, one year after Dr. Baichwal's graduation, the staff-student ratio at Grant Medical College was 1:6. At Graz and Innsbruck in Austria, the ratios were 1:11.3 and 1:16.8 respectively. Belgium's Bruxelles had 1:9.9 and Ghent, 1:23.2.[5] These European colleges enjoyed more recognition in Ontario.

In its reply to the Ontario Human Rights Commission, the college expressed reluctance "to draw conclusions from the examination results of a small group of candidates from one or two schools in any one year." It pointed out that "Indian graduates as a group have had a rising failure rate in the MCC [Medical Council Canada] examinations over the last five years—five times the failure rate of Canadians."

But, in our May 1966 letter to the college we enclosed Medical Council examination results, not for one year, but for more than forty years. Again, we noted that, while the Indian results may not have compared favourably with those of Canada, they compared very favourably with their comparable numbers from countries whose medical education the college had accorded greater recognition. Between 1919 and 1963, fifty-one graduates from India wrote the exams and achieved a pass rate of 76.4 percent. Belgium's forty-one, Greece's sixty-one, and Romania's forty-three graduates achieved pass rates for that same period of 56.09, 37.7, and 62.7 respectively.[6] Moreover, the relevance of the failure rate in the previous five years was somewhat questionable. After all, Dr. Baichwal had graduated as long ago as 1952.

Of course, the college could always argue, as it did, that none of these criteria were exhaustive. It purported to reach its conclusions on the basis of all the relevant information. At no point, however, was it possible for all such information to be readily accessible to outsiders. Indeed, outsiders could never know what other criteria the college might invoke at any given time.

There was another issue, however, that we raised. We cited the fact that, in its considerable earlier correspondence with the Department of Immigration, the college failed to mention that Indian medical graduates were in danger of being disqualified in Ontario. In its exchange of letters with the department, the college identified a number of countries whose medical facilities were in some jeopardy, as far as Ontario was concerned. Yet, notwithstanding the fact that the college's attention was specifically drawn to this issue, there was no mention of any danger to India. Indeed, the only such mention was that Indian degrees were then "accepted." In view of the fact that the college was explicitly notified that Indian medical graduates would be coming to Ontario, we contended that it was unfair to impose this ban retroactively.

Incredibly, the reply of the college to us was contained in one sentence. It declared simply, "No new evidence has been presented that would justify re-opening the case of Dr. Baichwal."

Contending that "a public licensing body should be required to furnish rational answers to rational questions," the Labour Committee for Human Rights turned its attention to the legal vacuum engulfing such questions. The committee became involved in a campaign for an appropriate amendment to the Ontario *Human Rights Code*. In this regard, the committee recruited some prestigious support. In July 1967, Canada's centennial year, Justice Bora Laskin of Ontario's Court of Appeal publicly endorsed the amendments for which the Labour Committee was campaigning. The judge was the keynote speaker at an international conference of government human rights commissions.

During the period in which the judge was preparing his remarks, he requested me to come to his office so that he could learn something of the latest issues in the field. By that time, I had known him for quite a number of years; he had taught me three different courses when I was a student at the University of Toronto law school and I subsequently served with him on labour boards of arbitration and on a CJC committee. My meeting with Justice Laskin exemplified the phenomenon of "turnabout." I sat in his office, holding forth on what were then contemporary human rights issues and he was taking notes.

In his speech at the conference, the judge made a strong statement in support of the amendment we were seeking. The audience applauded enthusiastically. After all that persistent campaigning, it appeared that the die was cast.

By 1972, the *Human Rights Code* was amended to provide that self-governing professional bodies would be prohibited from engaging in the kind of discrimination that was elsewhere unlawful. Another victory for the Labour Committee and its allies.

ENDNOTES

1   Gordon Donaldson, "Neighbors Rally Behind Negroes — Hate-Monger Loses," *The Telegram*, September 11, 1959, 3.

2   *An Act to Amend The Fair Accommodation Practices Act*, S.O. 1960–61, c. 28. Online: http://archive.org/stream/v1ontariobills196061ontauoft/ v1ontariobills196061ontauoft_djvu.txt.

3   "Legislation Expected On Housing Prejudice," *The Globe and Mail*, January 12, 1961, 5.

4   "Jewish Survey Charges Manpower Branches Accept Discrimination," *The Globe and Mail*, April 17, 1967, 1.

5   *World Directory of Medical Schools* (Geneva: World Health Organization, 1963).

6   Medical Council of Canada Annual Announcement, Examination Results, 1965, pp. 22–33.

CHAPTER FIVE

Community Organizing

*A*mong the objectives of any viable operation in race relations is the creation of self-help organizations that are designed primarily to serve the interests of some victimized minority group. During my tenure there, the Labour Committee became involved in a couple of such ventures.

The first one arose in the summer of 1962. Sid Blum asked me to go to Halifax and meet with a group of black people from an area known as Africville. Members of this group had written to Sid, complaining that, in their dealings with the Halifax city government, they always got the short end of the stick. So Sid asked me to try to provide whatever assistance we could. I went there, not knowing what kind of help I could — or should — offer these people.

I did know that the part of the country I was about to visit contained proportionately the largest black population in Canada. We believed, therefore, that there was likely to be proportionately more discrimination against them than would be found elsewhere. Despite the fact that my knowledge of the area was limited and the nature of my mandate was vague, I greeted my proposed trip with much enthusiasm.

A word about my first day there. Arriving in mid-August, I was met early on by a well-respected member of the Halifax community, Lloyd Shaw. I had learned that, despite his status as a successful businessman, Lloyd had been involved for many years in social democratic politics.

Indeed, he was then on the national executive of the New Democratic Party (NDP), as he had formerly served the CCF. My patrician socialist host turned out to be very kind and gracious. He spent a considerable period of time with me, and showed me the major sights of the city. I should also note that his later contribution to Canadian social democracy included his daughter, Alexa McDonough, who became the federal leader of the NDP.

According to prearrangement, I was joined a little later by then *Maclean's* writer, David Lewis Stein, whom I had known from my camp years. David was there to do a piece on the problems of Africville and my role in trying to address them.

By another prearrangement, David and I went to Africville on the morning of the day after my arrival in Halifax. The setting was hard to imagine: dilapidated houses, no flush toilets, and a sign over the well warning people to boil the water before using it. About four or five Africville residents joined David and me in the home of Leon and Emma Steed. Mrs. Steed was the person who wrote most of the letters to Sid Blum that requested our presence there. It soon became apparent that she was one of the principal leaders, at least of this group of Africville residents. The possibility of relocation was very much on everyone's mind.

One of the first questions I asked of this group was, "Do you want to move elsewhere?" One member of the group quickly replied, "Would *you* want to live here?" No one in attendance evinced any disagreement with this sentiment.

I thought, therefore, that it was important to create some kind of organization that could help these people in their dealings with the Halifax authorities. Such an organization might be able to provide a certain amount of expertise and, more important, a source of pressure for whatever negotiations might ensue and for whatever political decisions had to be made. I also had it at the back of my mind that the Labour Committee was interested in trying to develop some affiliated human rights organizations in such regions of the country. Perhaps, I thought, it might be possible to create an organization that could serve both of these functions.

Accordingly, I arranged for a meeting to be held in my hotel room on the following evening. I invited the Africville people, along with a number of other Haligonians (blacks and whites) whose names had been supplied to me by Sid Blum's office and some of the local labour leadership. On the designated evening, about a dozen such people gathered in my hotel room.

After a lengthy discussion about the Africville and general race relations situation in the area, I proposed that the assembled group and any others of their choosing constitute themselves: the Halifax Advisory Committee on Human Rights. The idea was that these people would participate as individuals and not necessarily as representatives of any other organizations. In that way, they could make quick decisions without having to endure the delay of seeking approval elsewhere. But, since they were all reasonably well connected with various organizations, they could, when necessary, try to enlist the support of those organizations behind any plans that this committee might undertake.

Our next step was a meeting on the following evening with Africville residents in the Africville church. About thirty residents attended. At the appropriate time, I addressed the meeting. My message was simple: "I have no magic answers . . . but . . . you're not alone anymore." I told them about the new organization that was now prepared to assist with their problems and work with them. I described some of the things that this organization, with their help, could do. I told them that I would continue to help as much as I could but that "I can't come back here every week or even every month."

Finally, however, I said to them that "If I have at least introduced a few people from Halifax to one another, I can go back to Toronto happy." As soon as my talk was over, Emma Steed rose in her pew and exclaimed, "Now we have friends who want to help us. This is the first time in our history that people from Africville have gone into a meeting like the one Mr. Borovoy called. We've done a lot and with the help of God, we'll keep going."

In response to another part of my mandate for the Halifax trip, I was careful not to confine the subject matter of my talks to Africville. I also discussed other action that could be taken on the general human rights front including a delegation to the relevant government minister calling for more publicity regarding the province's fair practices laws and the systematic testing of apartment buildings with black and white testers.

Thereafter, the Halifax Advisory Committee on Human Rights functioned on its own for a number of years. It became a regular feature of many of the negotiations for the relocation of Africville residents. While I periodically exchanged letters with some of the committee leaders, there was, in fact, very little help that I could provide from as far away as Ontario.

A few months after I returned to Toronto, David Lewis Stein's article appeared in *Maclean's* magazine.[1] A number of my Halifax friends told me that it went over well in their circles. Not long after the article appeared, I was a guest on the CBC television program *Front Page Challenge*. Africville was the main subject of my appearance there. I recall the show going well and being particularly relieved that one of the panelists, Gordon Sinclair, refrained from asking me the question he so often put to guests: "How much money do you make?" I didn't want to reveal how *little* I earned.

As things worked out, I did not get back to Halifax for about four years. One of the most heartwarming aspects of my return trip was the reception I got from Emma Steed. When I telephoned her and identified myself, she replied, "Bless my ears." By the time of this return trip, the Africville situation had been moving into high gear. Dr. Albert Rose, a Toronto housing expert, had visited and recommended a relocation program. Meetings between the committee and the city were ongoing as were negotiations. Indeed, it appears that this little organization that I recommended, the Halifax Human Rights Advisory Committee, met forty times between 1962 and 1967 and it became deeply immersed in much of the action with city hall.

In an effort to put some perspective on all these developments, a later book on Africville by sociologists Donald Clairmont and Dennis Magill contended, "Borovoy's Halifax visit and the political strategy he suggested were responsible for changing the direction of Africville relocation politics." Perhaps so, but as events there transpired, it became clear that there were many divisions within the Africville community. Apparently, a number of the residents did not welcome the idea of leaving the area. Ultimately, however, everyone did leave and Africville ceased to exist.

Controversy about Africville, nevertheless, continues to this day. It might be interesting to examine some of the arguments that emerged during the course of the relocation. According to Clairmont and Magill, my "political strategy of collaboration with outside groups prior to the forming of [an] indigenous organization can be compared with Saul Alinsky's approach. Alinsky emphasized that . . . it is necessary first to develop a strong people's organization using indigenous leadership."

In the result, according to Clairmont and Magill, "the unorganized Africville residents were collectively excluded" from the planning and negotiating regarding the fate of their community. Indeed, the authors believed that "the Africville people were regarded essentially as being . . . less than competent in knowing what was good for them." This is a theme that emerged again and again during the 1960s and early 1970s: disadvantaged people were being effectively denied participation rights in determining their own destiny. Not surprisingly, Africville became, for a number of commentators, a prime illustration of such "patronizing" politics.

At the same time, the commentary surrounding Africville contained some of the very fallacies that arose more generally. Note, for example, the following statement in Clairmont and Magill: "Unfortunately the [Human Rights Advisory] Committee did not build a strong community-supported Africville organization." Perhaps, this was indeed unfortunate. Nowhere, however, do Clairmont and Magill impugn the *Africville residents* for this omission. Why, for example, did the authors not say, "Unfortunately the Africville residents did not build a strong community-supported organization"? After all, weren't they the people who should have been expected to shoulder the key responsibility for doing what was necessary? Could it be that Clairmont and Magill also regarded the Africville people "as less than competent in knowing what was good for them"?

From my point of view, it was strange that Clairmont and Magill compared my strategy of creating political coalitions with Alinsky's approach of first building an indigenous organization. The authors made it sound as though Alinsky and I had some kind of ideological difference over how to deal with disadvantaged people. In fact, the key difference between Alinsky and me in those years was not ideological; it was economical. His organization would go into a community with hundreds of thousands of dollars and a number of paid organizers who could stay there for several years. In 1962, I had barely enough money to get home.

As a result, I could spend only a few days in Halifax/Africville. Moreover, why should the creation of an indigenous organization become a prerequisite for providing disadvantaged people with assistance that they have requested? After all, the Steeds and some of their friends from Africville invited the Labour Committee to go there and try to help them. Should we not, therefore, have offered whatever assistance we could? Didn't the individuals who requested our help warrant that help, even if their neighbours weren't interested?

As regards the Rose report, the book on Africville relates how the Halifax Advisory Committee convened a public meeting for Africville residents to discuss it. Apparently, only forty-one of those residents attended. Thirty-seven of them voted to accept the Rose report. Thus, the committee reported to the city that 90 percent of those residents attending the meeting approved the report. According to Clairmont and Magill, however, the committee's letter to the city "did not indicate that only 37 residents had voted in favour."

The implication was that the small number of participants at that meeting somehow invalidated their decision. But how often is any organization able to enlist the attendance of anything but a small minority of eligible participants? Yet, it would be a rare event when that fact was allowed to interfere with the ability of an organization to conduct its business. Why should the situation be treated so differently in the case of disadvantaged black people?

In summarizing the situation, Clairmont and Magill noted that the "relocation promise of dramatically improving life opportunities for Africville residents fell far short of realization." Perhaps the authors' standard of measurement was flawed? After all, how often does reform in the real world "dramatically" and so quickly improve people's lives? In embellishing their conclusion, Clairmont and Magill cited a survey on the basis of which they declared that "only 25% [of the relocated residents] reported themselves as 'very pleased' " with their new circumstances. Given the widespread resistance people often have to change, I would have thought that a finding of "very pleased" from as many as one in four, would have qualified as a positive outcome. Even more significant was the survey result that a majority was at least "somewhat pleased" (very pleased—25 percent; somewhat pleased—28 percent; not at all pleased—47 percent). The majority who were "at least somewhat pleased" had to include those who were "very pleased." Thus, 25 percent "very pleased" is added to the 28 percent "somewhat pleased" to make at least 53 percent—a majority—"somewhat pleased." In the real world, people's responses to change are rarely more favourable than that.

In any event, instead of carping over the inability of the Halifax Advisory Committee to create a Utopian situation, someone, at long last, should pay tribute to the dedication and hard work that the members of that committee made available, free of charge, to their impoverished Africville neighbours.

$\mathcal{T}$he ensuing subject should illustrate that, notwithstanding the foregoing, I was an enthusiast about indigenous organizations with indigenous leadership. It will be noted, however, that the circumstances surrounding what's coming are significantly different from those described above.

In the fall of 1965, I received an invitation to speak at a conference sponsored by the Indian-White Committee of Kenora. Dan Hill, who was also invited to speak there, prevailed upon me to go with him by train instead of by plane. So we embarked upon that twenty-six-hour train ride that served as a prelude to my next adventure. Although I didn't get much sleep, I did have enough time to think through the kind of speech I was going to give.

I recall the conference as being rather well attended with people from both the white and aboriginal communities. I believe that the greatest number of chiefs from the surrounding reserves were also in attendance. The theme of my speech was that, if you want to persuade governments to act, you must be prepared to raise hell. Very few people in the real world are highly responsive to reason, but most people can be influenced by pressure. As I might have said then, for the first time (it was repeated many times thereafter), pressure without reason is irresponsible, but reason without pressure is ineffectual.

Something must have connected. After my speech, I was beset by a number of the chiefs in attendance. One after the other, they began to recite for me a litany of grievances they had over the way they were being treated. They were hoping that I could give them some tips for how to exert pressure on the authorities. In the midst of a conference with all those people buzzing around, it was not possible for them or for me to really absorb the grievances they had and the advice I might give. I invited them, therefore, to meet me in my hotel room at 5 p.m. on the day that the conference ended.

It has often been said that, according to the culture of many aboriginal people, the clock is a virtual irrelevancy. Such aboriginal people, it is said, rarely show up on time for appointments they make. It will be appreciated, therefore, how astonished I was when I arrived at my hotel room at five o'clock on the day in question and found that all the chiefs were there waiting for me. At the very least, this conveyed to me how serious these leaders were about the proposed subject of our meeting.

Their complaints spanned the spectrum: abuses perpetrated by law enforcement, inadequacies in health care, a disproportionate amount of welfare compared with an inadequate level of employment, insensitivity in the treatment of alcohol, and pervasive racial discrimination. Having obtained a broad picture from them, I began to zero in on specifics. Since they were so eager for action, I wanted to see if I could get them to focus on specifics that had a reasonable chance of achieving some concrete gains. There is nothing like the experience of some success to encourage more effort thereafter.

There was no shortage of such specifics. A number of the reserves reported, for example, that each of them had suffered a health-related emergency because of a shortage of communication facilities in their community. As I began to poll them, I learned that a remarkable number of reserves had no telephones. In consequence, each of those communities was able to relate a story of its inability to get help when help was urgently needed. A number of the reserves complained that many of their people were forced to seek welfare because there was too long a hiatus period between their trapping season and the fishing season. As for alcoholism, I remembered something that Dan Hill had often criticized. Why should a well-financed agency like the Addiction Research Foundation be located only in the southern parts of the province and not in the north where its services appear to be so needed?

Since a good number of these aboriginal people's complaints related to the town of Kenora, I suggested that we stage an event in Kenora consisting of a march and a presentation to the town council. We would ask the council to take some action on its own and to petition the senior levels of government to adopt those measures that were clearly beyond the town's jurisdiction. Thus, we would ask the town to petition the federal authorities for telephones on those reserves that were bereft of them and to petition the provincial authorities to lengthen the trapping season and extend the coverage of the Addiction Research Foundation. In addition, we would ask the town to establish a mayor's committee to deal with local discriminatory practices and perhaps assist in obtaining jobs for qualified aboriginal people.

I was surprised at the speed with which these aboriginal leaders endorsed these ideas. I offered to cancel my flight that was scheduled for the next day and spend the rest of the week, preparing a first draft of a brief and going from reserve to reserve to organize the event we were planning. And this is exactly what I did.

Shortly after our meeting ended and the aboriginal leaders left for home, I went out for a walk. No sooner had I arrived at the door of the hotel, when I was intercepted by a group of community development officers who worked primarily for the federal Department of Indian Affairs. They had heard of my meeting with the aboriginal chiefs and they wanted to know what had transpired. When I told them that we were planning a march and a presentation to the town council, a look of shock appeared on the faces of these professed social animators. "How did you do it?" they asked me. My reply appeared to blow their minds: "I suggested it to them." Apparently, these people had been trained to avoid direct talk with the members of the communities they were supposedly trying to "develop." The idea seemed to be that if these community development people sat around long enough in the company of aboriginal people, something miraculous would happen spontaneously.

The next day, Monday, November 15 1965, I began to organize. One of the native leaders, Charlie Fisher, picked me up at my hotel and we set out to visit the reserves. Indeed, we spent the entire week this way — we met aboriginal people in their homes, in their churches, and in the out-of-doors. Not only did we drive for miles and miles and miles, we also took lengthy hikes in the woods and walked across frozen lakes. Everywhere we went, I repeated to the people we met the grievances that their leaders had disclosed to me. I also emphasized a recurring theme: the key to success is the direct participation of those most affected: the aboriginal people themselves. It was critical, therefore, that they turn up and take part in the planned demonstration.

And, while I was doing all this, I was repeatedly consulting the chiefs and other leaders about the wording of the brief and the logistics of bringing all those people so many miles to Kenora. One of those I consulted—as I did on many occasions—was Dan Hill. As the director of the Ontario Human Rights Commission, he was prepared to provide assistance. What he came up with was, as usual, ingenious. He would provide an "educational" grant to the Indian-White Committee of Kenora. They, in turn, were prepared to use a substantial amount of that money to charter buses so that we could bring the residents of all those reserves into Kenora for what was surely an "educational" meeting with the town council.

At one point, the press became aware that something newsworthy might be happening. (Of course, any planned event involving such a large number of people could hardly have been a secret.) From me, the press wanted to know how many native people were likely to participate. Here I had to tread a fine line: I wanted to avoid an anti-climax on the night in question and yet I wanted to ensure enough interest that the press would attend. Invariably, I would give the press a number that was less than I expected but enough to keep them interested.

The local media also began to raise questions about possible violence. If I had been prepared to be irresponsible, I might have more vigorously exploited the potential for violence. Of course, that was always a subject of interest to the press. I played down the danger of any imminent violence but pointed out that unmet frustrations could generate future violence. I also lashed out at those elements in the town that were fixating on violence. In this connection, I said, "People here should be less concerned about the town's image and more concerned with the problems of the Indians."

So often, events in the United States become a yardstick by which Canadians measure what happens in this country. A few months prior to what we were planning for Kenora, the civil rights march in Selma, Alabama, had occurred. The *Toronto Star* made much of its view that the two situations were comparable: "Just as southern whites blamed outside civil rights workers for Negro militancy, so officials here direct more of their anger against organizers from southern Ontario, chief among them, Mr. Borovoy."[2]

On the night in question, Monday, November 22 1965, our demonstration took place. The number of participants exceeded our most hopeful expectations: not merely 100 as the press had reported our predictions, or the 275 that the native leaders and I had quietly calculated, but 400 Indians marched four abreast down the main streets of Kenora. They filed quietly and with dignity into the legion hall that had been converted for the occasion into the town council chambers. No violence, no threats of violence, no drunkenness, no rowdyism, as had been predicted by our white opponents—a dignified demonstration from the beginning to the end. In the council chambers, the brief was read by two of the native leaders who had been deputized by their colleagues to perform this role, Peter Seymour and Fred Kelly.

The next day, the demonstration was headline news all over the country. It also triggered a raft of editorials and other media commentary. Numbers of reporters subsequently visited the Kenora area and reported more fully on the conditions there. Within only a few months of the event, the relevant governments swung into action. The federal government ensured that every reserve would have telephones; the province lengthened the trapping season so that the native trappers could look sooner to fishing rather than welfare for their living; the Addiction Research Foundation announced the establishment of a facility in Kenora; and the mayor of Kenora established a mayor's committee as we had requested.

My attention then turned to the question of follow-up. I thought it would be wise for the aboriginal people to capitalize on their victory and create for themselves, a viable organization that could deal with their grievances and interests on an ongoing basis. In this connection, I began to work on the chairman of the Human Rights Committee of the Canadian Labour Congress, Art Gibbons, himself an executive of one of the prominent railway unions. What intrigued me about Art Gibbons was his remarkable capacity for growth: at the time, he was well into his fifties. He not only became persuaded of the value of having the Canadian Labour Congress assist in the development of such an aboriginal organization, he became positively enthusiastic about it. Indeed, I remember him saying at one point, "I want this program so badly I can almost taste it."

Gibbons used his substantial influence inside the Canadian Labour Congress to persuade his colleagues that they should fund a special worker who would live in Kenora for at least two years and whose job would be to assist the aboriginal leadership there to create a self-help organization. The Congress soon approved the funds and Gibbons asked me to set about hiring the worker. By the time this happened, it was 1968 and I had already agreed to leave the Labour Committee for the Canadian Civil Liberties Association (CCLA). But the Association readily agreed to enter into a partnership with the Canadian Labour Congress on the Kenora program in which the Congress would provide the funds and the ultimate lay leadership and CCLA would provide my services both to hire and then to supervise the worker in the field. Shortly thereafter, I hired a young social worker, Patrick Kerwin, who agreed to deploy to Kenora and take up the job there.

Fortunately, Kerwin did not have to work at creating such an indigenous organization; his job essentially involved restoring one. For years, there had been a Treaty Council #3 comprised of the reserves in the area that were, in fact, constituents of the Treaty Council. Pat helped them revive that organization and attract funding for it so that it could, thereafter, function on its own. By the time he left the job and the area, Treaty Council #3 was a flourishing organization that (I might add) had a budget larger than any with which I had then ever worked. So much for my alleged differences with Saul Alinsky.

A word about some of the noteworthy human interactions involved in the Kenora project. One of them involved the special relationship I seemed to cultivate with Art Gibbons. The mother of a woman I was taking out around then spent some time in the company of Art and me. Without any prompting or questions, she commented that there was an electricity in our relationship. This, of course, coincided with what I was experiencing. After many of my talks with him, Gibbons seemed to completely imbibe my vision for what we might accomplish with that group of aboriginal people. Indeed, I think it's fair to say that, as we went forward, ours became a completely shared vision.

Another one of the human interactions I mention more for its humour value than anything else. A few days after the march, the now defunct (but then very much alive) *Winnipeg Tribune* newspaper carried a story with the headline: "Negro and Jew Spearheaded March of Indians." Apparently, the reporter had discerned that Dan had played quite a role behind the scenes in making the march become the success that it was. Although some people were offended at what they believed to be a racist undertone in the story, Dan and I wound up sharing many laughs over the incident. Fortunately, Dan's superiors in the government never made an issue of his involvement with the likes of me.

I relate a third incident of such human interaction because it may have significance beyond what actually transpired. One day several months after the march, I had a telephone call in my Labour Committee office from one of the young aboriginal leaders I had met during those critical times. He was telephoning me long-distance in a state of outrage over the fact that he had been ejected from a bus on which he had been travelling in the north country. Indeed, his call was probably placed within an hour of this ejection. He demanded immediate action from me and my organization.

I told him that I would send him the relevant forms so that he could file a complaint under the *Human Rights Code* and that I would follow through with it in Toronto. He replied angrily that this wouldn't do any good because, at the moment, he was stranded in the middle of nowhere and nothing short of immediate redress would satisfy him. I explained as patiently as I could that there was no way on earth I could restore for him that seat on the bus; he would have to be satisfied with subsequent action. With that, he hung up in an apparent huff.

A few months later, I ran into him at a conference in Winnipeg. In a hotel room that had been set aside for the conference participants, he accosted me in person and proceeded to berate me for my alleged failure when he had called about the bus incident. Again, I tried to explain that even Superman would not have been able to get him back on the bus at that time. With that, he became enraged and let loose a stream of invective. Among the comments he made at the time was the following: "You're just like all the other white men." When I heard that, I became angry. "Don't you dare talk to me like that," I retorted. I then let him know that I had no intention of taking such "crap" from him. I also added that whatever injustices he may have suffered did not exempt him from acceptable standards of reasonable behaviour. And, with that, I heaped a bunch of invective upon him. In an apparently escalating rage, he stormed out of the room and, for then, that ended the incident. (In retrospect, I was relieved over his departure; he was a big guy.)

Later that evening, however, the two of us were in a car with a number of other people, driving toward Kenora. To my surprise, he apologized to me. Of course, I wasted no time in accepting his apology. But I went on to offer him what might have been (I didn't know for sure) gratuitous advice. I counselled him that, apart from a marriage partner, he should not dwell on people's motivations. I said he would be wise to assume that virtually everyone he dealt with was a self-seeking son of a bitch. The only relevant question, I suggested, was whether those people could be helpful to his people. If they could, he should work with them; if they couldn't, he should ignore them. But, I insisted, don't get hung up with people's motives.

Our next interaction was the diametric opposite of those that preceded it. On January 2 1969, the woman I had been seeing rather intensively for the previous six months suddenly became sick and died, within a couple of days. Not long after that happened, I had a visit from that aboriginal leader with whom I had quarrelled so vigorously. He brought me a native drawing and, just above his signature, there appeared the words: "Your brother." Needless to say, I was deeply moved by that gesture of warm and genuine friendship. Months later, I was told about a television interview in which he referred to me. The interviewer asked him whether there were any white people he trusted. His answer included, "Alan Borovoy."

Of course, I am unable to provide a definitive explanation of his changed response to me. I could not help suspecting, however, that I may have been one of the few white persons who ever really treated him as an equal. In matching his unkind words with my own, I avoided any hint of patronization or condescension. *Anyone* who had treated me the way he did would have received the same response from me. There was simply no reason to treat him any differently. And I didn't.

A comparable incident might help to illuminate this point. A few years later, a number of the treaty council leaders invited me to participate with them in a consultation with the federal Department of Indian Affairs. During the course of their exchange, one of the native leaders became very angry over the position the government was taking. In sheer frustration, he called out to the bureaucrat who was heading the federal team, "You're full of shit." The head bureaucrat responded with the words, "This is very healthy; I'm glad you said that."

Not surprisingly, this response compounded the anger in that room. I don't suggest that the government officials needed to admonish the aboriginal leader who was uncivil to them. But there was also no need to *commend* him for it. Although, there is no guarantee that a rough response would have evoked a gentle rejoinder, there is every guarantee that a patronizing response would evoke a hostile rejoinder. At the very least, existing suspicions would be exacerbated.

Several years later, in the 1970s, a group of young aboriginal "warriors" from the Kenora area seized Anishinabe Park and held it at gunpoint. During the period of that occupation, I received a telephone call from Roy McDonald who had been the chief of the White Dog Reserve at the time of the march. He expressed considerable unease that those young aboriginal men had resorted to guns in order to deal with their grievances. In Roy's view, our 1965 march should have amply demonstrated to the entire aboriginal community that lawful, non-violent tactics could actually work. He was upset that the younger people had failed so badly to learn that central lesson from the march. For me, at one and the same time, I shared Roy's disquiet about the young people but also derived considerable solace from the fact that Roy and (as he indicated) so many of his generation had completely assimilated that lesson.

In the fall of 1990 on the occasion of the twenty-fifth anniversary of the march, I was invited to return to Kenora in order to participate in the festivities with many of the area's aboriginal people. At the time, they inscribed my name in the honour roll for Treaty Council #3. That was an honour I continue to revere.

ENDNOTES

1   David Lewis Stein, "The Counterattack on Diehard Racism," *Maclean's*, October 20, 1962, pp. 26–27 and 91–93.
2   Perry Anglin, "100 Indians in Kenora Plan Selma-Type Protest March," *Toronto Star*, November 20, 1965, p. 4.

CHAPTER SIX

Outside Activities

*A*t the Labour Committee, it was always permissible for staff members like me to become involved in outside activities. My Western counterpart, David Orlikow, for example, simultaneously served as an MP for the riding of Winnipeg North. And frequently I sat on concilia- tion and arbitration boards as a union nominee. The constraint I always observed was that such activities should create no conflict either with the objectives of—or the time commitment required by—the Labour Committee.

One such outside activity began before I started with the Labour Committee. In February 1959, the CJC hired me, on a part-time basis, to work for the elimination of the religious education program that was then mandated in the public schools of Ontario.

First introduced by the George Drew Conservative government in 1944, this Ontario law required two half-hour periods a week of Protest- ant Christian instruction. (Since Confederation, the Roman Catholics have been entitled to their own schools, publicly financed.) This pro- gram should not be confused with the traditional religious exercises featured in the public schools (the recitation of the Lord's Prayer and selected Bible readings without comment).

The program at issue here involved full-scale instruction (it's fair to call it, indoctrination). Note that, in one of the early outlines for the course, there appeared the following admonition: "Jesus Christ is more than a hero to be admired; He is the Revelation of God in history."[1] Undoubtedly, such statements represent the sacred beliefs of many people. Early on, however, I argued that the faith of some (or even, most) should not be taught as fact for all. Controversial doctrines of faith, such as the divinity of Jesus, are simply not incontrovertible matters of fact, such as $2+2=4$ and c-a-t spells cat. Public tax-supported schools have no business teaching them as though they were all philosophically and pedagogically of the same vintage. An exacerbating factor in this regard is that generally youngsters of the designated ages, regardless of their faith, are required to attend the public schools. The notion of compulsory indoctrination in a faith alien to one's home and family is repugnant to democratic principles.

Invariably, someone would ask: What's wrong with learning about any of the great religions in our society? And just as invariably, I would reply, "Nothing." Indeed, as I would often add, it's not possible to understand much of history or literature without an adequate knowledge of certain religious perspectives. But this religious education program was not designed to promote knowledge about Protestant Christianity or any other religious ideology. It was designed to promote a *belief in* a particular religious ideology, namely Protestant Christianity. And that was always objectionable.

If the philosophical arguments were not enough, there were always the official guidebooks and even the behaviour of some of the official lecturers. In describing the circumstances surrounding the crucifixion, one of the guidebooks made an insensitive reference to "these Jewish rulers bent on murder." In a suburban Toronto classroom, a Protestant minister (authorized as a teacher of religion) asked the members of an elementary school class to indicate whether they had been to Sunday School on the previous Sunday. Everyone, except one Jewish boy, indicated that they had indeed attended Sunday School. With that lone boy standing by himself, the minister proceeded to lecture the class on the importance of going to Sunday School.

Whenever Jewish or other minority group members complained about this program, they would be reminded that they could always exempt their kids from the classes. That right, of course, was a matter of law. But to flaunt the right of exemption at those people simply compounded the insensitivity that enveloped the whole process. After all, most of the religious minorities in our society have sought acceptance from the majority. They were, therefore, reluctant to have their young-sters singled out as conspicuously different from their classmates. The argument of the critics was that, by forcing religious minorities to face such a dilemma, the religious education program was effectively infrin-ging their freedom of religion.

One of the first items of business that confronted me when I began to work on this program was a request from a group of Jewish parents whose kids attended Wilmington Public School in North York. They were upset by the existence of this program and they sought the assistance of the Canadian Jewish Congress in doing something about it. Despite the Jewish majority at Wilmington, the school continued to conduct Protest-ant classes, as required by the law. I don't remember now who came up with the idea but I think it was truly inspired. It was suggested that, even though the right of exemption did not adequately address our objections to the program, we could nevertheless use it as a weapon.

While individual parents had their misgivings about invoking the right of exemption, collectively they would not face the same embar-rassment. So we organized groups of canvassers to go from door to door in the Wilmington neighbourhood and ask the parents to sign prepared exemption forms for their respective kids. In the result, we gathered, after a short period, signed forms exempting well over four hundred students from the religious classes. I remember thinking how very much I would have loved to see the expression on the principal's face when he received all those forms in the mail. The accommodation of so many exemptions could well paralyze the whole program.

Not long afterwards, we received an invitation to meet with Dr. Fred Minkler, the then director of the North York Board of Education. Of course, we were delighted to accept his invitation. He told us that there would have to be substantial changes in the administration of the pro-gram, because, without them, the authorities were simply incapable of facilitating so many exemptions (as they were obliged to do). At this point, our group recommended that the board use its discretion under the law to exempt the entire school from the program. (In addition to the right of parents to exempt their kids, school boards could request exemptions for any part or all of their respective jurisdictions and teach-ers could do likewise.)

Dr. Minkler expressed misgivings about our proposal. He said that such a solution was likely to produce the religious fragmentation of the school system. He urged us to think in terms of a solution that could obtain right across the township. We should not, according to him, press our advantage where the Jews had a majority to the detriment of those Jews who lived in places where they were in the minority. At the end of the meeting, a compromise arrangement found acceptance on all sides. The religious classes would be rescheduled to the period from 3:30 p.m. to 4:00 p.m. That was the period that was usually used to help the needy and detain the naughty. From our point of view, this was a terrific solution. The "3:30 plan," as it came to be called, would quickly make religious instruction the most unpopular program in the school. And that outcome suited us just fine.

News of the Wilmington settlement quickly spread through the surrounding neighbourhoods. Groups of Jewish parents came to see us from a number of nearby schools. We took them to see Dr. Minkler and, without hesitation, he extended the 3:30 plan to their schools. Of course, those schools, like Wilmington, had Jewish majorities. During the time that all these arrangements were made, Dr. Minkler secured a resolution from the board empowering him to keep extending the 3:30 plan when there was evidence that the religious program was creating "disruption."

Then came the situation that would test the integrity of the whole arrangement. Parents from ten additional schools, elsewhere in North York, asked us to help them get the 3:30 plan. But, while the Jews were in the majority at six of the schools, they were in the minority at the remaining four. When all of these parents asked Dr. Minkler to give their schools the 3:30 plan, he appeared to suffer an instant seizure. In granting the request for the six schools with a Jewish majority, he predictably said that there was no evidence of "disruption" at the other four schools. To this, we responded that there was no such evidence at any of the schools that received the 3:30 plan after Wilmington. He maintained, however, that in those schools with Jewish majorities, he could reasonably anticipate disruption.

At this point, our meeting grew tense and angry. "Are you suggesting that we try to disrupt the schools?" we asked him. Before he could answer, we complained that such a posture on his part was completely "irresponsible." Moreover, we charged that it was he, not we, who were now guilty of religiously fragmenting the North York school system. "What has become of your wish to promote a uniform system across the township?" we pressed him. There was nowhere he could go and nothing he could do. The unprincipled nature of his policies had finally borne their contaminated fruit. From there, we took our case to the board itself. But political stalemate on the board prevented any helpful solution from that quarter. In the result, delegation after delegation of critics appeared before the school board week after week. Even if it was not then possible for the trustees to make the recommended changes, the delegations and the editorials they triggered provided terrific publicity for the cause.

At a later time, different trustees were elected and the political direction of the board began to change. A revitalized board adopted two measures favoured by the critics: exemption from the religious program for all North York and a resolution calling on the minister of education to review the wisdom of the relevant law.

During the North York battles, another entity entered the fray on our side: the Ethical Education Association (EEA). This was a non-denominational group whose members came from many constituencies. Originating in Etobicoke, it began to appear in a number of different areas. Its president, Doris Dodds, was a well-spoken intelligent Etobicoke homemaker and activist in Unitarian causes. It became my role, on behalf of the CJC, to help strengthen EEA and our alliance with it. To this end, I probably had at least three lengthy telephone conversations a week with Ms. Dodds, and, of course, I attended virtually all of EEA's meetings. (I don't want to make any of this sound like a sacrifice; it was always a delight to talk to Doris Dodds.)

Many of those delegations to the North York board were combined efforts from the two organizations. EEA also served to attract liberal mainstream Protestants to the cause. Early on, educational historian Charles Phillips, an Anglican, came to us through EEA, as did scholar-author John Seeley and United Church minister Don Gillies.

One of the ways in which I responded to the abuses perpetrated under the religious education program was to work them into some of the many speeches I was then invited to make to various community organizations. At that stage of my life, I was rather hot-headed and full of piss and vinegar. As for my earlier reference to the Protestant minister who humiliated a Jewish boy for not attending Sunday School, I frequently expressed my rage. I remember saying to one group that I simply could not understand how the boy's father refrained from physically assaulting that minister.

As for the anti-Jewish references in the guidebooks, I remember, on one occasion, reading the contentious portion and slapping the book down on a desk and exclaiming, "This is the crap that's being peddled in our public schools." At that point, a number of people in the audience walked out. Perhaps that wasn't the best way to "win friends and influence people"? I hoped, however, that for everyone who walked out, more people were won over by my youthful passion.

On another occasion, I hit on a highly effective response to such abuses. I learned of an egregious situation in Niagara Falls. One teacher put the names of all her pupils on the blackboard. If they had attended Sunday School on the preceding Sunday, she inscribed a gold star beside their name; if they did not attend, they received a black mark. I told Pierre Berton about this practice and he wrote about it in one of his *Toronto Star* columns. Berton's style was particularly effective. He didn't preach; he simply told the story. Invariably, the point of the story would jump off the page and confront the reader. His column on this issue produced many additional allies for the cause.

One of the most show-stopping of these abuses came to our attention in the mid-1960s. A small group of Universalists complained to EEA of a particular practice in their area, a small place called Gosfield South, near Kingsville. The school board was in the habit of inviting representatives of a fundamentalist Christian group to provide the religious classes there. The issue, however, became what they, in fact, were teaching the youngsters of Gosfield South. Among other things, they reportedly taught the kids the following:

- If your faith is strong enough, you can defy the law of gravity.
- Insane people are devil possessed.
- Jesus literally cured the sick by spitting on their tongues.

When I heard all this, I salivated. I knew I had a winner. EEA, therefore, arranged for me, as its counsel, to lead a delegation to the Gosfield school board. The idea was for us to call upon the board to exempt its whole jurisdiction from the religious education program. Of course, I knew damn well that there was no way the board would grant our request. But I also knew that the confrontation would be extremely newsworthy. Just to make sure, I arranged for EEA colleagues to telephone the petitioning Universalists and ask them, in turn, to telephone as many ratepayers in their area as they could and tell them what was happening. I specified that, in each case, our friends should tell the ratepayers that a Toronto lawyer was coming in to attack religion in their schools. I knew that, across most of Canada, it was highly unpopular (a) to be a lawyer and (b) to be from Toronto.

It worked. The board meeting designed to deal with this issue attracted more than two hundred people. It was probably the largest turnout that the board ever had. And, to help matters even more, those ratepayers were hopping mad at me and my allies.

In the result, it was not my arguments but their reactions that ensured the newsworthiness of our encounter. They called us every name in the book: "pagans," "Communists," and more. Some of them also shook their fists at us. That made for terrific photographs that appeared in the newspapers. As expected, the board turned us down but the exercise triggered a wave of prominent media attention (the *Toronto Star* had it on the front page, as did many other newspapers). Editorials, commentary, feature pieces, appeared in the print and on the electronic media. I also got an opportunity again and again to make our arguments in all of these media.[2]

The late American radical Saul Alinsky referred to the kind of tactics we used as "mass *ju jitsu*." It involves deliberately antagonizing your opponents so that they are provoked into behaving foolishly. In this way, we used the strength of our adversaries against them and they made the case for us. Incidentally, I took with me on that trip, two Protestant ministers who supported us: one was an Anglican priest and the other a United Church minister. While the priest frequently wore his clerical collar, the United Church minister rarely did. But I pressured him incessantly because I thought it would be particularly helpful for us to have those two clerical collars on our side of the dispute. He finally agreed to do it but told me later that he would give himself permission to wear the collar only when his activities were *against* the church.

At some point in the middle of one or more of the foregoing con-troversies, the government of Ontario appointed a special independent committee to review the religious education program. The chair of the committee was J. Keiller MacKay, a former judge and Ontario Lieuten-ant-Governor. It might also be added that he was the founding president of the Canadian Civil Liberties Association (CCLA).

I had occasion to appear before that committee to present the EEA position on the issue. While the details have receded in my memory, there is one exchange that I expect never to forget. In the wake of the hearing, I approached a member of the committee, the late F.C.A. Jeanneret, a for-mer chancellor of the University of Toronto. At some time in the remote past, he had been my French teacher at university. When the formalities at the committee had ended, I went over to have a more personal reunion with him. I first asked him if he remembered me. He replied that not only did he remember me, he also remembered where I used to sit *when* I came to class. I could have anticipated no better proof that he did indeed remember me. I was a notorious hooky-player from lectures and classes.

In due course, the committee recommended the termination of the religious education program. Although no government action followed immediately, various school boards across the province discontinued the instruction, either through formal exemption or welcome atrophy. In the chapter dealing with my years at CCLA, I will deal with how we drove the final nails into the coffin of this pedagogical impropriety.

*S*ince 1951, I had been a member of the Community Relations Committee of the CJC. (Originally it was the Joint Community Relations Committee of the Canadian Jewish Congress and B'nai Brith.) Remark-ably, I first entered that committee as a representative of the Toronto Jewish *Youth* Council. In many ways, I felt like "The Man Who Came to Dinner." Until the time when the congress was effectively replaced, my tenure with the committee had been unbroken for sixty years.

For the longest time, I was in complete sync with the positions that the congress adopted. I was supportive, for example, of the congress advocacy of legislation against employment discrimination and, as indi-cated, I heartily endorsed its opposition to the program of religious in-struction in Ontario's public schools. My support was enhanced by the respect I felt for the then lay leadership of the committee. People such as Professor Jacob Finkelman, J.I. Oelbaum, Professor Bora Laskin (as he then was), Fred Catzman, J.S. Midanik, and professional staff such as Ben Lappin and Ben Kayfetz helped to cement my basic support for the activities of the committee.

At some point in the early 1960s, however, this situation began to change. Following the assassination of US President John F. Kennedy, the suspected assassin, Lee Harvey Oswald, was himself murdered before a host of spectators in the Dallas city jail. The killer in this case was a local resident named Jack Ruby. Not long after this second killing, a leaflet appeared in Toronto declaring that Ruby had killed Oswald before Oswald was able to reveal that "Communism is Jewish."

Various elements in the Toronto Jewish Community were unable to laugh this off as a harmless prank perpetrated by politically impotent people. Indeed, there was considerable upset in the disproportionately large community of Jewish Holocaust survivors in Toronto. More and more elements of the Toronto — and then Canadian — Jewish community began to call for remedial legislation to prohibit public expressions of racial, religious, and ethnic hatred.

From the beginning of this development, I was uneasy. I feared for the implications that such legislation could have on a viable free speech in Canada. At the time, I knew that long-term committee member Syd Midanik shared my misgivings.

The rumblings turned into a full-scale campaign. A congress delegation met with the federal justice minister and pushed hard to get such legislation. A Jewish Member of Parliament from Montreal, Milton Klein, introduced a private member's bill on the subject into the House of Commons. My kind of free-speech civil libertarians appeared to be in short supply within the leadership of the Jewish community. And, in the late 1960s, the CJC convened its regular national plenary sessions. During one of the debates, Milton Klein told the assembly that, if his bill were to become law, the hate-mongers in this country would think twice before opening their mouths. Approaching the microphone just after him, I declared that, if his bill were to become law, most of Canada would have to think twice before opening their mouths.

Indeed, I voiced an argument at that stage that has stuck with me ever since. I contended that a prohibition on the expression of "hatred" will inevitably imperil a lot of legitimate speech. Pointing out that freedom of speech is often most important when it expresses strong disapproval, I argued that the dividing line between strong disapproval and "hatred" was effectively indiscernible.

When the debate ended and a vote was taken, I found myself in a minority of no more than five against a majority of several hundred. On our side there were at least Syd Midanik, David Satok, Harry Arthurs, and me. From that point on, the congress became increasingly comfortable with various censorship measures. And I became increasingly uncomfortable with the direction the committee was taking. These issues manifested themselves in many different ways. For some reason, the CBC began to invite various Nazi crackpots on a number of its public affairs programs. Every time this happened, there were angry meetings of the Community Relations Committee. At one point, I protested to my committee colleagues that, if they thought the Nazi hate-monger danger was so great that it warranted special legislation, they could hardly object when the CBC decided to make such phenomena a subject of program interest. In short, I argued that my colleagues were "trying to have it both ways."

I also thought that the CBC was overdoing the attention it gave to these neo-Nazi elements. But I expressly opposed a legislative solution: I took the position that these neo-Nazi elements were too trivial to justify a special law. I remember my friend Louis Greenspan quipping that the CBC was now creating a "Nazi of the Week" show.

In the midst of all this, a German neo-Nazi by the name of Von Thadden announced an impending visit to Canada. The CJC wanted to organize a rally to express local disdain for Von Thadden and what he represented. In that connection, I was approached by the congress's new regional director Meyer Sharzer. He wanted me to organize such a Jewish rally. As long as the rally was not aimed at any government action to restrict speech in this area, I didn't have a principled opposition to what it was planning. Certainly, I shared the community's revulsion over the emergence of neo-Nazi activity. But, in terms of my personal priorities, I was not at all anxious to become embroiled in the organization of such a rally. I knew very well that it would be extremely time- and energy-consuming.

But Meyer Sharzer, whom I happened to like very much, was relentless. He kept confronting me with one argument after another as to why I should do it. For the longest time, I was able to devise plausible arguments in response. But then, he announced that he had the show-stopping argument. With all the energy at his command, he exclaimed, "Please." At that point, I accused him of being a "devastating polemicist." And I finally agreed to do it. Fortunately, the visit never took place and I was spared an assignment I really didn't want.

In addition to the congress embrace of censorship, it also came out, years later, in favour of public money to religious day schools. In view of the important role that I believed the public schools had played in the development of positive intergroup relations, I opposed this congress initiative as well. In all, I played the role of official dissenter for some forty years. Despite my continuing opposition to some of its central positions, my colleagues never removed me from the committee. Until the congress effectively passed from the scene, I happily continued to serve and, of course, to criticize.

I was the NDP candidate for the Ontario legislature in the provincial election that took place on Monday, September 25, 1963. (As indicated, social democratic politics was an outside activity quite acceptable for Labour Committee staff members.) At about 7:30 p.m., a half-hour before the polls closed, I left the campaign headquarters and went out for a walk. My objective was to compose a speech with which to console my campaign workers. I was expecting an electoral catastrophe.

Upon returning about a half-hour after the polls closed, I was rendered speechless by the scene that greeted me. Dozens of people were standing in front of a wall that contained incoming election returns from our riding. The atmosphere was electric. As new results were being posted, cheering ensued. I couldn't believe what confronted me. With more than half the polls reporting, I was in the lead. My supporters were ecstatic.

"Oh my god," I thought, "what the hell have I done?" At about the halfway point in the campaign, I had pretty well decided that the politician's life was not for me. Yes, I had had a reasonably good time in the campaign. There was a lot to being a candidate that was fun. But I realized that I much preferred the life of a pressure group activist. Many of the campaign issues simply didn't grab me. By contrast, virtually everything about the Labour Committee affected me deeply. Besides, as a pressure group activist, I could exert pressure; as a politician, I had to absorb it.

Just a few weeks earlier, I had had an epiphanous experience, while I was canvassing from door to door. At one home that I visited, the television was showing the US civil rights march on Washington. It was like a magnet, I stayed all afternoon, watching that magnificent display of humanity. It was the day that Martin Luther King, Jr., made his "I have a dream" speech. I remember thinking that portable pensions and the other issues in the political campaign came across as a major anti-climax, after the drama of the Washington event. It's not that portable pensions were unimportant; they simply lacked the drama and excitement of what was on TV. I yearned to return to my work for racial equality.

So there I was on election night, facing the very real prospect that I could become a member of the legislature. Fortunately, the shock of those early election returns did not last long. The incumbent, long-serving Liberal MPP, Vern Singer, soon pulled ahead — and stayed ahead. In the result, I lost by about five hundred votes out of the more than twenty thousand that had been cast. But, ever since, I have mused about how there were two very frightened people at the end of that campaign: Singer, because he thought he was going to lose and me because I thought I was going to win. I never ran again.

Indeed, very often I thought that it would have been more appropriate for my father to be our candidate at that time. He canvassed several polls for me and, according to the election returns, we did very well in those areas. I remember mentally dismissing his reports of positive voter reactions because I thought that, once he introduced himself as the father of the candidate, the voters would act positively out of mere politeness. In fact, however, he really did forge a connection with the voters. No doubt, his success was attributable to his very conspicuous honesty and integrity.

Even though it all came together for me during that afternoon I watched the march on Washington, the truth is that I had always harboured some doubts about how much I wanted to be a politician. Of course, in agreeing to run, I made a valiant effort to win. But, at the back of my mind, equivocation persisted. During the course of the campaign, that equivocation would surface in different ways.

After speeches or in telephone calls from voters, I would periodically be asked where I stood on the program of religious education in
the public schools. Contrary to the way many politicians might have
reacted, I was not remotely tempted to hedge. I stated my opposition
to the program with complete bravado. Of course, my well-established
track record on the issue may have contributed to my stiffened spine.

When I was consulting with my campaign workers about what material to put in our leaflets, I made a politically strange decision. I decided to include a press clipping that had appeared about a debate I had had
earlier with University of Toronto history professor Ken McNaught. The
debate at a meeting of the Spadina riding New Democrats dealt with
whether our party should advocate Canada's withdrawal from NATO.
McNaught said "yes" and I said "no." But, unlike other New Democrats
who reached the same conclusion, I made some hawkish statements
about the Cold War. And the press clipping reproduced some of them.
Since our campaign did not involve foreign policy, my use of that clipping could be seen as gratuitously foolish. It could well have turned off
some of my support. But I thought there was something educational in
putting across the fact that not all social democrats were adherents of
the peace movement.

As I was sitting in our campaign headquarters one day, I became
aware of a telephone conversation involving a campaign worker who
was sitting next to me. The caller, representing the Yiddish newspaper,
The Journal, was apparently trying to solicit an ad from our campaign.
One of his tactics was to suggest that it might not look good if it became
known that Borovoy and the New Democrats discriminated against Yiddish. At that point, I asked our campaign worker to hand me the telephone. I began by identifying myself to the caller as clearly as I could. I
told him, "I'm Alan Borovoy, the candidate. You should have no doubt
who you are talking to." He replied, "Oh yes, Mr. Borovoy." Then I said
as forcefully as possible, "Go fuck yourself." I embellished that saluta-
tion with some choice remarks about my attitude to blackmail.

Whatever else might be said about the foregoing anecdotes and descriptions, the very least they reveal is something less than unbridled
ambition to become a member of the legislature.

Notwithstanding my equivocations and misgivings, there were
times when I went beyond the call of duty to get elected. The three can-

didates—all Jewish—were invited to appear together at the Baycrest Jewish home for the aged. My opponents—neither of whom could speak Yiddish—brought interpreters. My people urged me to try it myself. Although my Yiddish was far from fluent, I agreed to give it a try.

It was a strange experience. When my opponents said something to which I wanted to respond, I wrote myself notes in Yiddish. Apparently, I got so immersed in what we were doing, I was actually thinking in Yiddish. Not only that, but I also got off some good Yiddish wisecracks. In response to a question about pensions, for example, I said, in Yiddish: About my two opponents, my Conservative and Liberal opponents, if someone asks them a question about bread, they answer about matzoh (actually, that line sounds more amusing in Yiddish). Where this came from, I have never figured out. Suffice it to say that I wound up bantering in Yiddish. Despite this heroic effort, I believe Singer won a plurality of the votes at that institution.

Until now, I have neglected to mention the third candidate, David Vanek of the Conservative Party. One night, Singer was unable to attend an interparty debate so David and I wound up debating each other. Someone asked our views about publicly subsidized legal aid. I responded in some detail, indicating support for a much expanded system. At that point, David turned on me and said, "I'll tell you where things are done Borovoy's way—in the Soviet Union. I prefer the tried and true system of British justice." I had a field day in reply. I told the audience that what I had been advocating happens to be the law in most Western democracies: in Norway, in Denmark, in Sweden, in France, in West Germany, in Holland, and even in the motherland of British justice, namely, Britain.

The next day, Vanek telephoned me at home and apologized. He acknowledged that the crack about Soviet justice was uncalled for and that he had deserved my retaliatory response. Of course, I accepted his apology immediately. Although I regret not having further dealings with Vanek after the campaign, I have often talked about him in the most glowing terms. I came away believing that he was a real mensch. Indeed, at one point I told Singer (whose campaign headquarters were almost next door to ours) that Vanek was too much of a gentleman for politics, "He isn't a mean son-of-a-bitch like you and me." It may be of interest to know that Vanek was later appointed a provincial court judge.

He was the judge who released nurse Susan Nelles from the charge of murdering those babies at Toronto's Hospital for Sick Children in the early 1980s.

In view of the results of that election, it's obvious that the riding was a hopeful one for the New Democrats. Of course, no new candidate would be offered a riding like that without having established some kind of reputation within the party. I'm sure that my public record with the Labour Committee was a big help. But I had also been somewhat involved inside the party. In this connection, for example, I have already mentioned my role as a debater for the campus CCF.

After graduation, I remained engaged. I worked in the campaigns of David Lewis and Val Scott. And I became a delegate at the founding convention of the NDP. I travelled there by car with my friend, Dennis McDermott, who was then the Toronto subregional director of the United Auto Workers (UAW). At the convention, I enjoyed much folk singing and good fellowship. I even made some friends there whom I would later see—two American fraternal delegates from the US Socialist Party—Sam Freedman who had been Norman Thomas's running mate in one of the latter's attempts to win the American presidency and Irwin Suall who was then with the Jewish Labour Committee and later with the B'nai Brith Anti-Defamation League.

I also became involved in a policy fight. One young delegate introduced a motion for our party to advocate Canada's withdrawal from NATO. I drafted a statement in reply and helped to recruit other young delegates to sign it. I remember deliberately muting my expressions so that the statement would be sufficiently palatable to people who did not see the Cold War the way I did.

Another one of my involvements before my campaign was the presidency of David Lewis's riding association. Indeed, I held that position in 1962 when he was first elected to Parliament. The most interesting part of that assignment, however, was the way I got it. When first approached by the riding executive, I refused. But one night, David himself telephoned me and started to apply the pressure. I resisted, telling him how busy I was. "I'm also busy," he replied, "and I have a wife and four legitimate children." How could I say "no" after that?

ENDNOTES

1   Anne F. Bayefsky & Arieh Waldman, *State Support of Religious Education: Canada versus the United Nations. Studies in Religion, Secular Beliefs and Human Rights*, vol. 3 (Leiden, The Netherlands: Martinus Nijhoff Publishers 2007) p. 687, Chapter 6: "Canadian Judicial Decisions."

2   Arnold Bruner, "30 Parents in Attack on Bible in Schools," *Toronto Star*, April 20, 1966, p. 1; N.A. "The Fundamentalists," *The Telegram*, April 21, 1966, p. 61.

part three

The "Civil Liberties" Years

CHAPTER SEVEN

In the Beginning

$\mathcal{T}$oward the end of 1967, I received a telephone call from Syd Midanik whom I knew from the Canadian Jewish Congress, the Hillel Commission, and the CCF-NDP. He was calling to invite me to have lunch with him and a downtown lawyer who had spent a number of years on the Toronto City Council. The purpose of the call and of lunch was to explore the possibilities of my becoming the top professional official of the Canadian Civil Liberties Association (CCLA). The association had been created a few years earlier, in 1964, as a resurrection of the long-standing but inactive Association for Civil Liberties that had been operated for a number of years on a voluntary basis by Toronto lawyer Irving Himel. The impetus for the new organization was a bill introduced into the Ontario legislature that threatened to create a number of new, sweeping, and frightening powers for the police forces of Ontario.

Although I was in the first group of people who had been asked to serve on the CCLA board of directors, I rapidly lost interest in the organization. It appeared to me that it was essentially a "fancy pants" lawyers club that was long on theoretical speculation and short on practical activism. Although, like most people, I harboured a great respect for Syd Midanik, I was unable to greet the subject matter of his call with much enthusiasm.

Shortly thereafter, I sought the advice of my good friend Dan Hill and found that he too was uninspired by the prospect of my switching allegiances to the CCLA. Dan also reminded me of the special role I had been playing. After all, the Labour Committee, at that time, was the leading race relations organization in Canada's voluntary sector. And, as the committee's director, I had become the leading professional activist in that same sector. Besides, as Dan reminded me, I was having a good time — so why change?

Not surprisingly, I considered Dan's advice, as usual, to be sound and sensible. I became disinclined, therefore, to become any more deeply involved in discussions or negotiations with the CCLA people. Not long after that, however, I received a visit at my Labour Committee office from my old friend Harry Arthurs, who by then was an Osgoode Hall law professor and a leading member of the CCLA executive. He told me, in all candour, that CCLA had become "moribund." According to Harry, the directors had decided to approach me because they had been impressed with the way I had been performing at the Labour Committee.

But there was more. Not long before their overture to me, CCLA had received — out of nowhere — a bequest of about eighty thousand dollars. On that basis, they believed that there was enough money available at least to build a viable foundation for the fledgling organization. Harry also told me that he was prepared to adopt and promote a more progressive approach to civil liberties than had been pursued by the rather conservative CCLA board until then. In view of the influence that I knew he had, I took such promises seriously. It was the same with his further undertaking to help me recruit a number of new people for our board who were more likely to share my vision. Potentially, the CCLA mandate was much wider than that of the Labour Committee, where the emphasis was pretty well restricted to race relations.

I told Harry that the timing was not good because it was beginning to look as though the Canadian Labour Congress (CLC) was going to come up with the money to finance the Kenora aboriginal project that Art Gibbons and I had been dreaming about. As I have said, my heart was set on my becoming involved in the development of an aboriginal self-help organization in that area. Harry replied that he could envision the creation of a partnership between CCLA and the CLC according to which the labour organization would pay the field worker and CCLA would make me available to supervise that worker. This was a terrific example of the kind of creativity that Harry often contributed to his organizational activities.

The aftermath of Harry's visit left me in a real tizzy. He had made the prospects of life at CCLA sound very exciting. Moreover, I had been experiencing a degree of malaise at the Labour Committee. Even though I had always very much enjoyed the work in that job, some recent developments had begun to worry me.

After all the fights that I had fought and won at the Labour Committee, I was becoming concerned that there might not be all that much new left to do. And, in the one new area that I had started to explore—the rights of aboriginal people—some of the Labour Committee's backers were less than enthusiastic. In this connection, it will be recalled that the Labour Committee embodied two partnerships: one involved the Jewish Labour Committee and the general labour movement and the second involved the Jewish Labour Committee and the Canadian Jewish Congress.

The first partnership was all for the growing work with the aboriginal community but strains had developed in the second partnership. The Canadian Jewish Congress had expressed opposition to that program. The Jewish Congress readily accepted the Labour Committee's work with blacks, but the aboriginal program went beyond the narrow framework of formal discrimination. The activity with aboriginals involved issues of poverty, deprivation, and social services that didn't necessarily relate to discrimination.

As matters evolved, a substantial amount of the Labour Committee's budget was coming from the relationship with the Canadian Jewish Congress. Over the years, a younger Jewish Labour Committee had been able to face down its Jewish Congress partners and wind up with the program it wanted. In the late 1960s, however, the leadership of the Jewish Labour Committee had become quite a bit older and less able to take on their Jewish Congress partners.

Indeed, I was beginning to worry about what would happen to the total program of the Labour Committee if and when the Jewish Labour Committee (JLC) passed from the scene. The viability of the program had always been so dependent upon the vitality of the JLC. Without the JLC's continuing involvement, the program was likely to be swallowed up by the bureaucracy of the CLC. In such event, much of the Labour Committee's particular activism in race relations would give way to the competing priorities of the general labour movement. In the result, a realistic consideration of the Labour Committee's future produced a rather bleak picture.

An aggravating factor emerged at the time of salary negotiations. I asked the chair of the JLC for a moderate salary increase (which I knew very well to be within the ability of the organization to pay). He made the fatal mistake of playing coy. His initial posture with me was one of counterproposing less than what I had requested. At that stage, his bargaining tactics simply served to intensify my declining confidence in the viability of the JLC. I knew very well that, if I persisted, they would pay what I was seeking. But their negotiating position had reduced much of my enthusiasm for the job.

At this point, I called Dan Hill once again. After listening to the totality of the foregoing, Dan did an immediate and complete about-face. He recommended that I go with CCLA. In his view, it was apparent that, in the near future, the JLC would be counted *out* and that, at the moment, Harry Arthurs could be counted *on*. I stewed for several more days and then announced my decision: I would leave the Labour Committee and take up the reins at CCLA. I set the date of the transition at May 1 1968. It was then mid-January. Of course, the idea of making such a move on "May Day" exerted a strong appeal on my sense of history. I doubt if anyone else attached comparable significance to the date I chose.

In some important ways, it was unfortunate that my scheduled date of departure was so far removed from the date of decision. The intervening few months brought me considerable pain. As soon as they learned of my plans, a number of the JLC leaders approached me and expressed deep regret over my decision. One of them took me to lunch and, during the course of our conversation, he told me that the people in the movement actually "loved" me. This was not the kind of expression that one expected from such people. I even had a call from one of the top leaders of the general labour movement—the United Steelworkers' district director Larry Sefton. Although I never knew Larry that well, I knew enough that I deeply respected him. His attention to me at that point was a great compliment. As a result of all these interactions, I found myself seriously questioning whether I had done the right thing. Again and again, I made the critical mistake of looking over my shoulder.

During this time, another factor began to weigh heavily on me. My decision had been largely based upon the bleak future that I anticipated for the Labour Committee. But what about CCLA? Until that time, no national civil liberties organization in Canada had been able to survive with any kind of full-time staff. While I always believed that I could do a creditable job, I had serious doubts about the extent to which the general community was prepared to provide funding for an activist organization based upon altruistic ideals. Of course, people would pay to protect their immediate self-interest but would they do so for ideals that were somewhat removed?

*D*espite all of the pressure and the pain, I hung on. Something deep down kept assuring me that I had made the right decision. Of course, I also found considerable solace when I consulted friends such as Dan Hill, Mel Finkelstein, and Millie and Owen Shime. On the first of May 1968, therefore, I entered the downtown office of the CCLA and began to work.

The work was probably the therapy that I most needed. As soon as I started to function in the new job, I started to feel substantially better. I began making plans and making decisions. With every passing day, I became more immersed in the new challenges before me.

It helped also to have readily accessible people whom I could trust. Just as I could consult with Sid Blum, Dan Hill, and Eamon Park at the Labour Committee, so too I could call upon Harry Arthurs and Syd Midanik at CCLA. I have already mentioned the reliability and creativity of Harry Arthurs. Syd Midanik was intellectually brilliant and morally unflappable. As for his intellect, he stood first in every class he was ever in at school until the last class where he stood second. As for his integrity, there is no one story that could adequately reveal it. But, one of the clients of his law firm was treated to a taste of it when he telephoned Syd in a panic because of an impending tax audit. "What should I tell them?" the client nervously asked. The answer was vintage Midanik: "Have you ever considered telling them the truth?"

As that anecdote reveals, Syd also had a wry sense of humour. When my first two-year contract with CCLA was coming to an end, I opened negotiations with the organization by naming an amount I thought I should earn for my next salary. When I asked Syd what he thought, he looked at me with a deadpan expression and said, "It's a little low." Not exactly the kind of response one expects from one's employer.

Two other people upon whom I grew to rely were June Callwood and Louise Arbour. June's selfless dedication was always an inspiration as was her moral courage. One measure of her courage was her willingness again and again to go public in support of positions that deeply offended many of her fellow feminists. I knew her well enough to know that their consequent attacks on her were very hurtful. In spite of the personal hurt she often suffered, June remained undaunted in the public expression of her "offensive" opinions. Louise's brilliance often provided us with ingenious legal arguments when we badly needed them. As will become obvious later, she could also be counted on for her courage.

After a very few days on the job, I made a critical decision. In early May 1968, I stopped all the fundraising activity that was going on at that time. In view of the "moribund" state to which the organization had sunk, I simply said that, at the moment, there was nothing to sell and it would be better not to try. My immediate intention was to focus on the program. The idea was to create enough activity and attract enough publicity so that our fundraising efforts might be more successful. And so I set about involving my new organization in the affairs of the community.

One issue of money, however, demanded early attention. Some months prior to May 1, the CCLA board had made an application for a grant from the US Ford Foundation. The grant was designed to finance a research project into the way Canada's criminal justice system was operating. The Ford Foundation contacted me and expressed an interest in the proposal but asked that we write a second proposal for a reduced amount of money. This was an offer that, of course, I couldn't refuse. I set to work immediately and got off a revised proposal within a couple of weeks.

As early as late July of 1968, the Ford Foundation told us that it had approved a grant of $85,500 US dollars. The combination of the $80,000 bequest and the $85,500 Ford Foundation grant meant that my new organization had enough funding to last a few years.

By the time that we learned of the grant, my program of involvement in the community was well under way. As early as May 7, I appeared before the Sarnia city council, in a delegation with—and on behalf of—the

Chippewa Indians of that region. This group of aboriginal people had approached me during my last few weeks at the Labour Committee. Since there was no staff in place at the Labour Committee when I left and since the subject matter of these aboriginal grievances contained civil liberties issues, I took the file with me to CCLA.

The Chippewas were complaining that they had effectively surrendered, in favour of the municipality of Sarnia, certain roads that ran across their reserve. Apparently, they had done so in the early 1950s on the strength of promises that the municipality would maintain those roads in proper repair.

Over time, however, that obligation was reportedly not observed. At the time of our delegation, for example, open ditches along the roads were allegedly "laden with weeds, accumulated garbage, and saplings." The native people also complained that clogged culverts created serious flooding and that during the summer, the roads were veritable dustbowls. Whereas the municipality's other roads were paved with asphalt, the roads across the reserve were reportedly "sprinkled with oil."

In order to attract public attention, our delegation travelled to the city council meeting by chartered bus; this involved about fifty or sixty of the residents. The ride enlivened spirits and promoted morale. At the meeting, we stressed the city's moral obligation either to "repair the roads or return the roads." On behalf of CCLA, I declared that our intervention was designed "to secure the principle that when state power is employed to deprive citizens of their property, the state should be obliged to fulfill its agreements with the citizens."

The event was well publicized. In the aftermath, the city undertook to keep the roads in proper repair. To my knowledge, this was done. While I lost touch with our aboriginal allies in the area over time, I believe that, if the city had faltered at any time soon after that delegation, we would likely have heard from our partners.

A little more than a week (May 15) after that meeting in Sarnia, I wrote to the Welfare Committee of Metropolitan Toronto. According to reports, Metro welfare officials had precipitously removed a number of welfare patients from the nursing homes in which they had been residing to places outside the Metro area. Apparently, the Metro authorities had come to believe that the quality of care was unacceptable, as was the cost. Having been authorized by certain relatives of the remaining welfare residents of Toronto nursing homes, we told the committee that "regardless of any differences between the Metropolitan welfare department and the nursing home operators, there is no justification whatsoever for uprooting innocent people" without their consent. In this connection, we contended that it is not acceptable to rely upon "instant consent which is secured from the sick, the elderly, and the helpless." We insisted that "due consultation is the essence of due process."

Of course, we publicized our letter. It appears that, not long afterwards, the Metro authorities discontinued the impugned practice. But the case served as a precedent for our many future attempts to apply the principles of civil liberties to the field of social welfare.

On June 3, I registered on yet another issue: expropriation. In the words of the CCLA brief on the subject, "early this year, without warning or notice, the Etobicoke Borough Council divested over 30 families [from the Meadowsweet area] of their homes and property." In our material, I attempted to put across certain principles that should influence state authority when it seeks to expropriate the private property of its citizens.

Our ability to attract public attention to our proposals was enhanced by the inclusion in our brief of a number of actual case histories. Having secured the permission of the affected people, we related the stories — with names included — of about a half-dozen of the Meadowsweet homeowners who suddenly found themselves facing the loss of the property upon which they were relying so heavily. In some of these situations, this was not their first expropriation. Their government had previously inflicted a similar hardship upon them.

We called for the enactment of appropriate by-laws that would provide adequate notice, an opportunity for affected parties to make representations regarding the necessity and desirability of the proposed expropriation, and sufficient compensation to enable the affected parties to compete effectively for comparable property elsewhere in the borough. We also asked the council to petition the Ontario government for the adoption of similar measures across the province.

Since that time, Ontario has made a number of improvements in its expropriation practices. Of course, it didn't hurt that the Meadowsweet expropriations were highly publicized and, around that time, the McRuer Commission on Civil Rights in Ontario published its report in which it also called for comparable changes in the law of expropriation.

In the midst of a public inquiry regarding the alleged misconduct of certain Ontario magistrates (July 1968), it emerged that some Ontario police had engaged in the practice of wiretapping, in apparent violation of a federal telephone statute. Just as inquiry commissioners would usually permit the participation of third parties whose reputations could be affected by what happens at such proceedings, we sought the opportunity to register on how the reputation of the administration of justice itself could be implicated by the wiretap disclosures.

In this connection, we called for the inquiry report to contain a "severe reprimand" of the responsible parties and a direct recommendation that such parties be prosecuted. We addressed squarely the argument of those public officials who claimed that this police illegality was needed to curb the illegality of others. We argued that it was "necessary to convince the public that unlawful activity cannot escape the legal processes, no matter how lofty the ideals or how exalted the office of the wrongdoers." We also called for a recommendation that the appropriate authorities create a new law to deal with the practice of eavesdropping. Although we were unable to get the reprimand or the prosecution, the federal government subsequently introduced a bill on electronic bugging. After sustaining a number of amendments, that bill became law a few years later.

*O*n August 8, we took part in a Windsor public meeting (that we had instigated) to protest the denial by that city's police commission of a carnival permit for the annual Emancipation Day celebrations of the local black community. A few months earlier, CCLA's help had been requested by Edmund Powell, the convenor of the Emancipation Day celebrations. Mr. Powell complained that, without the carnival, he would be unable to finance the entire celebration and accordingly he called it off. The police commission had based its decision on its concern that, during the previous summer, there had been race riots in nearby Detroit. The commissioners were afraid of a recurrence of such riots and the consequent risks to the safety of the Windsor community.

As CCLA's representative, I took the matter to court on behalf of Mr. Powell. I argued that carnival permits should be based upon the reliability of the convenor and the safety of his equipment. The invocation of riotous behaviour in Detroit was an "extraneous consideration" and, therefore, beyond the jurisdiction of the police commission. The court upheld the commission.[1]

Of course, the court never considered the ethical merits of the commission's decision; it addressed only the legal scope of the commission's statutory powers. Thus, it was appropriate for members of the community to make an issue of the ethical propriety of what the police commission had done. And it was also appropriate for such members of the community to generate political pressures in support of their position. Hence, the public meeting. In addition to me, the platform party included local politicians, clergy, and labour leaders. As a special guest speaker, we had a Michigan state legislator who subsequently became the mayor of Detroit: Coleman Young.

At the meeting, I quoted the chair of the police commission. Among his remarks were the following:

there is ample credible evidence of the possibility of riots if [the carnival permit] were granted. . . . [N]o group or committee of people can with certainty predict what might happen three months or three days from now. Riots are explosive, unpredictable, frequently spontaneous, and their causes irrational.

I noted that the chair was referring, not to the likelihood of riots, but to their possibility. And since he had said that no one can predict such matters with certainty, he might very well have been assuming for the police commission the power to ban Emancipation Day carnivals until the end of time. I argued that the position of the police commission "would force Mr. Powell to demonstrate that a riot was impossible. I have no difficulty advising Mr. Powell that it is impossible to prove that riots are impossible. . . . Riotous behaviour in Detroit," I insisted, "should not restrict lawful behaviour in Windsor."

I also drew the attention of the audience to the situation in Toronto. John Beattie, a self-styled Nazi, had obtained a permit to speak in a Toronto park and his right to do so was protected by more than one hundred police officers. I spelled out the following absurdity: "In one Canadian city, a licensing authority protects the right to advocate persecution; in another Canadian city, a licensing authority denies the right to celebrate emancipation." Even if we were unable to get the carnival permit for Mr. Powell, we scored heavily in the polemical rhetoric.

On September 9th, I appeared as CCLA general counsel before the York Borough Council. The issue concerned the attempt of Gregory Spears, an American draft resister, to be confirmed in the job of recreation coordinator with the borough. He had been initially hired to serve in that position but, during his probationary period, certain members of the council had questioned him about his evasion of the US military draft and his pacifist philosophy. When he was asked whether he would go to war for Canada, he replied that it was difficult to answer a hypothetical question but, in any event, he did not think that war ever accomplished anything. Apparently, it was this exchange that prompted the borough to deny him permanent status in the job.

I told the borough council that if CCLA had been representing Gregory Spears at the time of this interview, we would have advised him not to answer questions relating to his draft evasion and pacifist philosophy. In this regard, I declared, "[I]t is not proper for an employer to question an applicant about his personal philosophy unless that philosophy is relevant to the requirements of the job. . . . Gregory Spears' abhorrence of violence would in no way undermine his performance in the field of municipal recreation."[2] Thus, to deny him this position because of his beliefs effectively violates "the most fundamental principles of political and religious freedom."

In response to the suggestion that Mr. Spears might unduly influence some of the young people with whom he interacted, we responded that we would have no difficulty accepting a taboo on using such positions for the purposes of indoctrination. We argued, however, that "there is not one iota of evidence to indicate that pacifists in general or Gregory Spears in particular harbour a congenital predisposition to indoctrination." In this regard, we noted that no one was advocating "a similar interrogation of Conservatives, Liberals, New Democrats, soldiers, or vegetarians" who applied for jobs with the municipality. In the result, Gregory Spears returned to work as a York Borough recreation coordinator.

On October 8, I made a presentation to the Newmarket District High School Board. The subject matter of my presentation was the earlier suspension from school of teenager Tim Cressman.[3] His offence involved his refusal to shave his beard as his principal had instructed him to do. Initially, his parents had attempted to persuade him to comply but, when their son resisted and demanded a rational explanation, his parents decided to support him. They found themselves unable to provide a rational justification and they had raised him to expect parental support unless he was in the wrong.

At the time of my appearance at the school board, Tim had endured more than two weeks of suspension. I argued that our educational authorities are obliged to respect the unique personalities of their students. Since the young man's beard was an expression of his unique personality, the school had no business imposing such a rule upon him unless it was necessary for the fulfillment of the educational mandate. I asked the question: "If we prohibit the cultivation of beards, do we further the cultivation of minds?" My answer to this question was immediate and forthright: "There is no co-relation between hair length and brain growth." Moreover, I argued that the stated need to require the removal of Tim's beard for purposes of class decorum was refuted by the great numbers of "well-functioning high schools and universities in which beards are permissible and plentiful."

Although I cannot now recall the details of my interaction with the school board, I do remember this much: for some reason I continued to participate in the trustees' discussion well after my presentation was received and digested. And I used this opportunity to push and press them. What finally ended my participation was the ultimate decision of the school board to re-admit Tim Cressman to class with his beard and warts intact. The issue was much publicized.

On October 9, we hand-delivered a letter to the Metropolitan Toronto Police Commission. The commission had denied a Yonge Street parade permit to the Vietnam Mobilization Committee for Saturday, October 26, the international day of protest against that war. Instead, the applicants were granted a permit to march on Bay Street and University Avenue. The decision of the Police Commission was apparently based on a provision of its parade by-law that purported to prohibit parades on "ordinarily" busy streets "except on days when the places of business along the proposed route [were] closed."

The by-law also permitted busy-street parade permits during business hours if they had been held annually for more than ten consecutive years prior to October 1, 1964. Of course, a Vietnam-related parade would not be able to qualify under this exception because the Vietnam War hadn't been going on that long. Perhaps only the Santa Claus Parade or the Orange Parade could have been squeezed in under this exception. · But political protest usually arises in a contemporaneous context. As I pointed out in many speeches that I made on the subject thereafter, no one was likely at that point to seek a busy-street parade permit in order to protest Mackenzie King's conscription policies.

The only other way a busy-street parade permit could be granted was if the chair of the commission and chief of police considered the proposed event to be "under unusual circumstances of municipal, provincial, or federal importance." My letter to the commission set out a number of reasons why the application at issue should be regarded as being of such importance. I thought it might also be helpful to look at some examples of other parades that qualified in this way. In one case, an international convention of the Fraternal Order of Eagles was allowed to tie up Yonge Street for five hours on a Friday afternoon (usually, busier than Saturdays) with five thousand marchers and thirty-five marching bands. As an added bonus that I simply couldn't resist, I let the Police Commission know that, at the time it was given this special advantage, the Fraternal Order of Eagles was a racially segregated organization. I argued that a parade on the issue of the Vietnam War should be able to claim at least *equal* "importance" with a convention of the Fraternal Order of Eagles.

Unfortunately, we were not able to succeed on this occasion. While our letter was careful to avoid, at that stage, getting into the complexities of the commission's parade by-law, I am pleased to report that the by-law was subsequently replaced by somewhat less inequitable ground rules.

During the time we were considering our response to the parade by-law controversy, I had an amusing exchange over lunch with Syd Midanik. In view of the reports that Trotskyists appeared especially influential in the Vietnam Mobilization Committee, Syd asked me whether I thought we were being "used." My reply was, "I know goddamn well we are being used." Invoking the CCLA mandate, however, I said that, for us, such considerations were irrelevant. We had to get involved. Of course Syd agreed, as I knew he would. Like me, however, he felt a recurring need to tell *someone* that we were on to those bastards.

In early 1969, I was contacted by a small group of civil libertarians in Fredericton, New Brunswick. They wanted me to act as defence counsel in criminal proceedings that had been launched against a columnist on the student newspaper at the University of New Brunswick. He had reportedly rebuked the courts of New Brunswick for granting an injunction that ordered a particular radical professor to stay away from the university campus. In the course of his comments, the student columnist allegedly described the trial involving the professor as a "mockery of justice" and he labelled the courts "instruments of the corporate elite."

Remarkably, he was charged with contempt of court by "scandalizing the courts." This was an offence committed outside of the courtroom; it was designed to protect the reputation and standing that the courts were supposed to enjoy in society at large. The rationale was that, if such comments could freely be made, the courts could no longer command the respect of the community. There were precious few prosecutions on record for such contempts of court. Indeed, an expert on the arcane procedures associated with this offence was called out of retirement to act as the prosecutor. As a friend of mine remarked, the hearing wound up pitting the guy who wrote the book against the guy who never read the book.

I feared that my first meeting with the accused young man may have fallen short of inspiring his confidence in me. I simply couldn't resist the impulse to wisecrack. I told him that his name—Tom Murphy—was a terrific one for a martyr. I said that I could imagine future generations singing the "ballads of Tom Murphy." I also advised him that an effective defence for him might require me to make some unflattering remarks about him. Since he was accused of writing things that could undermine the prestige of the courts, I was going to try to show that very few people would be influenced by anything he had to say. Thus, his upcoming trial threatened to reduce him every which way.

Actually, I found it hard to fathom why the powers in New Brunswick considered it so important to go after someone like Tom Murphy. They must have started to imagine that the security of their precious little world was going to come apart. The spectacle in the courtroom bolstered these impressions. On one side, were the students, hippies, and radical professors, bearded and long-haired. On the other side, there were the pillars of the establishment, shirts, ties, business suits, and good grooming.

For some reason that I never discovered, the proceedings began before a three-judge panel in the New Brunswick Court of Appeal. This unusual procedure equipped me with my first argument: by starting in the Court of Appeal, they were effectively denying to the accused person, a right of appeal that the *Criminal Code* had conferred upon him. Of all the arguments I used, this one appeared to elicit the greatest interest on the part of the judges. Nevertheless, they dismissed it along with my free speech arguments.

On the subject of free speech, there has been a tendency over the years for judges to acknowledge that there must be a right to criticize the courts, as there is in the case of all other institutions. But many judges have been quick to endorse the kind of reasoning that emerged in a late-1960s criminal defamation case. While the judge in that case also acknowledged the right to criticize, he felt obliged to point out that "invective does not advance the truth." On many occasions my answer to that argument was that "a piece of writing devoid of invective is likely to be a piece of writing devoid of readers. . . . . When," I would ask, "is the last time you saw a line-up to buy the *Canadian Bar Review?*" Unfortunately, arguments like mine simply could not reach the judicial Neanderthals who then inhabited the New Brunswick Court of Appeal.

At one point during the trial, I attempted to introduce the results of a survey that our side had commissioned. We had recruited then McMaster sociology professor Lynn McDonald to try to determine whether Tom Murphy's point of view was having a practical influence on community perceptions of the judiciary. Having interviewed a large sample of people, she was able to compare attitudes to the courts on the part of those who had read Tom Murphy's material with those who hadn't read it. Not surprisingly, attitudes to the courts were essentially the same in both groups.

But the New Brunswick Court of Appeal resolutely refused to admit that survey into evidence. The judges essentially considered the replies obtained by Lynn McDonald to be hearsay and thus inadmissible. On this matter, I put up quite an argument. I said that the replies Lynn McDonald received to her questions were not being adduced for the truth of their contents but rather simply as evidence of what those people had said to the sociologist. She was a perfectly competent witness to testify that those remarks, in fact, were made to her. It was then my intention to ask her, as an expert, to provide an opinion as to what those replies meant. On that basis, I argued that hearsay was simply not at issue.

The New Brunswick judges stood (or sat) firm and refused to budge. They excluded the survey and dismissed my arguments. Of course, they wound up convicting my client.

Once the conviction was registered, the next issue concerned the appropriate punishment. The proceedings were adjourned for a few weeks so that, at the next session, the parties would address the question of sentence. In the meantime, our side focused on the publication of an apology to the court in the hope that this would mitigate the severity of what was coming. Traditionally, apologies are tendered for contempt of court.

When I arrived in the courtroom after the adjournment of a few weeks, there was a press clipping lying on my desk. It was an excerpt from the university student newspaper and it purported to be a column written by Tom Murphy during the recess period. The column was laden with the most biting invective about the courts and the judges. When court resumed, the prosecutor made a motion to file that column as an exhibit. It was clear that he intended to use it to offset the impact of any apology that the accused had made.

At that point, it was *my* turn to make an objection on the basis of hearsay. I simply declared to the court that there was not one stitch of evidence that Tom Murphy, my client, actually wrote the column. All they had was a piece of paper with derogatory remarks and his name. That was not evidence against him or anyone else.

The response of the judges was to grant a short adjournment (an hour or two) to see whether the prosecutor could come up with evidence linking my client to that column. During that intermission, I held my breath for much of the time. When the recess ended, the prosecutor announced to the court that he had been unable to find any linking evidence. I heaved a sigh of relief and that column was thereby excluded.

The prosecutor then pointed out that there must be jail time. If the penalty were only a fine, he intimated that "the organization" would pay for it and the accused would never learn any lesson from the experience. When the prosecutor referred to "the organization" he suggested that there must be money backing the accused because, after all, how were the travel expenses of his counsel being subsidized? At this not so subtle suggestion of conspiratorial influences behind me, I jumped up and recited to the court the names of key people on the CCLA board of directors. Those names included CBC broadcaster Barbara Frum, newspaper columnist Pierre Berton, author June Callwood, Conservative Party activists Dalton Camp and Julian Porter, and our president, Ontario's former Lieutenant-Governor J. Keiller MacKay. "An impressive array of subversives," I said to the court.[4] In the result, Tom Murphy was jailed for ten days.

Needless to say, the case triggered a raft of publicity. Even a new magazine, *The Mysterious East*, grew out of the case. It was a writer's field day. By the time the case ended, it was the spring of 1969. Almost a full year had elapsed from the time I had started with CCLA. I believe that all the public attention that we received from the various actions I had taken created a situation in which, at long last, we could do some effective fundraising.

*I*n the late summer of 1968, I went to New York with my old friend Mel Finkelstein, who had become CCLA's financial advisor. There, we met officials of the American Civil Liberties Union (ACLU) and they taught us how their membership development campaigns were operated. Upon our return, we adopted their mass-mail technique and never looked back. Our membership began to grow.

And so did our program. In area after area, CCLA mounted challenges of Canadian institutional behaviour. Our goal was to protect the fundamental freedoms endemic to the democratic system. So, we championed freedom of speech, security of the person, equal dignity, and procedural fairness. Our adversaries included governments at all levels: federal, provincial, and municipal. Our institutional targets included police departments, welfare administrations, health authorities, and boards of education. Despite our limited resources, we attempted to register all over the place. And we did.

Although it made sense to discuss my early CCLA period in a chronological way, it would be impossible to replicate that approach with regard to the ensuing forty years. I will treat what follows, therefore, on the basis of the various themes that prompted CCLA involvement.

ENDNOTES

1 "Decision Not to Allow Emancipation Day Carnival Upheld," *Globe and Mail*, June 15, 1968, 5.
2 CCLA, "Submissions to York Borough Council re. the Employment of Gregory Spears," September 9, 1968, p. 3.
3 CCLA, "Submissions to Newmarket District High School Board re. Suspension of Tim Cressman," October 8, 1968, p. 2.
4 *R v Murphy*, 1969 CanLII 164 (NB CA), online: http://canlii.ca/t/fx314.

CHAPTER EIGHT

Freedom of Expression

VILIFICATION

I have already related how the Canadian Jewish Congress got involved in a campaign to secure an anti-hate law for Canada. And I also recounted how, within congress circles, I expressed my opposition to that campaign. At that time, I was regularly employed by the Labour Committee and had no particular occasion to go public over my differences with the congress.

But all that changed when I went to work for the Canadian Civil Liberties Association (CCLA). It became part of my mandate to register publicly on the merits of the anti-hate law. And so I finally came "out of the closet," so to speak. Within several months of my inception at CCLA, the Parliament of Canada had a government anti-hate bill on its agenda. Since a Senate committee was holding hearings on the bill, that provided a platform for CCLA to register publicly and, of course, it did. By the time the issue arrived in this way at the doorstep of Parliament, the neo-Nazi provocations of the mid-1960s had largely abated. Without that backdrop, the abstract discussions regarding the terms of a bill were incapable of creating a comparable level of public controversy. Thus, CCLA was able to express its opposition and emerge nevertheless, essentially unscathed.

But, by the early to mid-1980s, provocations erupted again. This time, they centred on a particularly repugnant individual, Ernst Zundel, an immigrant from Germany. His message surpassed the traditional forms of anti-Semitic invective. He brazenly denied, flat out, that there had ever been a Holocaust. It's not hard to imagine the impact of this message on the Jewish survivors of Nazi persecution. As one writer so poignantly expressed the matter: It wasn't enough for yesterday's Nazis to extinguish six million Jewish lives, their modern sympathizers seek to extinguish six million Jewish *deaths*. The very repugnance of Ernst Zundel and his message effectively guaranteed that any CCLA effort to oppose legal censorship in his case would ignite a firestorm of controversy. And that, of course, is exactly what happened.

Initially, the Jewish Congress and its allies considered using the anti-hate law. It was not clear, however, that the denial of the Holocaust could be treated as the wilful promotion of hatred, within the meaning of the *Criminal Code*. In view of that, certain allies of the Jewish Congress raised the very real possibility that the Attorney General of Ontario would not consent — as the anti-hate law explicitly required before such a prosecution could proceed.

An independent element of the Jewish community (comprised largely of Holocaust survivors) retained a lawyer in order to launch proceedings under the false news section of the *Criminal Code*. This did not require the authorization of the Attorney General, and Zundel's behaviour was arguably more vulnerable to this section rather than the anti-hate law. According to the false news provision, it was an offence knowingly to disseminate false material that was "likely to cause injury . . . to a public interest."

Upon being called by the media to comment on the propriety of this prosecution, I expressed a vigorous dissent. The gist of my argument was that the false news section was capable of nailing commentators who did not bear the remotest resemblance to Ernst Zundel. Both in press interviews and in articles that I published, I provided examples of the kind of speech that this law was capable of targeting. If denying the Holocaust could authorize a criminal prosecution, what about denying the enormity of Stalin's crimes or denying the magnitude of the Inquisition? I also pointed out how frequently politicians accuse each other of lying. Indeed, they often tend to exaggerate their own claims and minimize those of their adversaries. In view of the fact that the false news law nowhere attempts to define the kind of "public interest" that must be injured, the dangers become obvious.

Even if those accused of this offence would ultimately be cleared because of inadequate proof that they had *knowingly* lied, they would have sustained a serious invasion of their rights. A critical danger to free speech is the very existence of a law that is capable of threatening us for engaging in normal democratic debate.

Unfortunately, my public opposition to the Zundel prosecution provoked the torrent of criticism I had expected. Long-time friends and colleagues within the Jewish community denounced the position I had taken. Some members of the Jewish community reportedly accused me of being a "self-hating Jew." Unavoidably, the CCLA dissent in the Zundel case fractured the long-standing alliance that had obtained between the congress and us.

As I recount the details of this regrettable schism, I feel impelled to qualify my remarks. Despite the magnitude of the public differences that arose between the Jewish and civil libertarian communities, it should be noted that, as far as the leadership of the Jewish community was concerned, these differences were essentially philosophical, not personal. During and despite the controversy, I retained my seat on the congress's community relations committee. Although the officers could easily have removed me, they never did. We continued to enjoy a friendly rapport in our personal interactions.

The Zundel trial (in 1985) turned out to be the disaster that our side had anticipated. There was a discussion in court over the monstrous proposition advanced by the accused that Auschwitz was not a Nazi death camp but a Jewish country club.[1] And the prosecutor, not the defence, called a non-Jewish banker to the stand and asked him if he was being paid by an international Zionist/Communist/banker/Jewish/Freemason conspiracy. As Toronto rabbi, W. Gunther Plaut, observed in the aftermath of the trial: If someone calls your mother a whore, that is not a fit subject for a debate. But the Zundel trial provided a platform — indeed, a pressure — to vocalize just such absurdities.

In the aftermath of the trial, the media descended upon me. One after the other called, requesting the CCLA opinion about the merits of the case. And, in interview after interview, I kept criticizing the false news law and the foolishness of such prosecutions. After a day of un-ending interviews, I remember feeling especially worn out. As I re-marked to my then girlfriend, I was beginning to understand why my media pronouncements were affecting me in this way. It wasn't the unpopularity of my position; I was used to that. But I was particularly struck by the hurt that I believe my comments were causing to so many of the Holocaust survivors. *They* simply did not deserve such unremit-ting repetition of this affront to their dignity.

A few days after the trial, I was invited to appear on an open-line radio program that was devoted to the case. At one point, the moderator announced that Ernst Zundel himself was on the line and, right after the ensuing commercial, he would be given a chance to speak with me. For-tunately, the commercial gave me an opportunity to think through how I was going to handle the situation. Of course, I had no wish to speak with him, either publicly or privately. After the commercial, Zundel ex-pressed praise and admiration for my various public comments on his case—all of which made me squirm in my chair. When the microphone was handed to me, I simply said, "While I feel obliged to defend Mr. Zundel's legal rights, I have no comparable obligation to treat him with respect." With that, we pulled the plug on him. And so, I did not talk directly with him then or, to my knowledge, at any other time.

When the Zundel case reached the Ontario Court of Appeal (in 1986), CCLA had a decision to make. Would we seek leave to intervene to chal-lenge the constitutionality of the false news law? If we did, we were very likely to aggravate the already tense situation between our long-time Jew-ish allies and ourselves. If we failed to seek such leave, we risked passing up a critical opportunity to attack a potentially repressive law.

Of course, we determined that we had to challenge that law. Signifi-cantly, there was very little opposition on our board to the proposed action. Most of us had resolved some time earlier that a civil liberties or-ganization worth its salt could not be deterred from taking such action because of concerns for its popularity.

At the time, however, there was at least one board member who took strong exception to our contemplated intervention: Irwin Cotler. Although he wasn't able to attend any of our board meetings to register his objections personally, he wrote us from his home in Montreal. The gist of his argument was that we should not risk dignifying a malevolence like Zundel. Better to defer our attack on the false news law until a more felicitous case came along.

The overwhelming board response to Cotler was that the real world is not so neat. There's no way to know when a more appropriate case would arise. In the meantime, however, the legitimate free speech of many constituencies could be threatened by the continued existence of this law. That's why we believed that we had to challenge it at the *first* opportunity. Accordingly, we rejected the idea of postponement and decided on immediate action.

Nevertheless, we still felt a need to do what we could to ensure public appreciation that the convergence of our legal positions did not represent any kind of alliance between the Zundel camp and CCLA. Indeed, as civil libertarians, it was important that we emphasize our hostility to what Zundel and his followers represented.

Zundel's lawyer, Douglas Christie, provided the basis for our next move. At the time, he was representing not only Ernst Zundel on a false news charge but also a former Alberta high school teacher, James Keegstra, on a hate propaganda charge. A number of comments attributed to Christie in the mass media created the impression that he not only defended his clients' legal rights but also endorsed their social views.

Not long before we filed our motion in court, I wrote to Mr. Christie, requesting a clarification of his position. My letter set out a number of the contentious quotes. In one of them, for example, he had been quoted as stating that his relationship with Keegstra began when he telephoned him "simply to commend the man's courage in fighting for what he believed in." Of course, we asked Christie whether this report was accurate. If so, we contended that it would reveal "a remarkable sense of perspective." When a man like Keegstra "abuses his position of trust as a teacher to preach hatred to a captive audience of teenaged students, his alleged courage is hardly the most significant thing about him." Again, we distinguished between defending Keegstra's legal rights and seeking him out "for moral commendation."

Acknowledging as we did the propriety of lawyers vigorously defending the rights of their clients "in or out of the courtroom," we noted that the situation is different when "those lawyers go outside of court to espouse their clients' *social views*" [italics in original]. At that point, we said that it was permissible to judge the situation, "not as one where lawyers were speaking for their clients, but as one where individuals were speaking for themselves." We also acknowledged the out-of-court right of lawyers to champion their clients' views but insisted that, if they did, we would be "entitled to treat them by the same standards as those by which we would treat their clients."

Calling upon Christie to "either effectively deny or adequately explain" the matters we raised, we told him that, unless he did so, our counsel had been instructed "not to cooperate" with him in any way with respect to the case, "except as may be strictly required." His reply contended that our letter was a "serious attempt to interfere" with his actions as counsel for Zundel and Keegstra. He said that he would refer our letter to his lawyer. That exchange of letters occurred during the summer of 1986. We have never heard from his lawyer.

But the fallout from that letter did not end there. Since that time, Christie opposed virtually every CCLA effort to intervene in his cases. He appeared less than moved by the fact that, in so many of those situations, our legal arguments would have served the interests of his clients. In most of those situations, however, we were granted leave to intervene, despite his objections.

One time we did not get leave was in the Court of Appeal in the Zundel case itself. When our lawyer arrived to argue the leave application, he was greeted by Zundel and his followers on the courthouse steps. They distributed materials containing a copy of my letter to Christie and their denunciation of me. Characterizing my letter as a "vicious, arrogant, and prejudiced diatribe," they contended that my letter dripped "with the hatred of one whose tribal prejudices have superseded any real love for civil and human rights." Following the inevitable publicity of this skirmish, one of my executive members telephoned me asking, "How much did you pay them to denounce you in this way?"

Although I never had much hope that my letter to Christie would help that much to repair CCLA's relations with the Jewish community, I did derive some satisfaction from the open hostility that we received from the Zundel entourage. I think that my attitude on this matter was heavily influenced by my experience during the 1950s in trying to ensure that despite some parallel positions, the Communists could not portray themselves as genuine liberals. That turbulent period impressed upon me the idea that those of us on the democratic left were morally obliged to keep the totalitarian left from identifying themselves with us. In taking the action that I did with respect to Zundel and Keegstra, I was simply applying the same approach to the authoritarian right.

But my interactions with Doug Christie didn't even end there. Sometime later, we wound up together on a CBC television show. The show dealt with a case where Christie and I had opposing views. Needless to say, I found that situation a much more comfortable one. Nevertheless, I had some uneasiness about appearing on a TV show along with him. I was afraid that, despite our differences, the mere fact that we were appearing together might create an impression of collegiality. But, after watching the show, my friend Louis Greenspan assured me that my contempt for Christie was conspicuous and those fears were therefore unfounded.

When I first arrived on the set, the producer asked me whether I had met Doug Christie who, at some distance to my right, was getting up with his hand outstretched to shake mine. Without even looking at Christie, I waved him down with my hand and told the producer that I knew who he was. In view of my letter to Christie and my instructions to CCLA counsel, I dared not shake his hand.

In the Keegstra case (in 1990), the Supreme Court of Canada upheld the constitutionality of the anti-hate law—four judges to three.[2] When the press asked me for a comment, I noted that, by the time the case reached the Supreme Court, Keegstra had been removed from the classroom, disqualified from the teaching profession, and ousted as mayor of Eckville, Alberta. By then, he was working as a garage mechanic. In addition to the free speech implications, I called the prosecution "gratuitous." "In my view," I said, "he should have been allowed to wallow in the obscurity he so richly deserves." The remarks attracted considerable publicity and I repeated them both in newspaper articles and in my book, *The New Anti-Liberals.*

In the Zundel case, the Supreme Court of Canada struck down the false news law. When the media asked for a comment on this case, I replied that it had become impossible to have a happy outcome. If the law had been upheld, freedom of speech would have been commensurately threatened. While I preferred that the law was struck down, I expressed regret that a "peripheral creep" like Zundel should be handed this opportunity for a moment of glory.[3] Certain officers of the Canadian

Jewish Congress subsequently expressed gratitude to me for the "sensitive" nature of my comments.

Throughout the years I debated these issues with some able people. They included Maxwell Cohen, then law dean at McGill; Irwin Cotler, who became federal minister of justice; Manuel Prutschie and Bernie Farber of the Canadian Jewish Congress; and David Matas, Mark Sandler, and Marvin Kurz of B'nai B'rith. In the case of Cotler, we often argued about these issues in private as well as in public.

At some point prior to the Keegstra hearing, I tried to persuade the Canadian Jewish Congress to join with CCLA in a joint approach to the federal government, asking for a reference on the anti-hate law to the Supreme Court. I argued that, in this way, Keegstra would be deprived of the kind of glory that had befallen Zundel. Although I did not say this to the congress, I had hoped that, through such joint action, we could telegraph publicly the existence of good relations between our respective constituencies. Unfortunately, the congress rejected this request and, as indicated, the Court upheld the anti-hate law.

In the New Brunswick case of Malcolm Ross, I pushed for a more nuanced position. He was a high school teacher who had published some reportedly vicious anti-Semitic material but apparently never expressed such views in the classroom. Here, I parted company with the civil libertarian purists who were hot to defend him. Instead of becoming mired in the facts of his case, I said that we should focus on the *criteria* by which his fate should be determined.

Both through the CCLA intervention in court and articles in the press, I advanced the view that the issue was not his freedom of speech but rather, his right to teach. And so we took the position that, on the basis of all the facts both in and out of the classroom, he should be subject to removal if the totality of his record created a reasonable apprehension that he would mistreat any of the youngsters in his charge.

When I had telephone calls from more purist CCLA members, I would invariably pose a hypothetical question: Suppose a teacher expressed a preference for sexual relations with juveniles? Wouldn't we be damn fools to put such a teacher in charge of a class of juveniles? He had a right to express such preferences but that need not be accompanied by an enforceable claim to a job that gave him access to vulnerable youngsters. By restricting ourselves in this way to the applicable criteria, we spared ourselves the burden of ploughing through the materials he had written. CCLA did take this position in court; but the decision, though largely against him, spelled out the principles differently.

Throughout the years, I saw my job as one of attempting to articulate critical distinctions. And so, these attempts appeared in most of our output across the board: media interviews, articles, essays, factums, and books. A key distinction that I kept harping on in the Malcolm Ross case concerned the nature of the restriction being imposed upon him. Almost invariably I would point out that, if he had been prosecuted for the reportedly anti-Semitic remarks he made, we likely would have lined up with the defence. But, when the issue concerned his claim to a position of delicate public trust as a teacher, our response was different.

In this regard, I experienced considerable disappointment over the attempts by the Supreme Court of Canada to spell out some of these issues. In both the Keegstra case dealing with the criminal offence of promoting hatred and the John Ross Taylor case dealing with telephone hate messages and the anti-hate provisions of the *Canadian Human Rights Act*, the Court was especially unhelpful.[4] And, at the time of its decisions, I was quite vocal in my criticisms.

In my view, the crunch issue concerned the word "hatred." I stressed again and again that there was no discernible way to determine the point at which strong disapproval turns into hatred. After all, as noted earlier, freedom of speech is often most important when it expresses strong disapproval. On many occasions I said that I would have been prepared to take a different position if the law had targeted incitements of imminent *violence*. But "hatred" was too fraught with ambiguity.

Nevertheless, the Supreme Court of Canada saw clarity where it didn't exist. In attempting to spell out the meaning of "hatred," the judges talked about "unusually strong and deep-felt emotions of detestation, calumny, and vilification," as though a litany of synonyms would adequately illuminate the problem. I contended that the judges could just as easily have declared that "hatred" means hatred. I labelled their explication "a tautology in disguise." It looked naïve, therefore, when the court attempted to assure the public that, if only adjudicators would "heed . . . the ardent and extreme nature of the feeling" within the definition, there was little danger that "subjective opinion" would prevail.

Before, during, and after the Keegstra hearing, I kept pointing to the number of *non*–hate-mongers who had been threatened under the anti-hate law. The targets of such threats included anti-American protesters, French-Canadian nationalists, anti-apartheid activists, pro-Zionist authors, and Jewish community leaders. And, I insisted, even if there was no lasting conviction or property seizure against them, their freedom of speech had suffered, nevertheless. I kept arguing that freedom of speech becomes less viable when you have to look over your shoulder in fear of facing legal processes simply for engaging in democratic discourse.

While there had been relatively little experience at the time with the anti-hate provisions of the *Canadian Human Rights Act* and its provincial counterparts ("likely to expose to hatred or contempt"), I was able to conjure up a number of hypothetical possibilities from my imagination. In time, however, actual situations occurred. Complaints were filed, for example, under the Canadian, British Columbia, and Alberta human rights statutes against *Maclean's* magazine and author Mark Steyn for an article of his which was deeply critical of the Muslim community. And, around the same time, right-wing commentator Ezra Levant faced an Alberta human rights complaint for publishing the contentious Danish cartoons in his western Canadian magazine. And, while they were all finally cleared, it cost them a pile of money to defend themselves. So much for the Supreme Court's assurances.

In other cases, there were splits among the adjudicators. In Saskatchewan, the human rights tribunal and the Court of Queen's Bench found "hatred or contempt" in a published ad showing a diagonal line running through two men holding hands and a reference to certain Biblical quotations. Those Biblical quotations had said that homosexuals deserve death because of their practices. Looking at the same material, the Saskatchewan Court of Appeal declared that the impugned publication did not amount to "hatred or contempt."

In a subsequent Saskatchewan case dealing with some leaflets distributed by an anti-gay activist, the Saskatchewan Court of Appeal had occasion to overrule both the tribunal and the Court of Queen's Bench with respect to other material.[5] In Alberta, there was a split between the Court of Queen's Bench and the tribunal.[6] At the time of my writing, the appellate court had not yet pronounced upon the controversy. The very least that can be drawn from these cases is that the terminology of the law is a good deal more murky than the Supreme Court had envisioned.

In certain jurisdictions, the law required human rights commissions to process all complaints. Other jurisdictions allowed the commissions to decide whether to become involved. Whenever a human rights law gave a human rights commission a discretion, there was a decision *against* taking action in the *Maclean's*-Mark Steyn case. In the view of those commissions, the remarks made by Mr. Steyn did not rise (or sink) to the level of "hatred or contempt."

In published articles, public speeches, and at a meeting of the Canadian Jewish Congress, I challenged this consensus. Mr. Steyn's remarks included the following: "[N]ot all Muslims are terrorists — though enough of them are hot for Jihad to provide an impressive support network."[7]

In this day and age, I argued, there is almost nothing worse that can be said about people than that they "support" terrorists. This means that they support the kidnapping, torturing, and decapitation of innocent persons. Can anyone be so confident that a future human rights commission would not designate such statements as "likely to expose" their targets to "hatred"?

It is not without significance that, in a letter to the editor purporting to answer one of my articles, Bernie Farber of the Canadian Jewish Congress invoked the very litany of synonyms by which the Supreme Court of Canada purported to define "hatred." Thanks to the Supreme Court of Canada, such semantic circularity had become inevitable.

In order to set the record straight on my approach to these matters, there is another issue I should address. Some people acknowledge the risks to freedom of speech in the anti-hate law but contend that, on balance, it is a risk they are prepared to take. In their view, the human dignity undermined by hate speech is simply more important than the right to free speech.

In my view, these people are not adequately mindful of the central role that free speech plays in the democratic system. Freedom of expression is the vehicle by which any of us can attempt to rally support for our various causes and interests. Debating is our civilized substitute for duelling. Experience has taught us again and again that injustice is less likely to endure — or even to emerge — in an atmosphere of free public debate. Under the glare of publicity, injustice tends to wilt and erode.

For this reason, freedom of speech is the prerequisite of all our other rights and freedoms. As a wise old trade unionist once observed, freedom of expression is the grievance procedure of the democratic system.

I readily grant that freedom of speech is not—and cannot be—an absolute. Admittedly, there are occasions when it must be restricted. But, if our system is to function as it should, such restrictions should be few, far between, and narrow. It should be appreciated, therefore, that in opposing our various hate speech laws, my goal has been to protect the viability of the democratic system. Even before there were any such laws, our society made considerable progress in containing the influence of hate mongers and their ilk. The experience amply demonstrated our ability to fight hate speech without restricting free speech.

On countless occasions, I was driven by this vision to take up causes and get involved in cases where freedom of speech was at issue. In this connection, I set my sights, during the mid-1990s, on the tort of civil defamation. A case arose in which Casey Hill, a well-respected Crown prosecutor, was publicly accused of certain wrongdoing. The accuser was a much-impugned organization, the Church of Scientology. In light of their respective reputations, Casey Hill was expected to win hands down.

Despite the similarities between the anti-hate crime and the defamation tort, I questioned whether the tort might nevertheless have a role to play in our democratic system. There was, after all, a respectable argument that the malevolent or irresponsible dissemination of deliberate falsehoods about identified individuals should not be allowed to escape all liability. Shouldn't personal reputation, therefore, be entitled to *some* level of protection?

Although there were critical differences between the hate crime and the defamation tort, I thought that legitimate free speech was threatened even by the tort. At the time, defendants could be nailed unless they proved the truth of their statements. Of course, that meant proof to the satisfaction of a court.

Suppose, despite mountains of research and painstaking effort, an accuser didn't know or hadn't learned about some relevant fact that simply could not have been known? I thought it was wrong that such a careful, responsible accuser should attract liability comparable to what we might contemplate for a malevolent or irresponsible accuser.

Where matters of public interest are involved, there must be elbow room to criticize, accuse—and exact accountability from—those who exercise or aspire to positions of power and influence. Without such opportunity, it would be impossible to have democratic scrutiny of those in authority. For these reasons, critics of authority must enjoy a generous amount of free speech.

It must be obvious that the requirement to prove the truth of purported statements of fact could not equip critics of authority with the elbow room they need. In pushing for a CCLA intervention in the Hill and Scientology case, I urged that we register on the shape of the law, irrespective of the facts. So, we never chose between Casey Hill and the Church of Scientology. In consultation with our then lawyer, Bob Sharpe (a subsequent justice of the Ontario Court of Appeal), we took the position that, where truth and the public interest were involved, defendants should need only to establish that, in all the circumstances, they believed and had reasonable grounds to believe the veracity of the statements they made. On the basis of our arguments, it was appropriate to examine the diligence and integrity of the defendants' research efforts. In the result, defendants would not have to be right, but they would have to be scrupulous.

Despite the arguments made by various participants and interveners like us, the Supreme Court of Canada reaffirmed the existing law.[8] Defendants would be held liable unless they proved the truth of their defamatory statements. Perhaps the judges could not see past the obvious good character of Casey Hill or the controversial record of the Church of Scientology. Of course, I cannot ascertain the mindsets and motives of any of the players. Suffice it to observe that the Court left the law in a sorry state. With some satisfaction, however, I note that, several years later, the Court proclaimed a defence of responsible public communication. In that case, my successors at CCLA intervened and pushed for the result that was achieved.

OFFICIAL SECRETS AND UNOFFICIAL DISPLAYS

In early 2004, ten RCMP officers ransacked the home of *Ottawa Citizen* reporter Juliet O'Neill. In the result, they carted off mounds of material belonging to Ms. O'Neill. This pervasive encroachment was conducted under the authority of the *Security of Information Act*, a federal statute passed in the wake of 9/11. Incredibly, that Act prohibited the disclosure—even the mere receipt—of material obtained in contravention of the law. In such respects, this law threatened to perpetuate some of the worst features of its predecessor, the *Official Secrets Act.*

Apparently, the Mounties suspected that a story published by Ms. O'Neill contained information unlawfully leaked to her by some members of the Force. The subject of the story was Maher Arar, a Canadian citizen who had been deported to his native Syria by the US authorities after they intercepted him in New York City. Public interest in the issue was ignited by reports that Mr. Arar had been jailed and tortured during his stay in Syria.

Even if the leakers of the information violated the law, why should a presumably innocent recipient be prohibited from further disclosing it? Even if the law would properly restrict the dissemination of truly secret or classified material, why should it do so in the absence of a claim that the disputed information is particularly sensitive? And, in view of all this, what conceivable justification could there be for the fourteen-year jail sentence that the law made possible?

Not surprisingly, we at CCLA salivated to take a crack at this law. So we recruited an able young lawyer, Stuart Svonkin, of the Tory law firm. He intervened for us and argued impressively that the law was unconstitutional. In striking down key sections of the Act, Ontario Superior Court justice Lynn Ratushny noted that the law "fails to define in any way the scope of what it protects."[9] Significantly, the government of Canada elected not to appeal her decision. The law and the country are better off for the removal of those sections.

Threats to freedom of speech are often unexpected and not anticipated. In the early 1990s, for example, Conservative backbench MP Bob Hicks introduced a bill that would have criminalized anyone who "wilfully burns, defaces, defiles, mutilates, tramples upon or otherwise desecrates the national flag of Canada." This appeared to come from out of the blue. I can't recall that this country was experiencing a particular problem over the mistreatment of our national flag.

On behalf of CCLA, I appeared before the relevant parliamentary committee and argued that so long as anyone owned a flag, such person should be allowed to mistreat it. It was a way for people to express critical opinions about the behaviour of our national government. Moreover,

I argued that the word "desecrate" was impermissibly vague. Noting that some people have been known to wear underwear containing a design of the flag, I asked, "Does this 'desecrate' or ennoble our flag?"

Without much further ado, the government let the bill die on the order paper. A fitting tribute.

In the early 1990s, certain opponents of free trade complained to CCLA that an anti-postering by-law in Peterborough, Ontario, was interfering with their right to communicate their views to the public. While CCLA had no position on the pros or cons of the free trade debate, it did have a position on the effective rights of anyone to engage in the communication of their views to their fellow citizens. Postering had become a time-honoured vehicle for public communication.

While the city had a legitimate interest in the problem of litter that resulted from the practice of postering, it should not address this problem by way of an indiscriminate ban on all postering. On this basis, we intervened in the case and attempted to challenge the constitutionality of the Peterborough initiative. On behalf of the Ontario Supreme Court, Mr. Justice Horace Krever struck down the by-law, noting that utility poles are used "to convey information on the part of individuals and governments, varying in nature from notice of garage sales, to notice of lost pets, to transit information, to voters' lists."[10] Ultimately, his judgment was sustained by the Supreme Court of Canada.[11]

UNDERMINING THE COURTS

In the fall of 1986, a pet peeve of mine once again reared its dubious head. Toronto lawyer Harry Kopyto was charged with contempt of court by scandalizing the court. Just after he had lost an attempt to sue certain RCMP officers for a "dirty trick" they had perpetrated against some Trotskyist leaders, Kopyto blurted to a *Globe and Mail* reporter that the courts "are warped in favour of protecting the police . . . they stick to the police like crazy glue." He wound up being convicted; his punishment was to be banished from appearing in the Ontario courts until he apologized for those remarks.

In chapter 4, in the context of the Tom Murphy case, I expressed my contempt for this branch of the contempt law. As I indicated in a CCLA statement on the Kopyto case, "In a democracy, there must be a right to speak harshly as well as nicely." While the courts have been quick to assure the public that it's permissible to criticize them, they have also noted that such criticisms must avoid invective and the imputation of bias.

In the CCLA statement, I said that freedom of speech "cannot viably coexist with such a demanding obligation to bite your tongue." Our statement then quoted Harry Arthurs, "Unless you assume that judges can't be biased or venal, there must be a right to say so."

With the release of the statement, we attempted to intervene in the appeal that Kopyto had lodged with the Ontario Court of Appeal. Unfortunately, the court denied our leave application but fortunately it went on to effectively hold that the offence of scandalizing the courts was a dead letter under the *Charter*.

But there were other kinds of contempt of court that continued to reign outside the courtroom. A pervasive and recurring source of contempt tyranny is the concept of "*sub judice*" which seeks to muzzle certain public commentary on cases that are before the courts. I believe that the rationale for this concept had something to do with helping to ensure a fair trial by discouraging commentary that might unfairly and unduly prejudice the adjudicative exercise. Whatever the origin, however, the practice has developed that, as soon as a case comes before the courts, public commentary remotely related to it often grinds to a halt. The response is almost Pavlovian. *Sub judice* has frequently wound up muzzling legitimate public discussion about important public issues.

Somewhere in the late seventies or early eighties, I began seriously to question the scope of the restrictions on free speech that appeared to be attributable to this doctrine. Indeed, the more I thought about the subject, the more I began to think that *sub judice* was perpetrating unwarranted censorship on the Canadian people and their institutions.

Early in 1980, for example, there was a press report that the police had conducted an investigation into a speech that had been made by black community leader Dudley Laws at the Contact School (an alternative school in the Toronto system). According to the lawyer for Metropolitan Toronto, the investigation had been triggered by "very intemperate and inflammatory statements" that Mr. Laws allegedly made to students at the school.

On behalf of CCLA, I wrote both to the chief of police and, after getting his lawyer's reply, to the Toronto Police Commission, complaining that a police investigation of such a matter represents a gratuitous intimidation of the intellectual freedom that is supposed to prevail in our schools. In short, my letter alleged that the police had no business investigating "inflammatory" speeches. Incredibly, one of the grounds upon which the police lawyer attempted to justify the investigation was contempt of court. Noting that a couple of police officers were then facing charges occasioned by a shooting incident, the police lawyer argued that the issue was *sub judice*. In the lawyer's view, the rights of those police officers could potentially be affected by Mr. Laws' speech.

In response, I contended that it was "preposterous to believe that such interests could be seriously imperilled as a consequence of a speech made in the setting" of that school. Moreover, I took issue with the selectivity apparently exercised by the police. In the words of my letter, "How many civilians have had the benefit of such police assistance to protect *their* comparable interests?"

In late 1983 the then Chief Justice of Canada, Bora Laskin, chewed out Ottawa lawyer Lawrence Greenspon for his involvement in a number of media interviews about his upcoming *Charter* challenge of cruise missile tests over Canadian soil. In arguing his case outside of court before arguing it inside, Greenspon, in Laskin's view, had come "close to contempt of court."

When I read of this exchange in the press, I was perplexed. I knew Bora Laskin to be a rational and even a progressive person. Had he been so thoroughly socialized by his monastic life in the judiciary that he had actually assimilated even the pap that the courts were then promulgating? After all, it could very well be argued that Greenspon's media interviews about his case were actually *promoting* the public interest. They could very well have helped to inform the public about the complicated issues in the case so that more people would be able to grasp the unfolding developments as they occurred. Without the kind of interviews that Greenspon had given, the public would be made excessively dependent upon press reports of the incomprehensible legalisms that were often voiced in court.

Wasn't there also an argument that Greenspon's client was entitled to his advocacy skills in media interviews? His client in this case was Operation Dismantle, a peace organization that had an interest in trying to persuade the public about the merits of its cause. Even though the case at that time was before the courts, the issue of cruise missile challenges was also very much before the government, Parliament, and the public. The democratic processes required the participation of everyone who is knowledgeable on the subject. Why should involvement in court restrict anyone's participation in the accompanying political debates?

Besides, what conceivable damage would Greenspon's public pronouncements inflict on the court processes? There was no question of his disclosing any matters of evidence that could prejudice a potential jury. He was dealing essentially with legal and policy issues that would be addressed by professionally trained judges. For such purposes, the adjudicators would not be confined, as they would be on questions of evidence, to what they hear in the courtroom.

We have seen similar scenarios on dozens of occasions. Of course, they don't always involve judicial rebukes of lawyers. Even more often, we see politicians avoiding and evading the discussion of important issues on the basis that some part of the issue is being litigated before the courts. But, in situation after situation, there was no threat whatsoever to the integrity of the court processes. The politicians had found for themselves a helpful way to avoid facing the music.

The more aware I had become of the destructive potential of this issue, the more I wanted to do something about it. But I also recognized that there would be very few court cases that could adequately present opportunities for challenge and precious little scope for briefs to government or testimony at legislative committees. I resolved, therefore, to engage in a form of guerrilla warfare. I would hit the issue in a number of the other ways that were available to me. As for the Laskin rebuke of Greenspon, I wrote an article about it in the *Toronto Star* and ventilated it again in my book, *When Freedoms Collide*.

I found other vehicles as well.

Earlier in the very year of the Laskin-Greenspon confrontation, I encountered another manifestation of the problem when I was a panelist at an Ontario Press Council forum dealing with the Grange Commission on the baby deaths at Toronto's Hospital for Sick Children. All the panelists received a lawyer's letter cautioning us about any statements we might wish to make on the controversial case involving nurse Susan Nelles. Since Nelles had launched a lawsuit against certain law enforcement officials, the panelists were warned to be particularly careful not to say anything that could influence a potential member of the jury. If it were alleged, for example, that the police had been out to "get" the young nurse, the speaker might be found in contempt of court.

I used my position on the panel to register my objections to this legal advice. Although I was in no position to question the opinion of the eminent lawyer who had sent us the letter, I did say that, if he was indeed right about the law, the law was truly an ass. My point was that a private lawsuit of the kind Ms. Nelles had launched should not be able to deprive the public of an important and timely debate about the police handling of her case. Everyone has an interest in determining at the earliest possible moment whether the police might have misbehaved.

Anticipating the arguments against me, I insisted that no one should be consoled by the oft-repeated assurance that freedom of speech in such matters was being delayed, not denied. I reminded the audience that this kind of litigation could take years. If there had been misconduct that went unchallenged, it could well be repeated against other people. And, after several years, there would be much less inclination for a vigorous debate. Why, I asked, couldn't the legal and political processes run concurrently? Why should the courts be allowed to exercise such a monopoly over whatever issues are brought before them?

The Grange Commission, itself, provided me with yet another opportunity to register on this hobbyhorse. At one point, a number of the nurses convened a public meeting to reply to those witnesses who had attacked them during the proceedings of the Grange Commission. This provoked Justice Grange to warn the nurses that, if they ever behaved this way again, he could well launch contempt proceedings against them. In particular, he declared that witnesses with standing at the commission should rely on the commission processes to give them a full and fair opportunity to protect their interests. They should not go to the public in this way with their complaints.

When I heard this, I high-tailed it to the commission hearings. I asked the commission counsel for an opportunity to make a short presentation to the commission and my request was granted. I told the commissioner essentially that his ruling was unfair. There was no valid reason why these nurses should have to endure what may turn out to be months under the cloud of the attacks that had been made against them. There was no reason why the commission should insist that anyone who appeared before it should be deprived of the right to register elsewhere. While we had a vigorous exchange, there was no formal resolution. In any event, no contempt proceedings were launched and the nurses effectively backed off.

A number of years later, I noticed some quotes in the media that reportedly emanated from then Ontario Chief Justice Charles Dubin. It was essentially a repetition of themes he had previously expressed. He was admonishing lawyers against arguing their respective cases in the media. According to him, proper respect for the court processes required that they defer to the court processes. He was especially incensed about the extent to which lawyers were using the media to advance their respective interests. The one virtue of Dubin's position is that he did not insist that those media commentaries necessarily represented contempts of court. As far as he was concerned, it constituted bad practice and showed a lack of adequate respect for the courts.

Having known Dubin from when he had acted as a lawyer for the Ontario Human Rights Commission, I invited him to have lunch with me so that we might have an adequate discussion of the subject. At this point, I should indicate that Charlie Dubin, as I knew him, had always been a very nice guy. Not surprisingly, he was gracious about my invitation and forthcoming about discussing the issue with me. Over lunch, I argued quite relentlessly that the public interest was the beneficiary of the very practice he was criticizing and that no legitimate public interest could be significantly damaged by it.

I also knew him to be a very smart person. I don't know whether I caught him at a particular moment of fatigue or I actually got the better of him in the argument. Of course, I believed the latter. After we talked for quite some time, Dubin finally said to me, "Okay, Alan Borovoy can make any statement he wants to the media." At this point, we both laughed. But I thought I should not pester him any further. I thanked him for the meeting and we went our respective ways.

BADGERING

At some point early in my CCLA career, I discerned a pivotal fallacy that was being committed on all sides of the free speech controversies.

One of the most illuminating expressions of it occurred in a 1951 judgment of the Supreme Court of Canada. In the course of commenting on what constituted permissible behaviour on labour picket lines, the Court made the following observations:

> There is a difference between watching and besetting for the purpose of coercing either workmen or employer by . . . argumentative and rancorous badgering or importunity . . . on the one hand; and attending to communicate information for the purpose of persuasion by the *force of rational appeal*, on the other [emphasis added].[12]

Some twenty years later, the Court expressed a similar theme. In the course of upholding an anti-demonstration by-law enacted by the City of Montreal, the Court argued that demonstrations did not really involve freedom of speech: "Demonstrations are not a form of speech, but of collective action. They are of the nature of a display of force rather than of that of an appeal to reason."[13]

Why were argumentative and rancorous badgering and importunity considered legally unacceptable? Why did free speech have to appeal to reason? These judicial declarations struck me as manifestations of bourgeois prejudice. Of course, acts and threats of physical violence had to be unacceptable. But why couldn't labour pickets and political demonstrators employ social pressure? Why couldn't they attempt to shame and embarrass those whose behaviour offended their interests? To confine freedom of speech to rational appeals is to load the dice against the less advantaged people of society. In order to compete with the more advantaged people, they must have recourse to non-violent political, economic, and social pressure.

While there is some indication that the courts have moderated their views about the relationship of free speech and demonstrations, other authorities in our society continue to reflect the old mentality. Thus, in the 1970s, the police prevented peace protesters from coming within a half a mile of Lytton Industries. The peace protesters were upset at this company because it manufactured the guidance systems for the American cruise missiles. But a bomb had been exploded near the plant a few months before the planned protest and the police chose to play it extra safe. Undoubtedly, they were helped in this regard by their belief that, in order for the protesters to express their views, it wasn't necessary for them to be so close. It never seemed to occur to the police that the protesters would have hoped to censure and shame those people who continued to do business with Lytton Industries. And *that* couldn't be done from a half-mile away.

In a letter to Ontario's then solicitor general I acknowledged that protesters could not expect to demonstrate wherever and whenever they pleased. But, I argued, the operative judgments should not be made by the police themselves. Their interests might propel them to keep the parties as far apart as possible. Citing my colleague, CCLA board member, Terry Meagher, I said that the system made the police "umpires of their own ballgame."

Similar restrictions were imposed upon protesters at the APEC conference in British Columbia during the 1990s and the Summit of the Americas conference in Quebec during the early 2000s. The British Columbia legislature did something comparable through a statute that purported to keep abortion protesters some 50 metres away from abortion clinics. And, in the early 1980s, the British Columbia Superior Court, on its own motion, issued an injunction against the civil service picketing of its courthouse. That injunction was upheld by the British Columbia Court of Appeal and the Supreme Court of Canada.

It's not without significance that, in the BC case, the Supreme Court made the point that the pickets could always express themselves elsewhere.[14] What appeared to be completely lost on the courts at all levels was the fact that it was legitimate for the union to attempt to shame those people who crossed its picket lines. Even if those people continued to cross because of a legal obligation to be there, the pickets might well have hoped that, by their presence, they would create enough discomfort to pressure the public into pressuring the government to resolve the labour dispute sooner rather than later and on terms more favourable to the union. Of course, it was not possible for the union to generate such pressures from miles away. No member of the judiciary who participated in this case evinced the slightest awareness of such considerations.

Of course, the Toronto Police Commission had inflicted a similar disability on the Vietnam War protesters when it steered them away from Toronto's busy Yonge Street. During more than one of these controversies, I made—and reiterated—the statement, "In Canada, we don't ban demonstrations, we reroute them."

In those situations where I fleshed out this statement, I frequently would invoke a British author who had made the critical point that there is a difference between freedom of communication and freedom of soliloquy. It isn't good enough, I would say, to relegate demonstrators and picketers to their respective bathtubs or even their backyards. They needed an audience and often they had to be close to that audience. At one point, I argued that demonstrators and picketers had to be close enough periodically to be seen and heard, if never "felt or smelt."

In late 1984, CCLA involved itself in a labour dispute where some of these principles were at issue. The managers of Toronto's Eaton Centre, the private sector corporation Cadillac Fairview Limited, issued an edict prohibiting the Retail, Wholesale Union from "congregating" in the indoor mall area adjacent to the Eaton's store. At the time, the union was attempting to organize the employees of the store.

Appearing on behalf of CCLA before a committee of the Toronto City Council, I argued that the city had a duty to "use its good offices" in an attempt to persuade Cadillac Fairview to rescind this restriction. The *Charter* rights for "freedom of association" necessarily required an opportunity for the affected parties to encounter each other and discuss the issues. But, since Eaton's workers enter and leave the store through the underground subway, these rights would become effectively impossible to exercise. I argued that, under such circumstances, freedom of association would have to be facilitated "through telepathic communication."

In yet another controversy, the claim to confront people more closely arose in a particularly poignant way. In the mid-1990s, the Mike Harris Conservative government of Ontario introduced a bill to impose curbs on panhandling in public places. Among the provisions of the bill, there was a prohibition against soliciting money at or near certain named public places. Those places included bus stops, taxi stands, bank machines, telephone booths, and public pay toilets.

Upon appearing before the legislative committee that had been established to deal with the bill, I attempted to resort to a certain amount of ridicule. I told the members of the committee that there probably was not a person in the room who had never run out of quarters at a telephone booth or had never encountered someone else who ran out of quarters. "Do you really want to make criminals out of such people?"

I asked. And then I said to them that, although I hadn't seen a pay toilet in the province for some time, I shudder what might happen if there were any left and someone had to use it. If such a person needed to go and had run out of change, I argued that it would be "in the public interest for them to ask for the money."

Of course, the room erupted into laughter. Significantly, however, the laughter did not influence the voting. The legislative committee and then the legislature enacted the bill without any amendments or changes.

THE PURSUIT OF TRUTH

In addition to its role in addressing grievances, freedom of speech is also a vehicle for pursuing and discovering the truth. In science and technology, a number of theories may openly compete in order to demonstrate their respective validity. The same is true for religion, philosophy, and politics. Ultimate questions concerning the meaning of life or more immediate questions concerning the selection of our government are resolved, not by edicts from on high, but by choices from down below. A number of the foregoing controversies involved the truth-discovering role of free speech as well as the grievance-resolving one. But there are yet other areas where the discovery of truth might be even more at issue.

At the University of Calgary in the early years of the twenty-first century, the administration imposed certain restrictions on the right of abortion protesters to publicize their views on campus. The university forbade the protesters from analogizing abortion to murder. On behalf of CCLA, I protested. In my view, this restriction cut the heart out of the anti-abortion argument. I thought that it ill-behooved a university, in particular to impose such limits on its campus members regarding key arguments about so central a social controversy. In the hope of enhancing the credibility of our arguments, I advised the university that CCLA is itself strongly pro-choice on the abortion question. But, I added, we believe not only in freedom of choice but also in freedom of speech.

Where campus controversies were concerned, it was not unusual for us to intercede to defend the free speech of the conservative protagonists with whom we least agreed. In one of the early cases during the mid-1970s, we complained to the president of the University of Toronto about the treatment accorded to the US conservative urbanologist, Edward Banfield. A small group of activists identifying themselves as members of Students for a Democratic Society (SDS) mounted the platform just before Professor Banfield's arrival and proceeded to physically block all the pathways to the stage. When Banfield arrived, they strongarmed him off the platform and his speech was never delivered.

Our letter to U of T president John Evans contended that the university had a duty to provide physical protection for the rights of its members to engage with visitors such as Edward Banfield. Because of Banfield's alleged racism, a number of U of T professors entered the fray, minimizing the importance of free speech. In their view, the key issue was racism not freedom of speech. American socialist writer, Irving Howe, had an apt description for such academics. He called them "revolutionaries with tenure."

As for the merits of their argument, I replied in the following way:

> The imputation of racism cannot justify the banning of speakers in 1974 Canada any more than the imputation of Communism could justify it in 1954 America. To say the real issue is the evil of racism is to legitimize the activities of generations of cultural and political vigilantes. It is to say that when an American university discharged Bertrand Russell, the real issue was the evil of atheism—or when some American campuses barred Malcolm X, the real issue was the evil of black nationalism—or when the Soviet Union exiled Solzhenitsyn, the real issue was the evil of capitalism—or when the Canadian government denied entry to Mulford Q. Sibley, the real issue was the evil of pacificism.[15]

Of course, our letter was released to the university press and distributed among interested organizations. Days later, the public learned that the university had suspended its official recognition of the SDS. Our next move probably persuaded the president of the university that it was not possible to pacify CCLA. One week after our original letter, we wrote again to the president, complaining that the reports had made it appear that the university action was taken without a prior hearing. Despite our anger over what those SDS activists had done, we still insisted that procedural fairness must be observed.

Somewhere around this time, universities in Canada began to prom-ulgate various measures restricting the scope of what people could say on campus and during campus activities. These measures took special aim at speech that could be seen as racist, sexist, or homophobic. The triggering and resulting intellectual climate is what we now identify as, "political correctness." It must be acknowledged that the impetus behind these restrictions was egalitarian, even humanitarian. The campus authorities were attempting to protect the sensibilities of their most vulnerable minorities. In curtailing *speech,* however, they risked encroaching on the free inquiry that is the lifeblood of the university. We went after various manifestations of political correctness on a num-ber of occasions.

A case that particularly dramatizes how political correctness under-mines the mission of higher education is that of Richard Devlin, a legal writing instructor at the Osgoode Hall Law School during the mid-1980s. One of the assignments he gave to his students involved their prepara-tion of legal briefs on the constitutionality of a hypothetical anti-pornog-raphy law. On a random basis, he divided the class into two: one side would argue in favour of the law and the other side would be against it. But some of the women in the class were upset because they wound up having to argue against their personal convictions.

The situation became exacerbated when Mr. Devlin learned that the sexual harassment centre at the university was making inquiries about him. This led to a meeting with him and two of the centre's counsellors. Although he was assured that he was not then the target of an official complaint, he reports the counsellors as saying that "one of the major criticisms" of his behaviour concerned the way he had divided the class for the assignment.

The counsellors reportedly claimed that Devlin's methodology in this situation could create serious distress for those who had to argue against their own personal opinions. It was even reportedly contended that some of the women were undergoing identity crises as a result of the assignment. According to Devlin, the counsellors warned him "if a similar situation were to occur again, there would be the possibility of an investigation to determine whether sexual harassment was actually taking place." Remarkably, this situation involved the university threat-ening a law teacher for employing *laudable* pedagogy. After all, a good lawyer must be able to advance and appreciate the arguments on all sides of a question.

What made this case even worse was the law review article Devlin subsequently wrote about it. In addition to revealing his fear over the incident, he also confessed to a significant measure of culpability for his impugned behaviour.[16] At that point, I simply couldn't resist taking a crack at him as well as the policy that was threatening him. In a *Toronto Star* column I was writing then, I declared that Mr. Devlin simply could not find a cat o' nine tails strong enough with which to beat himself.[17] In reply, he wrote an angry letter attacking me.[18] In this case at least, it has to be admitted that the canons of political correctness won a smashing victory.

Toward the end of 1993, mathematics professor Matin Yaqzan was suspended from the University of New Brunswick for writing an article in the campus press contending that, if a woman visited a man's quarters after hours, she was implicitly consenting to sexual intercourse. He also described date rape of "promiscuous" women as an "inconvenience" rather than a "moral outrage."[19]

In the course of suggesting that the impugned article might violate the university's policy on sexual harassment, the relevant academic vice-president noted that the policy prohibits behaviour that creates an intimidating, hostile, or offensive environment. Although the suspension was lifted shortly thereafter, the professor never returned to the classroom. He took early retirement under conditions that were not publicly disclosed.

In addition to devoting one of my *Toronto Star* columns to this case, I was invited, several months later, to deliver the keynote speech at a conference convened by the university to discuss the issue.[20] While I agreed that the impugned article was "an exemplary piece of foolishness," I deplored the suspension. I argued that, in a community of scholars whose role is to search for truth, the opinions of such a professor must receive "not disciplinary coercion, but critical discussion."

Among the other outside speakers who were invited to address the conference, there were journalist Sandra Martin, historian Michael Bliss, and MP Svend Robinson. I should note that Svend and I, while acknowledging that we had often been allies, engaged in a spirited argument to the apparent delight of the conference participants.

Another development worth mentioning about the Yaqzan case is the role of the student community. The UNB student union ran a series of ads in the campus newspaper in which they solicited student testimony that could be used in the administration's review of the professor's case. This action represented a significant departure from the historic role played by university students. In days gone by, they would have likely championed the free speech of their teachers and fellow students. In this situation, they were assisting the forces of persecution; indeed, they were even attempting to *facilitate* those forces.

In this connection, an apparently significant incident occurred at Ryerson University in the very early 1990s as well. The first complaint filed under that university's anti-harassment policy was against two engineering students for the remarks they reportedly made in criticism of the awareness day planned by the campus gay and lesbian club. Some two months after the complaint was filed, it was dismissed, but the dismissal was not based upon the substance of what they had said. Their comments were found not to be "unsolicited" within the meaning of the policy. Apparently, the statements of the accused students were made in response to questions that had been asked of them by a campus newspaper reporter.

Some months later, I was a panelist at a forum on the Ryerson campus. At one point, I suggested the possibility that those students might well have been subject to discipline if their remarks, in fact, had been unsolicited. I asked the audience whether such an outcome would be appropriate. No one in attendance even attempted to answer my question. I find it difficult to imagine that such universal silence would have greeted a comparable question at a Canadian university during the McCarthy period in the 1950s.

In fairness, I realize that the students' silence at Ryerson could have been attributable to a case of mass shyness. No such excuse was available, however, at the University of Western Ontario in the mid-1980s. There, the student council refused to grant recognition to a student organization that was dedicated to promoting a pro-Palestinian solution to the problems of the Middle East. According to the council's legal commissioner, "The stated purpose of this club has been transformed from a club to promote forums for debate of the Middle East crisis to a club to promote a specific solution for the Middle East crisis."

Upon being approached by some students in the rejected club, I investigated the situation and ultimately fired off a letter to the student council. Among other things, I pointed out that, on that very campus, there were groups dedicated to promoting Catholicism in particular, Christianity in general, as well as political clubs—Conservative, Liberal, and New Democratic. As I argued in my letter, if recognized clubs could pursue philosophies that were pro-Christian, pro-Catholic, pro-Conservative, pro-Liberal, or pro-New Democrat, why in the world should a club be rejected because it was pro-Palestinian?

At some point after the CCLA letter had been disseminated to the campus press, I was approached by certain students who had been involved in the decision to exclude the pro-Palestinian organization. We had, as they say, a "firm and friendly" meeting. I am unable to trace cause and effect, but it is worth noting that a subsequent student council reversed the policy and recognized the group in question.

Somewhere around that time, the student council at the University of Ottawa adopted a similar position to that of its counterparts at Western. It revoked the recognition it had granted to the Jewish Student Union. The basis for this action was the allegedly "racist" character of the State of Israel.

I regret that I did not learn of this case soon enough to get CCLA involved. In this situation, the student council radically altered the role that such councils have traditionally played. Instead of encouraging discussion and debate over issues like the Middle East, this council squarely arrogated to itself the right to determine what opinions its constituents ought to hold.

At Ottawa, it took interference from the university administration to redress what the student council had done. The administration restored campus recognition to the Jewish Students' Union.

In 2008, the year before I officially retired as general counsel of CCLA, I became embroiled in another controversy that grew out of the authoritarianism of Canadian university students. The national organization of university student councils called upon its constituents to adopt restrictive measures against student organizations that were promoting an anti-abortion position. Here, we were addressing ourselves to the effective right of organizations with such an orientation to function on the various campuses concerned. By and large, that meant the ability to rent facilities at a low cost, the advertising of its functions on campus bulletin boards, and some access to dissemination facilities.

At the time, we wrote a letter of complaint to the national organization and sent copies to its affiliates.[21] While the letter did precipitate some rational discussion, it also triggered a wave of hostile invective. It didn't seem to matter to the pro-choice authoritarians in the student community that CCLA was itself strongly pro-choice. Unlike the student councils that blasted us, we had established a high pro-choice profile: we had intervened in court, made presentations at parliamentary committees, and addressed rallies, all in furtherance of our pro-choice position. But that wasn't good enough for so many of our erstwhile allies in the student community. To them, we were, nevertheless, the enemy.

In many ways, the curbs on speech in Canadian university activities were provoked by the case of Philippe Rushton at the University of Western Ontario. In the late 1980s, Rushton, a psychology professor, attracted world attention with his research into the brain sizes and certain other physiological characteristics of three major racial groups. His conclusion was that Orientals had the highest intelligence, the white race was next, and, in third place, were the blacks. These findings ignited an explosive controversy.[22]

But, while a professor's methodology was a fair subject for disciplinary scrutiny, his philosophy was not. The controversy that engulfed Rushton exceeded the bounds of propriety. The then premier of Ontario, David Peterson, actually advocated that Rushton be dismissed. But other critics went even further. The Attorney General of the province ordered the Ontario Provincial Police (OPP) to conduct an investigation for the purpose of a possible prosecution under the anti-hate section of the *Criminal Code*. Apparently, therefore, it wasn't enough to fire a professor for such work, it was no less appropriate to *jail* him for it.

Despite my lifelong anti-racist philosophy, I spoke and wrote against the treatment that Rushton got. I called upon those who were upset by Rushton's research to seek, "not political influence to dismiss him, but intellectual arguments to rebut him."

In the spring of 2001, CCLA jumped into a controversy over an anti-Islamic article written by a law student at York University. His article accused that religion of being "oppressive, backwards, and brutal . . . an affront to basic human dignity." It also charged that Islam was "a hybrid ... of the worst elements of Communism and fascism coexist-ing in a monstrous symbiosis."[23] A fellow student filed an official com-plaint under the university's anti-harassment policy against the author of the article. In a prolonged exchange of letters with the dean of the law school, we argued that, as unpleasant as those criticisms of Islam were, the university should make it clear that they could not justify disciplin-ary action.

We attempted to make the case that, in preparing students to engage in the search for truth, the university had a duty to create a regime that was hospitable to a vigorous free speech. And, in anticipation of the perennial argument that civility should be observed, our letter made the following statements:

> Nor should there be any legal obligation [for such speech] to be ex-pressed in terms of endearment, tones of affection, or even according to the canons of Emily Post. Religious, philosophical, and political dis-putes often engage the deepest passions; it would be unacceptably artifi-cial to insist that such passions be removed from campus controversies. While the University must not tolerate acts or threats of physical vio-lence, it must be open to the most biting of criticisms.[24]

We asked for a declaration from the university that, even if the mat-ter was ultimately settled (as it later, indeed, was), the speech in ques-tion was not beyond the pale. Although the dean replied more than once that it was not proper for *him* to issue such a declaration, we asked more than once that he identify the official who did have such juris-diction. The events of September 11th effectively put an end to this ef-fort. In the meantime, the two students settled their differences; the key ingredient in the settlement was an apology from the critic to the complainant. We never did get any kind of acknowledgment that the impugned speech was protected. On the contrary, those letters from the law school made us fearful that, if the matter hadn't been settled the way it was, the student who criticized Islam could well have faced punishment at the hands of the university.

In the late winter of 2009 (a couple of months or so before I official-ly retired), I picked a fight with both Carleton and Ottawa universities. In both cases, the universities would not allow the posting of a cartoon in connection with "Israeli Apartheid Week." The cartoon showed a helicopter labelled "Israel" shooting a missile at a child whose shadow spelled out "Gaza."

It would be difficult to imagine more feeble rationalizations than some of those invoked by these universities to justify this censorship. According to one of the officials at Carleton, the poster contained "certain words or images [that] could be seen to incite others to infringe rights protected in the *Ontario Human Rights Code.*" Pointing out that the rights protected by the *Code* involve access to public market transactions such as jobs, housing, and various facilities, my letter to the university argued that there was simply no such connection raised by the poster. As we contended, "the cartoon is hardly the functional equivalent of a commercial sign stipulating that 'no blacks, Jews, or aboriginals need apply.' "

Carleton University also impugned the poster on the grounds that it was "insensitive to the norms of civil discourse." We criticized the idea that "of all the constituencies in our society," the students should be "uniquely required" to conduct their debates and discussions in the manner of the manor. Carleton never replied.

In the case of Ottawa, we did get a reply that appeared somewhat responsive to our criticism regarding the breadth of their policy. Their president contended, nevertheless, that the impugned poster was validly prohibited. He contended that it projects "an image that stigmatizes Jewish people as murderers of babies." In response, we argued that this interpretation could effectively suppress some of the most compelling images connected with public affairs. We cited a Pulitzer Prize–winning cartoon showing US soldiers firing at both Vietnamese and Iraqi civilians. The caption read: "Nothing changes." We suggested that, on the basis of the university's analysis, such cartoons could be considered the stigmatization of the American people "as murderers" of civilians.

Although this university president did not expressly say so, it may be that he was objecting also to the way the cartoon exploited the old canard of Jews murdering babies for their blood. In view of the centuries of anti-Semitism associated with this canard, it could have increased the unacceptability of the cartoon. In any event, the appropriate remedy would be for campus members to censure the publishers of the cartoon, not for any authorities to censor them. All of this led us to argue that campus speech should not be "so uniquely sanitized of expressive vinegar." Unfortunately, our second letter did not elicit a further reply from the University of Ottawa.

At some point in the spring of 2009, I received a letter from the University of Waterloo announcing its intention to award me an honorary Doctor of Laws degree at its impending fall convocation. Of course, I was pleasantly surprised. Apart from the odd speech throughout the years, I did not initially think that I had had any significant contact with that university.

On further reflection, however, it occurred to me that a little more than ten years earlier, I had had a great deal to do with Waterloo University. From about 1996 until 1998, I went to bat for a Waterloo professor who was facing potential discipline arising from a student complaint under that university's anti-harassment policy. At no point, however, did any representative of Waterloo link the doctorate with my earlier involvement. Indeed, I simply don't know whether there was any connection. When the announcement became public, I did receive a particularly warm letter from the professor whose cause I had defended. I also know that a number of the chief executives of the university, including the president, had changed since my involvement in the complaint. Nevertheless, the circumstances of that complaint were sufficiently strange to warrant a mention here.

In March 1996, a black female student filed a complaint alleging that her then sociology professor had made statements in class that were "racist" and "unbalanced" so as to cause her "undue stress, humiliation, and embarrassment." According to her, the professor had failed adequately to define such terms as "employment equity" and "affirmative action." Almost two years later—in February 1998—her complaint was finally dismissed by a professor from another university who had been requested by the president of Waterloo to adjudicate the matter. In the meantime, I wrote a number of letters to various officials of the university.

In a letter bearing a date in September 1996, I wrote to the Waterloo provost on behalf of CCLA. My letter contended that the complaint simply failed to disclose an offence under the policy. As to the charges that the professor had made "racist" and "unbalanced" comments, I noted that "there is no indication as to precisely *how*" he had done so. In this regard, it is interesting to compare my letter with the decision of the outside adjudicator. He said, "There is in fact no indication . . . of how [the professor's] behaviour can allegedly be characterized in these ways."

My letter contended that nothing in the university's policy "would make the expression of 'racist' or 'unbalanced' views *per se* an offence within the campus community." On this matter, the adjudicator said, "The expression of 'racist' or 'unbalanced' views *per se* would not constitute an offence however objectionable it might otherwise be." According to my letter, "The professor's alleged failure to adequately define 'employment equity' and 'affirmative action' addresses pedagogical techniques not ethical behaviour." According to the adjudicator, these allegedly inadequate definitions may speak to the professor's "failings as a university teacher but I do not see how they establish a foundation for a formal complaint to the Ethics Committee."

As to the complainant's charge that the professor had caused her "undue stress, humiliation, and embarrassment," I made the point that "professors are not obliged to avoid the expression of opinion that might give offence . . . the canons of academic freedom have long recognized that legitimate expressions of opinion can sometimes be hurtful." On this issue, the adjudicator declared it was not enough that one of the students felt uncomfortable; he said that discomfort is often the result when any of us are "challenged by ideas or opinions that clash with our own." On this score, I said the only conceivable obligation professors would have is "to avoid *gratuitous* offence." On the same matter, the adjudicator said that the policy required a professor's statements to be "gratuitously offensive."

I do not reproduce the foregoing in order to boast how smart we at CCLA are or to accuse the outside adjudicator of plagiarism. On the contrary, I think the matter was always a rather simple one to resolve. *That* is what explains the similarity between our analysis and that of the adjudicator. The factor that makes the university's handling of this complaint so objectionable is that it took so long for them to resolve a matter that should have been dismissed right at the outset. I point out in this regard that I sent copies of all my earlier letters to the president of the university so that he was apprised of our arguments almost from the beginning. In the meantime, of course, the impugned professor was forced to live under a cloud.

What, then, explains the failure of the university to resolve this matter at an earlier point and its involvement of an outside adjudicator? The culprit, in my view, was the state of political correctness as it then prevailed on the Waterloo campus and elsewhere. I am particularly proud that CCLA played such a forthright role in challenging the emanations and offspring of that regrettable campus phenomenon.

PORN

Historically, the censorship of pornography and obscenity was very much on the free speech agenda of civil libertarians. CCLA was no exception. Here, however, the fight involved philosophical objectives that went beyond the role of free speech in the redress of grievances and the quest for truth. Although some of those elements were present at some points and on some occasions, the fight against censorship of culture and the arts involved another objective entirely.

In culture and the arts, freedom of expression provides the basis for enrichment. To whatever extent people have the right to produce and consume as they choose in literature, films, art, music, and dance, they are enabled to enrich their own lives and those of others. When civil libertarians fought the forces of censorship, therefore, they were attempting to remove impediments on the pathways to enrichment.

Traditionally, the proponents of censorship tended to be conservative and right-wing. They were often perceived as sexual prudes who could not abide the fact that other people might be enjoying themselves. These people often thought of themselves as defenders of the faith and custodians of family values.

Somewhere around the 1980s, however, a new constituency joined the coalition that was advocating censorship. This new constituency tended to be progressive, left-wing, and even egalitarian. They saw pornography as a threat to equality. Where the earlier group of pro-censorship advocates tended to favour keeping men and women in their respective roles vis-à-vis each other, the latter group tended to be pro-feminist and very much in favour of "women's liberation."

As we became increasingly aware of feminist support for censorship, we became commensurately apprehensive over the welfare of CCLA.

After all, our membership had always been deeply supportive of the feminist cause and movement. At one point, our growing concerns impelled us to arrange a meeting between certain leaders of our organization and some of their counterparts from the National Action Committee on the Status of Women. Although the meeting was diplomatic and civil, it failed to produce a consensus. It became necessary, therefore, that CCLA challenge the growing influence of the pro-censorship feminists.

In the same way as we could not allow our alliance with the Jewish community to derail us on hate propaganda, we could not allow our associations with feminist organizations to derail us on pornography.

Somewhere around 1984, I arranged to appear before the Fraser Committee that had been appointed by the federal government to review this issue. In order to shore up my political flank, I found a woman with recognizable feminist credentials to appear with me. That woman was Louise Arbour, then a brilliant law professor at Osgoode Hall and subsequently a justice of the Supreme Court of Canada and special prosecutor of international war crimes at the court in The Hague. Despite what I insist was the able presentation of CCLA, the Fraser Committee recommendations were closer to the position of the National Action Committee than they were to ours.

Around the mid-1980s, the government of Canada introduced a bill that purported to rewrite the Canadian law on obscenity. But it was so wide in its scope that it appeared capable of catching a fair amount of legitimate literature. When the officers of the Toronto library board learned of the potential perils that librarians might face, they expressed their apprehensions in a letter to the federal minister of justice. His reply did not console the officials of the library. They then consulted me about what to say by way of rejoinder. I said that they should reply, not with verbal syllogisms, but with disruptive action. More specifically, I suggested that they close the libraries.

The idea seemed to capture the imagination of the chair and executive director of the library board. Their reaction inspired me to get to work. I went around to visit and attempt to buttonhole the members of the library board. It soon began to appear that we were gathering significant support. During this time, I made a speech at a conference of librarians. Because of their combination of mild manners and militant action, I labelled the librarians the "Clark Kents of political action." At the designated time, I appeared with one of my staff colleagues before the library board and officially recommended the action of closing the libraries. In the result, they closed all but four of their thirty-two libraries on Human Rights Day that year—December 10 1987.

There was one particularly amusing development at the library board meeting that made the decision. By pre-arrangement, I was met by a uniformed Canadian soldier whose assignment it was to drive me to Kingston that night where I was scheduled to make a speech the next day at the National Defence College. The setting, however, especially amused me. I had just made what was probably the most radical proposal that the library board had ever entertained. And then I received a military escort to take me to my next engagement. How I wished that the people on Grace Street could have seen me then.

The library event itself was quite a success. A few hundred librarians attended at the Hart House theatre and participated in the program we had planned. The platform speakers were author Margaret Attwood, filmmaker David Cronenberg, art gallery official Philip Monk, CBC broadcaster Erica Ritter, and me. As I remarked to David Cronenberg, this was the perfect strike. Neither the employees nor CCLA closed the libraries; library *management* did it. The publicity was quite phenomenal. My only regret was that city council did not make good on its threat to take legal action against the librarians' organization. That would have ensured even greater publicity.

Not long after this protest meeting, the government of Canada withdrew its contentious bill. In some ways, I was sorry that the government acted as soon as it did. I was in the middle of organizing a nationwide shutdown of museums. Indeed, I had already met with officers of the Canadian Museums Association. That action would have been nothing short of a ball.

But the prevention of a new invasion of free speech was not enough. The existing law of obscenity and child pornography continued to pose a threat. The obscenity section criminalized the "undue exploitation" of sex by itself or in combination with "crime," "horror," "cruelty," or "violence." The court said that such "exploitation" became "undue" if Canadians generally could not tolerate other Canadians being exposed to the material in question. The definition of "child pornography" was perhaps less vague, but no less contentious. It included material in which a person who was merely "depicted" as being under eighteen years old was merely "depicted" as engaged in explicit sexual activity.

During the 1990s, the obscenity and child pornography sections of the *Criminal Code* were tested in court and both were upheld as constitutionally valid. CCLA intervened in both and was ably represented by Sheila Block in the first case and Trish Jackson in the second one.

Proclaiming that its interpretation of the obscenity law was "intelligible," the Supreme Court spelled out how it might work. It said that material in which sex was coupled with violence would almost always be obscene and so will much material that is "degrading or dehumanizing."

But the portrayal of sex coupled with violence is a key feature of much legitimate art and literature. Consider, for example, the following: the rape of Leda by the god Zeus from Greek mythology; the medieval paintings that depict the rape of the Sabine women; and the famous rape scene from Ingmar Bergman's classic film, *The Virgin Spring*. Legitimate art cannot be confined to the portrayal of virtue. It must be able to depict more than hearts, flowers, and telephone books. The depiction of evil is crucial to the historic role played by art in our society.

While the notion of sex coupled with violence is excessively broad, the terms "degrading" and "dehumanizing" are hopelessly vague. Material that is degrading to some could be enriching—even helpful—to others. Consider, for example, how an earlier government bill warned that ejaculating onto another person could be deemed "degrading." Yet a book on AIDS prevention explicitly advised that such conduct could be healthy. Imagine arresting anyone for distributing material that is designed to save life!

As far as the child pornography section was concerned, we became involved in a case concerning a young artist named Eli Langer. A Toronto gallery was exhibiting drawings he had done in which he showed youngsters in sexual situations. Despite the fact that the drawings emanated entirely from his imagination (no live models were used), the Crown charged Mr. Langer with creating "child pornography." We attacked both the charge and the law.

As the ludicrousness of the situation became increasingly evident, the Crown finally withdrew the charge against Langer and proceeded exclusively against the drawings themselves—under the forfeiture sec-

tions of the *Criminal Code*. The judge declined to hold the law unconstitutional but he "acquitted" the material on the grounds that it had
"artistic merit." We continued to argue, however, that this was an elu-
sive defence: there was no way for artists to know *in advance* whether
their productions would pass muster. It followed, therefore, that the
creation of material dealing with child sexuality would be a hazardous
undertaking.

I incorporated these ideas into a brief and, together with CCLA board
member Trish Jackson, I flew across the country in August of 1999 to
meet with federal justice minister Anne McLellan in her home riding of
Edmonton, Alberta. The meeting was lengthy and contentious. When
we left, it was clear to us that we had not moved the minister. The political pressures on the other side were too great for us to dislodge. On
subsequent occasions, I appeared more than once before parliamentary
committees to argue our case once again. I also appeared, as did board
members Trish Jackson and David Cronenberg, in the press, on radio,
and on television.

On one occasion, I debated against a male ally of the pro-censorship feminists. He had attracted substantial publicity by arguing that,
as a psychologist, he felt competent to assess certain types of violent
pornography as dangerous to women. During the morning before our
scheduled evening debate at the University of Guelph, he arranged for
an intermediary to ask me if I had any objection to his actually showing
the audience, by way of a big screen, some of the impugned pictures.
Although I did not object at all, I delayed my reply so that he would
believe I was troubled by the prospect. After a seemingly respectable
period, I transmitted my acquiescence.

At one point in the debate, he presented some awful pictures to the
audience. (The audience was composed largely of students, some faculty, and members of the public.) After he finished showing the pictures and commenting on them, I pounced. "If you really believe that
exposure to these pictures is so dangerous to women," I asked him,
"why would you show them to an audience of so many strangers?" Even
if my argument did not contain an air-tight syllogism, it had an arresting impact.

Again and again in one forum after another, I argued that there was
simply no point in criminalizing the mere fictionalized depiction of

sexual transgressions. The only such transgressions that are worthy of the law are those in which a real person was unlawfully abused for the purpose of sexually arousing a subsequent audience. Thus far, my colleagues and I have been unable to persuade either judges or legislators to go along with us. In this connection, I had an amusing encounter in the aftermath of the Supreme Court judgment on obscenity. I ran into Mr. Justice John Sopinka who had actually written the judgment. Our chance meeting occurred in an Ottawa restaurant. I had known him both in law school and he had acted for us when he was in practice. When he saw me, he remarked that he had heard that I didn't like his judgment in the obscenity case. To which, I replied in the manner of counsel in court, "Precisely, my lord, precisely."

At the time I terminated my tenure with CCLA, it began to appear that we were making headway against the provincial film censorship laws. Of course, prior restraint—requiring things to be approved before they can be seen by the public—is a more pervasive intrusion than is subsequent prosecution. It's one thing to make people accountable for what they publish and show. But it's quite another thing to force them to have their material cleared before they can make it public. At one point, some of my wisecracks about this appeared in the press. I noted that it struck me as absurd that sexual material must be vetted before it can be shown but the disclosure of the most delicate defence secrets is subject only to subsequent prosecution. Conclusion: in our society, sex is more dangerous than a breach of national security.

ENDNOTES

1   Walter Stefaniuk, "The Zundel Trial: Rosy Views of Death Camp Challenged by Prosecutors," *Toronto Star*, March 5, 1988.

2   *R v. Keegstra*, [1990] 3 S.C.R. 697.

3   *R v. Zundel*, [1992] 2 S.C.R. 731. See also, Peter Small, "Jewish Groups Demand New Criminal Charges Be Laid Over 'Falsehoods,'" *Toronto Star*, August 28, 1992, A16.

4   *Canada (Human Rights Commission) v. Taylor*, [1990] 3 S.C.R. 892.

5   *Whatcott v. Saskatchewan (Human Rights Tribunal)*, 2010 SKCA 26.

6   *Lund v. Boissoin*, 2012 ABCA 300.

7   Mark Steyn, "The Future Belongs to Islam," *Maclean's*, October 20, 2006.

8   *Hill v. Church of Scientology of Toronto*, 1995 S.C.R. 1130.

9   *Canada (Attorney General) v. O'Neill*, 2004 ONSC 255, Ratushny J.

10 *Ramsden v Peterborough (City)*, 1991 ONCA 328 at para 6, 5 O.R. (3d) 289, Krever J.A. *[Ramsden]*.

11 *Ramsden v Peterborough (City)*, 1993 SCC 60, SCR 1084, Iacobucci J. *[Ramsden]*.

12 *Williams v Aristocratic Restaurants*, 1951 SCC 784, S.C.R. 762 at para. 1, Kerwin J. *[Williams]*.

13 *Dupond v. City of Montreal et al.*, 1978 SCC 201, 2 S.C.R. 770, at para. 3, Beetz J. *[Dupond]*.

14 *BCGEU v British Columbia (Attorney General)*, 1988 SCC 3, 2 SCR 114 *[BCGEU]*.

15 Canadian Civil Liberties Association, Toronto, March 22, 1974, A. Alan Borovoy, p. 2.

16 Richard F. Devlin, "Legal Education As Political Consciousness-Raising or Paving the Road to Hell," (1989) *Journal of Legal Education*, vol. 39, 213–30.

17 Alan Borovoy, "Campus Thought Police Give Substance to Phantom," *The Toronto Star*, February 1, 1993.

18 Richard Devlin, "A counter-attack in defence of political correctness," *The Toronto Star*, March 8, 1993.

19 Matin Yaqzan, "Opinion: Rape, Past and Present," *The Brunswickan* (Fredericton: University of New Brunswick), November 12, 1993.

20 Alan Borovoy, "Students Shout Down Free Speech," *The Toronto Star*, January 5, 1994.

21 Canadian Civil Liberties Association, Letters to Various Forms of Student Councils at Universities, re: Freedom of Expression and Association on University Campuses, October 27, 2008.

22 John Philipe Rushton, *Race, Evolution and Behaviour: A Life History Perspective* (Port Huron, MI: Charles Darwin Research Institute, 1995).

23 Stewart Bell, "Religious beliefs fair game for criticism: Osgoode Hall Dispute," *National Post*, June 11, 2001.

24 Alan Borovoy, "Letter to Peter Hogg, Dean, Osgoode Hall Law School," Canadian Civil Liberties Association, May 30, 2001, p. 2.

Law and Order

FUNDAMENTAL SAFEGUARDS

On a Saturday afternoon late in October 1968, I received a telephone call from a friend of mine, a woman in her early twenties who was a PhD candidate in psychology at the University of Toronto. Her call, from a local police station, was asking for my help. Some time earlier, she had been arrested at a demonstration against the Vietnam War and the police were still holding her. She was looking, of course, for the fastest and easiest way to secure her release from custody. But, during the course of our telephone conversation, she made a point of asking me to arrange for dinner to be fed to her "children." Knowing that she had no such children, I soon realized that this request had been made to impress the police at the station. Presumably, it was the way she obtained access to the telephone that was otherwise being denied her.

Within the next half-hour, I showed up at the police station and asked the officer in charge how I could get my friend out on bail. He replied that this discretion was reposed in the local justice of the peace. How, then, I asked, could I make contact with the justice? The officer replied that this could not happen for a few hours because the justice, at that time, was attending the opera; I would have to await his return.

When the justice finally did arrive, he ordered the release of my friend on her promise to pay a particular sum of money if she failed to show up for her trial. In her case, there was no reason to impose any additional fetters on her release; she was obviously a respectable person with no criminal record whatsoever. At her trial several months later, she was acquitted of the charge that had occasioned her arrest.

*W*hen I subsequently reflected on this experience, I became angry. My friend, an innocent person, had been forced to spend twelve hours in jail, not because of any misconduct of hers, but because the system had failed to accommodate her situation. Indeed, the most remarkable aspect of the experience was the absence of any intention to punish—or even hurt—my friend. Those in charge treated me and my friend in a polite fashion; there was no evidence of any rancour or hostility.

Since this incident arose so soon after I had taken over at CCLA, I began to see it as a metaphor for the problems of our criminal justice system. I learned to see the enemy, not as a practitioner of malevolence, but as the embodiment of indifference. The system was not particularly out to hurt accused people but neither was it particularly poised to help them. This is not to deny the existence of malevolence or even sadism in our law enforcement community; it is simply to see the issue in perspective. Only a minority are intentional wrongdoers; but only a minority are intentional *right*doers.

Within the next year and a half, CCLA became involved in a major project that tended to reinforce what I had learned from my friend's experience. With a grant from the Ford Foundation we conducted a cross-country survey of how the Canadian criminal justice system was working in practice. We interviewed accused persons and examined court records in Halifax, Montreal, Toronto, Winnipeg, and Vancouver. In all, we looked at several hundred cases. The time period under review was January 1970. We published our account of this project under the title: "Due Process Safeguards and Canadian Criminal Justice".

Since our survey took place prior to the major bail reforms of that time, we were particularly interested in the initial stages of the accused persons' experience. Although police officers then enjoyed a certain amount of discretion in how they launched the process, we found that 72 percent of the accused people in our survey were arrested rather than summonsed. An arrest, of course, constitutes a significant intrusion on a person's freedom. Perhaps even more significant, a majority of those arrested endured at least a few days of pre-trial confinement. Indeed, a majority of the accused spent at least twelve hours in custody before their bail applications were even processed. Shades of what happened to my friend!

The *Canadian Bill of Rights* (the *Charter* was at least a decade away) proclaimed the right of arrested people to "retain and instruct counsel without delay." Presumably, the idea was to ensure the earliest possible legal advice to minimize the risk that the arrested people—many of whom would be in a state of panic (and at least some of whom would be genuinely innocent),—would irreparably damage themselves. It is significant, therefore, that most of the accused persons in our survey said that they made statements to the police; they considered most of these statements to be self-incriminating; and most of the interrogations reportedly occurred before the accused person had consulted legal counsel. Indeed, about 30 percent of these arrested people claimed that they were denied their request to make a telephone call from custody. Even if those people had sought consultation with a lawyer, the system apparently rendered them often incapable of fulfilling that wish.

It has always been the case that a large number of accused people plead guilty. But our survey discovered that, in the case of those people, the system disposed of them in trials that lasted less than ten minutes. Remarkably, therefore, those court hearings, on average, totalled less than three hours. They rarely convened in the afternoons; their average daily adjournment time was as early as 1:25 p.m.

An exacerbating factor in the system was the nature of the pre-trial detention facilities. In the overwhelming number of cases, there was virtually no attempt to provide activities for the prisoners. Essentially, they just sat and waited. Those who were proven guilty and sentenced to confinement in penitentiaries usually had recourse to some kind of recreational facilities. By contrast, those who had not been found guilty and were simply awaiting trial, were subjected to a regime of oppressive inactivity.

In its conclusion, our report acknowledged that there were very few cases "of a sensational character." Our report did say that "our system can be characterized by its plethora of cursory trials, defenceless interrogations, needless detentions, and inadequate facilities." In the result, CCLA described the Canadian criminal justice system as "insensitive." Our report made the following observations:

> Rarely are we vindictive, but usually we are indifferent. We don't go out of our way to inflict hardship, nor, however, do we go out of our way to relieve it. Time and again, competing considerations weigh more heavily than the rights of the accused. So often these considerations represent little more than cost and convenience. We won't pay the money, we won't take the trouble.[1]

Following our well-attended press conference on the survey, we made striking headlines in the mass media. Our work proved to be highly newsworthy. It led also to numerous follow-up interviews. Despite the then brevity of my involvement with CCLA, I experienced the excitement of our organization's having made it big.

But there was even more. The Law Society of Upper Canada picked up on our material relating to the custodial interrogations without counsel. To their enduring credit, the leaders of the Law Society's legal aid committee instituted a system of publicly paid duty counsel to be available and accessible to people who are arrested at night. Presumably, police officers would no longer be able to claim that lawyers were unavailable when it was convenient to question the accused people.

While I very much appreciated the importance of this reform that the Law Society adopted, I became hungry for even more. In addition to the provision for paid duty counsel, I thought the law should contain some kind of prohibition on the power of the police to conduct custodial interrogations in the absence of a defence lawyer. I thought that there should also be a requirement for the police to advise arrested people of their right to counsel and a further requirement to facilitate the exercise of such rights.

Without the latter prohibitions and requirements, I feared that the safeguards in the *Bill of Rights* would become effectively stillborn. So we began to beat the drums for some such changes in the law. Of course, our survey provided a very helpful backdrop for our efforts. To the extent that members of the public were familiar with it, they would have experienced an enhanced consciousness. My reformist drives impelled me to do a little research. Whenever I became involved in such activity,

I invariably tried to get a handle on the resulting consequences for law enforcement. For me, it wasn't good enough simply to regurgitate civil libertarian dogmas; it was also necessary to engage in a cost-benefit analysis of what my proposed reforms would bring about.

I soon came upon some literature describing a study that had been done in the American city of Pittsburgh. The researchers tried to document what happened to law enforcement in that community after the US Supreme Court decided the famous case of *Miranda*.[2] That was the case that effectively instructed the police to desist from questioning arrested people without having observed the kind of safeguards that I had begun to promote here. The study found that, despite a drop in the rate of custodial confessions after *Miranda*, the conviction and clearance (or crime solution) rates remained stable. In short, the *Miranda* safeguards did not appear to have diminished the ability of the police to enforce the law.

Armed with this additional intellectual equipment, we met with the federal minister of justice and his Ontario counterparts and pushed for appropriate safeguards at both levels. I also wrote media articles and responded to many interviews where I was able to push these views. While the law did not formally change in our direction until the advent of the *Charter*, our activities probably served to raise the consciousness of decision makers and the public. When the *Charter* was being debated, helpful provisions were added and, after the *Charter* was proclaimed, some helpful judgments were rendered. Of course, we made a well-debated and well-covered presentation to the key parliamentary committee on the *Charter* and we participated by way of intervention in a number of the key court cases that construed and applied the *Charter*. In addition, I'd like to think that the decision makers were influenced by the relentless polemics we waged during the decade between the publication of our "due process" survey and the debates on the *Charter*.

ELECTRONIC BUGGING

As indicated earlier, a "law and order" issue that surfaced towards the end of the 1960s involved the police use of electronic bugging as an investigative tool. As the pressures built up, the federal government

introduced a bill that was designed finally to ensure that this police practice was brought under a regime of legal control. Not surprisingly, CCLA
found that the powers intended for the police were too wide and the safeguards intended for civilians were too narrow. And, when we appeared
before the House of Commons Justice Committee, that is exactly what
we said. Of course, we attempted to buttress our position with an analysis of the government bill. We also proposed a set of alternative powers
and additional safeguards for the politicians and public to consider. Our
presentation triggered a significant amount of comment and debate.

In one area, in particular, our proposals found their way into legislative amendments. Borrowing from the American experience, we recommended a mechanism for ensuring a greater level of accountability
when the police resorted to this surreptitious surveillance. We suggested
that, after a given period, the law should require the police to advise
those people who were the targets of police bugging. In recognition of
the possibility that, in certain cases, early notification could undermine
an investigation, we proposed a mechanism by which a court could
grant the police a postponement of this obligation.

Nevertheless, the then federal justice minister, Otto Lang, vehemently opposed our recommended safeguard. At the time, however, no
party commanded majority support in the House of Commons. Taking
advantage of this minority Parliament situation, the opposition parties
ganged up on the government and forced through an amendment to
the bill similar to what we had proposed. Otto Lang denounced it as a
"goddamned stupid amendment."

In the Senate, however, more conservative elements prevailed; our
amendment was excised from the bill. Not long after that, the bill returned to the House for additional consideration. Upon passing the bill
for a second time, the House restored our amendment and, this time,
the Senate let it become law.

Some months afterward, I was given the benefit of an insight into
what happened when the bill returned to the House. In a telephone call
that had been undertaken for other reasons, federal NDP leader, David
Lewis, related to me what happened. As indicated earlier, I had articled
for him and so we had somewhat of a personal relationship. He told me
how he managed, in particular, to win support for the amendment from
the Créditiste members of the House. He said that if he had simply

gone to them and talked to them about civil liberties, there was a good chance that they would not have appreciated what he was talking about. So he hit on a different ploy. He went to them and said that, if they supported this amendment, they could "kick the Senate in the ass and Otto Lang in the balls." *That*, Lewis reported, evoked a positive response from the Créditiste members. Thus, their support was added to that of the other Opposition parties and our amendment became law. Often, it's interesting to learn what actually makes history happen.

POLICE COMPLAINTS

In the mid- to late 1960s, the press was full of stories about conflicts between the police and various elements of the public. There were allegations of beatings, shootings, even killings. CCLA embellished this record with an affidavit about an incident alleging police neglect of a particularly troublesome kind. The incident happened during the arrest and subsequent confinement of a woman who turned out to suffer from a serious epileptic condition. Upon being taken into custody, she allegedly pleaded with the police to help her secure her medication. According to her, a simple telephone call to the hospital across the road from the police station would accomplish what she sought. She claims that her many requests were denied and, about a day or so after her release from custody, she suffered a serious seizure and collapsed in the street.

We made this story public through the medium of a letter, requesting a meeting with the then Ontario Attorney General, Arthur Wishart.

That meeting took place in late June of 1969. Reproducing the recent press accounts of alleged police misconduct, we called for a structural reform in the way civilian complaints should be handled. We argued that the police monopoly over the handling of civilian complaints must be ended. The system had to include a mechanism for the *independent* investigation and review of civilian complaints against the police. Police self-investigation would no longer suffice. Borrowing from our colleague CCLA's then secretary, Terry Meagher, we declared that "the police must no longer be umpires of their own ballgame."

Our brief to the Attorney General also called for an end to the non-police functions of police authorities, such as the granting of licences and the determination of parade routes for political protesters. In time, some such changes were made. But they rarely attracted much public scrutiny. Our proposed changes to the police complaints system, on the other hand, provoked a storm of political and public debate. The police weighed in against the proposal and other elements of the public surfaced on our side of the debate.

During the decades in the aftermath of that meeting, allegations of police misconduct were constantly in the media. There were beatings, shootings, and deaths attributed to police behaviour. On a number of occasions, those incidents provoked some kind of independent scrutiny, albeit on an ad hoc basis. Criminal lawyer Arthur Maloney, Catholic Cardinal Emmett Carter, and Mr. Justice Donald Morand were among those who headed up these various independent inquiries into police behaviour. Not infrequently, these inquiries produced recommendations for the kind of changes we were seeking in the way civilian complaints were to be handled. Even at the federal level, an inquiry conducted by Mr. Justice René Marin called for a greater level of independent involvement where complaints against the RCMP were concerned.

Early on, there was a development that had some interesting consequences. A story in the media reported that the Toronto Police Commission was initiating some proceedings against Syd Brown, the then president of the Metro Toronto Police Association. The trigger for this action was a picture of Mr. Brown that appeared on the cover of *Toronto Life* magazine; he was shown holding the tin cup of a beggar. Mr. Brown's purpose was to attract attention to the allegedly paltry wage levels under which Toronto police were then required to work.

I fired off and publicized a letter to the police commission in which I complained that the commission should not be exercising such authority over an officer who was acting in his capacity as a leader of the police union. A major point of my argument was that the police are denied the most elementary forms of self-help available to other employees, such as the right to strike. In my view, therefore, society must be particularly solicitous to ensure that there was no needless interference with the ability of those officers to advance their employment interests. Since the spectacle of civil liberties organizations going to bat for police was a rather rare one, we attracted a significant amount of publicity for that intervention.

Not many years later, I was on a television panel discussion with Syd Brown. The subject matter dealt with the police complaints controversy. I, of course, was making the case for the reforms we had been seeking and Syd was weighing in on the other side. At one point, he made an attempt at a show-stopper. He asked me whether I would favour similar reforms in the way lawyers were regulated. As it happens, I had thought about that issue over the years. So, I countered by making Syd Brown an offer: I said that I would agree to go with him to change the system for the lawyers if he would agree to go with me to change it for the police.

That exchange actually gave me an idea. Shortly thereafter, I telephoned Syd and offered him the support of CCLA for the reform of the way labour relations were managed for the police. And, sensing a softening of his stance over the handling of civilian complaints, I asked him if he would consider extending the support of the police association for the changes we were proposing in the way civilian complaints were being managed. Among other things, I suggested to him that the internal police handling of those matters was no more helpful to police respondents than it was to civilian complainants.

A few meetings then took place between some of them and some of us and an alliance was forged. We planned a joint delegation between the police association and the civil liberties association to call upon the then Solicitor General of Ontario, John MacBeth. Our delegation was going to request independent investigation and review of civilian complaints against the police and a more independent regime for the handling of internal relations between the police and their employment masters. The delegation took place a few weeks thereafter (October 1976) amid a fair amount of publicity. Our delegation was described in the press as "an unholy alliance."

I suspect that this delegation may have been the straw that broke the government's back. Not long afterwards, the new Solicitor General of Ontario, Roy McMurtry, established a pilot program for the city of Toronto: it contained an additional amount of independent involvement in the civilian complaints system. And, not long after that, a reformed system was extended throughout the province. Although we continued to press for even greater reform, we also appreciated the distance we had come.

In a subsequent visit to New York City, I told the then national director of the American Civil Liberties Union (ACLU) about CCLA's coalition with the cops. He said that, as far as he knew, what we did had no precedent in the United States. I have often thought that our alliance with the police must have satisfied all the criteria of a good social action project. It had the element of surprise; it brought about a political realignment; it generated substantial publicity; and it was a lot of fun. In the words of the song, "Who could ask for anything more?"

POLICE POLICIES

Earlier in my tenure with CCLA (in 1970), I was confronted with a news story about the fate of more than a dozen bookstore clerks who had been arrested for their role in allegedly distributing obscene material to the public at large. As clerks, they exercised no decision-making discretion concerning what would be sold in the bookstores that employed them. Nevertheless, they were facing criminal charges for the dissemination of the impugned material. Moreover, they were taken out of their respective stores in handcuffs.

Shortly thereafter, I made a date for the police commission to receive a delegation from the CCLA. At the inception of our meeting, the chair of the commission distributed across the table, copies of some of the material that formed the subject matter of the charges. He challenged us to deny the obscene nature of that material. At this distance (more than thirty-five years) from these events, I'm not quite sure how to explain my failure to object more vigorously than I did to the dubious tactic that the chair of the police commission employed. Perhaps I was too new at the time and perhaps I was cowed by the fact that other members of our delegation who were senior to me, didn't react that way. I am as convinced as I can be that if I were to face a similar situation today, I would let the police chair know what I thought of any such attempt to drown us in irrelevancy.

Notwithstanding those tactics, our delegation pressed on. We argued, of course, that we were not there to dispute the validity of the charges; that was for the courts to decide. Our objective was to question the policies that underlay the prosecutions. We argued that, in view of the vagueness in the obscenity laws, law enforcement should focus first on whether the material should be characterized as "obscene." There was a

Growing up

ABOVE: In Fauntleroy garb on Grace Street, late 1930s

TOP RIGHT: With a pony at my uncle's farm, 1943

BELOW: Managing editor of high school magazine, 1950

ABOVE: With my ever-loyal and helpful cousin Andrea Pearl Baltman. We were 14 & 4 then. Even at that age, she was competent.

Family and friends

With my father, Jack Borovoy, 1930s

Celebrating my birthday with my mother, Rae Borovoy, 1992

With my parents on my way to receive the Order of Canada, 1983

ABOVE: At family seder, 1970s

ABOVE: My parents, Rae and Jack Borovoy having a conspicuously good time at their 50th anniversary party (January 1979)

RIGHT: Dancing up a storm in the 1980s with (now Reverend) Dawn Clark

LEFT TO RIGHT: Rhoda Goldstein; my parents, Jack and Rae Borovoy; Berril Garshowitz; Louis Goldstein (to whose memory this book is dedicated); Murray Tojo Rubin at my folks' 50th anniversary party

LEFT, FROM LEFT TO RIGHT: Mel and Mindy Finkelstein; cousin Andrea Baltman; Andrea's mother, my auntie Ida Brown; and yours truly at my folks' 50th anniversary party

ABOVE: With my cousin Andrea and her son Stuart

LEFT: With Dan and Donna Hill

Three close friends: Owen Shime (right), the late Daniel G. Hill (first director of the Ontario Human Rights Commission), and the late Millie Shime

In song

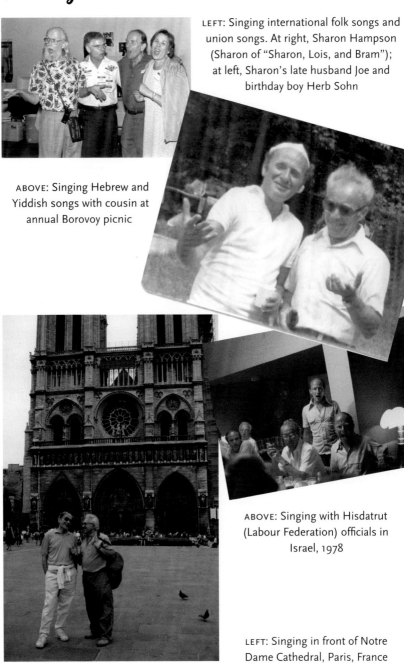

LEFT: Singing international folk songs and union songs. At right, Sharon Hampson (Sharon of "Sharon, Lois, and Bram"); at left, Sharon's late husband Joe and birthday boy Herb Sohn

ABOVE: Singing Hebrew and Yiddish songs with cousin at annual Borovoy picnic

ABOVE: Singing with Hisdatrut (Labour Federation) officials in Israel, 1978

LEFT: Singing in front of Notre Dame Cathedral, Paris, France

At work

At the CCLA office, 1980s

LEFT: Candidate for the Ontario legislature, 1963

ABOVE: In the CCLA office, 1976. Used for a profile in *Weekend Magazine*, September 4, 1976 (Photo: Richard Pierre)

ABOVE: In a panel discussion, 1970s

At Canadian Labour Congress (CLC) convention (1980s). I presented the
CLC Social Justice award to Donna Hill (seated beside me) and Daniel G. Hill
(at right). In the middle is their son, folk singer Dan Hill.

With 92 ½ year old Roger Baldwin, founder of the American Civil Liberties Union at
the United Nations in New York, 1976

In conversation

With my intellectual guru—philosopher Sidney Hook (1980)

In Israel with Terry Meagher, then Secretary Treasurer, Ontario Federation of Labour
and long-time executive member of the CCLA and the Labour Committee

In conversation with then Ontario Chief Justice Warren Winkler

In conversation with Ontario's then chief provincial court judge Sidney B. Linden

Travels

Punting on the Cam (Cambridge, England, 1993)

At my favourite place, the Tanglewood Music Festival (Massachusetts) — a frequent retreat

With Jonathan and Pammy Shime (off-spring of Millie and Owen) at the Tanglewood Music Festival

In retirement

With special friend, Myra Merkur, at the 2013 CCLA gala

With Canada's former Governor General, the Right Honourable Adrienne Clarkson (who frequently interviewed me in her former life at the CBC)

ABOVE: At Law Foundation award with old close friend Mel Finkelsten (left), and other friends Sheila Freeman and Mel's wife, Mindy (right)

ABOVE: Mark Sandler, then President of the Law Foundation of Ontario and Harry Arthurs, former president of York University

ABOVE: With my successor at CCLA, Nathalie Des Rosiers

ABOVE: With a favourite cousin from my father's side, Doreen Sears

ABOVE: Harry Arthurs perplexed because he feels obliged to say something nice about me at the Law Foundation

LEFT: Myra and I with idealistic cousin from my mother's side — Dr. Debbie Honickman

ABOVE: Getting a plaque
for 40 years of serving the
CCLA. With Board Chair
John McCamus (left) and
Education Director Danielle
McLaughlin

To A. Alan Borovoy,
General Counsel,
from the
Canadian
Civil Liberties
Association
with
gratitude
for forty years
at the barricades
may 1, 1968 ~ may 1, 2008

ABOVE: The plaque

ABOVE: At 50th reunion of high school graduating class in 2000 with Red
Petroff (left) and Murray Tojo Rubin (right)

Portrait © by Mendelson Joe

special provision in the *Criminal Code* for doing that; in our view, the employment of that provision should serve as a prerequisite to the laying of charges against any persons. Moreover, we argued that the only people who should even be considered for prosecution are those who effectively decide what material would be sold. Hapless store clerks should not become the targets of law enforcement policy. And, we contended that the use of handcuffs in such a situation represented unwarranted cruelty.

Needless to say, the then leadership of the police commission remained staunchly unresponsive to the merits of our argument. Nevertheless, I am not aware of anything similar happening thereafter. Of course, our delegation was well publicized at the time.

An important aspect of this issue did not dawn on me until sometime later: the policy of law enforcement. The police cannot enforce every law in the same way. Who decides which laws will be enforced in what ways? And, on what basis are such decisions made? This was a subject that began to engage an increasing·amount of my attention.

Much of the issue came to a head on the occasion of the 1981 Toronto bathhouse raids. One night in early February of that year, some two hundred police officers stormed into four downtown bathhouses in what was described as the largest single police operation since the 1970 invocation of the *War Measures Act*. In the course of what they were about, the police reportedly perpetrated a state of mayhem, including the terrorizing of those who were using the premises and the arrest of more than three hundred people.

The overwhelming number of the arrested persons were charged with nothing more serious than being "found-ins" on the premises of a common bawdy house. And their alleged misconduct involved nothing more serious than having sex with consenting adults. In this case, the impugned sex appeared to be of the homosexual variety.

I was appalled. It didn't take long for the press to seek out my comments. I kept asking and re-asking the same questions: Did the police have nothing better to do with their time? Which of our exalted officials came up with the bright idea for using the police in this way? Invariably, the answer we got from the police and even from the governing politicians was that the police were obliged to enforce the law as it is. If we wanted to change that law, we had to go to Ottawa and persuade the federal authorities.

I regarded such comments as an invitation to engage in ridicule. "When is the last time," I kept asking, "that you sent so many police officers to the stadium in which the Toronto Argonauts have their football games?" I would say that I didn't like to tell tales out of school but as a devoted football fan, I knew from firsthand observation that the illegal consumption of alcohol was rampant at those football games. Moreover, I would invite the press to imagine the deployment of two hundred police officers to crack down on jaywalking. Of course, jaywalking was also unlawful. Apparently, however, a decision was made somewhere in the bowels of the police department that those laws did not warrant the kind of enforcement that was employed in the bathhouse raids.

And, I continued to argue, even if the police felt obliged to lay some charges in connection with the bathhouses, why did they have to go about it in the way they did? Why, for example, did they feel it necessary to terrorize so many people who were doing nothing more than having sex with each other? As long as such found-ins were not inflicting their sexual activities on unwilling participants, unwilling observers, or children, their conduct, even if unlawful, could hardly be seen as a threat to the public interest. To whatever extent such a threat could be deemed to exist, it came from those who operated the bathhouses, not from those who used them. Would it not have sufficed, therefore, for the police simply to issue a few summonses to the proprietors?

Such questions and arguments formed the basis for briefs that we presented to various authorities. It all came together in a recommendation that there be a public inquiry into the raid. After an initial press conference in which we joined a number of others, we met with the then provincial Solicitor General, key politicians at the Toronto city council, and the Metro Toronto Police Commission. Thus, I had CCLA register on the issue in a number of forums. I also had occasion to appear and repeat the arguments in many media interviews. One of those media appearances became particularly rancorous. On a panel show hosted by former Ontario coroner Morty Shulman, I became involved in a back-and-forth slanging match. Citing the example of a somewhat contemporaneous police raid on a heterosexual swinging club, Shulman asked whether I had registered on that. I replied that I hadn't heard of that incident. At this point, he adopted an incredulous manner as if to doubt my truthfulness. I rejoined that I didn't pay as much attention as he did to these kinds of stories. And so, we went on fighting.

On one occasion, I had quite a set-to in private with a former mayor of Toronto who was then still on the council: June Rowlands. At the time, she was going out with a friend of mine and so we had had much occasion to see each other socially. And, while a friendly rapport always existed between us, we had sharp differences of opinion on the issue of the bathhouse raids. Neither of us managed to convince the other.

While those in authority provided us with recurring platforms on which we could repeat our message, the most we got in terms of results was an independent review created by the city of Toronto. While such developments were politically advantageous, they lacked subpoena power and some of the other instruments of coercion that the province would have been able to create. Although we weren't able to extract more official action than this, the decades that followed were accompanied by a marked improvement in the relations between the gays and the cops — indeed, it was a period in which gay-straight relations became a lot less contentious.

In the more immediate aftermath of the bathhouse raids, however, there was more trouble. Within a little more than two years, 130 men in the province of Ontario were charged with sexual offences arising from the police use of video cameras in public washrooms. In a number of cities — Orillia, Welland, Kitchener, St. Catharines, and Guelph — periods of such video surveillance were followed by large-scale arrests that attracted major media stories.

So often the mere mention of police video surveillance generates images of the most serious threats to our society: espionage, terrorism, organized crime. But in Ontario at that time, this sophisticated technology was used to crack down on buggery, fellatio, and masturbation. Essentially, the misconduct at issue involved simply having sex with consenting adults in those public washrooms. Once again, there was no question of their having inflicted their sexual preferences on unwilling adults or children. Ultimately, not one of these arrested men went to jail. All of which suggests that even then our society did not consider the impugned misconduct as a serious threat. Yet, in the publicity that followed, reputations were damaged, jobs were lost, and families were ruined. There was even a case of a reported suicide.

From the standpoint of my evolving views about the formation of police policy, I recommended to my colleagues that CCLA arrange to see the Solicitor General of Ontario; he was the minister responsible for the police. In March of 1986, a CCLA delegation called on the minister and registered its discontent with the kind of police policies that had produced the law enforcement actions in question. In the final analysis, however, we urged the minister to promulgate guidelines to the police in order to avert recurrences. Our brief—which we released to the press—was filled with rhetoric and provocative comments. We described these police tactics as "gratuitous voyeurism" and "lavatory overkill." We also asked, "To what extent did innocent excretion occupy police surveillance?" And we asked how the role of voyeur squared with the self-image of the officers who had to perform these assignments.

Acknowledging as we did that the police could legitimately feel a need to enforce the laws in question, we addressed the issue of alternative police tactics. We suggested, for example, that warning notices could be posted in these public washrooms. Such notices would be likely to convey the impression that the premises were under surveillance. That, in itself, would constitute a viable deterrent. We also recommended that those washrooms be periodically patrolled by uniformed officers. That would also constitute quite a deterrent. Our whole approach was based on the premise that the impugned misconduct by the washroom users was more of a nuisance than a threat. As we said, "The object of the exercise is to prevent the acts rather than to torment the actors."

Our brief explicitly called upon the minister to issue a new set of policy guidelines for the police to observe in such situations. Our brief and meeting were well publicized. In June of that year, a directive on the subject was sent to all chiefs of police. It was clearly designed to discourage the police propensity to engage in such excess. We particularly appreciated the fact that the directive began with the following words: "Following a submission from the Canadian Civil Liberties Association to the Ministry of the Solicitor General . . ."

As I became more involved with issues about policing, I began to take stock. In so many situations, the key issue was a policy one. This led to questions concerning how the policies were arrived at. Another factor I found troubling was the number of times that these policy matters were unnoticed. So often, it was only by happenstance that the policy came to light.

Just a few short years before the bathhouse raids, I became troubled by a development around Kenora and Fort Francis Northern Ontario. There was a strike at the Boise Cascade plant. And there were skirmishes on the picket lines. In case after case, the police not only arrested picketers for minor mischief but they also applied for and secured bail conditions requiring the arrested strikers to stay away from the picket lines. As a result, the picket lines became decimated.

Upon delving into the matter a little further, I noticed that I was unable to find any cases where such conditions had been imposed upon *non-strikers* charged with picket-line misconduct. Indeed, in one case a non-striking employee was released without such conditions even though he was accused of pulling a knife on one of the strikers. (Although it couldn't have been known at the time of his release, this man was subsequently convicted of the offence that led to his charge.)

Not surprisingly, the government was unresponsive to the criticism that CCLA made about these findings. But the incident contained a deeper significance. Somewhere, somehow, the law enforcement authorities in that area decided to treat strikers and strike-breakers by different standards. That was a policy issue that could well have gone unnoticed. Together with the arrest of those clerks in handcuffs, the bathhouse raids, and the video surveillance of public washrooms, the Boise Cascade arrests shed additional light on the issue of police policies.

At some point during the time that CCLA was involved in these issues, I participated in a related public panel discussion. One of my fellow panelists was Ontario's Attorney General—and also Solicitor General, Roy McMurtry. For me, such public gigs provided a platform for my message and an opportunity for wise-cracking. In the course of one of our exchanges, McMurtry quoted a passage from a Supreme Court judgment. When he finished, he asked in sarcastic tones, "What does Mr. Justice Borovoy think about that?" I paused conspicuously and then replied, "You know, I like the sound of that. Should I consider this an appointment?"

In mid-1994, another issue of police policy emerged. At a trial involving the black radical leader, Dudley Laws, the public learned that the Toronto police had conducted intelligence investigations of the black leaders in that city. Among the targets of this police surveillance was the late Wilson Head, a well-respected activist and academic. Of course, this disclosure was an unplanned development at a trial that dealt with other matters. Thus, this disclosure became another beneficiary of sheer happenstance.

INDEPENDENT AUDITS

As I reflected on all of these experiences, I became increasingly persuaded that an adequate level of police accountability was going to require the creation of a new mechanism. And so I hit upon the idea of an independent agency mandated exclusively to conduct—and report on—self-generated audits of police policies and practices. This agency would ask largely neglected questions designed to give the public deeper insight into how the police operate. Consider, for example, the following: Who decides and on what basis do they decide what the police do all day? How far, if at all, does the government participate in the policy development? How much does the government become involved in police operations? To what extent is the government entitled to knowledge of police operations? How far, if at all, are the police susceptible to the influence of bias? What indications are there that the police are becoming involved in unacceptable activities?

By the time that we developed the audit idea (from early to mid-90s), the complaints system introduced by Roy McMurtry had taken hold throughout the province. While we readily acknowledged that the Mc-Murtry approach represented a distinct improvement on the way police complaints used to be handled, we argued for even more reform. Granted, the McMurtry approach provided for a level of independent review, but the frontline investigations were still conducted mainly by the police themselves. All the while that the McMurtry system was being implemented, CCLA was pushing for a greater independent involvement in the actual investigations.

One place where we got independent investigations in Ontario was in the Special Investigations Unit (SIU) that was created to deal with certain criminal matters where police officers could be accused. So far, so good. But criminal convictions are especially hard to obtain against police officers. Thus, it remained important to get independent investigations in the disciplinary regime.

While we continued to press for such reforms in the complaints system, we also began to acknowledge that the changes we sought would not be sufficient. There had to be an independent audit system. A complaints system is inevitably dependent upon the willingness of injured parties to take on the police. This kind of courage is a relatively rare commodity. The complaints system also requires that the public have adequate knowledge of what the police are doing. But some police operations, such as the intelligence surveillance, are performed in secret so that the public cannot acquire timely knowledge of them.

To mitigate these disabilities, we argued for a system of independent, self-generated audits of police activities. In our view, the auditors should be equipped with a power of access to police records, personnel, and facilities. In the result, they should make a public report on what they have found. Since we so often found that those with decision-making power over the police were reluctant to exercise it, our plan was to ensure that the sole functions of the audit were to discern, disclose, and perhaps even propose — but not to decide. The incentive for them to do a thorough job would be the risk of embarrassment if they were to fail in the few functions they were called upon to perform. But once those reports were public, there would be additional pressure on the decision makers to do something about them. Thus, there would be a built-in pressure for reform within the system.

From that point until my retirement, we pushed our audit proposal on virtually every occasion where it had arguable relevance. We repeated it many times in our appearances before the Toronto Police Services Board; we made a point of including it in presentations to legislative committees and at meetings with the provincial Solicitor General; we also presented it at public inquiries, such as the ones on Ipperwash and Maher Arar. On at least one occasion, the Toronto board adopted a resolution calling upon the provincial authorities to legislate an audit system. The Arar inquiry made a recommendation that bore a heavy resemblance to our proposal.

But, despite these relentless efforts, we have not yet managed to have such an audit system translated into law. I was not above trying to develop some colourful way of attracting attention to our various presentations.

On one occasion, we had arranged a meeting with the New Democratic Party's Solicitor General, Allan Pilkey. Since his father, Cliff Pilkey, was a member of the CCLA board, I thought that the press might pick up on the spectacle of the father telling the son what to do. So, we arranged for the father to be a member of our delegation. Unfortunately, the event did not attract the contemplated level of publicity.

THE POWERS OF THE CIVILIAN MASTERS

Not long after we got under way with our various audit efforts, I discerned another missing link in the mechanisms for supervising the police. I began to notice how many times our politicians would disclaim any involvement with the day-to-day operations of the police. They kept insisting that they adopted a "hands-off" policy regarding such police activity. At the time of the controversies regarding RCMP wrongdoing, the then prime minister Pierre Trudeau contended that the ministers in charge of the RCMP should not even have a right to know what the Mounties were doing day by day. Indeed, Mr. Trudeau maintained that this posture was a matter of principle. There was, of course, a plausible rationale: the police must not become the instruments for any political party or ideology.

But, as I reflected on Canada's conventional wisdom in this regard, I was struck with a conundrum: How were the civilian masters supposed to exercise accountability for the police if they couldn't issue orders to them or even know what they were doing?

The way Canadian doctrine purported to resolve this dilemma was to distinguish police policies from their operations. On this basis, the civilian masters could direct policies but not operations. But, in order to exercise accountability for policies, it became necessary to have knowledge of operations. If the civilian masters were prevented from knowing about the operations, they could hardly be in a position to ensure police compliance with their policies.

As these questions continued to haunt me, I finally decided to seek advice outside my immediate circles. I telephoned Ian Scott who, by then, was no longer Ontario's Attorney General. When I told him about what was bothering me, he began to inundate me with stories of the frustrations he had encountered as minister, in his attempts to supervise the police. For example, he asked them to tell him what plans they had made to handle a big event that was about to occur in the city of Toronto. Instead of providing him with any details, the police kept assuring him that matters were "well in hand." No matter how hard Mr. Scott attempted to acquire the relevant details, he reported that he had been unable to do so. Thus, it became clear that he shared my disquiet over the conventional wisdom.

I turned next to criminology professor Clifford Shearing whom I had met when he was the research director for the Marin inquiry into the RCMP complaints system. He told me that he too had difficulty with the Canadian system. Since he had already become a supporter of our audit proposal, a consensus immediately arose between us as to how the civilian masters could intrude upon police operations without the relationship becoming vulnerable to partisan control. We both agreed that a good audit system would be able to detect any improprieties in the directions that the ministers would be giving to the police. In that way, there could be ministerial direction and knowledge without partisan contamination.

From there, I consulted with the leadership of CCLA and, not too long afterwards, I was able to secure board endorsement for the idea of giving the ministers and other civilian masters greater effective control over police operations. And, I began to push this idea as well—in articles, in my next book, in speeches, in presentations to inquiries, and in briefs to political authorities. In this area, the status quo has been particularly resistant to the kind of changes I had been advocating. I am hoping that my successors will carry on the campaign.

STRIP-SEARCHING

Somewhere in the mid- to late 1990s, we began to identify police strip-searching as a problem. A number of situations emerged in which the police were strip-searching arrested people in circumstances where there was no apparent need for it. Indeed, there was a widespread belief that some of the strip-searching was designed to intimidate. And, as usual, much of the strip-searching was perceived as little more than bureaucratic reflex.

I remember going to the Toronto Police Services Board more than once to complain that the police appeared to have needlessly strip-searched certain people they had arrested. We became particularly incensed that this would happen to arrested people who were very likely to be released in short order. On these occasions, we proposed certain guidelines that, if adopted, would limit police strip-searching to those situations where it was at least arguably necessary.

Then came the case that was to be known as the "Guelph strip search seven." Toward the end of 1997, a group of about seven women were arrested at a demonstration in Guelph, Ontario. They were part of a protest against an education bill that had been introduced by the Mike Harris government of that province. In the main, these women faced no charges; they were arrested pursuant to the police power for preventing breaches of the peace. They were held for several hours and then released without charge.

But, at some point during their incarceration, they were transferred to a provincial detention centre and there, they were strip-searched. Apparently, it was then the policy of that provincial facility to strip-search everyone it was holding. But the question arose: Why was it necessary for the Guelph authorities to transfer these people? According to the Guelph authorities, they were expecting that their lock-up would soon be too crowded to accommodate additional prisoners. But it was argued that, at the time of the transfer, there were vacant cells in the Guelph lock-up and also a gymnasium in which additional people could be held.

When this case was drawn to our attention, we decided to seek a remedy through the Guelph Police Services Board. The police complaints system that had been introduced by Roy McMurtry was about to go out of existence. The Harris government had effectively dismantled it and replaced it with a system that returned much of the power for handling such complaints to the police themselves. The Harris approach would allow appeals to an external body but the right to go there would arise only after the police had thoroughly processed the complaint.

Since I anticipated biased treatment from the complaints system, I arranged for CCLA to appear before the Guelph Police Services Board where we would request the board to provide for an independent review of the police conduct in question. Of course, I had no reason to believe that the Guelph Police Services Board would be significantly less biased than the Guelph Police Department but, at least in that forum, I could get a public airing of our point of view. Indeed, I believed that I could use the occasion to ventilate our objections to the retrograde measures conceived by the Harris government.

Accordingly, I made a presentation to the Guelph Police Services Board at its February 1998 meeting. Instead of acceding to our request or taking any other action, the board formally requested the Guelph chief of police to investigate the circumstances and provide a report to the board about the way her officers had handled these women. As I said to the press in the wake of the meeting, what was the point of seeking a report from the chief; she had already publicly praised the actions of her officers. And, I further mused, if the board should have a report on the matter, why hadn't one been ordered before this time? Why was there no report until the CCLA presentation?

Since the chief's report was not ready for the board's March meeting, it had to be held over until its April meeting. A couple of weeks before the April meeting, we wrote to the board and requested that it release the report prior to the meeting so that the public could respond to it at that time. The board rejected this request. Accordingly, we asked the board for an opportunity to make a presentation at its May meeting. In that way, we would be able at least to see the report before we responded to it.

Needless to say, the chief once more found that her officers had handled the situation admirably but, in our view, the report did not adequately explain why those prisoners had to be transferred where and when they were. Appearing once more before the board, we asked once more for an independent review of the relevant police behaviour. Not surprisingly, the board finally turned us down.

Having been directly refused (in May, for the first time), we decided that there was no avenue left but the dubious Harris complaints system. This time, we were able to persuade five of the women to sign complaint forms. I also arranged for them to consult a lawyer separately from us. All the while, I realized that the statutory limitation period of six months would soon be coming to an end. Since it was difficult to meet that deadline, I was curious, to see how fairly the internal process would exercise its statutory discretion if we were a few days late.

Big surprise—the Guelph police chief dismissed our complaints for being out of time. Wasn't that remarkable? We had originally appeared before the police services board in February; the board then asked for a report; the report wasn't ready for the March meeting; we asked for an early release of the report so that we cold comment on it at the April meeting but that was refused; at the May meeting, our request was directly rejected and then we filed complaints. Despite all of the delays that had been caused by either the chief or the board, *we* were dismissed for being out of time. Of course, I appealed the dismissal and the appellate body overruled the chief and reinstated the complaint. But, in the meantime, I had been enabled to effectively demonstrate the unfairness of the Harris complaints system.

But there was more. Upon overruling the chief, the appellate body handed the investigation of the complaints over to the Waterloo police. But the difficulty with this was that the Waterloo police had been involved with the Guelph police in the initial policing of the demonstration. In compliance with the statutory system then in effect, the Waterloo police investigated and then handed the matter back to the Guelph police. At that point, the Guelph chief again dismissed the complaints as "unsubstantiated." In our view, the chief was not entitled to make such a ruling at that stage of the complaints process and so we appealed once more to the appellate body. But this time, the appellate body denied our request without reasons. At this point, I summed up the process for the press: "First, the chief investigated her own department and found its behaviour acceptable; then her colleagues in Waterloo investigated and the chief again found in favour of her own department; and now [the appellate body] has dismissed the strip search complaint without providing reasons — not a very impressive track record."

We took the case to court. There, we obtained a unanimous judgment by three judges on the Divisional Court that the chief's interpretation of the statute was "patently unreasonable." The police appealed and, at the end of the day, all three judges on the panel at the Ontario Court of Appeal upheld the judgment of the Divisional Court. Six judges had ruled that the police interpretation of the statute was not only unreasonable but "patently unreasonable." Although we were prepared at this time to return the complaint to the system to deal with it on the merits, we found that the impugned officers had retired.

While there wasn't much left that we could do with the original complaint, the whole sordid story was of considerable assistance when the new Liberal government of Ontario decided to replace the Harris complaints system with a system that more closely resembled what McMurtry had done. Once more, the system would allow for greater external review but once more, it would fail to provide for external investigation as a general practice. And still, there was no provision for an independent audit system.

While the political processes were dealing with the defects of the Harris complaints system, the court process proved to be helpful regarding the substantive law concerning strip searches. In a case called *Golden*, the Supreme Court of Canada prohibited routine police strip searches as an incident of arrest. In this regard, I am proud to report that CCLA intervened in the case where we were ably represented by criminal lawyer Frank Addario. Fortunately, the power of the police to conduct strip searches had undergone a constructive change.

Before I finish my description of our involvement with strip searches, there is one anecdote that bears reporting. One night, while I was working late to prepare for a presentation on strip searches, a problem dawned on me. I decided to seek the advice of CCLA chair, John McCamus. And so, I telephoned him at home and asked the following question: "Is it more intrusive for the police to feel a prisoner's genital area while the prisoner is clothed or simply inspect visually when the prisoner is unclothed?" McCamus paused and then said, "Can you hold the line a moment, I want to turn the lights down." I laughed so hard I never did get the answer to my question.

TASERS

Toward the end of 2007, Canadians were confronted with a most unwelcome image on their television sets. The image featured RCMP officers administering taser shots upon an unarmed man in the Vancouver airport. Not long before the tasering occurred, the man had arrived on a flight from Poland. He was in Canada to visit his mother. Unfortunately, he did not have facility with the English language and so communication became difficult and, at certain points, impossible. In his frustration, he flayed about angrily and the Mounties were called in to subdue him. Despite their numbers and their brawn, the Mounties resorted to the taser. Shortly after they subdued the man, he fell ill and died.

There were shockwaves across the country. Many Canadians were outraged over the behaviour of the RCMP. Suspicions were triggered: How often do the police behave like that? So much of what the police do is invisible to the public. After all, it was the happenstance of a civilian-operated video that brought this incident to public attention.

In some ways, the worst aspect of the incident was the reaction in the upper echelons of the police and government. A case in point was the then commissioner of the Ontario Provincial Police (OPP), Julian Fantino. Commenting on the public outcry over the behaviour of the Mounties, he made the following statement:

> I've never heard the same kind of fired-up response when a police officer is killed in the line of duty. . . . I only wish people would scream as much when officers are killed in the line of duty.[3]

As I said at a protest rally organized by the Canadian Polish Congress:

> I can only wonder what planet Mr. Fantino inhabits. My recollection is that Canadians are invariably upset by such killing of police officers. Admittedly, however, there's a difference between that reaction and the one triggered by the tasering. When police officers are killed, people are upset but not necessarily shocked. They are not shocked, of course, when criminals behave like criminals. But they are shocked when they think that police officers may have behaved like criminals.

Another example of this insensitivity in high places was a statement made by Stockwell Day, the minister then in charge of the RCMP. He was responding to a Canadian Press finding that of more than five hundred cases in which the Mounties had used tasers in a previous four-year period, the victim of the tasering was unarmed in more than 75 percent of the cases. Mr. Day reportedly dismissed the finding as one simply of the odds. According to him, the RCMP stop some three million people each year and the vast majority don't have weapons. But neither, of course, are the vast majority tasered. I would have thought that the most significant factor here was that the vast majority of *those tasered* were not armed. Mr. Day has made some bizarre statements during the course of his career, but this one was worthy of special mention.

The deputy commanding officer of the RCMP in British Columbia was quoted as saying, "We don't see anything yet that causes us to question the validity of the use of the [tasers]." No basis even to question it? In a period of four and a half years from the time this weapon was introduced into Canada, eighteen people died shortly after having been tasered. The obtuseness of the RCMP in British Columbia was nothing short of remarkable.

No less disturbing was the announcement by the Ontario government that it had no plans to review its policies on tasering. Yet, in Toronto, Ontario's largest city, there was a guideline that permitted tasering not only to defuse violent and potentially violent situations, but also "for any other lawful and justifiable purpose." Despite everything that had happened, the Ontario government remained sublimely complacent.

CCLA began to call for a moratorium on the use of tasers "at least in those situations where lethal force would not otherwise be justified or in the absence of imminent peril to life and limb." Some of my comments on the subject appeared subsequently in the *New York Times*. We also used the occasion, of course, to flog our audit proposal. We pointed out that, if such an audit system had existed, it might have been able to act "as an early warning system to identify taser-related problems before a tragedy like this occurred."

THE EXCLUSION OF TAINTED EVIDENCE

Since law school, I have been intrigued by the issue of excluding improperly obtained evidence from the trials of accused people. I confess to having been somewhat impressed by my professor's argument against the American propensity to exclude such evidence. My professor asked, "Why should all of society be punished for the wrongdoing of a single police officer?" After all, the exclusion of such evidence could very well result in the acquittal of a guilty criminal. In my professor's opinion, it would be better in such circumstances to focus on punishing the delinquent officer.

But, as I acquired more experience on the job with CCLA, I began seriously to question the validity of my professor's proposed alternative. Where, in all of Canada, would we find a police department that was prepared to punish an officer whose misconduct helped to nail a criminal the police very much wanted to get? At one of the many debates and conferences in which I participated in the lead up to the adoption of the *Charter*, a Crown attorney echoed this sentiment: Don't exclude the evidence; punish the officer. In my response, I challenged the realism of that proposed alternative. But then, I proposed a compromise: If, by the time the case gets to trial, the delinquent officer has been charged or disciplined in a serious way, that should become a factor in favour of admitting the evidence against the accused person. If that hasn't happened, that should be a factor in favour of excluding such evidence. After I said that, I looked at the audience, smiled, and said, "You see how flexible I can be." No one at that conference took me up on the idea.

Of course, the ultimate provision in the *Charter* is also a compromise of sorts. It says that unconstitutionally obtained evidence is to be excluded if its admission would bring the administration of justice into disrepute. The problem was to determine how that condition was going to apply. I made a number of attempts to insinuate my ideas into the arguments that CCLA counsel made in court. I do note that the Supreme Court of Canada has laid down some helpful guidelines for resolving such disputes. In doing so, the Court explicitly rejected the then prevailing propensity to admit the evidence in those situations where the accused person was charged with a serious crime. As I suggested in an article I wrote at the time, the exclusion of tainted evidence might otherwise have had to be confined to situations where the accused was charged with nothing more serious than failing to get a dog licence.

While on the subject of dogs, I should mention that a CCLA intervention helped to bring about a ruling by the Supreme Court of Canada that dogs could not randomly be used to search for drugs on the premises of high schools. We were less successful in our efforts to persuade the political authorities to narrow the scope of a law enacted at the beginning of the twenty-first century that would allow the police in many situations to resort to law breaking as an investigative tool.

PUNISHMENTS

One situation in which we experienced considerably more success with the political authorities concerned the mid-1980s attempt to bring back the death penalty. Brian Mulroney had promised that, if he became prime minister, he would provide for another parliamentary free vote on capital punishment. (In the 1970s, a free vote resulted in the abolition of capital punishment and its replacement by certain mandatory penalties for culpable homicides.)

We decided to organize a rally against the return of the death penalty. And so, CCLA undertook to become a co-sponsor of a rally along with the John Howard Society of Ontario. The idea was to recruit the kind of speakers whose mere presence on the platform would convey substantial political clout. In the result, we were able to get the sitting Attorney General of Ontario, a former leader of the government party in Ottawa (Robert Stanfield), the primate of the Anglican Church, the moderator of the United Church, a Catholic cardinal, the president of the World Council of Churches, a leading reform Jewish rabbi, the president of the Canadian Labour Congress, the president of the National Action Committee on the Status of Women, journalist June Callwood, author Pierre Berton, criminal lawyer Eddie Greenspan, and, of course, I was there to represent CCLA. As a special platform guest, we had Lesley Parrott, the mother of a murdered young girl. Despite her anguish over what had happened to her daughter, she still felt the need to register against the death penalty.

We packed the Ryerson Theatre in Toronto with more than twelve hundred people, one hundred of whom couldn't be seated in the auditorium and therefore had to watch the proceedings on closed-circuit television in the gymnasium. We also arranged for a band to greet people as they arrived at the auditorium and then to usher speakers onto the platform. It was an exciting and moving evening.[4]

As the master of ceremonies, I attempted to generate excitement. One way I did this was to read to the audience letters of support that we received from the Attorneys General of Quebec and Manitoba. That helped to enhance the clout that was already represented there. Moreover, we arranged for a number of constituencies to travel to the rally by bus. They came from Kingston, Brantford, and St. Catharines. Autoworkers, doctors, religious groups, and John Howard chapters were represented there. One of my messages to the audience went as follows: "The polls measure the breadth of support but a rally tells you the depth of concern."

A little more than three weeks later, the House of Commons voted 148 to 127 against a resolution to approve "in principle" the return of capital punishment. The tide turned and we won.

A number of activities prior to the rally very likely contributed to our victory. Eddie Greenspan, a CCLA board member and criminal lawyer of some renown, appeared in several cross-country debates against an MP who supported the return of the death penalty. On several occasions, Eddie skilfully exposed the hollowness of the arguments against us. CCLA also collaborated with U of T psychology professor Jonathan Freedman in a study of jurors who had sat on first-degree murder cases that resulted in convictions. The study found that, in twenty-nine of thirty-two cases, at least one juror would have been less likely to convict if the death penalty had been available at the time. In fifteen cases, at least two jurors took this position. This survey helped us to demonstrate that the restoration of capital punishment would not only violate human dignity but it could also jeopardize public safety.

At some point around the mid-nineties, governments of Canada made several attempts to appear tough on crime. One of the most facile devices by which they did this was to enact a number of additional mandatory minimum jail sentences for various crimes. Every few years, they added another offence to the list and, in some cases, they even increased the amount of the sentences to be imposed.

Needless to say, we at CCLA were vehemently opposed to this overly simplistic way of dealing with serious crime problems. One case, in particular, helped us to dramatize the injustice of it all. Saskatchewan farmer Robert Latimer was charged with second-degree murder for having ended the life of his severely disabled daughter. Apparently he believed that this was the best way to relieve the pain she had been suffering virtually since her birth. Although the trial judge labelled the act a "compassionate homicide" and the jury also signalled its wish to be lenient, the appellate courts held that the mandatory minimum sentence for second-degree murder must apply. And so, Robert Latimer was ordered to be jailed for life with no chance of parole for ten years. The rigid nature of mandatory minimums brooks no exceptions for extenuating circumstances.

CCLA intervened in the Supreme Court of Canada to no avail. We also got involved in a nationwide petition in which more than sixty thousand Canadians asked the government to commute his sentence. The first time that Mr. Latimer went before the parole board, he was not successful. The board ruled that he showed no remorse. Indeed, he didn't. He always believed that what he had done served his daughter's best interests. On that basis, he found it impossible to show remorse.

Upon being interviewed by CTV following the parole board judgment, I exploded in anger. I said that no one authorized the board to brainwash the prisoners; its job was to assess whether those prisoners posed a risk to public safety. During Mr. Latimer's incarceration, I took a high-powered delegation to see the federal justice minister about the case. The minister was my old friend Irwin Cotler. Needless to say, the meeting was a friendly one. In addition to me, our delegation included former immigration minister Ron Atkey, former Saskatchewan premier Allan Blakeney, and Laval law professor Gisèle Côté-Harper. We pushed hard for an end to mandatory minimum jail sentences. Although Cotler had evinced considerable sympathy with our position, the government apparently felt that it might be too politically costly for them to go along with us.

I also had occasion to represent CCLA on this issue before a parliamentary committee. A number of the more right-wing Tory backbenchers were sitting directly in front of me. And I looked them straight in the eye and related the details of a significant case. A few years prior to the adoption of mandatory minimum jail sentences for a crime that dealt with the discharging of a firearm, the accused person, upon being convicted, was sentenced to twelve months in jail. The court of appeal reduced his sentence to six months and, in the course of doing so, said that both his impressive background and the fact that he was in a situation of high stress contributed to the leniency that it chose to grant.

It turns out that this particular accused person was a police officer and the offence he committed arose during the time he was chasing a fleeing felon. I asked the MPs sitting in front of me which of them was prepared to have this officer jailed for five years because that was the sentence the government was proposing for this crime. I kept returning to this theme again and again during the course of my presentation. Until this day—a number of years later—not a single one of those MPs has come forward in response to my question. So far, mandatory minimum jail sentences have apparently become an entrenched feature of our legal system. I regret that my retirement arose before our side was able to win a significant victory over this inexcusable injustice.

In May of 1980, Francis Pincivero, an Italian immigrant, was ordered deported from Canada to his native Italy for having committed a number of criminal offences here. Deportation is another punishment available for government to invoke as a way of ensuring the peace of the community. Of course, it is usable only against non-citizen immigrants.

Ordinarily, I would have paid no attention to Mr. Pincivero's plight. I thought it was ethically permissible for Canada to provide that immigrants could be deported if they commit crimes of moral turpitude within our borders. What attracted me to his case was the fact that he was thirty-one years old and had lived in this country since he first arrived with his family at the age of three. He reportedly did not know his native land and could not adequately speak its language. Moreover, he was married to a Canadian citizen and that marriage had produced a Canadian child.

Some years earlier, while Mr. Pincivero was a minor, his father reportedly applied for Canadian citizenship. For some unexplained reason, the application was not made on behalf of the man facing deportation. We speculated about the possibility that the family had harboured the mistaken view that all of its members would be covered by the application.

In the circumstances, I thought that deportation was a repugnant remedy for our government to invoke. And I said so in a letter to Lloyd Axworthy, the then minister of immigration. My letter complained that the government's proposed action would "deny this man residence in the only country he has consciously known." An exacerbating factor was the dilemma faced by his wife and child who either had to suffer the breakup of their family or the prospect of living in a country with which they too were completely unfamiliar.

On behalf of CCLA, I called upon the minister to take whatever action was necessary to ensure that Mr. Pincivero be permitted to remain here. In doing so, I pointed out that we did not seek that he be immunized from the other penal consequences of his criminal conduct. Our letter was released to the media where it was accorded significant coverage.

In the result, the minister did what we requested. And that required a few political somersaults. Having secured the cooperation of the US government, the Canadian authorities took Mr. Pincivero across the US border for a few minutes in order to fulfill the technical requirements of the deportation order. Then he was brought back into Canada on a minister's permit. All this was done because the letter of the law required that deportation orders be strictly implemented.

The Pincivero case exerted at least a minor impact on some of my social interactions. One of the members of the immigration appeal tribunal that originally issued the deportation order was a woman who has periodically wound up in some of my social circles. Whenever I have subsequently seen her, I have made a point of delivering a few barbs in her direction. Far from being a shrinking violet, she has shown no hesitation to respond in kind and, periodically, even to initiate some of her own. Despite the passage of some thirty years, I continue to regard that deportation order as an unconscionable impropriety.

On several occasions, CCLA on my watch has taken action against certain substantive provisions of our immigration law. In presentations to the minister and to parliamentary committees, we challenged the breadth of measures that were designed to protect national security. We complained, for example, about the provision that authorized the deportation of permanent residents involved in the "subversion by force of any government." Why, we kept asking, should Canada be so solicitous of *anti*-democratic governments as well as those that are democratic? Violence could well be the only way to purge a country of a tyrannical government. Why in the world should Canadian permanent residents be subject to deportation if they provided such assistance, for example, to an uprising in North Korea?

Still other measures provide for the deportation of persons who are "members" of an organization reasonably believed to be engaged in terrorism. Part of our complaint in this regard is that the statute contains no definition of the word "members." The fact is that many people become involved in organizations for a variety of reasons that have nothing to do with the security interests of our country.

Another section of the Act provides for the deportation of those who, it is reasonably believed, *will* engage in terrorism or other forms of hostility against Canada or its allies. Not infrequently, I have referred to this provision as "deportation by clairvoyance." Even if there is an argument for such wide powers in the case of those who are merely visiting this country, something tighter should be required to deport permanent residents. After all, they have pulled up stakes on the strength of this country's grant of ongoing residence. Despite the logic of our position, the foregoing provisions appear to have survived.

Elsewhere in our immigration law, we have enjoyed greater success. Traditionally, those facing deportation on security grounds could have been prevented from seeing certain evidence against them. Such evidence could be withheld if a judge thought there were reasonable grounds to believe that its disclosure would detrimentally affect Canadian security. Although the judge was required to prepare a summary, for the person's perusal, of the evidence that was to be used in this way, we argued that the system was unfair. Needless to say, a number of other organizations and persons expressed similar objections.

From the beginning, we contended that the law should provide for special security-cleared advocates who would be entitled to see *all* of the relevant evidence to be used but who should be prohibited from disclosing it to those slated for deportation. When I was questioned about this, I readily acknowledged the inadequacy of any system that ultimately deprived the affected persons of the right to see the evidence against them. But I argued, nevertheless, that allowing a security-cleared lawyer to see the material was the best way I could think of for striking a balance between fairness and security. I always felt obliged to acknowledge that our country's national security could well require that some material had to be kept secret.

One day, at a parliamentary committee that was considering these matters, there were two presentations: one from me and one from another organization that was objecting to the process. From the outset, I simply took the position that the matter should be handled by way of security-cleared counsel. But the other witness insisted that the people slated for deportation had to be able to see the material. Ultimately, he had to back down. Under close questioning from some members of the committee, his arguments became exposed as unduly doctrinaire and dogmatic. On this occasion, CCLA moderation became conspicuously the wisest way to proceed.

In addition to such presentations, we also intervened in a court case that was testing the existing provision. The court sided with us and Parliament ultimately changed the law in the direction that we had been advocating.

ENDNOTES

1 Canadian Civil Liberties Education Trust, *Due Process Safeguards and Canadian Criminal Justice* (Toronto: 1971), p. 48.
2 Richard H. Seeburger & R. Stanton Wettick, Jr., "*Miranda* in Pittsburgh: A Statistical Study," 29 U. Pitt. J. Rev. 1 (1967).
3 "Fantino Fires Back at Taser Critics," *St. Catharines Standard* (November 22, 2007). Online: www.stcatharinesstandard.ca/2007/11/22/fantino-fires-back-at-taser-critics.
4 Tom Spears, "Busloads flood into Metro for capital punishment rally," *Toronto Star*, June 4, 1987, A7.

CHAPTER TEN

𝒩𝒶𝓉𝒾𝑜𝓃𝒶𝓁 𝒮𝑒𝒸𝓊𝓇𝒾𝓉𝓎

EMERGENCY POWERS

In October 1970, the political landscape in Canada was sudden-ly — and perhaps irrevocably — transformed. After a decade of sporadic and mostly futile bombings, the Front de Libération du Québec (FLQ) pulled off a political kidnapping. One of its cells seized the British trade commissioner, James Cross, and hid him somewhere in the province of Quebec. In order to relinquish him, the FLQ demanded that the author-ities perform certain political handstands including: the release from jail of all FLQ members who had been involved in those previous terror-ist bombings and the broadcasting over the CBC of the FLQ manifesto.

It appeared that the idea was to humiliate the governments of Can-ada and Quebec. Such humiliation would undermine their authority with the people under their respective jurisdictions. That, in turn, would set the stage for an FLQ takeover of the province of Quebec. The FLQ object was to drive Quebec out of Confederation and establish there a government responsive to the doctrines of Marxism-Leninism

The then prime minister of Canada, Pierre Elliott Trudeau, owed his election, in large part, to the leadership he had provided against the forces of Quebec nationalism. In particular, he was hostile to any sug-gestion of Quebec's separation from the rest of Canada. Not surprisingly, therefore, he refused to implement the demands of the FLQ or even to engage in any negotiations with them.

As the entire country awaited a coherent response from the Quebec government of Robert Bourassa, the FLQ struck again. Within only a few days of the James Cross kidnapping, another cell of the FLQ seized Quebec's labour minister, Pierre Laporte. The brazenness of the FLQ action shocked Canadians from coast to coast; FLQ operatives grabbed Laporte in the middle of a touch football game in which he had been playing with members of his family. At this point, the FLQ appeared to have acquired the upper hand. The noose tightened around the political throat of the Quebec government.

A new group of players soon surfaced. A coalition of Quebec community leaders convened a press conference at Montreal's downtown Holiday Inn. This coalition included Quebec's democratic separatist leader, René Lévesque, Le Devoir publisher, Claude Ryan, and the presidents of Quebec's three leading labour federations: the FTQ, the CNTU, and the Quebec teachers' union. The coalition called upon the government of Quebec to effectively break ranks with the federal government; they urged the Bourassa government to negotiate with the FLQ kidnappers. And, as a further politically protective measure, the coalition called for a government of national unity—which would include coalition members—to replace the Quebec government during the course of this crisis.

The ensuing political tensions could almost be cut with a knife. All over Quebec, people were echoing the message of the coalition: "Negotiate with the FLQ." Large street demonstrations were planned for downtown Montreal. There were widespread fears that the impending demonstrations would be accompanied by severe violence. (Just months before, Montreal had witnessed a number of violent demonstrations in connection with a taxi dispute.) Moreover, many people feared that the FLQ would soon strike again.

Into the midst of this confusion, the federal government dispatched a number of combat units from the Canadian military. Armed soldiers began to patrol the streets of Montreal. On the steps of the House of Commons in Ottawa, a group of reporters encircled Prime Minister Trudeau as he was about to enter the chamber. They began to question him about the presence of armed soldiers in Montreal. His replies were typically testy Trudeau. He warned that law and order were more important than the feelings of some "bleeding hearts." When the reporters asked what he was going to do next, Trudeau replied, "Just watch me."

Indeed, the combination of tensions in Quebec and prime ministerial bravado provided the perfect backdrop for the next major development. In the wee hours of Friday morning, October 16th (about 3 a.m.), the federal government invoked the *War Measures Act*. (This was a stand-by emergency powers law, first enacted during World War I and last invoked during the Second World War.)

The operative regulation adopted under the Act proclaimed the existence of an "apprehended insurrection." With that, a new crime was created: membership in the FLQ. Those found guilty of this crime could be jailed for up to five years. But, even without being found guilty, they could be held on mere suspicion for up to twenty-one days, without bail and without even being charged. Moreover, the police were equipped with additional powers of search, seizure, arrest, and detention. Almost immediately following this invocation, police in the province of Quebec began to round up and detain many people suspected of radical and separatist proclivities. By the time of sunrise on October 16th, some two hundred new prisoners were being held in Quebec jails.

In a special broadcast to the country, Prime Minister Trudeau explained that this action had become necessary because of the terrorist activities of the FLQ. By way of additional explanation, he pointed to what he called the state of confusion in Quebec and the fact that the Quebec government had explicitly requested him to take this action. One consequence of the invocation that became immediately obvious was the virtually instant relaxation of the tensions throughout Quebec.

When the bottom fell out of Canada's political tranquility in this way, I had been general counsel of the Canadian Civil Liberties Association (CCLA) for approximately eighteen months. A year and a half's experience was hardly a sufficient background for me to draw on in order to grapple with the civil liberties implications of this unprecedented crisis. Indeed, I remember muttering something monumentally inconsequential when the press woke me on the morning of the sixteenth to tell me what Trudeau had done. But, as soon as I was able to gather my wits, I telephoned CCLA vice-president, Syd Midanik, and board chair, Eamon Park. The crisis situation demanded a crisis response: the three of us met later that morning in order to figure out what we were going to do.

In situations like this, it helps a lot to have compatible colleagues. In addition to being very capable individuals, both Midanik and Park were civil libertarians of the pragmatic school. Like me, they both shunned doctrinaire absolutes in favour of value balancing, risk weighing, and pragmatic analysis. The three of us resolved that CCLA should express strong misgivings about the government's action. Acknowledging the possibility that some circumstances might arise at some point that could justify what the government did, we were all prepared to take the position that the public record as it then stood was unable to perform this task.

We also decided to seek approval and authorization from the CCLA board at the earliest possible opportunity. On this basis, an immediate notice went out to all board members that a special meeting would be held on Saturday afternoon, October 17th. But we were in a rather peculiar position. Earlier that day, the CBC had telephoned requesting an interview for mid-afternoon. Since we did not wish to risk irrelevance, it was important that we be able to say something reasonably definitive during the course of that interview. Thus, we had to take a stand even before our board could weigh in on the matter.

I believed that between Midanik and Park there was sufficient clout to carry the rest of the board. A former chair of both the Metro and Toronto school boards, Midanik was widely and deeply respected for both his intellectual brilliance and ethical integrity. Similarly, Park, the assistant national director of the United Steelworkers and former CCF (social democratic) member of the Ontario legislature was a tough, no-nonsense labour leader who enjoyed substantial respect. We all knew that we simply had to act first and seek a mandate later.

On Friday afternoon, the CBC set up cameras in the CCLA office and proceeded to interview me regarding the organization's response to the invocation of the *War Measures Act*. While I cannot now recall the interview with clarity, my lingering impression is that it was not one of my sterling efforts. I confess that I was feeling somewhat wobbly about our position. I feared the early discovery of material that might vindicate the government's position. Nevertheless, I took what appeared to be the only tenable position we could take: the facts on the public record did not then warrant the magnitude of the intrusive measures the government had adopted.

Somewhere during the course of that afternoon, I received a telephone call from New York City; it was Arieh Neier, the then director of the American Civil Liberties Union (ACLU). He was calling to express the good wishes of his organization and to inquire whether there was anything they could do for us. While there wasn't very much of practical significance that the ACLU could do in those circumstances, I nevertheless very much appreciated that call of support. When you feel beleaguered, you are grateful for virtually any gesture of friendship that comes your way.

On Saturday afternoon, the next day, the board gathered at the offices of the United Steelworkers union. Many of our stars were present: Dalton Camp, long-serving national president of the Progressive Conservative Party; Julian Porter, civil defamation lawyer and Conservative Party activist; Walter Gordon, cabinet minister in both the Trudeau and Pearson Liberal governments; Barbara Frum, national broadcaster; June Callwood, journalist and author; Leon Weinstein, head of a national grocery chain; Dennis McDermott, subregional director of the United Auto Workers union; Terry Meagher, secretary-treasurer of the Ontario Federation of Labour; and, of course, Syd Midanik, Eamon Park, and yours truly. It is also of some interest to note that Barbara Frum brought along her elementary school-aged son, David Frum, who, in later years, would become a newspaper columnist and a speech writer in the White House of US president George W. Bush.

At the outset of the meeting, a quiet tension engulfed the room. After a period of such spontaneous silence, Dennis McDermott raised his head and asked, "Okay, which one of you bleeding hearts is going to go first?"

At this stage, I cannot recall who, in fact, did go first. It did not take long, however, for everyone to get into the act. As one opinion after another was expressed, it became clear that our board harboured an overwhelming consensus that the opposition I had expressed on television the day before was going to carry the day. But two of our directors dissented: Walter Gordon and Leon Weinstein.

The case of Walter Gordon deserves special mention. Having held senior positions in the last two Liberal governments, Gordon was a person to be reckoned with. Indeed, a few months earlier, we had broached the possibility of his becoming CCLA's next national president. (Our founding president, J. Keiller MacKay, had died around that time.) Many board members believed that Gordon's connections could provide a source of much-needed support for the organization.

Earlier on, however, one of my union colleagues expressed some caution about Gordon's suitability for our presidency. He pointed out that, even though Gordon was an ardent Canadian nationalist, he was not all that progressive on other issues. Indeed, during the months before that fateful board meeting, I had several interactions with Gordon that seemed to corroborate this admonition. On a number of such occasions, Gordon came across as a rather conservative nitpicker. By the time of our board meeting, and in view of his behaviour there, I had become convinced that, despite both his political eminence and personal pleasantness, it would be a mistake to make him our president.

This realization coincided with my deepening antagonism to what the government had done. In consequence, I began to push for increasingly stronger expressions of our opposition to government policy. Of course, it didn't hurt for me to sense Gordon's discomfort. Fortunately, the board accepted my recommendations. Not long afterwards, Walter Gordon submitted his resignation from our board of directors and I heaved a sigh of relief.

Saturday, October 17th was fateful for yet another reason. In the middle of the night, the body of Pierre Laporte was discovered in the trunk of a car located on a Montreal parking lot. He had been strangled to death by one of his FLQ kidnappers. By the time of this discovery, the CCLA position had been well publicized throughout the country.

I was not surprised, therefore, that our office telephones were being rung off the hook by scores of angry people who had called to express their indignation to us. But I was genuinely surprised and rather upset by a 2 a.m. telephone call that my parents received from a member of the public who was angry at me. While I thought of myself as fair game for public disapproval, my parents were not. Indeed, I was surprised that the caller had connected us. Apart from a shared last name (and there were a number of others in the telephone book who also had it), I had no idea how the caller discerned our relationship. For some years, I had not been living with my parents. Fortunately, my folks were good sports and good soldiers and they took it all in stride.

One of the reasons for the depth of the anger that people were feeling was the sheer savagery in what the FLQ had perpetrated. After all, kidnapping and murder are especially cruel. For this reason, virtually all of our material contained condemnations of the FLQ—and even statements of sympathy for their victims. And, while I never expected these statements to win any popularity contests for CCLA, I believed that our material should never ignore the human dimensions of the controversies in which we were involved.

As I write these words, I am reminded of the uneasiness I frequently feel about our various allies in CCLA's campaigns against injustice. In this connection, I have already alluded to the case of Walter Gordon and my uneasiness with conservative colleagues. I have also felt comparable uneasiness with respect to allies at the other end of the spectrum: those of a radical persuasion.

In this connection, I remember so vividly a conversation I had with a radical lawyer from the Law Union during the period of the FLQ crisis. Both of us had publicly registered our opposition to the government's invocation of the *War Measures Act*. But, on that day, I was feeling particularly feisty about some of our left-wing allies. And, after regurgitating my opposition to the federal government, I also expressed some heartfelt contempt for the FLQ. At that point, my "further left" colleague responded true to form. He referred to the behaviour of the FLQ as "bad tactics."

This response set me off. "Bad tactics?" I rejoined. "Repeat after me," I insisted, "it was a fucking outrage." "Try it," I said, "see if you can get your tongue around it." Why is it that certain left-leaning folks are unable to generate anywhere near the enthusiasm for condemning injustices on the left as they do when their targets are on the right?

All the while, however, my disdain for those emergency powers continued to grow. In addition to the two hundred or so Quebecois who were being held without bail or even charge, police abuses were being perpetrated all over the country. In Vancouver, hippies were being threatened; in Ottawa, there was a house raid by police against a member of the peace movement; the printing plates of the Guelph student newspaper were seized; and in Toronto, a Maoist organization suffered the confiscation of a thousand copies of its literature. Apart from the Guelph situation, not one of these incidents was remotely related to the

FLQ crisis in Quebec. And, in the case of Guelph, the printing plates were taken because they contained the FLQ manifesto.

As I appeared in one debate after another, and made one speech after another, I kept invoking all of these non–FLQ-related abuses. And I found myself resorting increasingly to wisecracks and ridicule. When I would mention the abuse in Guelph, I inevitably added, "The prospects of an insurrection in Guelph boggle the mind." (In this regard, I was chastened to learn sometime thereafter that the founding meeting of Canada's Communist Party took place in a barn outside Guelph.)

I was particularly derisive on the prohibition against membership in the FLQ. The relevant enactment provided that an inference of such membership could be drawn from a person's participation in meetings of the FLQ or in activities in which FLQ members also participated. Thus, I declared that a person could be in deep trouble if he had ever unknowingly gone bowling with members of the FLQ.

Of course, the enactment also provided that persons accused of such membership could always furnish evidence on their own behalf. But where, I asked, could people obtain corroborating evidence of *non*-membership? None of us has ever had another person shadowing us for our entire lives. On this basis, I argued that the FLQ crisis had become the first time in history that it was advantageous to be a Siamese twin.

In addition to arguing that, as it then stood, the public record could not justify the creation of such sweeping powers, I also contended that, without the emergency powers, the existing law was a very potent instrument against terror. Substantively, it was unlawful to perpetrate, attempt, aid, abet, and even counsel an act of terrorism. And it was also unlawful to conspire to commit such a misdeed.

Procedurally, the police could arrest, even without warrant, anyone they reasonably believed was about to commit an indictable offence. The *Criminal Code* continued to provide that anyone, not just a police officer, could use as much force as was reasonably necessary to prevent a serious breach of the peace. Moreover, the common law had always provided a "defence of necessity" for anyone who committed an illegality in order to avert a greater illegality that could reasonably be seen as imminent. It would take a lot, I argued, to demonstrate why these considerable powers were inadequate to address whatever dangers confronted the Canadian people and their institutions.

The autumn of 1970 was hectic and tense—debates, speaking engagements, media appearances, and innumerable meetings to create alliances and coalitions. At one point, we tried to work out something with Quebec's civil liberties organization, the Ligue des droits de l'homme. But it turned out that the Ligue was a good deal more conservative than we were. We kept on challenging the propriety of government policy; the Ligue focused on ensuring that the prisoners had access to toothbrushes.

Despite organizational differences, however, we invited the president of the Ligue, Jacques Hébert, to join the CCLA board of directors. He, of course, was a long-time personal friend of Pierre Trudeau's. But he was also an intelligent and fine man in his own right. Fortunately, Hébert agreed to join us and this helped us to forge an important alliance with elements in the province of Quebec.

During that same fall season, I was a visiting professor (once a month) at the Dalhousie Law School in Halifax. Another visiting professor at the same time was the eminent Quebec intellectual and poet, Frank Scott. Despite his lifelong credentials as a champion of civil liberties, he supported Trudeau's invocation of the *War Measures Act*. One late afternoon, I had the honour to sit beside Frank on a plane from Halifax to Montreal. During that entire flight, he and I argued about the emergency powers that Trudeau had invoked. Later that evening, Frank Scott and I joined Syd Midanik, Eamon Park, and a number of Quebec civil libertarians to discuss the emergency powers crisis. It was out of that meeting that we extended—and Hébert accepted—our invitation for him to come on our board.

During that same autumn season, my friend Irwin Cotler, then a law professor at McGill and special executive assistant to federal justice minister John Turner, invited me to attend an off-the-record session on emergency powers, with Turner and a number of others at a resort hotel in Montebello, Quebec. Other people who attended those sessions included Jerry Grafstein (later to become a senator), Marty Friedland (then a U of T law professor and later to become dean of the law faculty), Harry Arthurs (then an Osgoode Hall law professor and later to become president of York University), Fred Kaufman (then a justice of the Quebec Court of Appeal), Gerard La Forest (then a law professor at the University of Alberta and later to become a justice of the Supreme

Court of Canada), and Irwin's special friend, the brilliant Harvard law professor, Alan Dershowitz.

For a couple of days, we had the most fascinating discussions about when, if at all, emergency powers could trump civil liberties. It was an impressive group and, by the time the sessions were over, I went home thoroughly stimulated.

Another set of meetings worth recalling during that period began with an invitation for me to speak on a panel at a meeting of a small group of scholars at the John F. Kennedy School of Government at Harvard University. My fellow panelist was the then ACLU director Arieh Neier. The topic, of course, was emergency powers and civil liberties. Having just come from Canada where there was overwhelming support for the powers that the government had created, I was overcome by the skepticism of this group of scholars. At one point, I leaned back and found myself saying, "My, you guys have a healthy disrespect for your government."

I remember being impressed with Arieh Neier's contribution to the discussion. When asked whether the United States would be likely to respond to a terrorist crisis the way Canada had done, he replied in the negative. According to Neier, the United States would not create new powers; it was far more likely to abuse the old powers. A memorable person I met at that meeting was Roger Baldwin, the founder of the ACLU. We met again at the next meeting that was slated for a few days after the one at Harvard. I was invited to address a national board of directors meeting of the ACLU in New York City.

I cannot now remember how well I thought I had spoken at that meeting but, in the wake of my presentation, there was a motion on the floor for the ACLU to give CCLA a sum of money for coping with the crisis. As it appeared that a consensus was developing in favour of approving the motion, Roger Baldwin spoke up and warned his fellow directors that such a contribution might risk a lawsuit at the behest of any ACLU members who thought this represented a departure from the purpose of their dues money. His argument carried the day and the ACLU never made that donation. When I arrived home, however, I was greeted by a generous personal cheque from Roger Baldwin to the CCLA.

In early December 1970, James Cross was discovered in a Montreal apartment building. In order to secure his safe release, the government agreed to allow his kidnappers safe passage to Cuba. The kidnappers of

Laporte were also apprehended around this time. Within the next few months, the situation began to simmer down. The army was withdrawn from Quebec and the Quebec justice minister lifted his veto over bail.

On March 29 1971, a delegation from the CCLA met with federal justice minister John Turner. Again, the subject was "emergency powers." Our delegation consisted of our then president Syd Midanik, vice-presidents Eamon Park and Dalton Camp, Fernand Daoust, a Quebec board member and then secretary-treasurer of the Quebec Federation of Labour, and Charles Huband, the chair of our Manitoba affiliate (later to become a member of the Manitoba Court of Appeal), as well as myself.[1]

Noting how normalcy had been restored, the CCLA delegation called for the immediate termination of the emergency powers then in force and the withdrawal of all charges that were the progeny of those powers. I took particular pleasure in attacking an earlier statement of Trudeau's. He had said that, in order to revoke the emergency powers, he would need the "absolute assurance" of all police that there was "absolutely no more danger." "It is impossible to demonstrate that danger is impossible," I replied, "let alone *absolutely* impossible."

But the main focus of our presentation was to prevent any new peacetime emergency powers legislation. For months, Prime Minister Trudeau had been lamenting the fact that there was nothing to choose "between the *War Measures Act* and the *Criminal Code*." He contended that he had invoked the *War Measures Act* because there was nothing less in between. Accordingly, he had been promising such new legislation for months.

In the opinion of the CCLA, however, a new law of this kind would create an unwarranted threat to civil liberties. Since it would contain powers of a lesser magnitude than were in the *War Measures Act*, it could more readily be invoked. As a result, it would become likely that emergency powers would be in force more often and for longer periods of time. And, since the *Criminal Code* itself was so potent, there was simply no demonstrable need for a "mini-*War Measures Act*."

If anything, our delegation argued, the *War Measures Act* should be amended. In the words of our brief, "no conceivable emergency, including bloody war, requires so many powers and so few safeguards."

At the conclusion of our meeting, Mr. Turner stepped out into the hall where he was surrounded by reporters. (They had already been given copies of our brief.) We were delighted with Turner's response to the reporters' questions. For the first time, we heard a representative of the Trudeau government declare that the contemplated peace-time emergency legislation was not necessarily on the agenda.

This comment triggered in me the speculation that there was some division within the government about the desirability of such legislation and that Turner was using the meeting with us as a platform for expressing his personal opposition to the idea. Of course, I have never been able to verify whether my suspicions were valid but I am heartened by the fact that, until this day, no such legislation has been enacted and, some years later, the *War Measures Act* itself was replaced by something less draconian.

In the autumn of 1971—about a year after the FLQ crisis had begun—I had lunch with Jacques Hébert in a Montreal restaurant. By then, of course, the last year's emergency powers had been allowed to expire and normalcy appeared to have been restored. I was interested, therefore, in learning what I could about the reasons why the government had behaved as it did.

First, I tried a theory of mine on Hébert. I suspected that Trudeau had resorted to the *War Measures Act* because, after that Holiday Inn press conference convened by those Quebec leaders, he was afraid for the stability of the Bourassa government. He feared that, between the coalition and the Bourassa cabinet, there might have been a consensus to establish an "extra parliamentary" government that was more willing than Trudeau was to negotiate with the FLQ kidnappers. I should point out that, although I was sympathetic with Trudeau's wish to avoid such an outcome, I remained nevertheless opposed to his suspension of civil liberties. I believed that tough leadership could prevail without such extreme measures.

In any event, Jacques Hébert appeared to believe that the causes of the crisis were more straightforward. He left me with the distinct impression that the government had been moved by a substantial fear that more devastating FLQ violence was in the offing. The invocation of the *War Measures Act* was seen, therefore, as a way to cool out the tensions and restore everyone's confidence (including that of the government) in the viability of law and order.

Following the expiry of the emergency powers that had been created for the crisis, the *War Measures Act* effectively disappeared from the country's agenda. It made a short reappearance at a 1979 hearing of the Mcdonald Commission on RCMP wrongdoing. After that hearing, it went into hibernation for several additional years.

One spring morning in 1987, I received a long distance telephone call from Perrin Beatty, the new minister of national defence in the Conservative government of Brian Mulroney. Mr. Beatty informed me that he was calling as a courtesy to let me know that, on the very next day, he planned to introduce a bill that was designed to replace the *War Measures Act*. At the time, I was hard at work on my first book, *When Freedoms Collide*. Accordingly, my first response to Mr. Beatty's news was a wisecrack: "You can't do this; I have already written my chapter on the *War Measures Act*." I then explained to Mr. Beatty that my definition of a "premature social reform" is one that I haven't yet asked for.

Notwithstanding the considerable inconvenience that Mr. Beatty's proposed reform would cause me (I wound up dumping my chapter on this issue), I welcomed the news that Canada was to acquire, not an additional emergency powers statute but a substantially narrowed replacement for the existing one. But the bill itself which we were to see the next day turned out to be a significant disappointment. Like its predecessor, it contained vague, overbroad powers, tautological definitions, and inadequate safeguards. I produced a draft brief and circulated it to the CCLA board. By the autumn of 1987, we had a brief ready to go.

We met with minister Perrin Beatty and a group of his mandarins in Ottawa on October 5th. Our delegation, CCLA's then board chair Ken Swan and I, tore into the bill. High among the targets of our criticism was the failure of the bill to include a definition for the word "emergency." A "public welfare emergency," for example, was defined as an emergency whose causes included fire, flood, drought, and storm. As we argued, this tells us about possible causes of an emergency but it fails to tell us exactly what an emergency is. Nor was the problem adequately resolved by the bill's subsequent requirement that there be "danger to life or property, or social disruption, so serious as to be a national emergency." We told the minister that this was simply "an escalation of tautologies."

The bill also threatened to perpetuate one of the key defects of the *War Measures Act*. It provided that an emergency may be declared when it is considered to exist *in the opinion* of the federal government. As we contended, this might mean that an emergency could be deemed to exist whenever the government says it does.

Ken Swan and I were encouraged by the fact that, on a number of occasions during our meeting, the minister turned to his civil servants and asked for their replies to our criticisms. In our view, every one of their replies was conspicuously inadequate. When the minister was confronted by reporters at the end of our meeting, he said that he had been impressed with many of the points we had made and he undertook then to give our brief serious consideration.

On March 1 1988, I was joined by my staff colleague David Schneiderman for our presentation to the parliamentary committee that was dealing with this bill. Earlier, the minister had told the committee that he was "particularly grateful for the thoughtful and constructive consideration of this bill given by the Canadian Civil Liberties Association . . . it is certainly apparent from the second reading debate that it [CCLA's brief] had considerable impact."

Despite the minister's kind words, we unleashed a further barrage of criticism at the committee hearings. Following our presentation, the minister asked us and representatives of the Canadian Bar Association to meet in private with some of his top mandarins in an attempt to thrash out our various differences.

At that meeting, we held our ground once more and pushed hard for further reform. At this point, it's fair to say that the bill as finally enacted resembled our comments more closely than what was originally introduced. Consider a few examples. We had argued that the operative definitions were so broad that a public order emergency could be triggered by a conspiracy of multinational companies to raise the prices of certain vital commodities. A further amendment provided, however, that an emergency must endanger "the lives, health or safety of Canadians or seriously threaten the ability of the government to preserve the sovereignty, security and territorial integrity of Canada."

Originally, we had argued that an emergency might be deemed to exist whenever the government says it does. According to the amendments, an emergency may only be declared when the government "believes on reasonable grounds" that such an emergency exists. This provision paves the way for the courts to review the triggering circumstances. We also had argued that under the original bill's definition of a public welfare emergency, the causes could include the economic disruption caused by strikes in the post office, railways, or even in the auto industry. The amended bill flatly provided that such a labour dispute could not trigger an invocation of emergency powers.

With the proclamation of the new Act, I had no illusions that the millennium had arrived. I could well imagine, for example, that the courts would be reluctant to overrule the government in the event that circumstances were sufficiently tense. Yet we know that, on a number of occasions, the courts have indeed intruded where alleged national security interests were involved. Consider, for example, how in 2008 the courts upset the process for security certificates. Moreover, the prospect of possible judicial interference could well serve to deter overzealous politicians from unwarranted employment of emergency powers.

As with everything else we do, the test for me is not whether our efforts have made the world ideal or even good but whether it has been made significantly less bad, at least in certain areas. I believe that I can safely claim that much for what my colleagues and I accomplished on the issue of emergency powers.

RCMP WRONGDOING

On many occasions, I have mused about how my position as CCLA general counsel has required me to confront issues that my friends and I used to hypothesize about, as students. One of these issues involved the response of a democratic society to widespread police law-breaking that is designed to serve the interests of law enforcement or national security. Of course, the problem is relatively minor when it concerns only the self-seeking, sporadic acts of individual officers or small groups of them on frolics of their own. It becomes a different ballgame, however, when the transgressions are large-scale, recurring, systemic, and aimed at serving the public interest. After all, the police are supposed to enforce the law. But the rub here is that we would be asking them to enforce the law in the very teeth of their institutional cultures.

Canadian society was forced to address this conundrum in the late 1970s. As a result of a number of mishaps and coincidences, there tumbled out of Ottawa a host of allegations, revelations, and outright admissions that, for some thirty years, officers of the Royal Canadian Mounted Police (RCMP) had been committing a variety of criminal offences, including burglary, theft, arson, mail opening, the invasion of confidential records, and even false imprisonments and assaults. To make matters worse, it was acknowledged early that a great many of these misdeeds had served the interests of national security or law enforcement and that they had actually become matters of official RCMP policy. From all of this, it became clear that, with the blessings and even the instructions of upper management, members of the RCMP had committed *hundreds* of offences.

How do Canadian governments typically respond when they are confronted with a policy nightmare? Almost invariably, they create a royal commission. This situation was no different. On July 6 1977, a three-person royal commission on RCMP wrongdoing was created with Alberta Superior Court Judge David C. McDonald at the helm.

While we at the CCLA had no objection to the existence of such a commission at that time, we were haunted by an overriding concern: would all this evidence of wrongdoing be "on hold" until after the commission reported? In view of the magnitude of what was involved, we realized then that it might literally be years before there was anything resembling normal law enforcement with respect to all of this Mountie misconduct. In our view, that was simply an unacceptable outcome. Instead of facilitating police accountability, the advent of this royal commission was helping to avoid it.

CCLA resolved, therefore, to push for the immediate adoption of normal law enforcement processes. To whatever extent there was evidence of criminal behaviour that lay within the jurisdictions of the various provinces to enforce, the federal government should quickly turn over the relevant material to them. And, in those areas that are subject to federal enforcement (such as mail opening and the invasion of tax records), the feds should provide at once for normal investigation and prosecution.

On this basis, the existence of the royal commission could be advantageous: it could provide an independent body to monitor and evaluate the way the normal processes were operating. Moreover, at the end of it all, the royal commission could make recommendations regarding the nature and scope of the powers that would thereafter protect Canada's national security.

Not only did the federal government refuse then to invoke the normal processes of law enforcement against all that Mountie wrongdoing, but it also made some highly dubious statements about the police obligation to obey the law. No less an official of our government than the incumbent prime minister — Pierre Elliott Trudeau — made the following statements at one of his press conferences:

> What I am saying is that I am not prepared to condemn . . . the people at the time who might have done an illegal act in order to save a city from being blown up. . . . Policemen break the law, sometimes, I suppose, when they drive 80 mph in order to catch the guy who is escaping from a bank.[2]

It is significant that the prime minister said these things in the wake of a disclosure that the Mounties had broken into private premises to obtain copies of the Parti Québécois membership lists.

In a letter to the prime minister that was sent as long ago as November 16th 1977, the CCLA took issue with these statements and called upon Trudeau to explicitly correct them on the public record. That letter co-signed by our then honorary president Emmett Hall, a retired justice of the Supreme Court of Canada, past-presidents Syd Midanik and John Nelligan, our then president Walter Tarnopolsky, the chair of the board Doug Trowell, and myself, was also published as a full-page ad in the *Globe and Mail*.[3]

Trudeau's reply of December 9th 1977 expressed his disappointment that "an association of the stature of yours should have chosen to abandon thoughtfulness for polemics in its haste to enter the fray." He alleged that we had quoted "selectively" from the statements that he made at that press conference. He pointed out, for example, that, at the same press conference when he was asked whether he would condone illegal activities, he said:

> Of course not. You know I have always told the police that they have to observe the law and this is what my earlier statements made clear. They must observe the law and if . . . they break the law and we discover it, they will have to pay for it.

Our rejoinder letter of January 11th 1978 contended that the prime minister was trying to have it "both ways." If it had been his intention to convey to the press and the public his opposition to such police law-breaking, we said that it was inappropriate to theorize so irrelevantly on the periodic permissibility of what he had called "technical" breaches. Our letter then went on to argue as follows:

> Far from quoting you out of context, part of our complaint was that *in context* those statements were likely to be injurious [italics in original]. The press conference at issue here was the one which followed the revelation of the break-in against the Parti Québécois. In that setting particularly, it was improper to defend the idea of illegal break-ins. To invoke the inapplicable threat of atomic explosions and the invalid analogy of escaping bank robbers is to make it appear that you do not completely disapprove of the misconduct involved.

During the course of the same exchange, the prime minister also rejected our recommendation that, in response to all that RCMP wrongdoing, he immediately facilitate the invocation of normal law enforcement processes. Pointing out that "the mandate of Mr. Justice McDonald extends to just such investigations," Trudeau argued that, "duplication several times over of any enquiry . . . does [not] appeal to me as wise."[4]

Although the prime minister refused to budge on any of our recommendations, I had occasion to feel vindicated a few years later. At a banquet in Vancouver held in conjunction with a conference I attended, I wound up seated next to Robin Bourne, who had formerly been an upper-echelon official in the Trudeau hierarchy. A rather urbane and witty man, he told me that he had been part of a committee charged with the responsibility of drafting Trudeau's reply to our letter. Mr. Bourne revealed to me that Trudeau had told him and his colleagues that our letter was better than the one they had drafted for him. This was one time when I agreed with the Right Honourable Pierre Elliott.

Despite this rejection at the prime ministerial level, my colleagues and I didn't give up. In one forum after another (including several appearances at the McDonald Commission and before parliamentary committees), we kept pressing for recommendations that the federal government invoke normal law enforcement processes at that time. We also kept attacking—and ridiculing—Trudeau's statements about the possibility of permissible law-breaking.

The prime minister's remarks did not exhaust governmental ration- alizations for this police law-breaking. Some officials went so far as to argue that, when the RCMP committed surreptitious entry for law en- forcement or security purposes, they did not break the law at all. Former federal Solicitor General Jean-Pierre Goyer, for example, contended, "If the law authorized something, then the law authorized the procedures by which this was done." On this basis, Goyer insisted that surrepti- tious entry in order to plant electronic bugs was permissible.

Even if such an argument had some plausibility for post-1974 bug- ging, we insisted that it could not apply to any such entries before 1974. In 1974, Parliament officially authorized electronic surveillance. Prior to 1974, however, nothing in the law had expressly authorized electron- ic bugging. The law then simply failed to expressly prohibit the practice. On the strength of Goyer's reasoning, we argued, therefore, that, "The failure of the law to prohibit us expressly from serenading our neigh- bours could be read as authority to enter their property in the event that their walls obstructed the sound of our voices."

In the case of what became known as Operation Ham, the RCMP security service had surreptitiously entered a building housing tapes that contained the membership list of the Parti Québécois. The tapes were physically removed from the premises so that they could be cop- ied for further investigation. John Starnes, the then civilian director of the security service, said that, since the documents were to be copied, they were not "stolen" and thus there was no intention to commit an indictable offence. (One of the offences at issue was breaking and en- tering with the intent to commit an indictable offence.) Starnes also discounted the need for a warrant on the basis that this operation did not involve a search and seizure.

But the removal of the membership list, without permission, de- prives the lawful owner of its enjoyment, use, and possession during the time in question. As CCLA said to the McDonald Commission on this subject, "If that does not constitute a 'theft,' the word has lost its meaning." Moreover, to the extent that the officers who entered the premises had to look for the tapes, they must have been involved in a "search." And, to the extent that they removed the tapes, there must have been a "seizure." According to the CCLA brief, "To deny that such consequences were implicit in Operation Ham is to denude our language of its most common usage."

In some cases, RCMP officials frankly admitted the illegality of some of their activities. Assistant commissioner M.S. Sexsmith, for example, acknowledged that he did not need legal advice on the question of mail opening; he knew it was unlawful. Former commissioner W.L. Higgitt testified that steps were taken to centralize the control of mail opening because he and his colleagues did not anticipate early legislation to legalize it.

Indeed, such policies had developed to the point of anticipating how to protect those RCMP members who got caught and how to deal with those Mounties who refused to comply. As for the latter, Higgitt declared that non-cooperating members would not be disciplined but they could be transferred. This reminded me of Churchill's "distinction without a difference." Remarkably, Higgitt maintained that non-cooperating members were analogous to those who could not pilot airplanes because they cannot stand motion. Thus, such a refusal to break the law was viewed as a *congenital* disability.[5]

One of the most controversial misdeeds committed by the RCMP at the time in question involved the burning down of a barn in the province of Quebec. Incredibly, it emerged that the RCMP did this because certain FLQ activists then under surveillance were planning to hold a meeting in that barn. Apparently, however, the Mounties' bugging equipment could not adequately work in that setting. Thus, the officers had hoped that, by burning down the barn, they could induce their targets to convene their meeting in a place more hospitable to electronic bugs.[6]

An RCMP sergeant named McCleery claimed that the barn burning was not criminal because no one stood to gain from it and it prevented an even greater harm. According to McCleery, "If it was a question of a barn vs. a life, there was no question to me—it was the barn."[7]

"Faced with practical examples of actual law-breaking," we said to the McDonald Commission, so many RCMP apologists took "refuge in hypothetical justifications." Acknowledging that such arguments "appeal to our pragmatic natures," we rhetorically asked, "Who but the doctrinaire would not choose the destruction of a barn rather than a person?" And, referring again to Trudeau's comments, we said, "Who but a blind dogmatist would not prefer to have a law broken than a city blown up?" We pointed out, however, that these apologists invariably failed to "include a description of precisely *how* the impugned miscon- duct averted precisely *what* overriding peril [italics in original]. Instead of specifics, there are generalities; instead of clarity, there is confusion."

Another argument we put to the McDonald Commission cited the fact that the law in this country is not nearly as rigid or unresponsive to crisis as the foregoing rationalizations would tend to imply. If there really had been reasonable grounds to believe that a building contained a bomb set to explode, the police would not likely be fettered by the need to seek a warrant. In circumstances of such imminent peril, our law would seem to empower anyone, not just a police officer, to enter the premises and defuse the bomb. Moreover, accused persons in such circumstances might well have recourse to the common law defence of necessity.[8]

But what has prevented these possibilities from creating an open-ended and dangerous police discretion is the law's requirement that there be a situation of urgent and imminent peril. As we said at the time, "It is simply not believable . . . that such considerations are even arguably applicable to the bulk of the law-breaking with which this commission has been concerned."

A frequent source of confusion at the time concerned the law-break- ing that is committed to protect the cover of an infiltrator or an inform- er. A willingness to break the law could well have been seen as needed to win the confidence of those being spied upon. Apparently, Messrs. Higgitt and Starnes attempted, without success, to obtain guidance on this matter from the government. We admitted that this was a difficult issue but insisted nevertheless that it not "become entwined with all of the other incidents of law-breaking." We concluded this point with the following observation:

> The surreptitious entries, the theft of the PQ membership list, the barn burning, the mail opening, and the assaults committed on potential sources had nothing to do with protecting the cover of infiltrators and informers. Those acts were committed by police officers as police offi- cers, not by anyone who was pretending to be anything else.[9]

All of this polemicizing led, once again, to a proposal from us that the McDonald Commission recommend the immediate prosecution and disciplining of those RCMP officials who broke the law. Even at that, we were careful to point out that the adoption of such a response need not include every single one of the wrongdoers. The goal should be equality with the civilian sector. Where civilians are concerned, there is such a thing as prosecutorial discretion. Where leniency is observed with civilians, so too should it be observed with police officers. We pointed out that we were not seeking wholesale prosecution, but we did seek to avoid wholesale immunization.

During the four years from the inception to the conclusion of the McDonald Commission, we sang this tune on several occasions—don't wait for the commission to report; enforce the law against RCMP wrongdoers now. We repeated the message to the McDonald Commission itself on a number of the many occasions we appeared there. We had said it to Trudeau in that famous exchange of letters with him. It was also part of our presentation to the parliamentary committee that was vetting the government bill on mail opening. And, of course, I reiterated the message time and again in dozens of media appearances.

Not all of those efforts produced a serious interaction. Consider, for example, the parliamentary committee on the mail-opening bill. Montreal committee member Rod Blaker interjected at the outset a number of questions and comments suggesting that professor Irwin Cotler and I on behalf of CCLA may not have had a proper mandate from the organization. He asked whether our then forty-five hundred members had seen and approved our brief and the same with respect to our fifty-member board of directors.

I explained that there is no ongoing consultation with the membership or even the board of directors regarding the *details* of our briefs. (In addition to periodically telephoning and writing the office, the members could register at annual meetings and through the elections of the board.) On a more regular basis, memoranda are exchanged among the board of directors by mail, telephone, and meetings; this usually results in a consensus over the policies we will adopt. Then, a smaller committee is created that will express those policies in a written brief. Apparently bereft of arguments, Blaker repeated his questions again and again—and I, of course, repeated my answers again and again. After this went on for a considerable period of time, an opposition member pressed the chair for a ruling so that there could actually be a hearing on the merits of our proposals.

Not content with the foregoing digression, Mr. Blaker went on to digress some more:

I have not heard anybody question the credibility of Mr. Justice McDonald, with one exception, you, representing the Canadian Civil Liberties Association. To the best of my knowledge, I can recall no occasion in the House when opposition spokesmen have questioned the credibility of Mr. Justice McDonald, and I query the taste . . . of people representing civil liberties that they should in a brief to a Committee of the House of Commons, the Justice Committee, raise the matter of credibility in a judge.[10]

Both Cotler and I denied that anything in our brief even addressed the credibility of the judge. Indeed, we challenged Mr. Blaker to find anything that did so. Then, I made the following comment:

A comment on losing potential faith in the administration of justice, is not to be equated with an attack on the credibility of a particular commission. Our concern is that if these cases are allowed by the government to be within the exclusive purview of the McDonald Commission, the public is likely to lose respect and . . . faith in the administration of justice. That hardly suggests the kind of statement you are imputing to us with respect to Mr. Justice McDonald.[11]

During this time, Blaker had been scouring our brief. As though he had experienced an epiphany, Blaker exultantly raised our brief and exclaimed, "Here is the quote: . . . 'There is a very real danger that these delays will undermine the public confidence in the administration of justice.' " To which, of course, I replied, "That is precisely what I just said."

Blaker was still not satisfied. He declared, "I took it to imply that you are referring, not to the government administration of justice, but rather to the administration of justice, namely, the judge." And I replied once more, "Even at the most contorted reading, it could not be construed that way. And I do not even want to impute that to you."

As the rancorous exchange continued, I finally said to him, "Mr. Blaker, you are really no better now than you were in our last debate."

That last debate referred to a public meeting, a few months earlier, at the University of Ottawa law school in which we both participated. At that session, I repeated the CCLA argument that the government was duty bound to invoke the normal processes of law enforcement in response to the wrongdoings of the RCMP. Taking a deep breath and mustering all of the sanctimony at his command, Blaker admonished me about the impropriety of a civil libertarian assuming guilt without a proper trial. I leaned over the table between us, took the microphone, and simply said, "So let's see some trials." The audience laughed.

The audience realized, as apparently Blaker did not, that trials were all we were ever looking for; that is, "the normal processes of law enforcement." There was never any question of our assuming the guilt of any identifiable persons. We knew—as did the rest of Canada, with the possible exception of Blaker—that *some* of those Mounties were, indeed, guilty. The Force, itself, had already admitted as much. Too bad for Blaker that the facts undermined the impact of his theatrics.

It's not for me to analyze motives, but I suspected that, when CCLA appeared before the parliamentary committee, Blaker may still have been smarting over that put-down. It may also be of some interest to know that my colleague, Irwin Cotler, did try to restrain me during the course of the parliamentary hearing. At one point, he whispered in my ear, "Don't sink to his level." I responded to this effort with the words, "I *want* to sink to his level." Since I realized that Blaker's interventions had effectively derailed us from addressing the merits of our brief, I thought that I might as well indulge in a good fight. Besides, that encounter with Rod Blaker played to my "street kid" proclivities.

At one point, I hit on the idea of circulating a petition on RCMP wrongdoing. Of course, petitions are anything but new. But we gave this one a novel twist: each signatory had to contribute at least one dollar. While the politicians and public might believe that many people would easily give away their signatures, there would be less likelihood that people would be seen as so readily surrendering their money. Their willingness to do so enhanced the credibility of their signatures. Moreover, the petition could become a helpful source of fundraising at a time when we deeply needed it.

The face of the petition recited the highlights of all the RCMP wrongdoing and called for the immediate invocation of normal law enforcement to deal with it. Then there were spaces for people to write their signatures, print their names, and produce addresses. We sent the petition to our members and a number of sympathetic constituencies. We also arranged for it to be posted at a chair and table on the sidewalk outside our offices on Toronto's busy Yonge Street. An accompanying sign contained the words: "IF YOU BELIEVE THE POLICE SHOULD OBEY THE LAW, SIGN HERE."

Moreover, we provided for our booth to be attended by various CCLA celebrities including Margaret Atwood, Pierre Berton, Walter Pitman, Daniel G. Hill, and Robert Fulford. On each occasion that we had such a celebrity, we notified the press. The publicity was substantial. It was fuelled by an altercation that Pierre Berton had with a member of the public and a newspaper column by Bob Fulford. Margaret Atwood immortalized her efforts on our behalf in her book, *Life Before Man*. Random passersby were signing our petition at the rate of more than a dozen an hour.

In the result, we collected more than fifteen thousand signatures and more than seventeen thousand dollars. We lost no time in pointing out that our organization was then small and, in the midst of the campaign, there was a postal strike. At the end of the road, we presented the petition and a brief to federal Solicitor General Robert Kaplan. In addition to me, our delegation included Pierre Berton, Quebec labour leader Huguette Plamondon, Ottawa law professor Ed Ratushny, and former NDP leaders Tommy Douglas and David Lewis.

There was at least one other significant forum in which I called for the normal processes of law enforcement. In the late spring of 1982, I received an invitation to be the dinner speaker at the 109th annual area officers' mess of the RCMP. The attire was formal; the RCMP officers wore their red tunics and I wore my uncle's tuxedo.

Since those who invited me stressed that they had done so because they believed I was not likely to say only what they wanted to hear, I ensured that my speech reiterated my message about RCMP wrongdoing. But I had a special argument for them. Not long before this dinner took place, postal union president Jean-Claude Parrot was sent to jail for refusing to comply with special legislation enacted by Parliament to end a current postal strike. Part of the lesson was obvious: his benign motives in trying to help his members could not excuse his law-breaking—why, then, should the *Mounties* be able to get away with that kind of plea?

An exacerbating factor concerned the plight of Dennis McDermott, then the president of the Canadian Labour Congress. Although Mc-Dermott had supported the strike from its outset, there was considerable anxiety about whether he would do so once the strike became unlawful. McDermott decided that it would be improper for the Canadian Labour Congress to back the unlawful strike. And McDermott was subjected to hefty amounts of flak from within his own constituency.

I admonished my audience along the following lines: "You may not like Dennis McDermott but I assure you that, if double standard justice is allowed to prevail in this country, you will like his successors a lot less." As I said these things, I was looking directly into the eyes of a number of former commissioners who were sitting directly in front of me. At the time, it occurred to me that one or more of those very commissioners might have been implicated if the action I was urging were ever adopted.

At one point during my presentation, there was some heckling near the back of the room. I abruptly stopped speaking and called out to them, "It's okay to heckle, but you must do so loud enough so that I can hear you; I want to answer you." The heckling stopped and I was able to continue without interruption. (I should point out that my intent was not to stop the heckling. I meant what I said: I wanted to hear their wisecracks; I actually thought it could be fun to banter back and forth with them.)

To my complete surprise, I received a standing ovation at the end of the session. To this day, I am not sure why that audience of Mounties responded so favourably. Afterwards, one of the officers who had invited me said that I did not disappoint them; in his view, my speech was truly devoid of pandering. That alone, however, could not explain the reception I got. It remains a mystery to me.

I cannot leave the subject of the RCMP banquet without acknowledging what a stimulating audience those Mounties, in general, were. They asked good questions and made perceptive observations. A number of them were also a lot of fun. Before the festivities got under way, a couple of the officers invited me to go downstairs and have drinks with them. In issuing the invitation, they told me that they wanted to see whether I was any different in person from the way I was on their tapes. This provoked laughter all around.

Several months before that dinner, the McDonald Commission, at long last, released its report. In general, we were pleased with the rather straightforward comments that the commission made about the police duty to obey the law. The Commission was also helpful in establishing the illegality of some of the controversial practices that both the government and Mountie officials had tried to portray as lawful.

Unfortunately, the commission was not so helpful on the issue of the early prosecution and disciplining of those RCMP officers who had broken the law. Indeed, at one of CCLA's appearances before the commission (during the summer of 1980 when the hearings were almost done), Mr. Justice McDonald, himself, made the following statement:

> I would not want you to be under any misapprehension that this Commission is sitting on some huge volume of evidence as to what specific individuals in specific cases have done or planned to do.
>
> . . .
>
> I am concerned that anyone . . . is under some misapprehension that we have had a large number of investigators interviewing members of the RCMP for days and days and months, to find out about individual instances. That has not been the case and it would not have been humanly possible.[12]

Yet, during the CCLA presentation two and a half years earlier, the same Mr. Justice McDonald expressed the following reservations regarding the wisdom of transmitting evidence to the provincial Attorneys General:

> Would not any . . . provincial attorney-general, in effect, at least in the provinces where the RCMP is the contracted police force not have to form his own task force of investigators and lawyers? If that is so, isn't that exactly the kind of machinery which a Commission of this sort attempts to put together . . . would any provincial attorney-general be as readily able as this Commission is to reach across provincial boundaries?[13]

On the basis of Justice McDonald's earlier remarks, was it not reasonable to believe that the commission itself would investigate a substantial number of the allegations against the RCMP? Federal cabinet ministers of the day bolstered this impression. When asked why no charges had been laid in connection with illegal mail opening, the then justice minister Ron Basford replied as follows:

> for the very simple reason that any facts or reports I have seen do not contain the precise type of information that is required in the laying of charges against specific officers or constables. That is one of the precise purposes of the hearings of the McDonald inquiry, to put before them facts with sufficient precision so that if charges can be laid, they will be laid.[14]

Former Solicitor General Francis Fox essentially echoed these remarks when he said, "There are other allegations which have been made against the Force and they have all been referred to the Royal Commission in order that they may produce the evidence."[15]

In this connection, I invoke once more the response made by Prime Minister Trudeau when we called upon him to facilitate immediately the ordinary processes of law enforcement. It will be recalled that he said, "The mandate of Mr. Justice McDonald extends to just such investigations," and that "duplication several times over of any enquiry . . . does [not] appeal to me as wise."

Even as I reflect on these matters more than two decades later, I confess that I am infuriated all over again. More than four years after the federal government had admitted the involvement of the RCMP in hundreds of unlawful acts, I remain bowled over by the lack of response. Apart from appointing the commission, the federal government did nothing; apart from the province of Quebec, the provinces did nothing; and the McDonald Commission conducted only a handful of investigations.

A few months after the commission reported in 1981, the then federal justice minister Jean Chrétien wrote to his fellow cabinet minister, Solicitor General Robert Kaplan, and said that there would be no federal prosecutions over the allegations of RCMP wrongdoing. Chrétien's explanation of his policy was something to behold. In fact, it was so full of lame excuses and feeble rationalizations that, once more, a delegation from the CCLA arranged to see the incumbent minister of justice—Chrétien's successor, Mark McGuigan. The meeting took place in early January of 1983 and, in addition to me, it included CCLA past president Walter Tarnopolsky, vice-president Robert Stanfield, board member Marvin Schiff, and our then research director, Erika Abner.

Mr. Chrétien's letter contended that, apart from one possible case, the McDonald Commission had not referred to him a body of evidence from which prosecutors could decide whether charges were warranted against particular individuals. To this, our brief raised a critical question: "Why have so many of these investigations been left undone for so long?" After all, as we reminded McGuigan, the McDonald Commission had publicly declared three years earlier that, apart from a few special matters, it had not conducted case-by-case investigations.

Why, then, we asked, "didn't the government either explicitly assign this responsibility to the Commission, [at that time,] or make some other arrangements to get the job done?" In the words of our brief, "it is particularly inappropriate for a representative of this government to cite past investigative inaction as though it were a relevant factor today." At that point, we drove home the message: "The party most responsible for this inaction is the government of Canada."

Mr. Chrétien also made a point of invoking the fact that many of the limitation periods in the applicable laws had already expired. Indeed, he emphasized the fact that the limitation periods were "running during the nearly four years" of the McDonald Commission. Our reply to this probably sounded testy:

> Didn't the government of Canada know five years ago that, by deferring so completely to the McDonald Commission, it was incurring a grave risk that the limitation periods for some of the offences would expire? What the government has failed to acknowledge is that *it* must bear much of the responsibility for the lapsed limitation periods [emphasis in original].[16]

Chrétien's letter further exploited the expiry of the limitation periods. He said that it would not be proper for him to distinguish between those who would now be protected by the expiry and those who could not claim such a benefit. To this, we questioned whether "comparable solicitude is available to *civilian* wrongdoers." Indeed, we noted that, in fact, civilians would not enjoy such protection.

While he acknowledged that the mail-opening offences did not carry limitation periods, Mr. Chrétien did note the length of time involved—most of the mail openings had reportedly terminated in 1972. We argued, however, that it was not at all so unprecedented to prosecute for civilian misdeeds that were as old as these. But we also reminded the minister that, when these illegalities first became known, the year was 1977 and the events in question were much younger. "In any event," as we repeated our theme, "it is the *government* and no one else, which much bear the chief responsibility for the paucity of investigations and prosecutions" during the time in question.

Mr. Chrétien had also claimed that, within the RCMP, there was a general impression that the mail openings were properly authorized. To this, we pointed out that ignorance of the law has rarely excused civilian wrongdoers. Indeed, we pointed out that the courts would not have had the occasion so often to pronounce on the matter if governments had not so often prosecuted in situations where ignorance of the law might have been involved. In any event, we reminded the minister that testimony before the McDonald Commission acknowledged that key officials of the RCMP knew very well that the practice was unlawful; they had even taken steps to centralize the practice because they did not anticipate early legislation to legalize it.

Again, Chrétien had trotted out the argument that the RCMP mail openers were not likely motivated by personal gain. To this, we replied that no such considerations have been applied to civilian wrongdoers. And again, we noted that not long before our meeting with McGuigan, the government of Canada had prosecuted CUPW president Jean-Claude Parrot even though there was no indication that he had been motivated by such personal gain. The government had even urged that he be jailed. The double standards were overwhelming.

The Chrétien letter made special mention of the fact that the McDonald Commission recommended a regime for legalized mail opening. But why, we argued, should this justify immunity for the RCMP? In comparable situations involving civilians, no such immunities have been forthcoming. Even though the Le Dain Commission had previously recommended the abolition of the offence concerning the mere possession of marijuana, the federal government nevertheless prosecuted hundreds of civilians for that very offence. And, by then, it was universally acknowledged that the mere possession of marijuana was a minor offence. But opening the mail in the course of delivering the post was clearly a more serious matter.

On the basis of all these factors, we urged the government to initiate whatever prosecutorial action was then feasible and in accord with its general standards.

But the government of Canada remained recalcitrant. No federal prosecutions were ever launched on account of all that RCMP wrongdoing. While I cannot now recall the details of our interaction with Mr. McGuigan, I do remember that he became quite angry over our presentation. Perhaps, this was a reaction he indulged himself because he had known us personally. Indeed, at one time, McGuigan had been the chair of the CCLA board.

Apart from the then separatist government of Quebec, none of the provinces initiated prosecutions for the wrongdoing within their respective jurisdictions. At one point, the BC authorities seemed to rely on some convoluted arguments that the alleged wrongdoings were not unlawful at all. Ontario invoked pathetic arguments similar to those that had been advanced by Jean Chrétien at the federal level. All in all, I think it is fair to say that the response of the Canadian authorities was highly dismal. To use the words of the *Charter of Rights and Freedoms*, the behaviour of Canadian officialdom had "brought the administration of justice into disrepute."

THE BIRTH OF CSIS

One of the most important functions assigned to the McDonald Commission involved making proposals for how Canada's national security should be protected in the future. It was clear that when the commission came into being, the law and practice in this area were nothing short of a mess.

The RCMP security service had been unlawfully opening mail for some thirty years, but its leaders continued to insist that, because of its importance to national security, the practice should be legalized. The RCMP security service had surreptitiously entered the properties of many Canadians in order to conduct what it called "intelligence probes." There were arguments about the legality, propriety, and even necessity of such activities. The RCMP security service had created fake material and disseminated it in certain circles in order to disrupt some of the organizations it had under surveillance. There were arguments about whether the law should—or did—allow for such "dirty tricks."

And then, there were reports that the service had actually spied on a number of legitimate dissenters. These security targets included the separatist Parti Québécois, the Waffle faction of the New Democratic Party, the National Farmers' Union, the Canadian Union of Public Employees (CUPE), and the National Black Coalition. I have never heard a report or even a credible allegation that any of these organizations, as such, practised—or even preached—the use of violence as a tactic to promote their respective programs. A number of them, of course, sought to effect radical changes in our society but, to my knowledge, none of them were prepared to use anything but non-violent methods to achieve their aspirations.

Moreover, I will always remember the day when my father telephoned me at the CCLA office to tell me about a story in the *Globe and Mail* to the effect that Toronto lawyer Clayton Ruby had been wiretapped by the RCMP. My father asked whether I thought I too had been a target of their surreptitious efforts. My initial response, of course, was a wisecrack: "I should hope so—what's so important about Clay Ruby?" Of course, there was an overriding concern. If there was any truth in the story, what in the hell were the Mounties up to? Had they never mastered the distinction between subversion and dissent? I can well imagine that Clay Ruby had been a major irritant to various police departments. But I have difficulty picturing him as aiding and abetting sabotage or espionage.

Several years later—in the aftermath of 9/11—there was another similar media report: that the RCMP had spied on former NDP leader David Lewis for some fifty years. Soon after this report appeared in the press, I had a speaking engagement with the Canadian Association of Chiefs of Police. With the then RCMP commissioner Giuliano Zaccardelli and some of his top cohorts in attendance, I lashed out at this latest exposé of Mountie mania. I told them that I had knowledge of the matters about which I spoke. I had articled for David Lewis and had been the president of his riding association when he was first elected to Parliament. I was able to tell my audience that I personally knew David Lewis to have been a lifelong enemy of Soviet Communism. Indeed, he had been a prime mover in the effort to remove Communists from positions of leadership in the Canadian labour movement.

I berated the abysmal ignorance of those so-called intelligence officials who had so little intelligence about these important political phenomena. For certain right-wing yahoos, there is no difference between democratic socialists and totalitarian Communists. To my surprise, RCMP Commissioner Zaccardelli rose to his feet after my talk, and addressing me in front of everyone, said, "Alan, you have more friends here than you realize." This suggested to me that, at the very least, the twenty-first century version of the RCMP was experiencing some discomfort over what its predecessors had perpetrated.

Another revelation that emerged at the time of the McDonald Commission concerned the surveillance and "dirty tricks" that the RCMP had perpetrated against the Canadian Trotskyist movement. The Trotskyists, of course, did have a totalitarian ideology and did expect, at some point, to employ illegal tactics to overthrow democratic government in this country. But no evidence had surfaced suggesting that this movement had ever actually engaged in such activity.

It appeared that these would-be revolutionaries had lots of fantasies but little know-how. To cite a comment once made, in another context, by the late American radical, Saul Alinsky, the Trotskyists were incapable of conspiring to have lunch together. In the United States, thirty-five years of FBI investigations had failed similarly to yield any evidence of relevant illegality on the part of the Trotskyists in that country.

Between groups like the Trotskyists on the one hand, and all those legitimate dissenters on the other hand, it became clear that the RCMP security service had spent much time, effort, energy, and money investigating *lawful* activity. My colleagues and I at CCLA soon realized that our planned appearances at the McDonald Commission had to address this issue: what kind of powers and safeguards were needed in order to ensure that Canada's future security intelligence activities did not repeat the excesses of the RCMP?

In the late winter of 1978, the CCLA deliberations on this subject produced a bright idea: I should go to Washington and consult some of the experts there. The Americans had been dealing with these issues for many years and had developed a sophistication that was simply not matched in Canada.

In April 1978, with cherry blossoms blooming all around, I arrived in Washington. It was quite a day: I met with people from the US Senate Intelligence Committee, the US Justice Department, the FBI, and the American Civil Liberties Union. At the time, the Americans were in the midst of creating and implementing a number of reforms for the FBI's intelligence operations. In the wake of Watergate and accompanying disclosures, a consensus was developing in that country to restrict the scope of what the FBI could lawfully do and increase the viability of the safeguards for its potential targets. I returned to Canada full of information, ideas, and transcripts of Congressional hearings.

During the ensuing summer, I spent much of my time reading through those transcripts. I was deeply impressed with the calibre of the discussions. When the Americans do things well, they are effectively unequalled.

At the time, the key domestic national security issue in the United States concerned the amount of preventive intelligence gathering that should be permissible. In Canada, there was an overwhelming consensus that, in security matters as in most other things, "an ounce of prevention is worth a pound of cure." But, in the United States, there was much more sensitivity to the downside of prevention. The Americans seemed to realize that preventive intelligence gathering represented a threat to civil liberties. When the goal is prevention, there is a tendency to expand the amount of surveillance that is undertaken. More people are investigated and more aspects of their lives are examined. The idea is to learn as much as possible about as many potential suspects as possible. The result is an ever expanding net of surreptitious surveillance.

Indeed, during the many years that the American intelligence agencies were relatively unrestrained in their investigative mandates, they committed many promiscuous abuses of civil liberties. Their targets included a number of legitimate dissenters, such as the peace movement and the civil rights movement. It was discovered, for example, that the FBI had spied shamelessly on the personal privacy of Martin Luther King, Jr. The Canadian abuses to which I referred earlier, occurred during a time when the Mounties were subject to similarly few restraints.

Yet, an important question remains: To what extent did these civil liberties costs yield national security benefits? In Canada, there was simply no adequate way to make such determinations. But, in the United States, there were. The independent General Accounting Office (GAO) of the US Congress was given access to FBI records and, with these resources, it conducted periodic audits of the FBI's intelligence investigations.

In view of the pervasive and intrusive character of the FBI's activities, how much prevention was, in fact, achieved? Apparently, not very much. According to the GAO, "Generally the FBI did not report advance knowledge of planned violence." In 1974, for example, the GAO estimated that the FBI obtained advance knowledge of its targets' activities in only about 2 percent of all its investigations. Significantly, most of this knowledge related to completely lawful activities such as speeches, meetings, and peaceful demonstrations. As one member of the US Senate Committee noted, "The FBI provided . . . a handful of substantiated cases—out of the thousands of Americans investigated—in which preventive intelligence produced warning of terrorist activity."[17]

The paucity of these security benefits combined with the enormity of the civil liberties violations to produce pressures for reform in the way the United States handled security intelligence operations. Most of the efforts focused on attempting to articulate an investigative threshold requiring some evidence of criminal conduct. The common law democracies have generally required such evidence before they would allow state encroachments on individuals. Moreover, it was believed that, to whatever extent crime was involved, there was less chance of intruding upon legitimate dissent.

Then, the question became: How far in advance of the anticipated criminal acts would intrusive surveillance be permissible? Investigations too long in advance increased the risks to civil liberties; investigations too close increased the perils to national security. During my time in Washington, this debate was well under way.

From what I could discern in the media reports, my interviews with American experts, and the materials that were given to me, it appeared that there was then a consensus in the United States that the FBI's intelligence mandate had to be significantly circumscribed. Among the Congressional oversight committees, the US Attorney General, and the non-government organizations, each might have used different language but all seemed to agree that there should be no investigative activity unless actual crime was anticipated in the rather near future. While most of the participants in the debate still favoured some amount of preventive intelligence gathering, only one (of which I was aware) favoured virtually none at all: the American Civil Liberties Union (ACLU).

According to the ACLU, the authority to investigate citizens and resident aliens—especially with intrusive techniques—should require probable cause to believe that certain federal criminal acts had been, were being, or were about to be, committed. The ACLU would not even accept participation in a criminal conspiracy as a basis for intrusive investigations. To my US counterparts, conspiracy was too vague and nebulous a concept for such purposes.

My problem, then, was: What was I to recommend for CCLA? Like the Americans, I rejected the status quo in this country that subjected intelligence gathering to such little restriction. Nevertheless, my instincts told me that my colleagues in the ACLU had adopted an unwarrantedly narrow position. In the interests of national security, I had become persuaded that *some* amount of preventive intelligence could be acceptable. The only questions, in my view, were: How much? And, how would we ever articulate the permissible criteria?

After thrashing the issue around in my mind during most of the summer of 1978, I finally came up with one variant or another of the following:

> Citizens and permanent residents should not be targeted for intrusive surveillance unless, at the very least, there are reasonable grounds to believe that the matter under investigation involves a serious, security-related *breach of the law*.

I recommended—and my CCLA colleagues agreed—that a lower standard would be acceptable for the surveillance of people other than citizens and permanent residents, such as temporary visitors. Similarly, a lower standard could well be acceptable for less intrusive surveillance, such as trailing and source checking.

For purposes of my recommendations, "intrusive surveillance" meant electronic bugging, surreptitious entry, mail opening, the invasion of confidential records, and the deployment of covert informants and infiltrators. Since I was not proposing that CCLA actually attempt to draft the terms of a bill, I suggested that we provide examples of what we would mean by "serious, security-related breach of the law." My list of recommended examples consisted of espionage, sabotage, serious violence, extortion, and bribery impairing the operations of government.

In order to ensure that some amount of preventive intelligence gathering would be permissible, I was prepared to provide explicitly that the targetable offences could include attempts, counselling, aiding, abetting, and even conspiracies. Recognizing as I did that the inclusion of conspiracies could still cast too wide a net, I suggested that the law should require evidence not only of a conspiracy but also of some overt conduct in furtherance of it. This is the way I hoped we could strike a balance that would both allow for some advance surveillance but simultaneously keep it within acceptable boundaries.

We re-entered the fray with the foregoing proposals. First, we attempted to sell our basic approach to the McDonald Commission and subsequently to the federal Solicitor General, the Senate committee that vetted the government bill, the House committee that did likewise, and the House committee that did the five-year review of what ultimately became the *Canadian Security Intelligence Service* (CSIS) *Act*. And, of course, we regurgitated our position in umpteen media interviews and public forums. At every step along the way, we attempted to challenge those who favoured giving our intelligence agencies greater power. More specifically, we challenged them to conceive a scenario in which our proposed powers would jeopardize Canada's national security.

Although the McDonald Commission gave us a very fair and full hearing, it ultimately proposed much wider powers than those we had urged. The commission recommended giving Canada's security intelligence agency the power to use intrusive surveillance to investigate activities "directed towards or in support of" serious violence for the purpose of achieving a political objective within Canada or a foreign state. While the commission also said that it would be appropriate to investigate "activities intended ultimately" to destroy the democratic system, it said that *intrusive* techniques should not be used "so long as [such] organizations . . . stick to the methods of liberal democracy."

At this point, we thought that we detected some ambivalence. It seemed to us that the McDonald Commission had not resolved how much intrusive surveillance should be available for preventive purposes. We focused on this issue at a meeting with federal Solicitor General Robert Kaplan in February 1982. We cited a hypothetical set of circumstances: an incipient revolutionary group restricts its activities, for the moment, to soapbox oratory, literature distribution, and fundraising in the hope that it could acquire enough support for future resort to violence.

Our delegation argued that the *McDonald Report* made it very unclear whether such a group would be susceptible *now* to intrusive surveillance. On the basis of the words "intended ultimately" the answer might appear to be "no." But, on the basis of the words "activities directed towards," the opposite conclusion might be warranted. In support of this latter conclusion, our brief reproduced a quote that the commission had cited with approval:

> The primary objective of an efficient intelligence service must be to prevent any insurgency or terrorism developing beyond the incipient stage. Hence a high quality intelligence service is required *long before the insurgency surfaces* [emphasis added].[18]

The CCLA delegation argued that such ambivalence must be avoided. Once more, we argued for a much tighter mandate. As we said, "The detection of an insurgency so far in advance of its actual emergence may require not only discernment but also clairvoyance." In our view, such an approach would wind up authorizing needless violations of civil liberties.

On the issue of safeguards, the commission report came a lot closer to the CCLA position. It rejected the Trudeau doctrine whereby the minister in charge should be kept ignorant of the security service's daily operations. The commission also called for (as we had advocated) an independent agency that would be empowered to audit the activities of the resulting security service.

In one other area, however, we parted company with the McDonald Commission and apparently many others in this country. The commission proposed that this country's security operations be conducted by an all-civilian agency. This recommendation promised to accommodate those who were eager to divest the Mounties of their security mandate. While we didn't particularly quarrel with the idea of getting the Mounties out of this arena, we wanted Canada's security intelligence agency to also have police responsibilities. Our belief was that the prospect, faced by police, of having to defend their activities in court could help to reduce the propensity for committing civil liberties violations.

Some months after we had registered our pros and cons on the *Mc-Donald Report*, a bill was introduced into Parliament. The way it happened proved to be particularly nerve-wracking. On the day in question, I received a telephone call from the CBC inviting our comments as soon as the bill appeared. This meant going to the CBC and waiting for the bill to come across its teletype facilities. I have never been comfortable with the exercise of instant analysis. Not wishing to carry that burden all alone, I asked the then chair of our board, Ken Swan, to join me. (Of course, we could have refused but, in view of our deep involvement in this issue, we felt the need to give it a try.)

As it turned out, most of the bill's key provisions closely resembled the proposals of the McDonald Commission. Since we were already familiar with these measures, we were enabled to avoid the instant analysis that we had feared. In the result, I went on CBC television and blasted away.

But the bill contained one critical feature that was not in the *McDonald Report*: a power in the security intelligence agency to break the law when it was "reasonably necessary" to do so. This provision provoked a storm of protest. Editorials, newspaper columns, and media commentary from a wide variety of sources expressed strong opposition to the existence of this provision.

At CCLA, we decided to organize a public rally. We went all out to recruit important speakers and gather a large audience. We achieved both. On our platform that night, CCLA had its national honorary president, retired Supreme Court Justice Emmett Hall, Ontario Attorney General Roy McMurtry, Manitoba Attorney General Roland Penner, the Primate of the Anglican Church, the Moderator of the United Church, a representative of the Canadian Conference of Catholic Bishops, the president of the Canadian Labour Congress, well-known broadcaster and author June Callwood, criminal lawyer Eddie Greenspan, and I acted as Master of Ceremonies. The place of our meeting was Trinity United Church at Bloor and Robert Streets in Toronto. The place was packed: more than eight hundred people appeared to be hanging from the rafters.

As people were making their way into the meeting, at the beginning, reporters stopped a number of them and asked why they were there. Each one of them expressed bitterness over the new power that the government had proposed to create. Particularly noteworthy, were the number of people who pointed out that this was the first such rally they had ever attended. They were simply not used to protesting in this way. I believe that this factor was especially persuasive to those in government.

Shortly after the meeting began, we faced a potentially disruptive interjection. Feminist leader, Judy Rebick, stood up from the audience and asked to address the crowd on the subject of abortion. Although the greatest number of us were, like Judy, pro-choice, there was no way we were going to allow her or that ideology to undermine our rally. Indeed, as emcee, I simply said "no" to what she wanted.

While that stopped her for a while, she attempted once more to interrupt, when Roland Penner was invited to speak. She and some of her cohorts were particularly angry at him because, as Attorney General of Manitoba, he had already taken steps to enforce the then abortion law against Dr. Henry Morgentaler. Penner was especially effective in quelling her protest. Whatever the merits of her position, he said the important thing on that occasion was to resist the kind of power the federal government was attempting to create. He exhorted both her and the audience not to allow any other issues to sidetrack our protest. The audience applauded enthusiastically and Judy Rebick receded into the woodwork.

Our protest meeting precipitated a torrent of publicity. Not long afterwards, the government withdrew that contentious provision. I remember being particularly impressed with the behaviour of Ontario Attorney General Roy McMurtry. While he never expressed much opposition to many of the other measures that bothered CCLA, he was nevertheless front and centre on the provision that would allow CSIS to break the law. In addition to appearing the way he did on the platform at our rally, he spoke out several times in the media. On one occasion, he and I became partners in a debate at a convention of the Canadian Bar Association. Our opponents then were former federal solicitor general, Robert Kaplan and John Starnes, the former civilian director of the RCMP security service. Provincial Attorneys General are not always that helpful during the course of federal controversies.

While we at CCLA were pleased with the outcome of the rally, we felt the need to resume our efforts to change those other sections of the bill. So, we continued to beat the drums at other public meetings, press conferences, and hearings of parliamentary committees. There was consistency in our recurring theme: the powers of CSIS should be narrowed so that intrusive surveillance could only be used against citizens and permanent residents to investigate serious, security-related breaches of the law.

Invariably, positions like ours provoke a certain amount of "trivial pursuit." At a Senate committee hearing, there was a suggestion that our solicitude for citizens and permanent residents represented a breach of equality. One of the senators charged that our proposal amounted to discrimination against foreign visitors. All people should be treated equally, this senator thundered at us.

All that really means, I replied, is that the standards would be lowered for *everyone*. Although we favoured the adoption of *some* threshold for the surveillance of other people, it would be ludicrous to insist that they should enjoy the high standards we were advocating for citizens and permanent residents. Would you really insist, I asked the questioning senator, that a foreign visitor who comes here for a weekend and who has had no previous connections with this country, should be entitled to enjoy the same level of protection against intrusive surveillance that you would give citizens and permanent residents? Or, is it indeed your position, I pressed him, to *reduce* the protections for citizens and permanent residents?

At a hearing of the House committee, Svend Robinson, a New Democratic MP from Vancouver, sounded a similar theme. He asked us about possible CSIS surveillance of foreign embassy personnel. At this point, I remember turning to my colleague, Ken Swan, and whispering in his ear, "How do I tell this guy that I don't give a monkey's fuck about the Soviet bureaucracy?"

At these parliamentary hearings, I traded almost shamelessly on what I learned from those American experts I had consulted. Again and again, I told our parliamentarians that this bill would give our security intelligence agency more powers than their American counterparts had. This came up particularly in the case of electronic bugging against domestic security threats. As a result of a 1972 court case and other developments, the power of the FBI to engage in this particular surveillance technique had been narrowed to the point where it was only available under a general criminal law statute that required past, current, or imminent commission of certain actual crimes.

What was even more significant, I told our MPs, was that not a single US president since 1972 had even requested additional bugging power for these purposes. Until that point, those US presidents were Richard Nixon, Gerald Ford, Jimmy Carter, and Ronald Reagan. I then hit my audience with the punchline: "On the basis of this bill, the government of Canada has done something truly remarkable: it has made Ronald Reagan look like a civil libertarian."

As a result of a television debate in which I participated at this time, I became somewhat friendly with one of my eminent opponents: John Starnes, the first civilian director of the RCMP security service. After that debate, we had lunch together on a number of occasions. One of our luncheon get-togethers came up after we both appeared, consecutively, at a hearing of the House committee that was vetting the CSIS bill. I went first and then he testified.

During the course of his testimony, one of the MPs noted that what John was saying directly contradicted a point I had made earlier. My new friend acknowledged the truth of this and then assured the committee that he planned to thrash out the question with me at lunch on that very day. All this appeared in the transcript of the hearings. The transcript also managed to include a question from one of the other MPs: Who's paying?

At lunch, we got into a strange conversation. In response to a question of mine, John declared that he had been particularly upset some years earlier by the suspicion in some circles that he had been involved in plotting the assassination of certain foreign leaders. I found myself asking him why that, in particular, should be so upsetting. The look of shock on his face became even greater with my next question. Playing the Devil's advocate, I asked whether, apart from the limits of the law, he had any moral qualms about taking out a guy like Gaddafi? But, before he could answer, I burst out laughing. Can you imagine, I asked, what a field day the press would have with our luncheon conversation?

Later on, it occurred to me that perhaps this exchange could have happened—only in Canada.

Although the CSIS bill passed without any of the additional amendments we were urging, our efforts to change it did not grind to a halt. There were numbers of additional opportunities for us to ventilate our position. We also created a significant opportunity. We took the government of Canada to court over the powers of CSIS. Our argument was that those powers exceeded the constitutional boundaries that were set in the *Canadian Charter of Rights and Freedoms*. We took affidavits from a number of community activists who had experienced some peculiar coincidences that they suspected had been caused by CSIS investigations. Of course, we acknowledged to the court that, in view of the surreptitious nature of CSIS activity, we were unable adequately to *prove* the truth of these suspicions.

This issue became fatal to our litigation effort. By 2 to 1, the Ontario Court of Appeal held that, in the absence of adequate evidence, CCLA had no standing to pursue this case. The judges contended that there was "another reasonable and effective way to bring the issue before the court." In this regard, they relied on the fact that, in one earlier case, CSIS involvement had been established. But, in that case, the CSIS role was only discovered because the target wound up being charged—a development that preventive intelligence gathering attempts as much as possible to avoid.

Because of the surreptitious nature of what CSIS does, we argued that adequate evidence would usually be impossible to obtain. We were left nevertheless with a most regrettable precedent: to whatever extent this decision is allowed to stand, the citizens of this country will have been left denuded of an effective way to challenge the constitutionality of laws that authorize surreptitious surveillance in the field of national security.

We were down, but not out. We continued recurringly to attack the CSIS enabling legislation. Shortly after the creation of CSIS, an interesting new opportunity came my way. I was invited to lecture to CSIS trainees about the civil liberties implications of their activity. This occurred, once a year, more than a dozen times. I had a ball in my various attempts to challenge the thought processes of these bright young people.

Certain themes began to come together. One of the first things I did was to try to get them to see their mandate differently from the way they were being trained. I said to them, your job, of course, is to chase spies and terrorists. But, I insisted, your job also requires that you *not* chase non-spies and non-terrorists. I emphasized that *both* are vital ingredients of their mandate. After all, their overriding objective is to protect the integrity of Canada's democratic processes. That means frustrating the subversive efforts of spies and terrorists. But it also means that CSIS operatives, themselves, must avoid excesses that would undermine those very processes.

A phenomenon to which I wished to sensitize them was the democratic radical: the person who wants to bring about radical changes, even transformations, of our society but steadfastly avoids violence and other illegalities in the course of doing so. Examples of this phenomenon, of course, were available in the history of the RCMP security service: the separatist Parti Québécois and the socialist Waffle faction of the New Democratic Party, to name just two. I stressed that such groups are for the political processes to address and not for a security intelligence agency.

While acknowledging that it was quite proper for them to target dangerous undemocratic radicals such as the FLQ, I also counselled them to avoid intrusive surveillance of undemocratic, but non-dangerous radicals. The example that came to mind in this regard was the Trotskyist movement. I have already indicated how much time, effort, and resources had been employed against the Trotsyists with no result, because they apparently weren't doing anything worthy of official surveillance. When it came to organizations such as the Trotskyists, I emphasized the importance of distinguishing a threat to the state from a pain in the ass. The record indicated that the Trotskyists were very much in the latter category but not at all in the former one.

Other themes that came up in my lectures to the CSIS trainees involved the importance of the rule of law and the need, therefore, that they be scrupulous about obeying the law. This, of course, was the issue that ultimately doomed the RCMP security service.

I don't know why these annual lectures were discontinued but I regret it. They were such fun.

9/11 AND ITS AFTERMATH

With the fall of Communism at the end of the 1980s, much conventional wisdom believed that this world had arrived at the "end of history." At least, it was widely thought that major ideological conflict was a thing of the past.

All of that ended on September 11th, 2001. The deliberate infliction of death, destruction, and intense suffering on three thousand unarmed, innocent civilians in the continental United States revealed the existence of another—and deadly—ideological conflict. The democratic West was forced to face the enmity of radical Islam and that movement's ready resort to acts of terrorism as an ongoing weapon of struggle.

Virtually every nation of the Western World responded to the atrocities of 9/11 by enacting new legislation to equip its intelligence agencies and police forces with enlarged powers to face the threat of terrorism. Canada was no exception. In the fall of 2001, the government introduced a host of measures containing additional powers and, by the end of that year, most of these measures had become law.

While I had no doubts about the goal of ensuring that our democracy could defend itself, I had deep reservations about the means that were chosen to do so.

Consider the case of Liban Hussein, a Canadian citizen from Somalia. He had lived in Canada for several years during which time he built up a business that managed to support himself, his wife, his children, and a number of other relatives. One day early in the twenty-first century, he woke up to find that his name was on the federal government's newly created special list of those involved in "terrorist activities." With that, his assets were frozen, he was arrested, he was jailed, the Americans began extradition proceedings against him, and it became a crime for anyone to have certain dealings involving his property. Under the authority of our new anti-terror laws, he was suddenly transformed into a legal pariah.

Moreover, by virtue of such laws, all of these actions were triggered by a unilateral decision of the federal government. Admittedly, such "pariahs" could seek redress in the courts; and the courts could remove them from the list if they found that the government had acted unreasonably. This could restore a person's normal legal rights. But court cases often take time to produce results and, in the meantime, the ostracization process can do a lot of damage. After a period of time during which the contemplated boycott operates, the affected persons could be rendered bereft of resources with which to defend their interests in court.

Fortunately, Liban Hussein never had to go to court. After a few months of having to endure what the government had thrown at him, he was just as suddenly cleared of all wrongdoing. The government declared that there was no evidence whatsoever linking him to terrorism. But, according to his lawyer, he had already lost his business, and his life lay in ruins.

Despite the enormity of what this provision can wreak, it is not among the measures that were slated for "sunset" expiry. By contrast, the section on preventive detention would "cease to apply" unless, within a certain time, Parliament took affirmative action to extend its life. Yet the period during which a person can be preventively detained without judicial review is only a couple of days longer under the anti-terror regime than it is for the other offences in the *Criminal Code*.[19]

I have never quite appreciated why the incremental lengthening of preventive detention should attract so much hype and, by contrast, the relatively new power of government to list and impoverish has attracted so little. Perhaps it's because the notion of preventive detention—regardless of the actual details—has always been accompanied by an aura of intimidation. Moreover, apart from the Hussein case, there have been no further reports that the impoverishing power has actually been used. There have also been rumours that Mr. Hussein received compensation in the wake of his ordeal.

Nevertheless, I used my many platforms—parliamentary hearings, speeches, media interviews, articles in the press, and my book *Categorically Incorrect*—to keep the pot boiling over this power.

My argument has had two prongs: in the first place, it seemed likely that anyone slated for the government's list would already be under intense surveillance, thereby increasing the ability of the authorities to intercept any potentially dangerous conduct and, secondly, there is no reason why the decision to list should not be subject to judicial review *before* it goes into effect.

This prohibition against dealing with the property of a terrorist group extends beyond those on the special list. All of us must avoid such transactions even with terrorist entities that are not on the list. This raises the question: how are we supposed to know what others are terrorist entities? In order to stay out of trouble, many people might well avoid dealing with anyone who appears to be Arab or Muslim. Again, this provision does not appear to have been enforced. But, if it were, it's not hard to imagine the injustices that could be caused.

In addition to the foregoing, I complained that the definition of "terrorist activity" was so broad that it could include lawful conduct and non-violent forms of civil disobedience. In common with the situation when the *War Measures Act* was last invoked, we received a heavy volume of telephone calls. This time, however, the bulk of the calls favoured our position.

Shortly after the bill was introduced into Parliament, I wound up in a radio exchange with my old friend Irwin Cotler, then an MP before he became justice minister. He was largely defending the bill and I was attacking it. Toward the end of our debate, he announced that he had delegated some of his students to research the issue. Their conclusion, he proudly reported, was that the bill did not infringe the *Charter*. My response was "First, you asked us to trust the government and now you want us to trust your students.

ENDNOTES

1   Canadian Civil Liberties Association, Submissions to the Honourable John
    Turner, Minister of Justice of Canada re: Emergency powers, March 29, 1971.
2   "PM not prepared to condemn those in raid," *Globe and Mail*, October 31,
    1977, 7.
3   Canadian Civil Liberties Association, "The RCMP, The Government, and
    the Rule of Law: An Open Letter to the Prime Minister of Canada," *Globe
    and Mail*, November 19, 1977, 14.
4   Pierre Elliott Trudeau, "Reply to CCLA letter of November 16 1977" (Decem-
    ber 9, 1977), 4.
5   Canadian Civil Liberties Association, "Toward A Charter for the Royal Can-
    adian Mounted Police," submission to the Commission of Inquiry Concern-
    ing Certain Activities of the Royal Canadian Mounted Police (Ottawa: 1980),
    p. 12.
6   Canada, Commission of Inquiry Concerning Certain Activities of the Royal
    Canadian Mounted Police, Testimony of William Higgitt, vol. 85 (Ottawa:
    1979) p. 13963 of transcripts.
7   *Ibid.*, Testimony of Donald Mcleery, vol. 81, p. 13321.
8   *Perka v The Queen*, [1984] 2 S.C.R. 232. Dickson J.; Section 8(3), *Martin's
    Criminal Code 2010*, p. 36.
9   Canadian Civil Liberties Association, "Toward A Charter for the Royal Can-
    adian Mounted Police," above note 5, p. 12.
10 Canada, Parliament, House of Commons, Standing Committee on Justice
    and Legal Affairs, Minutes of Proceedings and Evidence (Issue no. 34, p.
    46, June 1, 1978) 30th Parliament, 3rd session, 1977–78.
11 *Ibid.*, p. 50.
12 Canada, Commission of Inquiry Concerning Certain Activities of the Royal
    Canadian Mounted Police, Testimony of the CCLA (Ottawa: 1978), pp.
    28961–64 of transcripts.
13 *Ibid.*, p. 2391.
14 Ron Basford, Canada, House of Commons, *Debates* (January 31, 1978), p.
    2384.
15 Francis Fox, Canada, House of Commons, *Debates* (November 1, 1977), p.
    510.
16 See above note 5, p. 25.
17 See John T. Elliff, *The Reform of FBI Intelligence Operations* (Princeton:
    Princeton University Press, 1979).

18 Report of the Commission of Inquiry Concerning Certain Activities of the Royal Canadian Mounted Police, Part V, Chapter 3, "The Scope of Security Intelligence," p. 436; Paul Wilkinson, *Terrorism and The Liberal State*, (Toronto, Macmillan/MacLean-Hunter, 1977), pp. 133–35.

19 *Criminal Code*, R.S.C. 1985, c. C-46, ss. 83.3, 6.(a) & (b) and s. 83.3(7)(c)(ii). Also See A. Alan Borovoy, *Categorically Incorrect: Ethical Fallacies in Canada's War on Terrorism* (Toronto: Dundurn Press, 2006) p. 180.

CHAPTER ELEVEN

Dignity and Equality

$\mathcal{T}$o begin this chapter, I find it useful to quote from one of my recent books:

> Democracy is the only system in this world that puts a premium on human dignity. Even though people differ in all kinds of ways, for example, in ethnicity, proclivity, and even ability, the democratic system considers them equal in *dignity*.[1]

Not surprisingly, therefore, a sizeable amount of my activity and that of the Canadian Civil Liberties Association (CCLA) focused directly on the threats to dignity and equality faced by many of our fellow citizens. We had occasion to go after our state institutions for both the hurt they presumed to inflict and the help they declined to provide.

RACE, RELIGION, AND ETHNICITY

By the time I left the Labour Committee, a lot had been accomplished in the field of human rights, particularly in race and ethnic relations. Virtually every jurisdiction in Canada had laws against such discrimination in employment, public accommodations, public licensing, and housing. Moreover, virtually every jurisdiction had a human rights commission with full-time staff to administer, enforce, and educate with respect to these laws.

Needless to say, my interest in racial and ethnic relations did not expire with my departure from the Labour Committee. But, with changes in the nature of the problems, there had to be commensurate changes in the way I addressed those problems. I began to learn, for example, that a significant amount of job discrimination was being practised by employment agencies. Numbers of employers who wanted to avoid hiring certain minorities would delegate such dirty work to these agencies. Minority group members who sought employment through these agencies would typically have no way to know when they were being improperly passed over. After all, they would have no way to know the identity of the agencies' customers.

Over the years, therefore, I instigated a number of surveys into how various employment agencies would react to discriminatory job orders. During the fall of 1980, for example, CCLA telephoned twenty-five randomly chosen employment agencies across the country—in Halifax, Toronto, Winnipeg, and Vancouver. In each case, our tester posed as the representative of an American firm that was planning to locate rather soon in that community. In the course of the discussion, which was ostensibly designed to find out what kind of services the agency would perform, our tester asked whether the agency would agree to screen out non-whites.

Only three of the tested agencies expressly refused; five responded in rather vague terms but did not refuse; in seventeen cases, there was no doubt about their willingness to comply. Indeed, many of them expressed considerable enthusiasm for the assignment. Here are some of the replies:

- "I'm a businessman . . . if you don't want a black, we don't send a black. If you don't want any Indians, we don't send you any Indians. . . . My business is to make a placement and make some money. I'm going to send you what you want."
- "So it's white and bright."
- "Well, that's why you go through an agency."
- "I like to get it from my clients right up front. . . . If they don't want non-white people, well heaven's sake, tell me right now and I won't send you non-white people."

The results were broadcast first on CTV's *W5* and subsequently picked up by a number of other media. In the aftermath of the publicity, CCLA in Halifax, Toronto, and Winnipeg pressed their respective governments for follow-up action. Most of the affected governments at least wrote to the employment agencies and reminded them of their obligations under the law. In Ontario, the response was somewhat more aggressive. We called on the minister of labour to launch a program of auditing the employment agencies irrespective of whether complaints had been filed. The minister announced that he intended to recommend that the law be amended to require the agencies to keep fuller records of their activities so as to render the agencies more amenable to auditing procedures.

The more I learned and reflected on the issue of racial and ethnic discrimination, the more I began to encounter a largely unaddressed problem: systemic barriers. The clue to the existence of this problem was the apparently widespread inequities we found in various sectors of the economy. Despite the fact that human rights legislation had been on the books since the early 1950s, we discovered numbers of situations in which racial minorities were hardly in evidence.

At some point in the 1970s, one of my executive members told me that he had never seen a non-white firefighter in the city of Toronto. Of course, I did not know how many fires my colleague was in the habit of attending. But his observations obviously required further investigation. I set out, therefore, to learn how many non-white firefighters there actually were in Toronto.

Of course, the first problem was: How do you get that kind of information? I could just imagine that if we had telephoned the fire department and asked them directly, they would likely have told us to get lost. So, we came up with a ruse. Our researcher telephoned all twenty-seven fire stations then existing in Toronto and told them that he was the adult leader of a group of young people whom he wished to take on a visit to their respective fire stations. But, since he had some visible minorities in his group, he wanted to take them there when one of their visible minority firefighters was on duty. (For those who might balk at such deceptions, I am reminded of the Anglican priest who once told me that, when you are doing God's work, you are entitled to be as wise as a serpent.)

In the result, our survey established that, of the more than eleven hundred firefighters then employed in the city of Toronto, no more than two were from visible minority groups. I put this in a letter to the Toronto mayor and released it to the press. It made the front page of that day's *Globe and Mail*.

By the time I arrived in the office (between 10 and 11 a.m.), there was a message on my desk telling me that the mayor wanted to see me in his office at 1 p.m. that very day. When I showed up, the mayor appeared most responsive to my ideas for affirmative recruitment efforts within the visible minority communities.

I was also able to identify a systemic barrier that had been impeding the city's employment efforts. At one time, those who wanted to be firefighters telephoned to city hall and had their names put on a special list. On the basis of the length of time a person had been on the list, the personnel people would attempt to fill vacancies as they arose. The problem with this approach is that immigrants suffered an obvious handicap: they wouldn't have been in the country long enough to establish the requisite seniority on the list. Thus, we were able to come up with an example of a discriminatory effect in situations where there was no necessary evidence of a discriminatory intent. It was a situation of an unreasonable recruitment policy producing an inequitable consequence. That had to change.

At the very least, of course, the city could undertake to post publicly all employment vacancies as they emerged. Such a measure would ensure that competitions for job openings could be conducted on a level playing field. We also recommended a number of outreach efforts the city could adopt so that a multiplicity of racial and ethnic groups would learn of job opportunities and be encouraged to come forward. My understanding is that the city, in fact, acted positively on a number of our proposals.

As the years went on, I pushed for an expansion of outreach efforts to ensure a greater level of non-white participation throughout the economy—particularly in places where their involvement appeared to be virtually non-existent. And, almost every time that we approached government to be more vigorous and imaginative with its outreach efforts, we came up with newsworthy material to bolster our recommendations.

In the late 1970s, for example, we conducted a survey of some five hundred jobs in the banks of Kenora, Fort Francis, and Sault Ste. Marie. Despite the large population of aboriginals living in those areas, only two of the five hundred bank jobs were held by people of native origin. And one of them was part-time. The obvious question, of course, was how in the world could we get such information. The idea is always to make it look as though you are investigating for something else. So, we talked to bank managers and personnel officials and told them that we were interested in finding out just where native people were inclined to work. By making our survey look as though we were interested in the choices made by aboriginals rather than the preferences exercised by employers, we found it much easier to get the information we were seeking.

In the case of the corporate sector, we looked at promotions that were announced with pictures in the *Financial Post* for the year 1976. In all, we examined more than 1,900 photographs of this kind. Even when we excluded those pictures that left us unsure of racial characteristics, there were still more than 1,900 photographs left. In the result, only 6 of those jobs went to visible minorities. In a 1991 survey of 1,200 jobs in Sudbury and Sault Ste. Marie retail establishments, we found that, despite large aboriginal populations in the area, only 3 such jobs were held by native people. Significantly, the places surveyed had at least 100 employees and a number of them had as many as 300 employees. In a group of such establishments that included more than 850 employees, there was not a single native job holder.

All of this material found its way into letters, briefs, and presentations that CCLA made to cabinet ministers, legislative committees, and human rights commissions at both the federal and provincial levels. They helped to fuel our ongoing program to expand job opportunities for visible minorities. We called on governments and employers to post job openings in the minority press, insert a racial equality pledge in their general advertising, and even offer financial incentives to various minority group organizations for seeking out qualified occupants to fill the available jobs.

We pointed out that such proposals could comfortably coexist with a ban on reverse discrimination. CCLA also acknowledged that, in certain situations, even numerical goals could be acceptable. For such purposes, however, the failure to fulfill any numerical goal should not automatically result in liability; it should simply mean that the employer would then have the onus to justify the selections that were made. Admittedly, this proposal would shift the traditional onus. I was not, however, about to lose any sleep over it. After all, the employers would have the relevant information. They would know why they chose the employees they did. To this extent, we agreed with the proponents of affirmative action that the human rights legislation then in place had proved inadequate for the purpose of achieving greater equality.

In the early 1990s, I became engaged in a human rights controversy, miles from Ontario. I received a telephone call from an old friend of mine who was then the president of the British Columbia Federation of Labour. Because of my involvement with human rights commissions, he was inviting me to be one of the speakers at a protest rally in Vancouver. The Social Credit government of that province had just introduced legislation to demolish much of the existing welfare state. One of the proposed measures involved the virtual gutting of the BC Human Rights Commission. By way of purporting to answer its critics, the BC government declared that it was seeking to accomplish nothing more than it had undertaken to do in the recent BC election campaign.

Some forty thousand people showed up to participate in the rally. While my speech readily acknowledged the government's campaign promise to institute widespread cuts in social services, I replied that "there are cuts and there are cuts." Then came my punchline: "A mandate for circumcision is not a mandate for castration." That crack wound up in the media. I was especially pleased that it made the widely read newspaper column written by Allan Fotheringham. While the rhetoric on our side played well, the political responses were not as favourable. At the time, the right-wing Social Creditors had the votes and our side did not. This reminds me of some dark humour that emerged following the Spanish Civil War. Left-leaning people would often say, "Our side may have lost the war, but we had the best songs."

Over the years, racial problems continued to strike. Not infrequently, they became especially acute in relation to the police. During an eighteen-month period, at the end of the 1980s and the beginning of the 1990s, three unarmed black youngsters were shot by the Toronto police. At around that time, the Donald Marshall Inquiry in Nova Scotia revealed how blacks and native people received a different kind of justice from what was available to affluent whites. In Manitoba, further double standards came to light between the police and aboriginal people. A task force on racism appointed by the Ontario government revealed that in significant sectors of the community the police were quick to harass and slow to assist the non-white citizens of that province. While I was on the job, CCLA registered on all of these issues—through a combination of briefs, letters, and personal appearances. On one such occasion, I authored a piece in the *Toronto Star* in which I called for an independent audit system to address these systemic issues that had surfaced in our various police forces.[2]

In the early 1990s, a racial issue of a somewhat different kind afflicted our community. It concerned the plans for a theatrical production of the musical *Show Boat* at the North York Centre for the Performing Arts in Toronto. In one editorial after another, Arnold A. Auguste, the publisher of the black newspaper *Share*, focused on the fact that the author of the play, the producer of the version coming to Toronto, and the North York mayor slated to welcome the production were all Jewish. In view of everything the Jews had suffered, Auguste wrote, how could they of all people be so insensitive to the feelings of blacks? Whenever he was criticized for the way he harped on this theme, Auguste would reply with the irrelevant affirmation that those central characters in the drama were indeed Jewish.

As veterans of many campaigns in which blacks and Jews had collaborated to bring about human rights laws and the creation of enforcement mechanisms such as the human rights commissions, Dan Hill and I co-authored another piece in the *Toronto Star*. The following represents the centrepiece of the argument that our article made:

> It's one thing to protest the actions of those responsible for bringing *Show Boat* to Toronto. But it's another thing entirely to make their ethnic origin a factor in the protest. It's no more acceptable, because of some high profile examples, to make a Jewish issue out of *Show Boat* than it is to make a black issue out of crime.[3]

With such admonitions, Dan and I were attempting to contribute to the healing of the wounds that had been caused by the controversy and the restoration of the kind of black/Jewish collaboration that had characterized that earlier period in Ontario/Canadian history.

Another racial issue arose during the summer of 1990 when the Mohawk Indians set up barricades to prevent the town of Oka, Quebec, from physically encroaching on land that they claimed to own and had planned to use for burial grounds. The town of Oka was intending to build a golf course there. Despite all the pleading, petitioning, and presenting, it became apparent that the town authorities had finally planned to treat the land as theirs; a golf course on that land would serve as a *fait accompli* and forever resolve the dispute against the claim of the Mohawks. In order to prevent that from happening, the Mohawks, with masks on their faces and guns on their shoulders, set up the barricades and blocked public roads.

The affected authorities went to court and obtained an injunction ordering the Mohawks to dismantle the barricades. The Mohawks refused and, in doing so, they acted in defiance of the law. The Quebec police staged an early July raid for the purpose of enforcing the court order. In the ensuing melee, one of the officers was shot and killed.

I reacted to these events essentially in two ways: in the first place, I had CCLA petition the Quebec government to create a public inquiry around the police action. While acknowledging the obligation of the Mohawks to obey the law, I raised a number of issues concerning the behaviour of the police. Was a raid at that time necessary? Were there no alternative courses of action open to the authorities? Were there any attempts to negotiate with the Mohawks? In short, was there no viable alternative to what the police did?

In the second place, these events galvanized me to write a book that had been germinating in my mind for some time. There was a mindset in the community that I felt the need to question. People seemed to assume that there were only two courses of action available to aggrieved people like the Mohawks: employ polite but impotent entreaties or engage in militant law-breaking. My book, entitled *Uncivil Obedience*, was designed to outline a third alternative: how to raise hell *without* breaking the law.

Later in the summer, the Canadian army was called in to enforce order in the Oka dispute. Despite the army's apparent exercise of restraint at the inception of its involvement, there were reports of questionable behaviour on the part of some of the soldiers. According to at least one reporter, for example, the soldiers actually precipitated a clash by screaming obscenities at Mohawk women one night after the television cameras had been withdrawn. As a result of such reports, CCLA called upon the federal authorities, this time to order a public inquiry into the way the army executed its mandate.

But one of the developments that proved especially contentious was the apparent attempt on the part of the army to prevent communications between the reporters in the aboriginal compound and their editors outside. This time, *we* took the federal government to court. We filed a motion in federal court to keep the army from blocking these communications. A few days later, however, the court rejected our application for an injunction. Around that time, the Oka stand-off ended. For CCLA and me, the actions we took at that time were a way of trying to ensure fair play for the oft-mistreated aboriginal people. While we were unable to sort out the complexities of their land claims, we thought the least we could do was to promote greater equity in the processes by which the governments purported to deal with their various grievances.

In mid-June 1990, a ten-year-old grade 4 student in a Scarborough public school was removed from her class for wearing a T-shirt with a Palestinian flag and a slogan bearing the words: "We fight for our right." Soon afterwards, I wrote to the school board complaining of the school's action. In response to the explanation that the impugned T-shirt violated a ban on political statements advocating fighting and violence, I argued that this could prove to be a most unacceptable guideline. Given the refusal of Nelson Mandela to disavow violence, I contended that the policy could wind up prohibiting students from wearing T-shirts in support of the black South African leader. My letter attracted reams of publicity.

Unfortunately, the action we took precipitated a number of telephone calls from members of the public (including members of our organization) complaining of our involvement in the case. What stands out in my mind at this point is an admonition I had occasion to make to those CCLA staff members who were fielding these telephone calls. I told them that they were showing a tendency to be more apologetic for our actions than the situation legitimately warranted. I said that it would be better policy for us to be less defensive and more aggressive. I thought that we should have told those callers how unacceptable it was to make little children the targets of conflicts over the politics of the

Middle East. By the time that summer came to a close (September 20), the family of that Scarborough student received a letter of apology from the school board officials. In an editorial comment on the issue, the *Toronto Star* made special mention of the CCLA involvement.

In May 1985, I renewed the battle against Ontario's 1944 program of religious instruction in the public schools. Noting that the equality rights section of Canada's new *Charter of Rights and Freedoms* had just come into force in April of that year, I told the minister of education, by letter, that the religious instruction might well violate the anti-discrimination provisions of both the *Charter* and the *Ontario Human Rights Code*. The *Charter* guarantee for freedom of religion and conscience was also at issue. Instead of simply promoting *knowledge about* various religious ideologies, I argued that the Ontario program appears "to promote a *belief in* a particular religious ideology," namely Protestant Christianity.

I cited examples to prove my point. In Elgin County, the written curriculum instructed the teacher to point out that "only through the blood of Jesus can . . . sin be taken away." In Norfolk, the material counselled the teacher to help students "realize that a heavenly home is being prepared for all who believe and trust Jesus as Saviour." While acknowledging that such doctrines are sacred to many people, I contended that the place to promote them is in a church, home, or Sunday School, not in the public schools. "It is incontestably unfair in the setting of the universal public school system," I argued, "to teach the faith of many as though it were fact for all."

I also took a shot at the right of parents to exempt their kids from the contested instruction. My letter contended that, while necessary, exemption rights create a dilemma for dissenting parents: "They must choose between subjecting their children to indoctrination in a faith alien to their home and the embarrassing conspicuousness which often attends religious-motivated withdrawal from the classroom." My letter also advised the minister that CCLA had been urged by numbers of people to launch a court challenge of the impugned instruction. Accordingly, I called upon him to spare everyone the expense and rescind the regulations.

By the spring of 1985 when I renewed CCLA's campaign against Ontario's religious instruction, the situation had changed substantially.

Some of the larger school boards such as those in Toronto and North York had exercised their rights under the law and dropped the course entirely. Others had watered it down so that it was barely recognizable. Indeed, it appeared that my political battles of the 1960s had helped to win significant victories. By the mid-1980s, however, certain particularly egregious practices had survived, for example, the programs in Elgin and Norfolk counties. I realized, therefore, that we could not rest on the laurels our successes had brought. So, I stirred the pot once again.

Since no remedial action had been indicated by April 1986, CCLA launched a court challenge. We sought to restrain both Elgin County and the Ontario government from continuing the religious courses. In order to avoid a finding that we lacked the standing to pursue the case, I found us a partner: the Millington family of Elgin County. As adherents of the Baha'i faith, they were often at odds with the religious classes in Elgin County. After one of the classes had taught that non-Christians would go to Hell, for example, the Millingtons' ten-year-old daughter suffered nightmares that the devil was chasing her and that she was burning in Hell.

Notwithstanding such experiences, the Millingtons declined to exercise their right to withdraw the girl from the religious classes. The little girl insisted that her withdrawal from the classroom on such grounds would represent a worse experience for her than the nightmares had created. In the interests of maximizing the pressure on the Elgin County school board, I appeared before one of its meetings and, upon relating this story, I asked that, pending the end of the court case, Elgin County should seek exemption from the religious education program. The school board members asked no questions and made no comments. Their chairman simply said that the matter would be referred to a special committee that had been created to consider the matter. All in all, I think it's fair to say that the school board created a pretty pathetic spectacle on the night of my appearance there.

Despite the able advocacy of our special counsel, Robert Sharpe, the Divisional Court of the Ontario Supreme Court in a 2 to 1 decision in 1988 upheld the constitutionality of the impugned religious instruction. But another highly skilled special CCLA counsel, John B. Laskin, had more success in persuading a unanimous three-judge panel of the Ontario Court of Appeal to strike down the religious program as unconstitutional. At around the same time, the Ontario court struck down the program of prayers in the public schools.

Victory, at last! I had been fighting this issue for more than thirty years: first, on behalf of the Canadian Jewish Congress; then, on behalf of the Ethical Education Association, and finally, on behalf of the Canadian Civil Liberties Association. It felt damn good.

In addition to stopping the public schools from promoting religious faith, we have also tried to stop public funds from supporting religious schools. One of our first forays into this battle occurred in the mid-1980s. As a swan song before his impending retirement as the long-standing premier of Ontario, Bill Davis instigated the introduction of a bill to provide additional funding for the Roman Catholic separate schools. Until that point, the public funding of those schools terminated at the end of grade 10. The bill in question promised to provide such funding for grades 11, 12, and 13.

This government action threatened to activate the proverbial electric fan. Letters to the editor flooded the newspapers; protest meetings were organized; and public rallies were conducted. At the next provincial election, the Progressive Conservative Party lost its majority in the Ontario legislature.

My position and that of CCLA were against the bill. We didn't want to allow a bad situation to become even worse. In our view, public funds should not support religious segregation. We always thought it was unfortunate that the Confederation agreements and the Canadian Constitution guaranteed the survival of public funding for the Protestant separate schools in Quebec and the Catholic separate schools in Ontario. In our view, the consequent religious segregation deprived our community of an excellent opportunity to strengthen religious integration in our society. Mindful as we were of the interreligious tensions throughout the world, we thought that it would be wise social policy to head off such destructive developments at the earliest possible stage. And so, we believed that public funding should be available only to secular, integrated public schools.

This philosophy became an important factor in the way we participated in the public campaign. At one of the rallies against the bill where I was asked to speak, I became aware of an undercurrent of anti-Catholic hostility. I was determined to do whatever I could to ensure that this campaign did not wind up fuelling anti-Catholic bigotry. Upon approaching the microphone at the rally, my first words were, "We are not here to oppose the Catholic Church; we are here to support the public schools." I cannot describe the relief I felt when those words were greeted with substantial applause from the assembled protesters. Wherever I could, I tried to promote this theme as the dominant message of our campaign.

Soon after the bill was introduced into the legislature, the government established a reference on it in the Ontario Court of Appeal. There was a felt need to untangle the legal and constitutional arguments triggered by the bill. In a close 3 to 2 decision, the court ruled that the government's initiative was constitutional. At the time, I commented that, if the *Charter* is to fulfill its expectations, "the courts should construe the application of the freedoms in it broadly and the exceptions to such application narrowly; in this case, the court did it the other way around." In some respects, our side sustained an even greater defeat in the Supreme Court of Canada. That Court held that, under the Constitution, public funding until the end of grade 13 was not only allowed but it was also required.

A related issue in which I became embroiled during the mid-1990s concerned the campaign to acquire public funding for certain non-Catholic religious schools. An alliance of Jewish and fundamentalist Christian schools went to court claiming an entitlement to public funding equal to what was available for the Catholic separate schools. This case precipitated another disagreement I was to have with key segments of the Jewish community. Of course, I weighed in against the claim they were making.

To be fair, I must acknowledge the legitimacy of their case. In view of the funding available to the Catholic schools, there was a real argument that it was unfair to deprive other religious schools of comparable benefits. Indeed, when the issue had been entirely in the political arena, the Jewish schools said they were content to receive such funding only for the secular part of their curriculum. I must also acknowledge the substantial hardship faced by many families who had to pay full fare for their kids to attend their religious schools—in addition to their share of the tax load for the public schools.

On balance, however, I thought that the consequent situation would be worse if they received the funding they sought. The more religious groups that were able to get such funding, the more would likely be seeking and getting it. At some point, I feared that even numbers of mainstream Protestants would be impelled to open separate schools. As time went on, this could well transform the public schools into veritable "ghost towns." Ontario would then be faced with a completely balkanized school system. We could effectively lose the immense benefits that the public schools currently confer upon our society.

The *Toronto Star* reproduced my remarks to a press conference dealing with a related issue. My comments were published in a section called "Worth Repeating." The following is a much-abridged version of what appeared:

> When youngsters from diverse backgrounds play together in the schoolyard, work together in the classroom, and eat together in the cafeteria, they have the opportunity to develop habits of intergroup rapport and respect that could last a lifetime. . . . If we have learned anything from the terrible experiences of the 20th century, it is that intergroup tension is endemic to the human condition. . . . We should, therefore, do everything we can to shore up the instruments of tolerance in our community.[4]

At the end of my address, I called upon the government to eschew the public funding of religious schools.

Needless to say, CCLA intervened in court in opposition once more to the official Jewish position. While I had many arguments with Jewish friends about the position we adopted, this issue never quite elicited the hurt that accompanied what we did on hate propaganda. In the result, the Supreme Court of Canada ruled in late 1997 that the applicants had no constitutional entitlement to the funding they sought.

Another tactic adopted by the rather resourceful proponents of such public funding was an argument they made to the Human Rights Committee of the United Nations. In that forum, they enjoyed a little more success. In 1999, the Human Rights Committee declared that the funding scheme in Ontario constituted unacceptable discrimination. While such declarations were relatively unenforceable, they nevertheless exercised a level of moral influence. As might be expected, the media began to carry stories in which a number of people claimed that the way for Ontario to avoid the stigma of discrimination was to provide the non-Catholic religious schools with a significant level of public support.

This development exerted an irresistible pressure upon me. I simply had to answer the world body's de facto contention that CCLA was supporting a regime of religious discrimination. This was the time, I thought, for us, at long last, to register on the whole question at issue here. I consulted with a number of my colleagues in the leadership of CCLA and secured their endorsement for what I wanted to do. The next time the press called, I argued that the way Ontario should address this issue of religious discrimination was not to supply funding to the non-Catholic religious schools but rather to withdraw funding from the Catholic religious schools. In that way, CCLA finally registered on the main issue.

The next time that the funding issue surfaced in a big way was during the Ontario provincial elections, late in the first decade of the new millennium. John Tory, the leader of the Conservative Party, undertook that, if elected, he would provide public funding to the non-Catholic religious schools. All hell broke loose. The incumbent Liberal government immediately joined issue and ensured that those religious schools could not look forward to such public support. Numbers of community organizations—religious and otherwise—immediately jumped into the fray.

As expected, we at CCLA attempted to do our part. We became involved in the publication of a major advertisement in the *Toronto Star.* The ad consisted of a strong statement against the funding of non-Catholic religious schools and—even more important—endorsements from many eminent community leaders. Our supporters included a number of former moderators of the United Church, well-known former politicians, writers, and labour leaders. We made especially sure that the list included prominent Jewish names so that we could telegraph to the government and general public that the Jewish community was split on this issue. In that way, we attempted to dilute the impact of the Jewish support for such public funding.

Perhaps one of the most impressive names we were able to recruit was that of the first mayor of Thunder Bay, Saul Laskin. In addition to being a highly respected public figure, he was also well known and properly revered in the Jewish community. Of course, he was the younger brother of Canada's first Jewish chief justice: Bora Laskin. In this regard, I was particularly pleased to have been the one who recruited him. Although we had never met, we had a perfectly delightful conversation in both English and Yiddish. In fact, our telephone call wound up with a pledge I made to him that I would take him to an upcoming meeting of my Yiddish-speaking luncheon circle. Unfortunately, he died before I was able to make good on that promise.

While our ad probably made a substantial contribution to the political campaign against the funding proposal, it also provoked angry criticism. Among our critics in this regard was the *Jewish Tribune*, the organ of the B'nai Brith organization. An editorial in that publication rapped CCLA for its alleged hypocrisy in attacking the John Tory proposal but maintaining silence on the Catholic school question. As indicated, we had not been silent at all on the Catholic issue. I have already related how some years earlier, we had called for the abolition of Catholic school funding. At the time, I had to conclude that diligent research was not one of the positive traits enjoyed by the B'nai Brith organization.

Fortunately, the Tory initiative was defeated. We thought, however, that this would be a good opportunity to renew and repeat our opposition to the public funding of the Catholic schools. Of course, we could not include a statement of such opposition in the ad that responded to the John Tory proposal. Not all of our co-signatories to that ad were prepared, as we were, to take on the Catholic funding as well. But, a few days after the publication of the ad, CCLA, acting on its own, sent the education minister a brief outlining our objections to the funding of the additional religious schools and our arguments against the current funding of the Catholic schools. The gist of our position was that such funding could well undermine the public schools that serve such an important integrative function in our society. (Even if the withdrawal of public funding from the Catholic schools would have required a constitutional amendment, that already had happened with such schools in the province of Quebec.)

At this time, the media response was substantial. Both my colleague Noa Mendelsohn Aviv and I were interviewed by numerous newspapers, television shows, and radio programs, and we appeared in several public debates.

Unfortunately, the increased media attention was not accompanied by significantly more votes. During the melee that greeted our involvement in the debate, it became increasingly clear that we were not likely to win an early victory on the Catholic school question. At that point, I began to fashion a somewhat different strategy. Instead of putting all our eggs in the basket of an all-out political victory, we should attempt to nibble rather than to bite. The Catholic schools are vulnerable in a number of other ways. We might enjoy some success by way of piecemeal attacks on some of their practices.

In 1999, we intervened in court against an attempt by supporters of Catholic school funding to strike down a section of the Ontario *Education Act* that would deny to Catholic schools the right to prefer Catholics in their employment policies. The section had stipulated that all their employees, regardless of creed, should be treated equally as long as they respected Catholic doctrine. But an Ontario superior court judge struck down that section as incompatible with the Canadian Constitution. The judge effectively ruled that Catholic schools may give employment preference to Catholics. This judgment was upheld by the Ontario Court of Appeal and the Supreme Court of Canada refused to hear it. Thus, I was unable to succeed in my first attempt to invoke the new strategy of whittling away at the Catholic system.

Before I go very much further, I should be careful to point out that CCLA was always prepared to defend the right of religious institutions to use religious criteria in the selection of their employees. We drew the line, however, at those religious institutions that were receiving public money. Our argument was that, as a condition of obtaining public funds, they should be obliged to comply with public standards. And so it was with the Catholic schools. The moment they stopped accepting public funds, we were prepared to defend those discriminatory practices.

The next case of "whittling" arose in 2002. A gay student at a publicly funded Catholic high school won a preliminary injunction allowing him, over his school's objections, to bring his boyfriend as his date to the school prom. In *Fab* magazine I was quoted as saying that it was wrong for school authorities to reject one of their students on the basis of sexual orientation. I declared that "if Catholic school boards have religious practices that may be at variance with public standards of fair play, then they ought to confine their financing to their own sources."

I am happy to report that my successors at CCLA have given every appearance of continuing to apply this strategy. Noa Mendelsohn Aviv, the organization's equality rights director, has shaken things up with her support for "gay-straight alliances" in some of the tax-supported Catholic separate schools.

I hope that CCLA's "whittling" strategy continues. Exert pressure for a greater acceptance of gay lifestyles in one school and more openness to pro-choice arguments in another school. If our people can succeed often enough in whittling down or even eliminating some of the more discriminatory practices at these schools, there could come a time, at least in some schools, in which their distinctive traits might be effectively lost. In such situations, those schools could become either less religiously Catholic or less publicly financed. Several nibbles have the capacity to inflict a bite.

My secularizing campaign also reached beyond Ontario. In late November 1997, I testified on behalf of CCLA before the joint parliamentary committee on the Constitution. At issue was a proposed amendment to the Canadian Constitution which, among other things, would relieve Newfoundland of the obligation to finance seven denominational school systems and require the new public schools to provide "courses in religion, not specific to a religious denomination." My testimony expressed support for ending the public financing of the religious schools and an admonition about the kind of religious material that might be involved in the new public schools. I repeated to the committee the key distinction that CCLA had made on a number of previous occasions, "It is perfectly permissible for the public schools to promote *knowledge about* many religions [but not] a *belief in* any particular religion." The amendment passed.

Although we worked to reduce the intrusion of religion in some situations, we tried to protect it in other situations. The British Columbia College of Teachers refused to certify the teaching program at Trinity Western University, a private Christian university. According to the college, the university's code of conduct, which requires students to sign a pledge not to be involved in homosexual activities, predisposed its graduates to discriminate against gay students. CCLA took the position that, *by itself,* the mere signing of a pledge to personally abstain from homosexual activities is no reason to conclude that such signatories will discriminate against gay pupils; teachers should be assessed according to their conduct, not such beliefs.

Moreover, since Trinity Western did not get public money, we believed that it should be free to deny admission to those who did not share its religious philosophy. As our court factum declared, "Unless religious institutions can exclude non-adherents, religious and cultural pluralism would be impossible, and minority religions would be particularly vulnerable." To my colleagues and me, the presence or absence of public funding was the material issue.

Fortunately, the Supreme Court of Canada upheld the arguments that we made. This included siding with us on the issue of whether the College of Teachers could apply *Charter* principles in its decisions. The lower courts agreed with the university that the college had no business using the *Charter* in this way. On this branch of the case, CCLA differed. We argued that the college was right to apply the *Charter* but wrong in the way it did so. It felt good to win all around.

On a number of occasions, we went to bat for adherents of the Sikh religion. In one case, Via Rail had twice removed a Sikh law student from its trains. This action responded to passenger complaints about his kirpan, a ceremonial dagger which his religion requires him to carry. In a letter to the then transport minister of Canada, I questioned the "selective" nature of the railway's concerns for safety. After all, I noted, "Youthful passengers carry hockey sticks, skates, and baseball bats when they travel by train. It does not require an extreme exercise of imagination to envision how such instruments could readily become weapons." I also noted that first-class passengers are provided with eating utensils that often include knives. As I argued, "Does Via management believe that the ability to pay first-class fares makes these passengers a more acceptable risk?" Moreover, kirpans could be sheathed in such a way that they couldn't be readily dislodged.

In the Supreme Court of Canada, we went to bat for a teenage Sikh boy who was suspended from a Quebec school for carrying his kirpan on school property. Our side won both times. Via Rail changed its policy and the Supreme Court of Canada ruled that the boy could wear his kirpan in school.

Incredibly, there was also a controversy regarding the Sikh turbans. While the kirpan arguably raised an issue of safety, the turban involved nothing more than aesthetics. Nevertheless, it took some time before the government of Canada agreed to allow Sikh members of the RCMP to wear their turbans. Significantly, the RCMP responded faster and more readily to this Sikh claim. As for the government, I publicly accused it of having "dithered irresponsibly" before accepting the "perfectly sensible recommendation" to let the Sikh officers wear their turbans.

But our office was flooded with mail and telephone calls bitterly attacking our stand. The following are some excerpts from our mail:

- "Sikhs and their turbans in the RCMP? No! No! What kind of motley crew will we finish up with?"
- "Why is society forcing me to wear a turban? . . . I have the right not to be subjected to any manifestations of Sikhism in my dealings with society."
- "I think it is disgusting that our government officials have been pressured for fear of appearing racist, to the demands of this religious group!"
- "Canada is nothing but a bastardized country now and your [sic] helping it to 'look' like one too!"
- "I am sick and tired of having our laws used to defend foreigners."

At some point after I had absorbed this kind of invective in our Ontario office, I happened to be visiting Calgary. There, I was invited to appear on an open-line radio show on the subject of turbans and the RCMP. I started by taking a very aggressive position. When the microphone was handed to me, I stated openly and forthrightly that, in my view, there was nothing of redeeming merit to be said against allowing Sikh officers to wear their turbans. I made it very clear that I was raring to do battle with anyone who had the temerity to advance such an unwarranted position. I was surprised (and perhaps a little disappointed) that none of the callers took me on. As I recall, they were all on my side. What an anti-climax! Needless to say, the government of Canada finally relented and the Sikh officers were allowed to wear turbans.

In late 2001, we defended a born-again Christian printer against an accusation that he had breached the *Ontario Human Rights Code* by refusing certain services to a gay and lesbian organization. Earlier, a board of inquiry had held that he was guilty of discrimination on the basis of sexual orientation, fined five thousand dollars, and ordered to provide the requested services. Our argument was that, under the *Code*, he was required to provide such services to gay persons but not to gay causes.

By the same logic, we reasoned that gay printers should be entitled to deny services to fundamentalist religious groups who denigrate homo- sexuality. Similarly, a black printer may not refuse potential customers simply because they are white but may refuse those who are promoting white supremacy. In this way, we hoped to champion both freedom of conscientious objection and the integrity of the *human rights code*.

SEXUAL LIBERATION

During my time with the CCLA, our society underwent profound changes. One of the most noteworthy involved the rights of women. No longer content with being submissive housewives or subservient stenographers, a growing number of women rebelled. They sought more meaningful work, a better quality of education, and an end to discrimination.

These changes comported well with the philosophical orientation that I had been developing. I found myself in enthusiastic agreement with the direction in which the women's movement was heading. Not surprisingly, therefore, CCLA, during my watch, took on some feminist causes. Indeed, I believe that we got involved in at least one set of such issues even before any women's organizations did.

Consider, for example, the plight of impoverished women seek- ing welfare assistance. When we first became involved in these issues during the late 1960s, most jurisdictions observed what came to be called the "spouse in the house" rule. That is, those seeking or getting welfare were subject to complete disqualification if they lived with a member of the opposite sex "as husband and wife." The $64 question, of course, concerned the meaning of this epithet. In practical terms, it often meant that the meagre income of applicants and recipients would be put at risk if they shared their premises with lovers. Women were disproportionately affected.

The injustice of it infuriated me. Disadvantaged women wound up severely penalized for daring to enjoy the kind of warm relationship to which most of us aspire. And, even before they were cut off, these women were subjected to the indignity of intrusive investigations and embar- rassing interrogations. Welfare officials reportedly looked through the homes of their welfare clients, checking to see whether there was any evidence of a male cohabitant. In those situations where such cohabitation was apparent, it was not unknown for the welfare clients to be questioned about relationships with children, parents, teachers, and religious institutions. There were even reports that some welfare officials evinced an interest in their clients' sleeping arrangements.

The inevitable question was: "Why?" The rule was so unnecessary. Critics like me asserted that we would not likely have objected if the welfare authorities had reduced the *amount* of welfare assistance to those who were cohabiting. Suppose, for example, the deserted or separated wife was living with a girlfriend or an old aunt? In such circumstances, it would not have been unreasonable—unless there was evidence to the contrary—to assume that a cohabitant, male or female, was contributing something for food and rent. But, if the cohabitants were not legally obligated to provide the kind and continuity of support that spouses generally owe one another, the complete cancellation of welfare benefits should have been out of the question. (Mutual support obligations could have been triggered by certain family laws in those situations where a man and woman cohabited for a few years and/or had children together.)

My colleagues and I were so incensed by the unfairness of this rule that we continued to protest—from the late 1960s when we first got involved until the early part of the twenty-first century when the Ontario Court of Appeal, with us intervening, finally struck it down as unconstitutional. Our tactics involved the writing and publicizing of letters to those in authority, the presentation of briefs in delegations to the cabinet ministers in charge, the conduct of a nationwide survey, scores of media interviews, newspaper articles, a number of court interventions, and a key section on it in my book, *When Freedoms Collide*. I think it's fair to say, therefore, that we in CCLA were not simply expressing a dissent; we were fighting like hell.

One such tactic proved to be especially significant: our March 1970 delegation to the Ontario welfare minister, John Yaremko. I got the bright idea that our impact would be considerably strengthened by the participation of our then president, the Honourable J. Keiller MacKay. A former superior court justice and a former Lieutenant-Governor of Ontario, Mr. MacKay embodied status and prestige. It appealed much to my sense of drama to have this pillar of the establishment going to bat for the poorest people in society.

The message was not lost on the press. We got lots of media coverage, including the major front-page story in the *Toronto Star*. The headline for the day, lifted from our brief, declared that, in important respects, people on welfare were being treated worse than those suspected of the most heinous crimes. While our brief dealt with a range of welfare issues, it included a special section on the "spouse in the house" rule. Also of particular interest to impoverished women were our proposals for reducing the oft-invoked insistence that, in order to obtain the help they sought, deserted wives would have to take their husbands to court.

In the early 1970s, CCLA was confronted with another issue that had become central to the movement for women's liberation: abortion. At that time, the law denied the right to obtain an abortion unless a specially designated therapeutic abortion committee determined that the procedure was needed in order to save the woman's life or preserve her health. A growing number of women recoiled at the idea that any-one but themselves should be empowered to exercise such control over their bodies. As far as they were concerned, it was an indignity to sus-tain such interference with their physical autonomy.

I have little doubt that the overwhelming number of CCLA board members were then—as they are now—in favour of a woman's right to choose. But there was then a serious impediment to our ability to register publicly in this way. Two key people, our president John Nel-ligan and our honorary president Emmett Hall, were opposed to our position. Despite these differences, Nelligan, a pillar of the Ottawa bar, and Hall, a former justice of the Supreme Court of Canada, were stal-wart civil libertarians who had demonstrated a genuine loyalty to our organization. But I was afraid that if we publicly expressed a strong pro-choice position, there could have been a serious split in our ranks. It could have proved very costly for us to lose both a president and such a distinguished honorary president in one shot. After having been on the job only a bare few years, I very much wished to avoid such an outcome.

I began trying to craft a statement that could command an inter-nal consensus. After several attempts, however, I became increasingly convinced that no such statement was possible if it aspired to do more than pussyfoot around the issues. I became very upset at the possible realization that I would have left the forthrightness of the Labour Committee to be a milquetoast at CCLA.

A wise insight that I had imbibed some years earlier surfaced in my psyche at that point. If otherwise like minds cannot agree on substance, they might well come together on process. What we knew about the operations of the therapeutic abortion committees suggested that they were havens of arbitrariness, inconsistency, and chaos. I feared nevertheless that, even if I could forge a consensus on our board to attack these committees, a statement thrown into the political arena could leave us vulnerable to some embarrassing questions. We might easily have been asked, for example, what would we propose to replace the system then in existence? Such questions could have smoked out the differences among the members of our board. I concluded, therefore, that, in the political arena, a statement of this kind could be too risky.

Then, I hit upon what turned out to be the life-saving idea: intervene in court. At the time, Dr. Henry Morgentaler, the Montreal abortionist, was being prosecuted and his case was soon slated to be heard in the Supreme Court of Canada. Why not, I thought, intervene in the case simply to argue that he should be acquitted because the therapeutic abortion committees infringed the *Canadian* (Diefenbaker) *Bill of Rights*? That was a line of argument we could vigorously pursue in the context of a court case. As such, we wouldn't need definitive answers on the ultimate shape of our abortion laws and we would not look like pussyfooters to anybody.

The CCLA board was quite taken with the idea. But we faced a rather formidable drawback. Interventions in court had always been a rarity in Canada. In the few cases that we knew about, there was unanimous consent among the contesting parties to allow the intervention. It soon became apparent that the Quebec prosecutor would likely be apoplectic at the prospect of an intervention from us. Nevertheless, we soldiered on. In my view, our tactical objectives regarding the abortion issue could be served even if we attempted without success to intervene in the Morgentaler case.

In the company of a few others who had also hit upon the idea, our counsel presented our intervention application to the then chief justice of Canada, Bora Laskin, my old teacher. We all made news. Despite the vigorous objections of the Quebec prosecutor, Laskin granted intervener status to a number of the applicants, beginning with CCLA. I do believe that was the first time in Canadian history that outsiders were allowed to intervene in a court case, without the consent of all parties.

In order to embellish our factum and take advantage of the excellent platform provided by Supreme Court cases, we conducted a survey of the policies and practices at a number of therapeutic abortion committees across the country. As a result, our factum was able to document what was actually happening on the ground in several communities. The survey revealed wildly disparate conduct on the part of those who were supposed to be exercising a judicial function. Two examples come to mind. Certain committees made it a practice to reject abortion applications if the woman had requested such permission on some previous occasions. Another committee reported that it would reject an application from some women unless they agreed to a tubal ligation. Our factum did not fail to raise the question: What do such criteria have to do with the woman's life or health?

In this, our first experiment with such court interventions, we wanted to make the best impression we could on the court, the press, and the public. So we asked high-profile lawyer Eddie Greenspan to act as our special counsel for these purposes. Even way back in the early 1970s, he was already a veteran of many court cases. He also brought with him his own considerable legal talent and a deft way with the press. I should add that he not only acted without fee but he also absorbed the expenses himself.

I remember being particularly moved at the time by the behaviour of our anti-abortion president, John Nelligan. Being the good civil libertarian that he is, he objected strongly to what we were learning about the therapeutic abortion committees. Despite his own posture on the substance of the abortion law, he nevertheless insisted that those administering that law had to use fair procedures. On one occasion, I can even recall a suggestion from him that we attempt to recruit some women to cooperate with us in an attempt to test some of the therapeutic abortion committees. Nelligan's involvement demonstrated the success of the CCLA policy. We united on the process even though we were divided on the substance. It's not without significance, however, that the media began to identify us as a "pro-choice" organization. For political purposes, image was the dominant consideration. Thus, on the abortion issue in the early 1970s, I was able simultaneously to have and eat my cake.

Although that court intervention helped me to preserve intact the unity of my organization, it was not able to succeed in the four corners of the Morgentaler case. The court rejected our arguments that the therapeutic abortion committees violated Canada's statutory bill of rights. Morgentaler himself was convicted. Of course, all this occurred in the early 1970s, years before the adoption of the *Canadian Charter of Rights and Freedoms*. In the late 1980s, after the proclamation of the *Charter*, another prosecution of Henry Morgentaler found its way to the Supreme Court of Canada. This time, the Court held that the therapeutic abortion committees did indeed violate the *Charter*. In that case, the Court struck down the abortion law and Canada was left without any criminal restrictions on the decision to have an abortion.

Despite the limited nature of our success and our objectives in the early Morgentaler case, we began to realize that we had discovered something with that experience in court interventions. We recognized that such interventions could be a useful vehicle for advancing the objectives of the organization. From that point on, going to court in this way became an integral part of the CCLA program. By the time of my retirement, we had intervened in almost one hundred cases. I know also that my successors have kept up a steady stream of court interventions. It's almost amusing to realize that this part of our program began as a way of getting me out of a tight political spot.

Following the court decision that struck down our last abortion law, the government of Canada made an attempt to re-criminalize the procedure. A bill introduced by the then justice minister Doug Lewis stipulated that abortions could be allowed if a doctor considered the physical, mental, or psychological health of the woman to be threatened by the pregnancy.

According to a Canadian Press story at the time, "Alan Borovoy . . . led a parade of witnesses" before the Senate committee that was vetting the bill after it passed in the House.[5] Focusing especially on the hopelessness of assessing mental conditions, I cited studies showing that psychiatrists differed widely in their diagnosis of mental illness. In one such study, two skilled psychiatrists attempted to diagnose twenty mental patients for depression. They both agreed that six of the patients were suffering from clinical depression, but they *disagreed* as to which six. I told the committee that much of psychiatric diagnosis was effectively a "medical lottery." I urged the committee, therefore, to reject the government bill as unfair.

After the pummelling that a number of us administered, the Senate became deadlocked and the government finally decided to withdraw the bill. So far, no replacement has surfaced. I think it's appropriate to observe that the heavens have not fallen over the state of our abortion laws.

By this time, CCLA had come all the way out of the closet with a substantively pro-choice consensus. Emmett Hall had died and John Nelligan had been succeeded as CCLA president many times over. In my testimony before the parliamentary committee and at a press conference convened by the National Action Committee on the Status of Women, I argued that, instead of dwelling on the mysteries of embryonic life, our society should focus on the limitations of governmental power. Even if the fetus could be considered a "person," it did not follow that such a "person" should be able to invoke the coercive power of the state to keep it within the body of someone who doesn't want it there. By way of summary, I declared, "compulsory organ sharing is repugnant to democratic principles."

This was also the position that we took in the case of Chantal Daigle, a Quebec woman whose estranged husband had obtained a temporary injunction to restrain her from having an abortion. Through the very talented John B. Laskin, our special counsel who intervened for us in the case, we argued that whatever interests the father of the fetus might have, they did not extend to controlling what the mother did with her body. Fortunately, the Supreme Court was with us.

One Sunday after the controversy had subsided, I received a telephone call at home from a man who identified himself as "Henry Morgentaler." Until that point, he and I had never met and we had never talked to one another. I responded to his self-identification with the words, "What took you so long to call?" From there, we went on to have a delightful conversation. Not surprisingly, we wound up talking Yiddish to each other. He had called to recruit me to speak to a training clinic he was conducting for doctors. I accepted and, in fact, did participate as he had requested.

Following the clinic, we had a number of lunches together and I had the privilege of taking him to one of my Yiddish-speaking luncheon circles. In person, I found him to be a lot of fun. Indeed, he exhibited a much keener sense of humour than a number of his supporters did. He good-naturedly teased me, for example, because of CCLA's defence of those who were picketing his abortion clinic. Some of his supporters, however, were not nearly as good-natured about the CCLA position.

In any event, I think it's fair to say that CCLA made a significant contribution to the liberal state of Canada's current law on abortion.

Another issue that angered equality-seeking women was the potential ordeal they anticipated, if they ever dared to complain of having been the victim of a sexual assault. One such ordeal would have been perpetrated upon them by the very legal system to which they had turned for redress. Not infrequently, the female complainant in a sexual assault case was subjected to a demeaning inquisition on her sexual history. An apparently deliberate tactic of many defence lawyers was to portray the woman as a tramp whose testimony could not be trusted.

Understandably, a growing number of women protested this indignity that the justice system kept foisting on them. As they saw things, it wasn't enough that they were so often casualties of sexual assault; they could also be made to endure public humiliation if they complained about it. The upshot of their protests and campaigns was an amendment to the *Criminal Code* that severely restricted explorations in court of any sexual interactions the complainant may have had with anyone other than the accused.

In the mid-1980s, the accused in a sexual assault prosecution called upon the court to strike down this "rape-shield" law as a violation of the procedural fairness required by the *Canadian Charter of Rights and Freedoms*. As a frequent intervener in *Charter* cases by then, we at CCLA realized the need for us to resolve the difficult dilemma posed by the impugned law. As the *Globe and Mail* commented at the time, if this law were struck down, women would again be exposed "to the kind of persecutional questioning that occurred in the past." If it were not struck down, "innocent people [might well] go to prison."

In an attempt to resolve the dilemma, CCLA convened a board meeting in November of 1986. It's not without significance that the majority of those attending the meeting were women. It's also noteworthy then that, with only one dissent, the board decided CCLA would support the constitutional challenge. The consensus at the meeting was that the rape-shield law created too many fetters on the ability of accused persons effectively to defend themselves.

But my colleagues and I remained uncomfortable over the outcome that a successful constitutional challenge could produce. While the overwhelming number of us favoured getting rid of the rape-shield law then in place, we also wanted to prevent a return to the "bad old days" when female complainants could so readily and unfairly be pilloried in court. We thought it would be wise, therefore, to petition the government for action in the legislative arena. Accordingly, I wrote to the minister of justice in December 1986. Warning of the very real prospect that the rape-shield law then in existence would be ruled unconstitutional, I argued that a legislative solution was the best way to go. To that end, my letter even made specific proposals as to how a better balance could be struck between fairness for the accused and privacy for the complainant.

Not surprisingly, the government failed to act on our recommendations. In consequence, the rape-shield law lingered longer as a monument to Canada's capacity for injustice. In addition to the constitutional challenge that had inspired our board meeting of November 1986, our letter to the minister of December 1986, and the contemporaneous comments of the *Globe and Mail*, there was finally a decision by the Supreme Court of Canada in August 1991. To a great extent, the Court adopted the approach that had been advocated by the CCLA. The rape-shield law was struck down as an unconstitutional infringement of fairness for the accused but guidelines were promulgated to ensure reasonable privacy for the complainant.

The CCLA presentation before the Court, my comments to the media, and my subsequent writings on the subject pointed out myriads of ways that the law could suppress strongly probative evidence favourable to the accused. Suppose, we suggested, an accused claimed that his sexual interaction with the complainant was consensual but she attempted to extort money from him by threatening to charge him with rape if he refused to pay her a given sum of money? And suppose, upon hearing that she had done this on previous occasions, the accused sought to produce that history to the court? Under the rape-shield law we were challenging, this would have been impossible because it represented a previous, non-exempt sexual encounter with someone other than the accused. It should be clear, we in CCLA contended, that the suppression of such evidence could very well produce an unfair trial.

Numbers of feminist leaders reacted with fury. *Toronto Star* columnist Michele Landsberg, for example, denounced the above scenario as "male-invented" and "silly," while flatly asserting that "women don't falsely report rape."[6] These comments appeared in a column that bitterly attacked Justice Beverley McLachlin who wrote the Supreme Court decision and me and my colleagues at CCLA for making such arguments before the Court. Feminist leaders such as former CCLA board member Doris Anderson and Christy Jefferson of the Women's Legal Action Fund (LEAF) also took shots at CCLA. Many others joined in. Some fifty CCLA members openly resigned from the organization and one could only speculate about how many other members followed suit without telling us.

It may be of interest to note that a real American case some years earlier addressed a situation in which an accused man tried to introduce evidence that the complainant charged him because he had ended her sexual affair with his son. A similar scenario emerged in a subsequent Quebec case.[7] If our feminist adversaries had had their way, the accused men in those real cases would have been deprived of the right to effectively impugn the motives of their accusers.

A key component of the Supreme Court judgment—and the CCLA presentation to the Court—seemed to get buried in all the angry exchanges. The Court judgment promulgated a number of guidelines that would continue to impose *some* restrictions on exposing the complainant's sexual history. And no one mentioned that CCLA had urged the Court to do it. Indeed, CCLA was the only party before the court that had addressed, in this way, the rights of the accused *and* of the complainant. Neither the prosecution, nor the defence, nor the feminist interveners had taken such a position. Ironically, our much-criticized organization might have actually helped to ensure that some amount of the rape-shield law survived the constitutional challenge. Indeed, we may have contributed more to the achievement of this objective than did the feminist organizations that were attacking us.

Our presentation before the Court had identified some of the recurring fallacies on the basis of which the rape trials of the past had subjected the complainants to those demeaning ordeals. One of those fallacies was the assumption that women who were sexually promiscuous were also ethically promiscuous and, therefore, not believable. The other fallacy was that women who agreed to have sex on a number of other occasions were more likely to have consented in the case of the accused. We asked the Court expressly to disallow evidence of past sexual conduct to the extent that it was influenced by those assumptions. And we also called for a procedural hurdle: Before evidence of past sexual encounters could be admitted, the trial judge would have to be persuaded of its probative value in a special *in camera* hearing convened for that purpose. As indicated, the Court bought the thrust of our proposal.

During the course of the controversy, I wrote the new justice minister Kim Campbell and recommended some beefing up of the privacy safeguards for complainants. As usual, I released the letter to the press. A few days later, I was shocked to learn that I was again the target of barbs in Michele Landsberg's column. She accused me of "late blooming," implying that I was making these concessions to the feminist perspective in order to reduce the heat to which CCLA and I had been subjected. I must say that the "late blooming" crack really pissed me off. After all, my letter represented the continuation of a position we had adopted before the courts and that I had expressed in a letter to a predecessor justice minister some *five years earlier*.[8]

The day that the column appeared, my secretary buzzed my office to tell me that Barbara Frum was on the telephone. Upon picking up the phone, I said, "So, it's my foul-weather friend." I knew that she was calling to express her solidarity with me, in an attempt to console me for the attack I had sustained in Landsberg's column. Although I very much appreciated Barbara's overture, I didn't really need it. I wasn't so much threatened by the Landsberg column, as I was angered by it. In any event, that gesture was so typical of Barbara Frum. She never failed to call if she remotely suspected that a friend of hers might be hurting. I readily describe us as "friends" in part, because I played a very important role in her life: some thirty years earlier, I had introduced her and her husband.

While Barbara Frum was distinguishing herself as perpetually thoughtful and compassionate, some other colleagues were noteworthy for their courage. Louise Arbour, then a criminal law professor at Osgoode Hall, took on the feminist establishment by acting as CCLA's pro-bono counsel at the Ontario Court of Appeal stage of the rape-shield challenge and June Callwood stood up to her long-time feminist colleagues during the political polemics on the issue. CCLA treasurer, Elaine Slater, also stepped into the arena with her impeccable credentials as an egalitarian activist (she had worked for the Congress of Racial Equality in the United States). Slater wrote to those CCLA members who had resigned, telling them that, as a grandmother of both males and females, she was especially concerned about the fairness of sexual assault trials to both genders. It was not easy for any of these women who surfaced so boldly on the issue but, despite the hostility it engendered, they were prepared to do it anyway.

Our experience with the rape-shield law is important not only for what it achieved in making sexual assault trials fairer, but also for what it demonstrated about the role of interveners in court cases. It showed how the justice system can benefit from having perspectives other than those of the main parties. Our experience in that case provided helpful fuel for our ongoing efforts to win greater acceptance for the involvement of outsiders.

The issue of employment equity (or affirmative action by which it has been known in the United States) served both to unite and divide CCLA and mainstream feminists. We were united over the need to improve upon the anti-discrimination performance of Canada's human rights laws and commissions. Despite more than three decades of laws—and full-time enforcement of those laws—against ethnic and gender discrimination in employment, for example, sizeable pockets of job inequity were persisting. Taking the position that human rights commissions must no longer be content to "sit on their formal jurisdictions waiting for complaints to come along," we began to urge their involvement in "self-initiated" efforts to promote the employment of disadvantaged groups in areas where such groups had been underutilized.

By itself, that position was acceptable to our allies in the mainstream feminist movement. The issue of numerical goals, however, was another matter. The employment equity plan at the Ontario College of Art dramatized the differences that developed. Despite apparent parity of talent in the available job pool, women had hardly made a dent in achieving academic positions at the college. Thus, there was an understandable lack of confidence in those responsible for hiring at that institution. The solution, according to mainstream feminists, was to provide that, for the ensuing decade (the 1990s), the preference would go to women in *all* jobs vacated by retirement. Even then, as some proponents of the plan acknowledged, women would have only 37 percent of the jobs — still a distance away from the stated objective of 50 percent.

In my 1999 book, the *New Anti-Liberals*, in briefs, and in press commentary, I charged that the plan inevitably discriminated against men. Rationalizations poured into the political arena. Since men traditionally had the advantage, it was contended that equity required — or at least allowed — favouring women for a while. According to a cabinet minister in Ontario's Bob Rae NDP government of the early nineties (Brian Charlton of management board), this advantage would be only temporary; it would abate as soon as parity was achieved (in his estimation in about fifteen years).

I challenged the ethics of this position. Why, I asked, should innocent men today be punished for an advantage those of their gender enjoyed in a previous generation? If you want to provide redress for what happened yesterday, I argued, you must compensate those specific individuals who were improperly excluded at that time. It is palpably unfair to compensate *someone else* just because of comparable genitalia.

While we in CCLA agreed that numerical goals might have a place, we maintained that the number of females to be hired in that plan had to be closer to 50 percent than to 100 percent. That was because of the assumption that men and women were equally divided in the art college's relevant job pool. We said that it was wrong to make overall parity the long-term objective of the program. We insisted that the objective must be short-term: no discrimination now and hereafter.

Thus, while we joined forces with the women's movement in supporting such bold initiatives, we differed on critical details. They were more supportive of the legislation enacted under the New Democrats in the early 1990s. That legislation stipulated that one of its objectives was to produce a racial, ethnic, and gender mix in most workplaces that would mirror the distribution in the community at large. CCLA and other critics contended that the NDP approach would be unable to avoid reverse discrimination. In any event, we contended, there was no earthly reason why every workplace should have to reflect the general picture.

In the result, the New Democratic Party lost the next Ontario election to the rather Neanderthal Conservatives under Mike Harris. The new legislature lost little time in repealing the New Democratic legislation on employment equity. The Tories appeared similarly uninterested in the more moderate forms of employment equity urged by CCLA. In commenting on these developments, I made the statement in newspaper columns and speeches that left-wing confusion had spawned right-wing reaction. CCLA and the mainstream feminists had found unity again — in defeat.

Women were not the only beneficiaries of the sexual stirrings for equality during the 1970s and thereafter. Homosexuals of both genders, by the droves, started to pour out of the closets in which they had sought sanctuary. Capitalizing on the demands made and victories won by women and ethnic minorities, the gay community began to insist on comparable treatment for themselves. They complained of abuse at the hands of the police, discrimination by employers, and inequities on the part of most state institutions with which they had dealings. Not surprisingly, we at CCLA were prepared to side with them in many of their battles.

At some point during the late 1970s, I was called by the press to comment on the recent discharge of a steward at a prominent horse-racing club. The discharge had been provoked by the revelation that the steward was gay. When the personnel people were called for their side of the story, they said they were concerned that, if he got into a relationship with one of the jockeys he had to assess, his judgment could become impaired. Essentially, they discharged the steward in order to avoid a conflict of interest over the duties he had to perform.

When all of this was drawn to my attention, I raised the possibility that heterosexuals were also potentially vulnerable to such awkward dilemmas. After all, there are many situations in our society in which those of a heterosexual orientation are required to pass judgment on members of the opposite sex. Consider, for example, how this analysis could affect our judges, various employers, and even medical personnel. Thus, my conclusion was: "Only eunuchs can be trusted."

As I have already indicated, CCLA was on the barricades in defence of gay people in a number of ways during the 1980s. These battles included the bathhouse raids in Toronto and the public washroom tactics of police in Orillia, Welland, St. Catharines, and Guelph. The culmination of many of these cases was the delegation I have already described in which we urged the Solicitor General of Ontario to issue directives that called upon the police to avoid the foregoing tactics and focus instead on less intrusive ways to enforce the relevant law.

In the early to mid-1990s, I used the column I had in the *Toronto Star* to go to bat once again for victimized gay people. On the appropriateness of allowing gay couples to adopt children, I questioned the kind of arguments that some alleged experts were using against the idea. A psychiatrist had published an article in which he argued that, according to statistical studies, heterosexual couples represented the best bet for the mental health of youngsters who were being adopted. In my column, I argued that "statistics don't adopt children; *people* do." Even if it were true, I argued, that heterosexual couples make for the best mental health environment, such a fact could not validly vitiate the eligibility of any particular gay couple. Such an assessment had to be done on an *individual*, not a statistical, basis.

I also challenged the local Catholic cardinal because of an article in which he had written that society must avoid policies that could promote homosexuality as a possible virtue. To this, I countered that the operative criterion in any particular case must be concerned not with the elevation or denigration of the homosexual lifestyle but rather, what was in the best interests of the children whose fate was being determined.

In the late 1990s, the Surrey Board of Education in British Columbia rejected a request that it approve certain books for educational use in kindergarten and grade 1. The books in question had portrayed families headed by same-sex couples as normal and socially acceptable. It appeared that the board was attempting to appease many of its ratepayers who claimed that the disputed material offended their religious sensibilities. And the vote cast by at least one of the trustees seemed to have been influenced by her own theological objections to homosexuality.

Some of the parties who had sought acceptance of the material wound up taking the board to court. At the Supreme of Court of Canada, CCLA intervened to make the argument that no one's beliefs about God had any business determining the policies of a public school board. Fortunately, the Court overruled the decision of the board on this question.

In the early 2000s, there was a reference in the Supreme Court of Canada regarding the constitutionality of same-sex marriages. The Interfaith Coalition on Marriage and Family, which was composed of certain Islamic, Catholic, and Evangelical organizations, contended that, by altering the conception of marriage in order to recognize same-sex unions, "Parliament would be failing to manifest equal concern for the interests of the members of the religious faith communities represented by the Interfaith Coalition as well as other Canadians, who will be marginalized from full participation in civil society."

In my 2007 book, *Categorically Incorrect*, I wrote that "the magnitude of the non sequitur here is simply breathtaking." CCLA intervened in the case and set about to challenge the coalition's analysis. We questioned how equality between gay and straight marriages rendered the religious believers in the coalition less equal members of society. And we questioned how such action would marginalize them from full participation in civil society. On the basis of this logic, we argued that the abolition of slavery in the United States could be said to have marginalized white Americans and the granting of full civil rights to Jews could be seen as having marginalized Gentiles. At the end of the day, the coalition lost and the egalitarians won. To my knowledge, the sun has continued to rise in the East and set in the West.

Having taken the side of the gay community in all of the foregoing disputes, we parted company with at least some of them over issues concerning freedom of speech. A nurse in Saskatchewan had his licence suspended because, among other things, he made statements expressing profound hostility to gays. And a preacher in Alberta was sanctioned by the local human rights commission because a letter he had written to the press was seen as hateful toward gay people. In both cases, CCLA intervened to protect the free speech of those who had attacked the gays. In the course of doing so, we expressed our own contempt for the contents of what the nurse and the preacher had said. But, we argued, state coercion was not an appropriate remedy for such misconduct. Fortunately, some gay organizations sided with us on this issue. At the time of my retirement, the courts had not yet definitively resolved these cases.

WELFARE AND THE WORKPLACE

No civil liberties organization worthy of the name can afford to ignore the influence played by economic factors on the personal freedoms of those affected. Two of the principal sources of such influence are employers and government. To the extent that employers are able to determine the various conditions of work, they are enabled to impose substantial restrictions on the freedoms of those they employ. Similarly, as increasing numbers of people become dependent upon various government programs for their respective incomes and, in some cases, even sustenance, such people become increasingly vulnerable to state restrictions on their freedom. If your employer requires that you surrender certain freedoms in exchange for your job or the government makes such a surrender a condition of your eligibility for government assistance, the potential implications for civil liberties become obvious.

In an earlier era, civil liberties organizations took up the cudgels to protect the rights of workers to organize and bargain collectively with their employers. The power of unions was often seen as a necessary (if not always, sufficient) counter-balance to the power of employers. In those situations where collective bargaining was viable, civil libertarians were often content to let the parties determine for themselves the state of their civil liberties in the workplace. They were able to do this, of course, through the give and take of the collective bargaining experience.

Notwithstanding the progress on the collective bargaining front, however, some situations have continued to need the special contribution of the civil liberties perspective. One such situation arose in the late 1980s. Employers—of both the public and private sector variety—began to require that their current and prospective employees surrender specimens of their urine for the purpose of drug testing. In view of the fact that a person's urine contains a host of information about health and lifestyle, this employer practice came to be seen as an infringement on the workers' personal privacy.

CCLA became heavily involved in the issue. In addition to writing and speaking on the subject in umpteen places, I testified before a parliamentary committee and orchestrated CCLA's involvement in court cases where this practice of employers was being challenged.

The essence of my argument was that urine specimens reveal a lot of personal information but virtually nothing that is relevant to the jobs at issue. The most a urine test can provide that is arguably relevant is information that the tested person had been exposed to the drug in question (principally, marijuana) within a period of a few days or possibly even weeks of the test. It provides no information as to the amount that was consumed or the impact, if any, that exposure to the drug may have caused. In particular, the urine test yields no information as to whether the affected person is — or was — impaired from the contact.

Again and again, I made the point that it would be quite permissible, from our point of view, to subject employees to a test of their fitness to perform the jobs in question, at the time that they report for work. Such a test would possess the virtue of supplying relevant information and nothing beyond it. We were advised, for example, that a number of eye-hand coordination tests had been devised for just such purposes. In any event, as we argued, there was simply no excuse for the all-encompassing urine test. Our argument applied even to those jobs that were safety-sensitive. If a test reveals nothing about impairment, what difference would it make if the person being tested was a pilot or a janitor?

On this basis, I testified before the House of Commons transport committee. I urged the MPs to resist the American demand that Canadian pilots and truckers be subjected to the urine tests. Calling these tests a "urinary witch hunt," I said that, just because Ronald Reagan and George Bush are the leaders of the free world, does not mean that we must follow them "in a stampede to the urinals."

At my instigation, CCLA challenged in court the drug-testing programs at both Imperial Oil and the Toronto-Dominion Bank. At Imperial Oil, we applied the above argument that such testing was inapplicable even in that company's safety-sensitive jobs. At Toronto-Dominion, we went a step further: There was no safety problem at all, unless the employer was concerned about an epidemic of paper cuts. We won both cases, not on the privacy grounds where it made the most sense, but under the human rights statutes where the argument concerned discrimination on the basis of perceived handicap.

In view of the role played by collective bargaining in reducing the power inequality between employers and employees, civil libertarians had to be concerned about the fairness of certain labour laws. In the mid-1980s, a member of the Ontario Public Service Employees Union (OPSEU) challenged the right of the union to use his conscripted dues money for political purposes outside of collective bargaining. He challenged, for example, the right of the union to contribute "his" money to the New Democratic Party (NDP) and even to the Ontario Federation of Labour which had enacted a pro-Palestinian resolution at one of its recent conventions. Since the issue was coming up in our courts, I was faced with the question of whether CCLA should intervene and precisely what position it should take.

I consulted some colleagues at the American Civil Liberties Union (ACLU). That organization had confronted and had purported to resolve this dilemma. An ACLU specialist in this area advised me that, in those cases where employees are required to pay union dues as a condition of employment, the union should be confined, in its use of such money, to strictly collective bargaining purposes, narrowly defined. Political contributions of the kind made by OPSEU should not be allowed and the affected employees should be entitled, therefore, to deduct the proportionate amount from their conscripted dues payments.

I balked. Why, I asked myself, should unions of all the institutions in our society be barred from treating as their own, the money that is paid to them for performing their respective services? Moreover, while the dissenting members' "freedom of association" is infringed by this arrangement, what about the comparable freedom of those other employees who happily accept the political contributions that are made with their money? In short, I began to see the issue as a conflict of freedoms of association. And, to whatever extent the courts acquired the power to supervise the political contributions made by such unions, freedom of association for the majority would suffer a commensurate encroachment.

Freedom of association means that the members of voluntary organizations such as unions must be able to determine, on the basis of their own criteria, how to spend the money collected by the unions. Given that decisions at the political level can have an enormous impact on what happens at collective bargaining, the right sought by the dissenting employee in this case could have substantial consequences. It would be fair, I thought, for the courts to help ensure that the decision-making processes in the affected unions were truly democratic. But, beyond that, the members, not the judges, should determine how best to spend their money.

Accordingly, CCLA intervened in the case and argued along the fore-going lines. The Supreme Court of Canada found for the union.

Every now and then, CCLA would spend its resources and energy in defence of a single individual—particularly, if the circumstances had wide repercussions. On this basis, we took up the case of Alice Kolisnyk who was suspended without pay in October 1984 from her job as a teacher of nursing at Mississauga's Sheridan College. The reason for the suspension was Ms. Kolisnyk's refusal to undergo a chest x-ray for tuberculosis. According to the college, the law requires annual chest x-rays for hospital employees who have a positive tuberculin reaction. But she claims that her positive reaction was a result of a vaccination that she and her generation of nurses were required to have.

The nursing teacher argued that such frequent x-rays could increase the risk of breast cancer, thyroid cancer, and certain leukemias. As an opening gambit, we called upon the relevant cabinet ministers to inter-cede in order to have the suspension delayed until such time as the case could be dealt with at arbitration. Significantly, new guidelines were then being prepared that were likely to provide some relief against an-nual chest x-rays. This provoked from me the comment that "to disci-pline this employee at this time bears at least some resemblance to conducting an execution in the midst of a parliamentary debate on the abolition of capital punishment."

At a benefit meeting for Ms. Kolisnyk, I rhetorically asked, "Did Alice concoct this relationship between cancer and x-rays out of whole cloth? Should she be prosecuted for spreading false news?" In addition to these flourishes of rhetoric, I was also careful to point out that we in CCLA were not necessarily saying that Alice Kolisnyk had struck the right balance between the costs and benefits of the annual x-rays; we merely said that there was a reasonable basis for her assessment.

At one point several months later in the spring of 1985, the nursing teacher was unceremoniously informed that the college was reinstating her with full back pay and benefits. In a letter to the college newspaper, Ms. Kolisnyk expressed her gratitude to all of her supporters, making special mention of OPSEU's Sean O'Flynn and CCLA's Alan Borovoy.

Just as employers have used economic clout to diminish the free-doms of their employees, so has the government used its superior fi-nances to reduce the freedoms of many citizens. A key difference, of course, is that, in many areas, the government enjoys monopolistic control over what's involved. One of the most critical areas in which the government exercises such economic power is in the provision of welfare assistance. An exacerbating factor here is the poverty suffered by those who seek welfare assistance. This factor makes such people especially vulnerable to governmental demands.

Early on, I became sensitive to the numbers of ways in which welfare procedures differed from those that prevailed in other situations. In January 1971, I complained to the Ontario minister of Social and Family Services about the plight of a deserted Etobicoke wife and mother of four children, ages one to seven. A couple of weeks earlier the family's welfare allowance was suddenly and summarily terminated. The letter informing her of this decision simply said, "Your allowance is suspended as of December 1, 1970 as information on our file indicates you are not living as a single person." The letter made no effort to inform the woman about the information that produced this decision. Nor was she given any opportunity to explain, question, or dispute the verdict she faced. Regrettably, cases such as this one were not isolated. They occurred again and again to people on welfare.

Small wonder that our well-publicized delegation to the minister of March 1970 contained the statement that, in some respects, the indigent on welfare have fewer legal rights than those suspected of the most heinous crimes. Traditionally, our society had proclaimed and observed the principle that no persons should be made to suffer the loss of liberty or property without first being given the opportunity to know and dispute the case against them.

Remarkably, the Ontario Court of Appeal was then of little help. It effectively declared that, since welfare recipients have a right to a subsequent hearing before the welfare appeal tribunal, there is no right to a prior hearing before the Family Benefits Director. Our complaint to the minister pointed out that a hearing before the appeal tribunal might not occur for weeks and that "*any* delay could produce irreparable damage to the family dependent on welfare." To punch home the point, I resorted again to rhetoric: "Retroactive payment cannot provide retroactive sustenance."

Fortunately, the Ontario legislature provided some helpful medicine. In the summer of 1971, new legislation stipulated that thereafter the

Director of Family Benefits would be required to provide welfare recipients with both advance notice when their allowances were in jeopardy and an opportunity to challenge the basis for the proposed government action.

Another flaw in the welfare process that used to drive me around the bend was the failure to publish the judgments of the welfare appeal tribunal. Again and again, I argued that, since the administration was always a party in welfare appeals, it would always know the state of the jurisprudence. But without published judgments, the claimants would not know. Another complaint I made in the early years arose from a practice by which certain municipalities required those receiving welfare to provide a signed statement giving the administration a certain amount of continuing access to their premises. On a number of occasions, it appeared that welfare officials took advantage of this practice to justify intrusive searches of the residences occupied by welfare recipients. Happily, both of those practices have since been remedied.

I cannot resist the impulse to tell one more anecdote related to my experience with welfare matters. A small town in the Ontario north country simply refused on one occasion to honour the decision of the welfare appeal tribunal that it restore a suspended welfare allowance. An official in the Ontario ministry offered immediately to pay the claim out of provincial funds and then simply deduct it from the subsequent subsidies that the province pays to such municipalities. In the meantime, however, I was having delicious fantasies about sending the bailiffs into the town's offices to seize and cart off typewriters, furniture, and other town possessions. Imagine going to such lengths to pay off a welfare recipient. The prospect of such publicity was enough to make me salivate. Too bad I won that dispute so easily.

DISABILITY

People with disabilities face a multitude of impediments in their ongoing efforts to navigate the rivers of life. Within the last couple of decades, the various institutions of our society have adopted a number of measures to help these people overcome such impediments. Not the least of these measures are amendments to our human rights laws that explicitly prohibit discrimination against people with disabilities. A critical factor enhancing the ability of our human rights laws to achieve their objectives is the recurring requirement that our various institutions make reasonable efforts to accommodate people with disabilities.

In the main, these recent measures have addressed the issue of how the government can affirmatively help those who suffer disability. For CCLA, the focus was on how government could stop *hurting* the people in this constituency. In particular, we took on the laws that provide for the forced hospitalization and treatment of those who are considered mentally ill.

Toward the end of 1976, we were approached by Burton Perrin, a psychology student at York University. He had recently written a Master's thesis that analyzed 200 certificates on the basis of which certain persons in Ontario actually suffered various periods of involuntary civil commitment between January 1972 and May 1973. Mr. Perrin advised us that his research had shown widespread defects in the committal procedures under review. We were sufficiently impressed with Mr. Perrin's initiative to undertake a follow-up on our own.

Our first step was to acquire reputable legal opinions. With Mr. Perrin's permission, we turned over copies of the certificates (with identifying material deleted) to Kenneth Howie of the Thompson, Rogers law firm and John Sopinka of Fasken, Calvin and asked them to assess the legal adequacy of the material. Needless to say, both these lawyers were highly respected and neither of them was involved in the leadership of our organization. Thus, we were able to combine both recognized skill and perceived objectivity.

In the result, both lawyers agreed that at least 142 of the 200 certificates (70 percent) failed to satisfy the requirements of the *Mental Health Act*. Each of the lawyers, however, impugned even more of the certificates. Significantly, one of their letters to us contained the following qualification: "We might add that, in reaching this conclusion, we may have erred on the high side and given the benefit of the doubt to some of the applications under consideration."

Accordingly, I had little difficulty in pronouncing publicly that *at least* 70 percent of these certificates violated the minimum safeguards in the law. That was no mean achievement. All that the law then required in order to authorize an involuntary commitment was that the person involved suffer from a "mental disorder of such a nature or degree so as to require hospitalization in the interests of his own safety or the safety of others." There was no definition of "mental disorder" and no attempt to specify what magnitude of risks to "safety" had to be reached. In short, the statutory language was vague and question-begging. To us at CCLA, it was simply unacceptable that anyone's freedom could be so comprehensively invaded on the basis of such incomprehensible criteria.

In order to reduce the risk that such vast power could be readily abused, the Act required the certificates of commitment to set out the facts, observations, and allegations upon which the assessments were based. This is essentially what was missing in the certificates examined by Mr. Perrin and our lawyers.

The certificates were loaded with conclusions and devoid of explanations. It is especially significant to note the virtual absence of anything relating to "safety" in the bulk of the material. Without a lot more, the allegations that did appear, such as "unmanageable," "uncooperative," "leaves hospital," and "unpredictable" hardly constituted a proper, let alone a legal, basis for such encroachments on liberty.

Neither Mr. Howie, nor Mr. Sopinka, neither Mr. Perrin nor CCLA could deny the possibility that there might have been adequate grounds for the commitment of the persons discussed in these certificates. But, even apart from the strict requirements of the law, the issue involved more than inadequate form-filling. While it was always possible that, despite an inadequate certificate, there might have been grounds for a commitment, it was also possible that in such circumstances the grounds might *not* have existed. Unless such grounds are spelled out, how could anyone know and whom could anyone trust? Just as the incarceration of suspected criminal offenders requires concrete evidence in court, so does the commitment of the suspected mentally ill require concrete explanations in the authorizing certificates.

We put most of the foregoing material in a letter to the minister and released it all to the press. The publicity made the front page of the *Globe and Mail* and it obtained prominent coverage in other media. The minister did not take long to grant the request with which our letter concluded: we were invited to meet with him within a few weeks. At that meeting, the CCLA delegation argued the case for changes in the law. Pointing out that so much of psychiatric diagnosis is based on value judgments, we argued both for tighter criteria and more exacting procedures.

Our arguments were buttressed with a description of recent studies, such as the ones we cited when the Federal government attempted, after the Morgentaler case, to re-criminalize abortions. Other studies found that insanity ratings went up when patients expressed a distrust of psychiatrists and went down when they expressed trust.

The risk of diagnosis influenced by value judgments appears to exist even in the case of the more serious psychotic disorders where the patients are seen to be suffering from delusions. The problem, however, is that entire religions have been based upon phenomena that will look, to many, like delusions. Moses, for example, considered himself a messenger of God, and Jesus claimed to be the son of God. Is the man who seeks to chuck his family for the priesthood exhibiting admirable dedication or unacceptable craziness? If he claims that he got the call from God, do we conclude that he is inspired or nuts? In any event, what language could possibly articulate an appropriate dividing line?

After the meeting, the minister requested that representatives from CCLA have a further meeting with representatives of the Ontario Psychiatric Association (OPA). Although that meeting turned out to be civil and friendly, it got nowhere on the issues. Perhaps our attempts to reach a consensus were somewhat undermined by some public commentary involving me and a former president of the OPA. He had said that if the kind of amendments we were seeking found their way into the law, the only freedom that would be experienced by the vast majority of mentally ill people would be the "pseudo freedom to lose their job, their family, their self-respect, and their marriage." I lost little time in pointing out that, while the interests that the psychiatrist identified were worthy of protection, they had very little to do with "safety." I raised the possibility that perhaps the doctor and his colleagues had been interpreting the existing criteria as protective of such interests. If so, he would have been effectively admitting improprieties in their commitment practices.

On the other hand, if all this was an argument on their part for a broadening of their power, we took issue with that as well. In our view, criteria that were broad enough to protect the kind of interests to which the doctor had alluded, would incur a sizeable risk of empowering forced hospitalization on the basis of the decision maker's value judgments. We argued that psychiatric training does not provide any special competence to determine, for example, whether the protection of a particular marriage warrants involuntary commitment. As we contended, "The choice between marital stability and personal liberty requires an ethical, not a clinical, evaluation." Despite the benevolence of the motives involved, we insisted that there was no reason to prefer the value judgments of physicians as against those of anyone else. Moreover, in our view, only the prospects of serious bodily harm and serious physical impairment could possibly justify the kind of power that was at issue in this dispute.

In the result, the law was changed in the direction advocated by us. Not surprisingly, we continued to press for more. On this score, however, we did not succeed. Indeed, years later, the Ontario government headed by Mike Harris rolled back some of the changes that our efforts had helped to bring about. In the result, Ontario was left with a committal law that represented a partial, but diminished, victory for the CCLA.

ENDNOTES

1   A. Alan Borovoy, *Categorically Incorrect: Ethical Fallacies in Canada's War on Terror* (Toronto: Dundurn Press, 2006) p. 21.

2   Alan Borovoy, "The Case for an Independent Police Examiner," *Toronto Star*, May 25, 1994, A17.

3   A. Alan Borovoy & Daniel G. Hill, "Ethnicity of 'Show Boat' Producers is Wrong Issue," *Toronto Star*, April 19, 1993.

4   Editorial page, *Toronto Star*, May 25, 2001. See also, Caroline Mallan, "Public hearings sought on tuition tax credit; Tory plan denounced by education advocates, lawyers," *Toronto Star*, May 25, 2001.

5   See, for example, *Brantford Expositor*, February 1, 1990. See also, Graham Fraser, "Borovoy Joins Fight Against Law on Abortion," *The Globe and Mail*, October 3, 1989, A11.

6   Michele Landsberg, "Rape Shield Law Offered Protection," *Toronto Star*, September 10, 1991, D1.

7   "Sex History Questions Barred, Accused Dad Wins New Trial from Quebec Appeal Court" *The Lawyers Weekly*, April 3, 1992, 2.

8   Michele Landsberg, "'Slut' Incident Sheds Light On Widespread Chauvinism," *Toronto Star*, September 24, 1991, F1.

CHAPTER TWELVE

General Reinforcements

$\mathcal{T}$hose who are serious about civil liberties will focus not only on specific laws and their accompanying safeguards, but also on general measures that would serve to bolster the public's commitment to the entire enterprise. Thus, we at CCLA found ourselves debating the merits of a constitutionally-entrenched bill of rights, the kind of public education that we undertook, and even the extent to which we ought to seek or accept money from the government.

THE CHARTER

When the *Charter* made its first appearance on Canada's political agenda around 1980, it provoked a rather telling debate. That debate revolved around the limitation clause in section 1, on the basis of which the freedoms set out in the *Charter* were to be "subject to such limitations as can be demonstrably justified in a free and democratic society."

I am unable now even to estimate how many telephone calls I received from the press, asking whether this provision would effectively annihilate the freedoms in the remainder of the document. But I can say that we were deluged with such inquiries. It became clear, therefore, that much of the press and the public regarded the rights in the *Charter*, not as human-made measures to be weighed against other interests, but as edicts descended upon us from the heights of Mount Sinai.

I don't know whether my replies to those telephone calls conveyed the impression that I was a veritable Benedict Arnold who was prepared to betray my civil liberties mandate or whether I was regarded as simply too confused to be helpful. But I told each and every one who called that, even if the *Charter* did not contain a limitation clause, the courts would inevitably read one in. The mistake, I said again and again, was the apparent perception that the rights in the *Charter* were a series of absolutes that could not be abridged or modified under any circumstances.

I had no trouble characterizing such doctrines as intellectual garbage unworthy of serious people. I readily acknowledged that the rights set out in the *Charter* could well be entitled to special treatment, that is, they should not be abridged without a compelling justification. But it nevertheless remained clear to me that "special" was not a synonym for "absolute." As vital as the principles in the *Charter* were, there would always be some circumstances in which they could be overridden. Indeed, sometimes those rights were in conflict even with each other. What do we say, for example, to a newspaper that, on the eve of a serious criminal trial, publishes much of the evidence and blatantly calls for a conviction of the accused person? It is at least arguable that such an article could prejudice the jury and thus jeopardize the fairness of the impending trial. Which of the competing rights, therefore, should prevail: the right to a fair trial or freedom of the press?

I had occasion to tell a number of my callers that, even though the United States claimed the rights in its Bill of Rights could not be abridged, the Americans may not really mean it. When they decided they were in favour of curbs on certain speech (for example, incitements, defamation, obscenity) they were faced with the problem of how to reconcile such a law with the fundamental freedom of speech in their Bill of Rights. One of their solutions was simply to challenge the extent to which the utterances in question were really forms of speech at all.[1] In some situations, they characterized what they sought to suppress as primarily action, not speech. I told those who interviewed me that it was far more preferable to determine up front that these rights could be modified than to resort to dubious labelling as a way of addressing such problems. What couldn't be denied, I insisted, was that there would always be some situations in which our precious freedoms could legitimately be abridged.

*U*navoidably, the criteria on the basis of which such abridgements would be based had to be expressed in broad language. It was simply not possible that a constitutional document could contain, in specific language, the myriads of possibilities that, over time, could justify potential restrictions on our freedoms. It was inevitable that various value judgments would be invoked to justify the exercise. The key question became, therefore, whose value judgments were appropriate to the task.

Those who favoured the constitutional entrenchment of our civil liberties believed that, because of their ostensible neutrality, the courts should be the ones whose value judgments ought to prevail. I took the position that this deference to the judiciary represented a form of tyranny. Why, I asked, should the raw value judgments of appointed judges trump those of elected politicians? After all, politicians are accountable for their judgments to the people who elect them; at the recurring elections, the people can turf the politicians out of office. By their very nature, judges owe no such accountability. I thought, therefore, that constitutional entrenchment was profoundly undemocratic.

The situation is different when judges are called upon to apply ordinary statutes. In that context, the role of the judge is to discern and implement the will of the legislature. Statutes are generally drafted in much more specific language so that the judge is better able to determine what the legislature wanted. But the constitutional exercise is a different ballgame. The judges then rule on the propriety of the legislative will itself. Since constitutions are drafted in much broader language, the judges are effectively forced to rely, more often, on their own value judgments. It's at this point that the system threatens to become tyrannical.

Those who favour entrenchment argue that the very invulnerability of our judges to the popular will is what makes them so much more qualified to deal with constitutional principles. According to the argument, there is a better chance that judges, rather than politicians, will defend unpopular causes. Invariably, these debates invoked segments of the American experience where the courts showed a willingness to overturn years of racial segregation and to curb the powers of the police. On many occasions, I have responded to this argument by pointing out that, for the most part, the American judiciary behaved so nobly during a rather short period of US history: the 1960s when Earl Warren was the chief justice of the US Supreme Court.

But another argument that I have used invokes the American experience during the thirty-five years at the beginning of the 20th century. During that period, the Court used the US Bill of Rights to strike down legislation limiting the hours of work, prescribing certain minimum wages, outlawing child labour, and regulating employment agencies. Declaring that "liberty" in the Bill of Rights can apply to liberty of contract, the US Supreme Court almost dismantled the welfare state.

*W*hen the issue came before CCLA, I found myself in a real quandary. For the above reasons, I was really against the whole idea. At the same time, key people on my board were strongly on the other side, including our national president Walter Tarnopolsky. He had spent years in and out of government and the academy, pushing the idea of an entrenched bill of rights. I became disquieted over the potential optics of the situation; how was it going to look for a civil liberties association to oppose the entrenchment of fundamental freedoms? Moreover, during the period set aside for debate, there was simply not enough time for me to try to convince so many people (even if one were to assume that, in a more ideal situation, I would have been able to do so).

I hit on a possible compromise. Instead of calling for a complete withdrawal of the proposed *Charter*, I borrowed a concept from the statutory Bill of Rights that then existed at the federal level: a "notwithstanding" clause. I created a draft brief for my colleagues to consider. It would provide for a power in both federal and provincial legislatures to enact, at an open session, a measure which would suspend the application of the *Charter* to any law, within their respective jurisdictions, whose continued existence was considered of overriding importance. Of course, it was much less cumbersome to employ a measure such as this rather than undergo the complex procedures of constitutional amendment. But, while the invocation of a notwithstanding clause would be much easier legally, it could still create problems politically. Governments might shy away from using it because of the potential stigma that would accompany the spectacle of their having nullified anything as important as a fundamental freedom. I circulated my proposed brief among the CCLA board and nervously awaited their response.

The first response came by way of a telephone call from our president Walter Tarnopolsky. His message was more in sorrow than in anger. Indeed, there was no anger at all, just sorrow. He simply informed me that, if we were to publicly advocate such a measure at this stage of the proceedings, he would feel obliged to resign the CCLA presidency. He was simply too bound up with the quest for the *Charter*. He almost seemed hurt by my effort. He was, in fact, one of the nicest people I have ever known. And I acknowledge no small dimension of discomfort in taking him on this way.

The next call I received was from the old boss of my articling years, David Lewis. His message was more in anger than in sorrow. He said, "what's gotten into you guys, you and Alan Blakeney [the former New Democratic Party Premier of Saskatchewan who was then also on our board] " "But you're a socialist" I reminded Lewis, "what accounts for your faith in the judges?" As we were regurgitating our favourite arguments, a very simple truth was emerging. There was no way I was going to be able to sell my idea to the CCLA Board.

I came up, therefore, with another tack. Our brief to the joint Parliamentary Committee on the Constitution would begin with a disclaimer that we were not about to address the principle of whether or not Canada should have constitutionally entrenched rights. For the purposes of our presentation, we treated that issue as having been settled. Our brief would focus on what rights should be entrenched and how they should be protected. Fortunately, the government's draft was so bad that our Board was unanimous in criticizing it. Over time, I have learned to rely on the incompetence of our government to rescue me from internal conflicts within my organization.

Our delegation was composed of our then president Walter Tarnopolsky, past president Syd Midanik, and me. Both Walter and Syd were staunchly in favour of entrenchment. Nevertheless, Midanik made cross country headlines with his comment, "Thanks, but no thanks". This comment succinctly and beautifully expressed the disappointment of many Canadians in the government's initial draft of the *Charter*. The body of our presentation went on to set out a detailed critique with specific proposals for change.

A few months later, the federal minister of justice, Jean Chrétien, came up with an amended *Charter*. In doing so, he acknowledged the influence of a few organizations, one of the most prominent being CCLA. At one and the same time, we avoided an internal split and even wound up congratulating ourselves.

By the fall of 1981, the Canadian people were disappointed once again: A clear majority of the provincial premiers rejected the *Charter* that had emerged from the federal House of Commons. There followed another period of wrangling. Then Jean Chrétien and the attorneys general of Ontario and Saskatchewan worked out a compromise that finally won the support of all the parties except Quebec. And what was that compromise? You guessed right. It was a notwithstanding clause. Yes, it bore a heavy similarity to what I had proposed to my Board the year before. Regrettably, I was unable to claim any credit for it because the deliberations at the CCLA Board, of course, were confidential.

This time, our Board split into three: Eddie Greenspan, Mary Eberts, and Irwin Cotler remained such staunch entrenchers that they wanted CCLA to oppose the new notwithstanding clause; then there was my group which included Don Smiley and Harry Arthurs who, like me, thought that the notwithstanding clause might actually redeem the *Charter*. The third group was essentially the "swing" group: Walter Tarnopolsky, Syd Midanik, and Ron Atkey. They did not like the notwithstanding clause but they believed that, without it, there would be no *Charter*. On balance, they preferred a *Charter* with the notwithstanding clause to no *Charter* at all. Besides, they believed that, in practice, it was not likely to do much damage. In the result, CCLA effectively accepted the notwithstanding clause and, at that point, our internal schism was at an end.

Next, my group had to face the challenge of how to respond to situations in which the *Charter* might be used to vindicate an important civil liberties principle by nullifying a law enacted by an elected legislature. I have never much cared for the kind of purity that was prepared to accept defeat in the interests of abstract principles. At my urging, therefore, CCLA began to increase and intensify its program of court interventions.

Inexplicably, however, the courts began, at that point, to cut back substantially on the third party interventions they were prepared to allow. To me, of course, this made absolutely no sense. Unlike ordinary cases, *Charter* litigation had the capacity—and was often even designed—to affect the fundamental rights and freedoms of large swaths of people in various sectors of the community. At this point, the courts should have been more—rather than less—hospitable to the assistance of outsiders. And so, we began to write articles, briefs, and letters in an attempt to influence judicial policy.

Somewhere around this time (the mid-1980s), the Ontario Court of Appeal rejected a CCLA bid to intervene in the prosecution of Nazi sympathizer, Ernst Zundel. We wished to challenge the constitutionality of the false news law under which he was being prosecuted for having publicly denied the reality of the Holocaust. The following day, the CBC asked that I come into the studio around noon to do an interview on how the court handled our application. In those days, I often walked the two mile distance from my apartment to my office. As I made my way across Nathan Phillips Square that morning, I was deep in thought about how I was going to comment on the court's decision. At some point in the Square I had the epiphany that resolved my problem and I expressed it in the interview.

In response to the interviewer's on-air questions, I declared, "because of the decision by the Ontario Court of Appeal to exclude the Canadian Civil Liberties Association from the Zundel case, the free speech rights of wide varieties of Canadians are going to be upheld by a lawyer who is taking his instructions from an avowed Nazi. How does that sit with you?" This reply was picked up in several quarters with the result that there was some embarrassment among the powers that-be.

In the meantime, the Supreme Court of Canada asked the Canadian Bar Association to create a committee to act as a liaison with the court on the policy questions surrounding interventions. That committee held hearings in order to broaden the participation and to provide the committee with assistance in its deliberations. When I appeared for CCLA, my first point was to express disapproval at the monopoly on this matter that the court had given to the legal profession. I argued that the *Charter* belonged to the entire community, not just to the lawyers and it was, therefore, inappropriate that the lawyers should play this special role. As to the merits of a broader policy on interventions, I went through a myriad of arguments, calling for the courts to change their policy. My colleague, Ken Swan, wrote a scholarly essay on the question and the Globe and Mail's Kirk Makin produced a very helpful column.

From that point on, the courts appear to have adopted a much more welcoming policy.[2] With very few exceptions, CCLA has been allowed to intervene whenever it has made the request. To date, this has happened more than a hundred times.

EDUCATION

In the late 1960s and early 1970s, Ontario Supreme Court Justice Edson Haines made headlines with a public attack on the right of silence that accused persons have enjoyed for centuries in our legal system. In his view, it made no sense to deprive the criminal justice system of testimony from the person who is likely to know the relevant facts better than anyone else. In taking this position, he readily dismissed the applicability of the historic justifications for the rule. There is no longer a court of Star Chamber and accused people can no longer be legally subjected to the rack, the whip, or the thumbscrew. Indeed, evidence could well be excluded from the resulting trial if it was obtained through any physical abuse of the accused person.

But despite all of the progress our society has made with such matters, those who were telephoned by the press to respond to Justice Haines, kept invoking the old history as if it were currently relevant. In short, they relied more on ritual than on reason to defend the right of silence.

This basic pattern has emerged in other situations as well, for example, when the *War Measures Act* was invoked, when the public learned that the RCMP had been breaking the law for some thirty years, when the anti-hate law was enacted, and when new anti- terror measures were adopted after 9/11. In so many cases, members of the public accepted governmental infringements of basic civil liberties without a whimper or they resorted to hollow ritual to justify their objections.

For these purposes, I do not take one side or the other in the foregoing conflicts. At this point, I am content simply to point out that every one of these issues raised genuine matters of principle and, to a great extent, the public reactions were a far cry from what was needed.

*A*s I mused about all this, I became increasingly convinced that something vital was missing from our educational system. The courses and curriculae were full of factual content relating to history and to civic institutions. Virtually nowhere, however, was there any attempt to impart anything about the philosophy of democratic institutions. We learned what was there but not why it was there. Generation after generation emerged from our school system without the remotest clue of what our society is basically about. The more I thought about it, the more I came to believe that the Canadian Civil Liberties Association could play an important role by way of redress.

One of the first ideas that hit me in this regard happened to coincide with some nudges I was getting from a colleague in the Canadian Labour Congress, Jim MacDonald. He had been urging me for some time to write what he called a "primer" on civil liberties. The result of his advocacy and my thinking was a booklet which I entitled "The Fundamentals of our Fundamental Freedoms". It purported to explain, in (hopefully) readable language, the philosophy behind the fundamental freedoms of the democratic system. Our organization made it available for use in the secondary schools, the universities, various levels of civil service, and organizations in the voluntary sector.

Shortly after we published and began to distribute this booklet, I was approached by my colleague, Danielle McLaughlin, CCLA's Director of Administration. She had been hired some years earlier to handle and oversee the administrative responsibilities of the organization. But I was always aware that, as a university graduate in liberal arts, her talents were not being adequately used at CCLA. She suggested to me that our organization should attempt to promote and even conduct civil liberties seminars in the high schools. I thought that was a good idea and I encouraged her to start working on it.

Danielle followed up—in spades. She talked to potential funders, leading educators, and she started to write draft grant proposals. Early on, it became obvious to both of us that we had something unique to sell. Unlike so many others, CCLA's program in the schools was not going to focus on imparting information or teaching techniques. The substance would be philosophical and the style would be Socratic.

For a number of years, I had believed that an educational program must seek primarily to make people think. And one of the best ways to do that was to jar them psychologically. Throw ideas and materials at the students that would disrupt the complacency of their value structures. Since there is a natural tendency to seek comfort in such matters, there would be an incentive to address disruptive thoughts and ideas. This would set the stage for some hard thinking. And that's exactly what we wanted. Our approach was not designed to promote our ideas; our objective was to stimulate them to come up with their own ideas. And, as they began to experiment with possible alternatives, we were there to point out the flaws and the fallacies. In short, we conceived of ourselves as intellectual agitators.

What we began to push in the school system mirrors what I had been doing for many years as a university teacher. I have taught courses at the Dalhousie law school, the University of Toronto Faculty of Social Work, the Windsor Law School, the political science department at Glendon College, the Faculty of Law at the University of Toronto, the Department of Canadian Studies at Glendon College, and at Glendon's School of Public Policy and International Affairs. In every one of these courses, I have been the perennial questioner.

Two of my students' reactions best express the impact of my efforts. The students in one of my courses told me that they invariably came out of my class with a headache. I thanked them for the comment and told them that this reaction enhanced my sense of fulfillment. Another student introduced a paper she was writing by telling me that doing a paper for me reminded her of a story in which a mother presented her son with a red tie and a yellow one and said he could choose one of them as a gift. When he chose the yellow one, she questioned him: "Didn't you like the red one?" In addition to amusing me, that reaction was also a source of fulfillment.

Danielle's program took off. The Law Foundation of Ontario agreed to provide substantial funding and Danielle recruited members of the staff and board to serve as teachers. By today, the program reaches thousands of students each year and all the English-speaking teachers' colleges in Ontario. She is beginning to consider ways and means of extending the program to other provinces. In Toronto, CCLA has partnered with the school board in convening annual civil liberties conferences for hundreds of high school students every year. By now, we have done more than fifteen such conferences. Just as our teaching generally avoided pushing any particular views, my public speech making was shameless in its advocacy of my various opinions. No one speech, of course, could hope to convey the panoply of my opinions. For those purposes, I used writing. Throughout the years, I have written many op-ed articles on the controversies of the day. For three and a half years in the early to mid-1990s, I wrote a fortnightly column for the *Toronto Star*. The space restrictions of such articles preclude any attempt at depth. For those purposes, I began also to write books. While books can go deeper, they reach a much smaller number of people.

In my first book, *When Freedoms Collide*, I attempted to provide a written workshop on pragmatic, non absolutist value balancing and risk weighing as a problem-solving exercise. In repudiating both pervasive absolutism and subjective relativism, I attempted to set out how, nevertheless, there could be objectivity in values. In view of how careful I tried to be in my repudiation of absolutes, it won't be surprising to learn that I'm still annoyed when commentators attribute to me a belief in "absolute free speech."

My second book, *Uncivil Obedience*, was an attempt to show political activists a variety of ways they could raise hell without employing violence or any kind of illegality. I began that book by attacking the extremes of both what I called "mindless militancy" and "reluctant moderation". I said as clearly as I could that pressure is the prerequisite for success.

Notwithstanding how careful I attempted to be on this score, commentators keep insisting on attributing different positions to me. Alberta's Dominique Clément, for example, contended that "rational debate" was the "cornerstone of the CCLA's modus operandi." Clément would have considerable difficulty in reconciling that characterization with my recurring comment: "pressure without reason may be irresponsible but reason without pressure is ineffectual." He also alleged that CCLA had "scrupulously avoided disruptive tactics." How does he square this with the rallies we have organized on capital punishment and the powers of CSIS? And what would he say about the way we orchestrated the shutdown of the overwhelming number of Toronto libraries in protest against a federal pornography bill?

In my third book, *The New Anti-Liberals*, I took on long-standing allies for the extremism they have recently adopted: feminists who support the censorship of pornography, a rape shield law that would incapacitate accused sexual assaulters from using legitimate defences, and employment equity that would needlessly promote discrimination against white males. My targets also included minority groups who favoured the censorship of alleged "hate propaganda" and the provision of public money to religious schools, as well as members of university communities who have become slavish devotees of "political correctness."

In my fourth book, *Categorically Incorrect*, I tried to draw some distinctions between what I consider sensible responses to international and domestic misconduct. The following probably best summarizes the theme of this book: "Internationally, key fallacies stem from an undue respect for a rule of law that does not exist. Domestically, key fallacies stem from an undue neglect of a rule of law that does exist."

GOVERNMENT MONEY

At some point in the late 1970s or early 1980s, the department of the Secretary of State for the government of Canada offered CCLA and a number of other organizations $3,000 for our involvement in a federally-initiated project. While I cannot now remember the precise date or any details of the project, I do remember that the issue came before a meeting of our board of directors. The chair of the meeting decided to elicit everyone's views by going around the table, in order.

The response that has been indelibly grafted on my psyche is the one made by Dalton Camp. He simply said, "for $3,000 I can't be bought". Both the humour and the analysis resonated with the other members of the Board. Indeed, as far back as I can remember, the CCLA Board was opposed to our taking government money, even on a project basis.

Undoubtedly, this policy helped to ensure a perpetual state of poverty for CCLA. Of course, there were a number of attempts, over the years, to change that policy. Those advocating it would always insist that the level of integrity in our organization would be able to resist seductive entreaties from the government.

In my view, those arguments invariably missed the point. My approach to the issue depended less on what we might do than on what we might not do if we got government money. It was the realization that, even for CCLA, the government was not always wrong. Periodically, it would adopt policies—even controversial ones—with which we did not particularly disagree. My worry was the public perception of us as an organization if, after receiving government money, we declined, in principle, to challenge some controversial government measure. It might then appear that we were motivated by the hope for additional government money. It's obvious that such a situation would undermine our organizational credibility.

In the interests of ensuring our reputation for independence, I have continued, therefore, to oppose CCLA's taking government money. For these purposes, it's wise to remember that, regardless of individual issues, CCLA and government would always be structural adversaries.

Somewhere in the 1970s, the government of Canada requested me to go across the country and conduct race relations workshops with a number of staff members from the department of the Secretary of State. I was happy to accept the assignment and, in fact, did so. A few days after it was all over, I received a personal cheque from the government for more than $700. It represented the fee the government had decided to pay me for having accepted its assignment.

I'm sure that my next move would have been capable of making history, if it had ever become public. I sent the cheque back to the government with a polite note advising the responsible parties that, as the full-time director of the Canadian Civil Liberties Association, it was my personal policy not to accept such government money.

Some years later, a friend of mine told me that he had written to the Attorney General for Ontario, requesting that the government make me a Queen's Counsel (QC). While I thanked my friend for having thought of me in this regard, I urged him officially to rescind the request. When he assured me that he could honestly claim the initiative had been all his and not at all mine, I replied that I was afraid it would be perceived as the consequence of collusion involving me. It was important to me that neither CCLA nor I ever create the appearance that we had our hand out to government.

THE VOLUNTARY SECTOR — THE CANADIAN CIVIL LIBERTIES ASSOCIATION

A critical element in the panoply of general reinforcements is an organization with a civil liberties mandate, in my case, the Canadian Civil Liberties Association (CCLA). The organization provides a continuing vehicle to raise questions, launch actions, reconcile conflicts, and educate people. Its very existence has served to ensure that the wielders of power are constantly under scrutiny and that the issues of civil liberties are constantly before the public.

Not many years ago, I became aware that a number of my board colleagues were harbouring fears for the continuity of the organization. These fears had been provoked by the extent to which the CCLA appeared dependent on the activity of one person: me. Almost alone, I had represented the organization at parliamentary committees, legislative committees, royal commissions, public inquiries, and at demonstrations, rallies, press conferences, and media interviews. I had also orchestrated CCLA involvement in court and I had instructed counsel on the policies of the organization.

My colleagues' concerns impelled me to accelerate the pace of some changes I had been planning. I began to involve my staff colleagues more directly in leadership roles. I divided the program and assigned a staff colleague to direct each part. With that, they began to represent the organization in all of the ways that I had and they began taking the kind of initiatives that had characterized my work. They proved to be very good indeed.

Initially, I felt some pangs when media people would come to the door looking for them and not for me. But, after a while, I experienced some sense of fulfillment at the way my colleagues were growing. It was becoming increasingly clear that the organization would quite handily be able to survive my tenure. In setting the stage this way, I fulfilled one of the most important functions of democratic leadership: I helped to ensure my own dispensability.

ENDNOTES

1   Z. Chafee, *Free Speech in the United States* (Cambridge: Harvard University Press, 1946) p. 150. Sidney Hook, *Pragmatism and the Tragic Sense of Life* (New York: Basic Books, 1975) pp. 89–90. And see the dissenting judgment in *Cohen v. California*, 808 U.S. 15 (1971) and the cases cited therein.

2   Robert J. Sharpe and Kent Roach, *Brian Dickson: A Judge's Journey* (Toronto: University of Toronto Press, 2003) pp. 383–89.

part four

The Rear-View Mirror

CHAPTER THIRTEEN

Unforgettable Persons and Moments

$\mathcal{A}$mong the factors that generally reinforce our values and commitments are the people we meet and the moments we share. In my life, there have been a number of unforgettable people and experiences. I have already mentioned and even described a number of those people: Sid Blum, Dan Hill, Syd Midanik, Harry Arthurs, John McCamus, Ken Swan, Sydney Goldenberg, June Callwood, Louise Arbour, Henry Morgentaler, and David Lewis, to name only a few. I have also referred to the role played by personal friends such as Millie and Owen Shime, as well as Mel Finkelstein and Berril Garshowitz.

As far back as I can remember, I have had heroes. During my teen years, the football player, Joe Krol, and the entertainer, Al Jolson, were my major heroes. And, as more serious matters began to occupy my range of interests, I started to acquire new heroes. Toward the end of high school, US presidential candidate Henry Wallace and then US Supreme Court Justice William O. Douglas served in this role for me until I became attracted to irresistible arguments that questioned the thrust of their opinions.

From university on, I have much admired Walter Reuther who, from the mid-1940s until the late 1960s, was the international president of the United Auto Workers (UAW) union. In addition to his innovative moves in collective bargaining and his progressive influence on the political scene, I was taken with his involvement in the quest for racial equality. When Martin Luther King, Jr., moved his civil rights campaign from the Deep South to the urban north, his co-leader in many of his marches was Walter Reuther. At the 1963 civil rights march on Washington (where King made his "I have a dream" speech), UAW signs and placards were all over the place. Indeed, this prompted me to complain at a subsequent conference of the US Jewish Labour Committee that, unlike the UAW, the AFL-CIO was nowhere to be seen at that historic march. Sometime afterward, Reuther orchestrated UAW support for Cesar Chavez and his farm workers union.

Another facet of Reuther's work that caught my imagination was his creation of the UAW Public Review Board. This was Reuther's response to the US Congressional campaigns to root out racketeers in the labour movement. Rather than wait for punitive legislation, Reuther set up this board, a panel of eminent citizens from outside the union who were given the power to adjudicate grievances that union members had against the union itself.

After my dubious flirtation with the US presidential aspirations of Henry Wallace, I welcomed Reuther's anti-Communism. He fought the Communists inside and outside his union. Inside the union, he supported liberal and social democratic candidates for union office who, like him, were determined to reduce the impact of Communism on his organization. Outside the union, Reuther supported Harry Truman's containment policy against the Soviet Union. When Soviet leader Nikita Khrushchev visited the United States, Reuther was on hand to ask him embarrassing questions about that country's repressive policies. At the end of the 1960s, Walter Reuther himself was killed in a plane crash, amidst suspicions that his enemies had done him in. My admiration for Reuther has survived, nevertheless.

About two decades after the foregoing events, I received a telephone call from the president of the newly created Canadian Auto Workers (CAW) union. Months earlier, that president, Bob White, had led the Canadian affiliates out of the international union. But the leaders of the new Canadian union were determined to preserve and perpetuate much of the idealism that they had encountered in the parent union. One manifestation of this idealism was the insistence on having a public review board in the new Canadian union. Bob White called to offer me the first chairmanship of the Canadian Public Review Board. What a marvellous coincidence this was for me! I was offered the chance to implement some of the very idealism I had admired so much. Needless to say, I accepted Bob White's offer and I have been serving in that position ever since. Despite some of our rulings that have run counter to the Union's interests, Bob White and his successor Buzz Hargrove frequently made a point of affirming their respect for the role that the Board was playing. As of the date of writing, we have had relatively few interactions with Buzz Hargrove's successor, Ken Lewenza. But his loyalty to this process was revealed by the fact that the Public Review Board was preserved when the CAW amalgamated with the communication workers.

Members of the Public Review Board are usually invited to sit on the platform during conventions of the CAW. At a few of these conventions, I found myself seated beside Walter Reuther's younger brother, Victor. It wasn't simply the family relationship that I found impressive. Victor Reuther had been a key UAW functionary and had worked alongside his older brother during most of Walter's battles. I exploited the opportunity and interviewed, questioned, and cross-examined Victor Reuther about so many of the UAW's campaigns. I also asked him his impressions of US president Franklin Roosevelt, American philosopher John Dewey, trade unionist Sidney Hillman, to name only a few of the all-stars from that era whom he had met personally. The chance to relate this way to Victor Reuther proved to be an unforgettable experience with an unforgettable person.

As a result of the intensity and duration of my involvements with the labour movement on this side of the border, I got to know—and know a lot better—many more Canadian labour leaders. Perhaps the most unforgettable of this group was Dennis McDermott who, starting as a factory worker at Massey Ferguson in the 1940s, became a UAW staff representative, then regional director of that union for Canada, and finally in the 1970s, president of the Canadian Labour Congress (CLC). He was tart-tongued, tough-minded, and gutsy. During a television interview on one occasion, he talked about the futility of becoming embroiled in public fights with certain kinds of people. But it was his words that were memorable: "Don't get into a pissing contest with a skunk."

Dennis was passionately committed to human rights, racial equality, and civil liberties—small wonder that we forged an enduring friendship.

When the going got tough at the Labour Committee and CCLA, I always knew that I could count on the regional director of the United Auto Workers and then the president of the Canadian Labour Congress (CLC). Another orientation we shared was our anti-Communism. Dennis became a loyal ally of Walter Reuther in the attempts to weed out Communists from influential places in the labour movement.

A central feature of his character was courage. It has been said, and rightly so, that the test of courage is not so much the willingness to take on adversaries, but the willingness to stand up to allies. *That* requires real courage. During his presidency of the CLC, Dennis was enmeshed in a controversy with a number of the affiliated unions. On the basis of a previous arrangement, he was due to speak at a convention of one of those affiliates. When Dennis appeared on the platform, he was the target of booing and catcalls. True to his character, Dennis stood his ground. He looked out at the audience and said, "More than a million trade unionists elected me president of the CLC; you can bet your sweet ass I'm going to speak." And, of course, he did.

During the last year of his life when he was already retired, Dennis attended a convention of the CLC. He was upset by the anti-Israel position being taken by a number of the CLC affiliates. At that stage of his life, he could have afforded to bask in his glory as a former CLC president. But not Dennis. He felt things too deeply. When he saw a wrong that had to be righted, that became his priority. So, he circulated a letter at the convention, tearing a strip off those who were baiting the State of Israel.

We don't often attribute sentimentality to a person with an acid tongue. But, in fact, Dennis had a sensitive and sentimental side. After many years of association with him, I was surprised to learn that he wrote poetry. I also remember him filled with emotion delivering a eulogy at the funeral of David Lewis. And, when I stepped down from the podium at a CLC convention after paying tribute to Dan and Donna Hill, the winners of the CLC social justice award, Dennis threw his arms around me and hugged me in front of the whole convention. No doubt, his heart probably explains his profound commitment to social justice.

Dennis also had a delightful sense of irony. A fellow trade unionist with whom he often enjoyed arguing was Louis Lenkinski, a Jewish Holocaust survivor who, for many years, had been a member of the

Jewish Labour Bund, an organization that had questioned the wisdom of the Zionist enterprise. When a delegation from Israel's labour federation, the Histadrut, visited the CLC, Dennis, the non-Jewish Zionist, chose Louis, the Jewish non-Zionist, to act as their host. Even though this assignment was Dennis's way of somewhat sticking it to Louis, he must have realized that, in fact, Louis and the people from Histadrut would relate very well to each other.

I also enjoyed and came to cherish my friendship with Louis Lenkinski, and with Terry Meagher, the secretary-treasurer of the Ontario Federation of Labour (OFL). Louis had many of the characteristics associated with the Jewish Labour Bund. He was secularist, socialist, Yiddish-speaking, universalistic, skeptical about Zionism, and hostile to Communism. Like many other Bundists, he made his peace with the Jewish State of Israel, once it was created. In this regard, I remember consulting him when I was invited to address a Zionist demonstration in front of the Soviet Embassy in Ottawa at the time of the 1967 six-day war. I playfully asked him whether he was more anti-Zionist or anti-Communist. He had little difficulty in advising me to accept the speaking engagement. "When a Jewish community is under siege," Louis said, "you help them. What difference does it make *where* that community happens to be located?"

Like so many others with whom I have been associated, Louis had a mischievous sense of humour. When the issue of hate propaganda was very much in the news, I was often the sole dissenter at meetings of the Canadian Jewish Congress Community Relations Committee. Although the members of that committee overwhelmingly favoured the anti-hate law, I was outspoken in my opposition to it. One day Louis telephoned to tell me that the Jewish Congress leaders had held a meeting and reached the decision to sew back on my foreskin. He was always happy to tease me.

While Louis who had started in the labour movement with the upholsterer's union wound up as an official of the OFL, Terry Meagher who had started with the bartender's union became Louis's boss, upon becoming secretary-treasurer of the OFL. Terry was intelligent, good-natured, and full of fun. At one point during an OFL convention, Terry drew me aside and escorted me to an area inhabited by a caucus of ultra–left-wing unionists. He walked over to one of them, put his arm around the man, and proclaimed loudly to me and others around that this man was his "favourite Commie."

During those years, Terry and Louis enjoyed a very close friendship. That friendship spoke volumes about both men. Louis, the Jewish Holocaust survivor, and Terry, the Nova Scotia Irishman, undoubtedly overcame mountains of prejudice that bedevilled other people from similar backgrounds. Not surprisingly, Terry was a steadfast member of the Labour Committee for Human Rights and a long time executive member of the Canadian Civil Liberties Association. He served both organizations with distinction.

Beyond the labour movement, a number of other unforgettable people came into my life. One of the most noteworthy of this group was Roger Baldwin, the founder of the American Civil Liberties Union (ACLU). I first met Roger when he participated at that 1970 meeting of American scholars at Harvard's John F. Kennedy School of Government during the time of the FLQ crisis in Canada. Although we met again a couple of days later at the national ACLU board meeting in New York, our most serious encounter occurred in 1976 at the United Nations in New York. He had agreed to take me on a guided tour of the UN. Early on, I challenged him about the way the ACLU was handling the case of the late Elizabeth Gurley Flynn, a functionary of the US Communist Party. Back in the 1930s, the ACLU had put Ms. Flynn on its board of directors. But, in response to the Stalin-Hitler non-aggression pact of 1939, the ACLU board expelled her. Following her death and some of the amelioration of American anti-Communist tensions, the ACLU board "rehabilitated" her.

I told Mr. Baldwin that I thought the ACLU was wrong at each stage of the Elizabeth Gurley Flynn saga. I think that her Communist Party membership should have initially raised questions about her suitability for the ACLU board. After all, the act of joining the Communist Party committed its members to the pursuit of activities that were inimical to the survival of political democracy in this world. While the ACLU should have been prepared to defend the civil liberties of Communist Party members within American society, service on the ACLU board was another matter.

Since I questioned whether the ACLU should have initially put Flynn on its board, expelling her after the Stalin-Hitler pact was not un-acceptable but it was done for the wrong reasons. She was expelled because people were offended—even if rightly so—by the Communist alliance with the Nazis. But her potential unworthiness to serve on the ACLU board went deeper than the one incident. It follows as well from the foregoing that her posthumous "rehabilitation" was also misconceived. In the absence of evidence that she warranted exceptional treatment despite her Communist Party involvements, she should have been disqualified from service on the ACLU board throughout the entire period in question.

Despite my lingering disagreement with Roger Baldwin's position on this matter, I was impressed with how well he argued. After all, he was then ninety-two years old. And, while I am in the course of admiring his exceptional fitness, I remember being particularly impressed by the speed with which he dictated letters in his office. Of particular note was his wit. As he was taking me through the UN and introducing me to various delegates who all seemed to know him, one of them said, "Mr. Baldwin, you're still active." To which Roger Baldwin replied, "Why not, I'm going to be inactive for a long time." He died a few years later at the ripe age of ninety-seven. I feel privileged to have spent this time with him.

In the fall of 1992, I visited South Africa as part of a Canadian program to exchange ideas and experiences with the reform movement in that country. It was an exciting time. Apartheid had just fallen and Nelson Mandela had been released after twenty-seven years in prison. Negotiations were under way to enfranchise the long-oppressed black and "coloured" people and provide for future transfers of power.

The itinerary that had been planned for me included a number of leaders from the African National Congress (ANC) and Judge Richard Goldstone who had ruled, from the bench, against certain aspects of the apartheid program. These meetings turned out to be deeply engaging. But one person was not included that I very much wanted to meet: Helen Suzman who, from her platform in the South African parliament, waged a one-person campaign for many years, against the apartheid regime. Fortunately, my request was granted and I wound up meeting alone with Helen Suzman in the recreation room of her home, for an hour and a half.

I came away highly impressed. It was essentially Suzman's courage that got to me. In addition to the years of fighting alone against the National Party government, she then took on her allies in the anti-apartheid movement. When they were calling for a worldwide boycott of South Africa, she publicly opposed them. In her view, such a boycott would disproportionately injure the very blacks whose interests she was trying to advance. It isn't necessary to agree with Helen Suzman's opinions on this matter in order to appreciate her willingness to stand alone against virtually everybody, when she thought it was right to do so.

Suzman also enriched my insights into the paradoxical nature of the South African regime. Although the regime perpetrated the unmitigated evil of apartheid, it permitted a certain amount of democratic practice including press freedom, judicial independence, and tolerance for opposition parties. Although the regime frequently jailed those who openly challenged it (blacks, "coloureds," and whites associated with the ANC), they repeatedly assured Suzman of her right to criticize.

In response to support he had received when he was in jail, Nelson Mandela appeared to have warm relations with Yasser Arafat, Muammar Gaddafi, Fidel Castro, and the South African Communist Party. Suzman, however, expressed considerable skepticism about such allies. In an era when white liberals were being denigrated from all sides, Helen Suzman was helping to restore their good name. She made me proud of my association with that constituency.

The itinerary for my South African visit contained an item for dinner at the residence of the Canadian ambassador. Having been travelling for a good part of the day in question, I was able to arrive about an hour before the scheduled dinner. I was shocked by what greeted me. I learned that the dinner was being held in my honour. Apparently, the ambassador had heard me speak when he was a student at the University of Manitoba during my visit there a number of years earlier.

Despite the fatigue I felt from travelling, I was sufficiently wide awake to experience a level of discomfort over this news. The dinner was slated to include about a dozen leaders from the African National Congress (ANC). I realized that they would expect me to make a speech. Since the people at the residence were good enough to give me a room with a couch where I could lie down for a while, I used that period of solitude—not to rest—but to figure out what the hell I would say in my speech.

When I was actually called upon to speak at the dinner, I told the audience that in making the arrangements he did, the ambassador had played a dirty trick on me. It must have been clear to him that he and I were the only people in that room who had never been in jail. I then told the group in attendance that, in planning things the way he did, the ambassador was illustrating the key differences between the way the South African and Canadian governments treated their critics. The South African government jailed them; the Canadian government made dinners in their honour. I said that the ambassador knew very well that, if news of this dinner ever reached Canada, I could be ruined.

Even before I had heard of Saul Alinsky, the fabled American organizer of the poor, I had used one of his signature tactics: the deployment of human bodies so as to inflict disruption on the operations and institutions I sought to influence. In his book, *Rules for Radicals*, he provided an example of such a tactic that he had conceived but subsequently found it unnecessary to use. In an effort to exert pressure on Chicago's mayor, Richard Daley, Alinsky devised a plan whereby members of his organization would occupy the toilets at Chicago's O'Hare Airport. In Alinsky's words, this could have amounted to the biggest "shit-in" that had ever been organized. He believed that, within thirty minutes, it could have created bedlam in the airport. In Alinsky's view, this tactic also had the virtue of avoiding illegality.

While I suspect that a compelling argument would be available to demonstrate how this tactic might violate Canadian law, I have used the essence of it in less contentious circumstances. In this regard, I recall how my colleagues and I in the Ethical Education Association and Canadian Jewish Congress went from door to door recruiting the parents of a particular North York school in Toronto to sign forms exempting their youngsters from religious instructions classes. It will be recalled that this tactic effectively paralyzed the religious education program and forced the director of education to negotiate with us. In view of the fact that the law had already provided a right to exemption, I think we could easily have established the legality of what we did.

Once I began to read Alinsky, however, I profited even more from what he had to say. In this regard, I recall how we persuaded the Toronto library board to close the overwhelming number of its libraries on a particular day, in protest against a federal pornography bill. The ensuing publicity and experience of disruption may well have been the critical factors that finally persuaded the government to withdraw the bill. As I explained at the time, the legality of this tactic would have been hard to impugn. Neither the employees nor the consumers closed the libraries; library *management* did.

I am pleased to relate that in the late 1960s and early seventies, I had occasion to appear on three different panels with Saul Alinsky. He proved to be every bit as delightful a character as his books had portrayed him. Indeed, one evening I was with him and a handful of community organizers, talking late into the night at a Montreal restaurant. It was stimulating, educational, and fun.

So much for my unforgettable moments with people who are generally on my side of most social conflicts. But I also have had many unforgettable times with political and social adversaries.

Somewhere around the early 1980s, I found myself in a public panel discussion with the conservative American professor Allan Bloom. He was the author of what was described as "an intellectual bestseller": *The Closing of the American Mind*. His book was an attack on the shallow relativism that he believed was inherent in American liberalism.

Despite — or maybe because of — my substantial differences with him, I had a lot of fun in our exchange. He was a witty and spirited debater. For what must have been a couple of hours, we kept trading quip after quip. Members of the audience subsequently told me that they thought our debate was "terrific."

At one point, Bloom, who was seated a little behind me on the platform, leaned over and commented quietly on one of my arguments. Rather graciously, he said, "That was a good response." At this point, I turned toward him and, pointing to the audience, I said, "So, tell *them* that." I was sorry to learn, a few years later, of his untimely death. He was a formidable and enjoyable opponent.

At some point in the early to mid-1990s, I developed the habit of joining a group of people who used to gather every Saturday afternoon at Toronto's Coffee Mill restaurant. Early on, I discovered the right-wing author and newspaper columnist, George Jonas. As I recognized that so much of his philosophy was diametrically opposed to mine, I started to seek him out at those Saturday afternoon get-togethers. I hungered for the polemics I knew that I could have with him.

He didn't disappoint. On many Saturday afternoons, he and I had some marvellous arguments. He was smart, witty, and fun. From my point of view, he emerged from our discussions as a most worthy defender of an unworthy philosophy.

Some years after these Coffee Mill encounters had ended, one of George's columns in the *National Post* was devoted to me. Under the title "Borovoy Sees the Light," Jonas reacted to an article I had just written in the *Calgary Herald* newspaper. In that piece, I lashed out at those provisions of Canada's human rights laws that purported to restrict expressions that were "likely to expose" people to "hatred or contempt" on such grounds as race, creed, and colour.

In acknowledging that I had had a significant role in the creation of these human rights laws and the human rights commissions that were designed to enforce them, I said that it had never occurred to my colleagues and me that these laws were ever going to be used to suppress the expression of opinion. George contended that he had explicitly warned me against such a development during the course of our Coffee Mill exchanges. As far as he was concerned, I simply hadn't paid enough attention to his advice.

In a letter to the editor, I pointed out that my colleagues and I at the Canadian Civil Liberties Association opposed these anti–free-speech measures from their very inception. Therefore, I had no need of the Jonas advice. Others jumped into our dispute. A letter was published from Eddie Greenspan who differed with my version of the facts, and other letters came from Louis Greenspan and Sydney Goldenberg who agreed with my version.

In my letter, I acknowledged that I was and remained a supporter of the human rights laws to the extent that they curbed discriminatory behaviour. As for the restrictions on free speech, however, I noted that the CCLA had intervened as long ago as 1990 to challenge the one in the federal human rights law. I also pointed out that the CCLA had opposed the anti-hate section of the *Criminal Code* as long ago as 1969. Moreover, in 1977, I had written to the federal authorities to complain when the federal human rights restriction first appeared. I wound up my letter to the *National Post* on a positive note: "Despite such inaccuracies and the utter wrong-headedness of [Jonas's] general philosophy, I confess that I still enjoy reading his columns."

Another right-winger worthy of mention here is my law school classmate, Hal Jackman. I would have to think very hard to remember any serious discussions that I have had with him, but he has nevertheless generated a lot of fun. When he participated in debates and discussions at the university, he often performed a spoof on himself. He was generally known to be the offspring of great wealth. But in his speeches, he frequently focused on the value of "getting back to the land" and "working with our hands."

At law school, he began to consider me the class Communist. Even though this occurred at a time when my orientation was becoming increasingly *anti*-Communist, Hal was not daunted. As a gift, he brought me a book outlining the history of the Soviet Communist Party. He also started to call me "Comrade." From that point on, that was the way he has addressed me.

One incident has particularly lingered in my psyche. Hal had become Lieutenant-Governor of Ontario and I was attending a reception at his official quarters. As I began to go through the rather long receiving line, he noticed me from the other end of the corridor. Despite the solemnity of the occasion, he called out, "Comrade." Hal was not fazed even when the dignity of the occasion might have required him to be otherwise.

My law school associations generated yet another unforgettable moment. At one of our class reunions, a former professor, under the influence of alcohol, approached me and planted a kiss on my forehead. That gesture was accompanied by the following statement: "I'm so fucking proud of you."

Perhaps the greatest, single, intellectual influence on my life came from the eminent American philosopher, Sidney Hook. As I have indicated earlier, I began reading his articles and books as long ago as the 1950s. Indeed, I have never stopped reading him.

What particularly impressed me about Sidney Hook was his ferocious independence. On domestic economic matters, he was very much the social democrat. But that coexisted with a more right-wing side to him. Since the 1930s, he was a virulent anti-Communist, even to the point of writing many treatises attacking the mushy-headedness of liberals on that subject.

At some point early in his development, he became and remained a leading expert on the philosophy of Karl Marx. Such expertise, of course, never diluted the vehemence of his anti-Soviet position. A champion of human rights for racial minorities, he expressed considerable skepticism about the quotas that had been designed to *benefit* such racial minorities. In any event, what impressed me most was not the extent of our agreement on the subjects of the day (we also had a number of disagreements), but the quality of his analyses of those subjects.

I particularly profited from reading Sidney Hook's explications of the philosophy propounded by his mentor, the great John Dewey. But Dewey couldn't write to save himself. Sidney Hook, on the other hand, had a colourful and free-flowing style. Hook was amusing, entertaining, and convincing all at once. Based upon my reading of Sidney Hook, I became pleased to call myself a pragmatist in the tradition of John Dewey.

In the spring of 1980, I received a call from an old friend of mine who had been living with her husband in La Jolla, California. She related to me how, under my influence, she picked up one of Sidney Hook's books and read it. She was so excited by what she had read that she telephoned Sidney Hook at the nearby Hoover Institute. When she told him about me, he asked why I had never called him. Of course, that's all I needed to hear. We had a few telephone calls, back and forth, and we exchanged some materials that each of us had written.

A couple of weeks later, I received a letter from Sidney Hook, praising the essays of mine that I had sent him. He told me that he had already reached the conclusion that I should be a professor at a leading university. He made me feel like a bar mitzvah boy who had recited his assignment without a mistake. All this led to an invitation that I come and visit him at his Vermont summer home when I was slated to be at the Tanglewood music festival in Massachusetts later that summer.

That visit to Sidney Hook's cottage in the summer of 1980 led to a series of eleven visits between that time and his death in the summer of 1989. Typically, we would arrive at his place in time for lunch and then sit down to an afternoon of delicious polemics. We also met once in New York and once when I took him and his wife out to dinner in Toronto. It's hard for me to describe how overjoyed I was at this relationship. When I received the news of his death in July 1989, I was saddened not only by the passing of this noble spirit but also because it had taken me so long to make contact with him.

Among my unforgettable experiences was my April 1988 speech at the Ottawa rally for the Japanese Canadian redress campaign. Rather than describe it myself I reproduce, in slightly edited form, an account of my participation, as it appeared in the book published by the organizers of the campaign:

> No one there would forget Alan Borovoy's dynamic speech, which ended: "We know that we cannot adequately guarantee tomorrow, but we want to do whatever we can do. That's why you have our support. Because it's the only way we know how to say to ourselves, to you, to each other, and to posterity, Never again, never again! This will bloody well happen, never again!" Borovoy's rousing speech had many in tears; it made an overwhelming impact.

While I consider many of my family members to be unforgettable, one of them deserves special mention in this context. I refer to the late Albert Garshowitz, whose mother was one of my father's oldest siblings. In all, my father was the youngest in his family of eight—five brothers and three sisters. My mother was the oldest of four brothers and two sisters. Thus, as an only child, I was bereft of siblings but awash in cousins.

Albert Garshowitz was one of some forty first cousins that I had. But what made him special was his role in Canada's armed forces during the Second World War. Although a number of other cousins also served, I believe it will become clear why I have singled out Albert. In the early 1940s, Albert joined the Royal Canadian Air Force (RCAF) and rose to the position of wireless air-gunner. As such, he became involved in one of the most dangerous operations of the war: the famous dambusters raid. The object of the raid was to destroy certain dams in Germany's Ruhr Valley. This destruction was expected to flood key sections of that country's industrial heartland, thereby weakening its capacity to make war. The operation was made so dangerous because the bombs required the planes to fly particularly low (under the radar and about sixty feet from ground level).

Like many others who participated with him, Albert never returned. Although I was very young when I last saw this illustrious cousin, I remember how good naturedly he played with us kids. I used to see him at the annual Borovoy picnics. (They occurred every year from 1938 until shortly after their seventieth anniversary in 2008). Those in my generation were in the habit of climbing all over Albert. And his response was always affectionate and fun-loving. I also remember the lovely letters he sent to my parents and me, from the various places where he was stationed. I'm sure other Borovoy relatives were treated with the same thoughtfulness.

Then came the news — first, he was missing in action; then, he was presumed dead; and, with the discovery of a charred body containing his dog tag, we had to accept the awful reality: Albert had been killed. It's not hard to imagine how I reacted, thereafter, whenever I heard the anti-Semitic canard that Jews were not doing their part for the war effort.

In March 1991, Rob Pritchard, then president of the University of Toronto, asked me if I would accept an honorary doctorate from the university. I was delighted to say "yes." At the time, this would have been my third honorary doctorate (I had already received them from Queen's and York), but this was special because the University of Toronto was my alma mater.

Nevertheless, I was aware of one problem that had the potential to interfere with the plan. The librarians at the U of T were then on strike and had picket lines at many of the university's facilities. I told Rob that, in all fairness, this might create a problem for me. Since the convocation ceremonies were not slated to occur until June, he suggested (and I agreed) that I respond in the affirmative and that we should set aside the issue until later.

But, as the months rolled on, I couldn't help noticing that the librarians were still on strike and that they were still picketing. I became increasingly uneasy. By late May, I felt it incumbent upon me to decide how I would handle the situation.

On May 31st, I sent a letter by courier to Rob Pritchard advising him that I was not prepared to cross the librarians' picket line in order to receive an honour from his university. Whatever else might conceivably justify crossing such a picket-line it was not appropriate to do so here. In the appendix, I have set out a copy of this letter so that I need not repeat here the analysis that I ultimately found persuasive. Later on that same day, however, I received a telephone call from Rob Pritchard. He asked me whether I had decided irrevocably not to accept the degree or whether it would make a difference if the parties had settled their dispute by then. Of course, I told him immediately that, once the dispute had been resolved, my interest in the matter would be at an end and I would then be delighted to attend and receive the degree. At that point, Pritchard told me to start writing my speech because he had every reason to believe that they were on the verge of a settlement. I laughingly chastised him for settling the matter before I could publicize what I had decided to do, and thereby claim some credit for the settlement.

Even though the parties had already resolved their differences by the time of convocation, the university was not prepared to let me escape without being publicly teased about the decision I had made. That was an obviously unforgettable moment.

The other awards in my life have also made a considerable impact—albeit with less controversy. I got the Order of Canada in the spring of 1983. My then girlfriend who lived in Kingston suggested that we use the travel money to rent a limousine from Kingston to Ottawa. Prior to the trip, I made a number of peanut butter sandwiches for us to eat along the way. The incongruity much appealed to me: eating peanut butter sandwiches on route to receive one of the highest honours that our country provides. I regret that I was unable to persuade our driver to share this delight with us.

I'm glad that both my parents were alive when I got the Order of Canada and somewhat earlier, a doctor of laws from Queen's University. But, despite the number of years that had elapsed since the death of my grandfather in 1948, I thought much about him with every honour I received. I have continued to think of him as my earliest partner in my liberal politics. Another image that kept coming back to me on these occasions was our gang on Grace Street.

A few years later in the mid-1990s, CCLA retained the services of a marketing expert. As a result of his advice, we applied to place an advertisement about our organization in *NOW Magazine*. The ad was cleverly titled, "Does CSIS Bug You?"

Not long afterwards, we received a reply from the magazine rejecting our proposed ad. The reply contended that our ad might be viewed as "offensive" to a number of their readers. This letter evoked hysterical laughter in our office.

Our rejoinder, very much tongue in cheek, commended the magazine for the sensitivity it was showing to its readers. But we asked how *NOW* could square this reply with the ads it was already carrying. Such ads included "brown and yellow showers" and "we'll lick your boots." Our accompanying note asked whether our ad would be more acceptable if we changed the heading from "Does CSIS Bug You?" to "Does CSIS BUGGER You?"

We rushed to mail our rejoinder so that we could publicize it in other media. It was too good an opportunity to lose. The *Toronto Star* obliged us with a funny story. After that, *NOW Magazine* offered to publish our ad for free. I should point out that our thanks went to Tony Doob for coming up with that show-stopping punchline.

At some point around 2007 or 2008, I finally decided that, after forty years, it was time for me to retire from my job at the Canadian Civil Liberties Association. I began to fear that, at seventy-seven, if I hung on very much longer, a number of my board colleagues would lose faith in the continuity of the organization. I was not prepared to take the risk that the organization would be unable to survive my tenure. I set my departure date for July 1, 2009.

On the evening of April 28 2009, a retirement banquet in my honour was held at Toronto's Royal York Hotel. For me, this was an unforgettable event, if ever there was one. The crowd was estimated at six hundred. It included retired judges, sitting judges, three chief justices, and much of the cream of the Ontario bar. I was roasted by the best — Justice Ian Binnie of the Supreme Court of Canada, Justice Robert Sharpe of the Ontario Court of Appeal, former Osgoode Hall law dean John McCamus, former York University president Harry Arthurs, and our master of ceremonies, noted criminal lawyer Eddie Greenspan. The speakers sounded like stand-up comedians. Again and again, the packed audience exploded in laughter.

Eddie couldn't resist comparing me with my illustrious successor, Nathalie Des Rosiers. He said that Nathalie was "a graduate of the Harvard Law School and Alan is a graduate of Harbord Collegiate." The newly elected president of the American Civil Liberties Union attended in person and addressed the audience. Her predecessor, the charming Nadine Strossen, appeared by way of a videotape. It was clear that the audience had a terrific time. For me, it was a memorable way to leave the job that I loved so much.

Penultimate Perspectives

Of course, I label what I say in this chapter, penultimate, rather than ultimate, perspectives. At this point, neither I nor my successors could hope to know the ultimate ones. If any readers wish to know those, they will have to consult my executors.

During the summer of 2008, I joined the hundreds of thousands of people who sat glued to their respective television sets, watching the convention of the US Democratic Party. Senator Barack Obama of Illinois was seeking to become the first black president of the United States. At issue during that summer was the leadership of the Democratic Party. The victor at the convention would become the party's standard bearer in the impending fall elections.

My attention was particularly arrested by the litany of speeches, seconding Obama's nomination. More than anything else, I fixated on the number of *white* delegates who were expressing their support for him. Of course, he had no shortage of black delegates on his side. But all that white support was truly newsworthy. After all, this was the very country in which less than forty-five years earlier, three young civil rights workers had been so brutally murdered—with impunity. It was also the country whose Southern communities had been so recently pockmarked with "Whites Only" signs on publicly accessible facilities. And it was the country in which the national army had so recently been called out to escort young black students into school. So much change in so little time.

As I watched one white delegate after another declare support for Senator Obama, I felt my eyes fill up with tears. Indeed, I had the feeling that if I tried to speak, I would have been all choked up. Why, I asked myself? Why did this development in the United States overwhelm me with so much emotion? It's not that I was such a strong supporter of Obama. To be sure, I had—and continue to have—my differences with him. But it was the *phenomenon* of Obama that was getting to me.

Part of the answer was obvious. I had spent so much of my life in the pursuit of racial equality. From my boyhood brushes with anti-Semitism to my later professional involvements on behalf of blacks and aboriginals, the cause of equality had long occupied a front and centre position on my personal agenda. I had even enjoyed several interactions with US civil rights leaders: I was one of a small group of Torontonians who was chosen to have lunch with Martin Luther King; I publicly thanked King's aide, Ralph Abernathy, for a speech he made to Toronto's First Unitarian Church; I sat on a platform with James Farmer, the leader of the Congress for Racial Equality; and I polemicized about civil rights a number of times with American labour leaders at conferences of the US Jewish Labour Committee.

But the more I thought about the depth of my responses that summer day in 2008, the more I thought there must be more to it than the foregoing. As my reflections intensified, I was struck by an intriguing thought: Obama represented the vindication of a point of view I had developed more than fifty years earlier. During the late 1950s, I had come to believe that the United States must prevail in its Cold War conflict with the Soviet Union. In general, of course, there was nothing particularly remarkable about a Canadian siding with the United States in that way. Lots of Canadians harboured similar views. But not that many of my fellow citizens, who were politically left of centre, felt the way I did.

Granted, there was no paucity even of left-leaning Canadians who argued that Canada should remain within the American alliance. Only a small number would have had our country opt for a neutralist course. But the arguments of the majority of left-leaners were cast primarily in tactical, not ethical, terms. They said, for example, that Canadian interests would be better served within, rather than outside, the American fold. They also contended that, given Canada's geographical proximity to—and economic dependence upon—the United States, a neutralist position was completely unrealistic.

I found very few left-leaning Canadian small "l" liberals or social democrats who were prepared to argue aggressively that pushing for an American victory was a matter not only of tactics but also of ethics. From at least the late 1950s on, I considered American paramountcy in the Cold War a moral imperative. No commercial, logistical, apologetic, or defensive posture would suffice for me. I supported the US-led alliance primarily because, in my view, it was the only morally appropriate stand to take.

The reasons for my position were central. For all of its faults, inadequacies, and imperfections, the United States was essentially a democracy. The Soviet Union, on the other hand, was a totalitarian dictatorship, and a repressive one at that. To quote a wise old trade unionist, the US unlike the USSR, had a grievance procedure. Americans were free openly and publicly to seek and attempt to mobilize the support of their fellow citizens for the redress of their various grievances. In that kind of system, it was at least politically possible for minorities—to use the words of the civil rights ballad—to "overcome." By contrast, the Soviet system was effectively closed to opposition interests and points of view. Thus, even though I was—and remain—very critical of many of America's misdeeds, there was no question about where I would be in the crunch.

I don't want to exaggerate. I never had to pay an exorbitant price for my Cold War politics. Since the overwhelming amount of my activity was in the domestic arena, my foreign policy views were rarely of wide interest. But there were nevertheless a few occasions when I felt the sting of my colleagues' disapproval. During the Cold War years, I got involved in a number of debates and panel discussions about international affairs. Quite often, an opponent or fellow panelist would be a peace activist who considered the United States at least as evil as the Soviet Union. In those situations, I would usually turn my verbal guns on that activist. In the left-of-centre circles I often inhabited, my views on such matters evoked a range of negative reactions—from disapproval, to contempt, to even hostility.

Thus, in Obama's success, I could genuinely feel that my bouts of unpopularity had been redeemed. Against all the odds, Barack Obama and, to a great extent the black community, had indeed "overcome." His victory vindicated my judgment. American democracy had proved its ability to produce meaningful reform. Small wonder, therefore, that I responded the way I did to the events of summer 2008. In the process, I also learned something significant about myself. It had become evident that, in my panoply of values, the defence of democracy occupied a position of centrality.

In the course of recalling the activities of my career, I have become conscious now—as I might not have been at the time—of the role played by this priority in the formulation of my policies and decisions. It might be useful, therefore, to review some of my previous actions in light of my overriding commitment to the preservation of the democratic system.

Remember how CCLA and another human rights organization diverged on the issue of how much access deportable persons should have to classified material that would be used against them? We were both testifying at a parliamentary committee. Initially, CCLA's fellow presenter argued that fair play required such persons to have complete access. From the outset, I argued that security-cleared lawyers should have such access on behalf of those slated for deportation, but they should also be prohibited from disclosing the classified contents to their "clients." As I related earlier, that other organization, under close questioning from members of the committee, ultimately softened its position.

At the end of the day, it became quite clear that the position CCLA took was the more prudential of the alternatives available. By opting initially for the extreme position that it did, the other organization was risking its credibility. Even though that much is clear, I have had some further thoughts that might be illuminated by my commitment to democratic survival. Because of that commitment, I did not want anyone reasonably suspected of terrorism to have access to my country's national security secrets. For me, the position I took at that committee was not simply sound from a tactical standpoint, it was also required by my ethical beliefs.

Admittedly, the compromise could impose some fetters on the ability of lawyer and client to consult freely. On balance, however, I believe that our proposal represented the *least bad* position that could have been adopted.

When it came time to make recommendations regarding the scope of the power that the Canadian Security Intelligence Service (CSIS) should enjoy, we proposed another compromise. The government of Canada bill provided for wide powers of preventive intelligence gathering; in the US, the ACLU would have narrowed the powers of intelligence agencies so that, in key situations, there would have to be probable cause to believe that certain criminal *acts* had been, were being, or were about to be, committed.

As far as the intrusive surveillance of citizens and permanent residents was concerned, we agreed with the ACLU that there should have to be reasonable grounds to believe an actual *crime* was involved. But, unlike the ACLU, we were prepared to allow *some amount* of preventive intelligence gathering. We differed with the ACLU in our support of the idea that CSIS could intrusively spy on citizens and permanent residents in the event of a conspiracy to commit serious security-related illegalities. But, like the ACLU, we feared the tremendous potential for abuse in the very concept of conspiracy. Thus, we suggested that there should have to be evidence of overt conduct in furtherance of any such malevolent plan. In this way, we hoped to provide our democracy with adequate power to ensure its self-protection but not an amount of power that could readily be abused.

Further retrospective reflection indicates that a number of the positions CCLA and I have taken over the years would have helped to de-polarize public opinion on the issues about which we were commenting. It is probably obvious that a de-polarized political climate would contribute to the enhancement of public confidence in the democratic system. The greater the consensus, the more likely the stability.

I have already related something of the relentless battle we fought against mandatory minimum jail sentences. The unfairness of those penalties was particularly evident in the case of Saskatchewan farmer Robert Latimer. Having been convicted of second-degree murder for ending the life of his severely disabled twelve-year-old daughter, he wound up being sentenced to jail for life with no chance of parole for ten years. Characterizing Latimer's role in the death of that little girl as a "compassionate homicide," the trial judge gave him a more lenient penalty. But, on appeal, the harsh sentence was imposed because it was the minimum required by the *Criminal Code* for second-degree murder.

After having been rebuffed by both the courts and the government, we borrowed an idea from British law: a *presumptive* minimum sentence. Acknowledging, as we had to, the horrendous nature of certain crimes, we could appreciate the need for the law to appropriately denounce the conduct in question. In any event, what we found most objectionable about mandatory minimums was their rigidity. Our whole point was that there must be some relief against rigid harshness. And so, we proposed that crimes such as murder might carry a presumptive minimum, so long as there was provision to bypass it in exceptional circumstances. I am hoping that this type of compromise might yet help to rid our society of those unjust mandatories. And, in the process, we could help to blunt the sting of the whole debate about appropriate punishments.

Through the medium of the *Charter*, Canadian law at long last was going to provide for the exclusion from court of much evidence that had been obtained in violation of constitutional principles. Shrinking from the prospect of a comprehensive ban on the use of tainted evidence, the *Charter* set conditions; such evidence was to be excluded if its admission would bring the administration of justice "into disrepute." By way of telegraphing our accommodation to some such exceptions, we recommended at least one situation where the courts might permissibly lean in favour of admitting the evidence. That situation was one in which the delinquent police officers were themselves charged or disciplined by the time the main case got to court. Otherwise, we argued, the courts should lean in the opposite direction. A compromise of this kind might well help to avoid—or at least reduce—the erosion of public confidence that so often accompanies these controversies.

In the case of extremists, we often both defended and denounced them. Take, for example, the purveyors of hate. On the one hand, we publicly criticized the prosecution of anti-Semitic teacher James Keegstra, but publicly supported his ouster from the mayor's office of Eckville, Alberta, his removal from the classroom, and his banishment from the teaching profession. In that way, we promoted both freedom of speech *and* ethnic dignity. In the case of Keegstra's lawyer Doug Christie, we petitioned to intervene in court on his side of the constitutional argument but we also wrote to him insisting that he account for some of his public statements that seemed to endorse the bigoted views of his contentious clients. While we opposed the prosecutions of both James Keegstra and Ernst Zundel, we questioned whether anti-Semitic author Malcolm Ross should be teaching in a New Brunswick high school. Again, there was something principled in our position for both sides of the debate — a net plus for Canadian democracy.

In certain media interviews, I challenged the propriety of the surveillance that both the RCMP and CSIS had conducted against Canadian Trotskyists. I argued that such surveillance was largely gratuitous; we saw no evidence that the Trotskyists had ever gone beyond fantasizing about revolutions. But I couldn't let the occasion go by without also taking a shot at them. On the subject of Trotskyists, I said, "There is a difference between a threat to the state and a pain in the ass." The viability of our democracy stood to be enhanced by the willingness both to defend and attack dubious elements on the margins of our community.

On employment equity I was supportive in some respects and critical in others. In view of the persisting inequalities after so many years of human rights legislation, I thought that the idea of requiring affirmative initiatives had some merit. I could even go for numerical goals. But the goals had to be sensible. It was not acceptable to punish today's generation of innocent white males because of the benefits conferred upon their predecessors of an earlier generation. To whatever extent it became possible to make a reasonable estimate of the number of the disadvantaged people that would be hired if there was no discrimination, such a number might well be worth becoming an equity goal. At one and the same time, we could embrace what was helpful in the concept and reject what was harmful in some of its manifestations.

On the rape shield, CCLA took what was then a unique position. While the prosecutors and feminist intervenors attempted to preserve the rape shield then in existence, the defence was attempting to nullify it in its entirety. We complained, not about the existence of such a shield, but about its scope. In its existing form, we considered it a threat to a fair trial. But if it were done away with completely, it would leave female complainants unwarrantedly vulnerable to invasions of their privacy.

Our argument attempted to identify some of the recurring fallacies on the basis of which the rape trials of the past had subjected the complainants to these demeaning ordeals. One such fallacy was the assumption that women who were sexually promiscuous were also ethically promiscuous and, therefore, not believable. The other fallacy was that women who agreed to have sex on a number of previous occasions were more likely to have consented in this case. We asked the court express-ly to disallow evidence of past sexual conduct to the extent that it was based on those assumptions. But we also called for a procedural hurdle: before other evidence of past sexual encounters could be admitted, a trial judge would have to be persuaded of its probative value in a special *in camera* hearing convened for that purpose. Once more, CCLA was attempting to de-polarize the situation. The court bought the thrust of our proposal.

On the infamous "spouse in the house" rule for welfare recipients, we argued that it was unfair to disqualify those people (in the main, women) just because they were cohabiting with a member of the op-posite sex. But, we acknowledged that, since two can live more cheap-ly than one, there might be an argument for reducing the *amount* of welfare assistance available to the recipient. This was another situation in which our approach could have helped to de-polarize the conflict. Ultimately, the Ontario Court of Appeal adopted a position, not unlike the one we advocated.

I hope it is clear from all the foregoing examples that de-polarizing compromises need not—and in these cases, did not—dilute any of the principles we were fighting for. Indeed, I would not have advocated any policy positions that I believed would have had such an effect.

*M*y life's work—first, the Labour Committee and then the Can-adian Civil Liberties Association—represented the fulfillment of cer-tain teenage fantasies. I dreamt of having a vocation in which I could fight for social justice, using creativity, oratory, publicity, and the ability to write and to organize.

My two jobs had it all. Not the least of it, they provided an outlet for my evolving ethical orientation. In that way, I felt indulged. I spent a virtual lifetime, implementing in my concrete work, the philosophy that was developing in my abstract thoughts.

It was obvious that, in the kind of work I was doing, I faced pub-lic policy decisions involving ethical choices, often difficult ones, just about every day. For whatever it's worth, my choices were not based on any attributions of Divine Will. Indeed, since my mid-1950s visit to the Mormon Tabernacle, I have thought that the attribution of Divinity engulfs the believer in hopeless contradictions.

My philosophy has eschewed both transcendent absolutism on the one hand and subjective relativism on the other hand. Although I have aimed for objectivity in my value choices, I've had to acknowledge that such objectivity was necessarily a limited one. It was an attempt to resolve ethical conflicts on the basis of the values and interests shared by those who stood to be affected by any particular problem or issue.

As I have indicated a number of times, my approach has been pragmatic. It has not posited any one value or truth, religious or secular, that would apply to every problem in every place at every time. The truths have been multiple and shifting. There has been no all-purpose anchor to which everything had to pay homage. Thus, I grew to abhor doctrinaire thinking that attempted to deduce policy from any stationary abstraction. In my world, a plurality of values and truths had to be perpetually balanced and weighed against each other on the basis of the shared values and interests in the situations where they arose.

*F*rom the beginning, I realized that my chosen work would be seen, at least, as somewhat strange. After all, why would a lawyer—with all that earning potential—choose occupations with such limited income possibilities? I remember so well the first time I had occasion to tell anyone outside of my immediate circles about my first full-time, post-graduate employment. It was in a conversation with the father of a young woman I was dating. I had come into their home, ecstatic with the news that I was going to be working for the Labour Committee for Human Rights. The man was visibly perplexed. "But when are you going to practise law?" he asked me. I know now that I must have come across as a visitor from Mars.

Needless to say, that conversation has been replicated in many different ways, many times over the years. Indeed, I have gone through much of my life in the belief that I was being perceived as some kind of weirdo. No matter, my life has generally been a happy one. My work, of course, has contributed immeasurably as have my family and friendships.

A number of years ago, I began to believe that, to be happy, we humans needed to have self-transcendent goals. We couldn't achieve happiness merely by appeasing our sensory appetites. That's why I started to think of rich playboys as desperately unhappy people. Essentially, they had nothing to live for. It was all-important, therefore, to have goals beyond our sensories. A genuine love relationship (parental, spousal, etc.) could do it as can work that is creative and helpful. My work provided just the kind of self-transcendent goals that would do the trick. And they did. Thanks largely to my work, I have had a most happy time.

Now that my regular career is virtually over, it's hard to avoid the inevitable questions as to how I would assess the trade-offs between career and family. Although my work provided a terrific source of fulfillment, was it worth the lack of wife and children? Of course, to express the issue this way, is to accept uncritically the assumptions that people have often made.

The fact is: there was no conscious trade-off. I never *decided* against having a family. Indeed, I always believed that I would have one. As far as my conscious decision making was concerned, the failure of the fates to deliver a family felt more like cosmic coincidence than wilful intention. Do I regret the outcome? In truth, I must answer this the way I have answered many of the issues that have confronted me—yes in some respects and no in other respects.

Without the burdens of family responsibility, I was free to focus on the work that I loved so much. Of course, there was a genuine advantage in not having to worry about driving the kids to hockey practice and not having to endure with them those interminable waits in doctors' offices. There was also a major disadvantage. I have gone through life deprived of spousal intimacies and parental pride. I have no doubt that I have missed a lot. In the result, however, I am not pained or upset. I feel more wistful than anything else.

Since there is no way for me to relive the past, I have no wish or need to resolve these questions. Fortunately, work, family, and friends have furnished me with a rich and happy life. Even if I didn't have a spouse, I have some of the most marvellous former "girlfriends" anyone could ask for. Even if I didn't have kids, I have had wonderful, enduring friendships. And I had my work. All in all, a highly rewarding mix.

For all of which, I am deeply grateful to whom or to what—beyond my friends and family—I still don't know.

As for the family, I have already mentioned the liberalism of my parents. Unlike so many others, they never felt the need to fashion their offspring in their image. They accepted my heresies with complete grace. But it wasn't until I started to observe interactions in other households that I came to realize just how special my parents were.

Other family members have also played a pivotal role, starting with the maternal grandfather with whom I shared so much, in life, politics, and humour. My perennially helpful cousin, Andrea (Pearl) Baltman, has been particularly important in this regard. I'm unable to evaluate the significance of the fact that we are both the only surviving offspring of the only two sisters in my mother's family of four brothers. But I can't help suspecting the influence of that providential development.

Beginning with the gang around Grace Street, my friendships have always been key in my life. Earlier, I described the impact of my friendship with Louis Goldstein. Unfortunately, he did not live to see his fiftieth birthday. Some of those early friendships have remained with me ever since, particularly those with Berril Garshowitz (1940), Mel Finkelstein (1941), and Murray Tojo Rubin (1944). At university—more particularly at Camp Ogama (1955)—I met and made friends with Millie Rotman and Owen Shime, who later became her husband. The three of us remained the closest of friends until Millie's untimely death in 1982; my friendship with Owen persists to this day. Other Camp Ogama friends who remain in the fold to this day are Sydney Goldenberg and the camp owner (Sydney's uncle) Joe Goldenberg (early 1950s).

In my political campaign, I became—and continue to be—friends with philosophy professor Louis Greenspan (early 1960s). As for later friendships that have endured: (now Reverend) Dawn Clark and Cyril Levitt (1980s) and Merrilees Muir (1990s). Judging by the values we shared, I believe my friendship with Calgary lawyer Sheldon Chumir (1980s–1992) would still have been going strong if it had not been cut short by his premature death. Not the least of my most recent friendships is the central one I now enjoy with Myra Gula Merkur who has generously provided both hearth and heart.

A number of people helped much in my work life and became friends beyond that: Dan and Donna Hill, Sid Blum, Terry Meager, Louis Lenkinski, Dennis McDermott, Marv Schiff, Syd Midanik, John McCamus, and Ken Swan. With Harry Arthurs, it was the other way around. He started as a personal friend and became a work colleague.

*S*ince I have already reached a ripe age, I feel the need (perhaps gratuitously) to include some advice for my younger colleagues and successors.

What people believe is often less important than *how* they believe it. More than once, I have respected certain open-minded opponents more than narrow-minded allies. And, in recent years, I have developed considerable contempt for knee-jerk reactions such as those on the left that indiscriminately condemn whatever Israel does and those on the right that indiscriminately applaud whatever Israel does. Both have forsaken analysis that is reflective for that which is reflexive.

My colleagues have often heard me say, "Beware of your allies." This is not to say that we should not seek and try to keep allies. They are often a prerequisite to victory in a case or cause. But there is a downside. The larger a coalition gets, the harder it becomes to wage our battles according to our best lights. Large coalitions could tend to become excessively conservative or excessively radical. The kind of nuanced arguments that I have been advocating here often become difficult, if not impossible, to sell to a wide group that is not particularly used to our type of advocacy. Seek and have partners, by all means. But use these alliances and partnerships in very limited ways so that they cannot undermine our day-to-day activity.

Respect, but don't worship, "the people." Democratically motivated organizations often defer more than they should to the judgment of the people at large. The fact is that, not infrequently, the people have dreadful judgment. Even if that judgment must be obeyed, it need not, therefore, be revered.

How do I square such remarks with my democratic philosophy? Although I don't have very much faith in the people, most of the time I have even less faith in the government. Thus, I favour ultimately letting the people choose but letting governments govern in the meantime.

The power of governments to make decisions must co-exist nevertheless with the right of people simultaneously to generate protests and
periodically to replace their governments. A sensible democracy must
make no assumptions that any constituency has superior virtue or wisdom. *No one*, therefore, deserves our unreserved trust. In any event, we
should try, with rational persuasion and lawful pressure, to correct our
respective governments and our fellow citizens, when we believe they
have gone wrong. Such attempts are what we call acts of "leadership."

The beginning of wisdom is the recognition that, whatever we humans do, it's likely to turn out badly. It's wise, therefore, to avoid fantasizing about human capability. But, even if we can't make the situation
good, we can make it less bad. So, the conscious objective of our efforts
should be, not to achieve the ideal or even the good, but the less bad. It
would be sensible, therefore, to renounce the quest to create Heaven on
earth—and focus instead on reducing the Hell.

I credit this perspective for the fact that I have never suffered the
"burn-out" that so often afflicts social activists. Not infrequently, burn-
out results from the disillusionment that accompanies the experience
of defeat in a cause or conflict. But, when you have a more realistic view
of human proclivities, you are not as likely to be disillusioned. You get
adjusted to—indeed, you even derive some fulfilment from—the incremental nature of the gains to be made. All of this will help to explain
my characterization of defeats as victories I haven't *yet* won.

We should attach a high priority to having fun. It's often such fun to
kick the ass of the establishment. And there's no reason to be deprived of
it. Indeed, such a priority can enhance the quality of our activism. Those
who are so "dedicated" that they don't see or appreciate the humour in
life run the risk of developing a bad digestive system—and even of getting pimples. So, for heaven's sake, relax and have a good time.

Now, that I have gotten all this off my chest, I can turn my attention
to my last great challenges. On that subject, Woody Allen has made a
most compelling remark. He said that he doesn't fear death; he just
doesn't want to be there when it happens. Thus, it will be appreciated
why I have come to regard procrastination as a virtue, worthy of being
cultivated.

Letter to Robert Pritchard

CANADIAN
CIVIL LIBERTIES
ASSOCIATION
229 Yonge Street, Suite 403
Toronto, Ontario M5B 1N9
Telephone (416) 363-0321

ASSOCIATION
CANADIENNE DES
LIBERTES CIVILES
229 rue Yonge, Suite 403
Toronto, Ontario M5B 1N9
Téléphone (416) 363-0321

May 31, 1991   <u>BY COURIER</u>

J. Robert S. Prichard
President
University of Toronto
Toronto, Ontario
M5S 1A1

Dear Rob:

You will recall that, in late March when I accepted your
kind offer of an honourary doctorate, I noted the presence
on campus of labour picket lines and indicated that, if
they should persist, they might pose a problem for me at
the time of convocation. Indeed, you were gracious enough
to acknowledge this when we saw each other on May 22nd.

It is now beginning to appear that my worst apprehensions
may actually be realized. The current library strike looks
as though it is going to endure for a while and there is
every reason to believe that the strikers will picket the
convocation facilities and ceremonies. That being the
case, I am obliged to face squarely how I should respond.
In view of your kindness to me, I believe you are entitled
to know not only my position but also something of the
process by which I got there.

The situation has been a very difficult one for me. On the
one hand, I have had many involvements with the labour
movement for many years. I could not easily take action
that I knew would exacerbate the pain of striking workers.
On the other hand, I don't much admire reflexive behaviour.
The fact that I might have general sympathies with the

2

labour movement does not mean that this particular union is right
in these particular circumstances.

Ideally, outsiders, faced with the prospect of entering a picketed
establishment, should attempt to evaluate the competing equities
between the parties. There have been many situations in which that
would be a relatively easy exercise. Penny-pinching, union-busting
employers, for example, can exert little weight on the scales of
equity. But most disputes today may well not be amenable to such
black and white characterization. Sorting out shades of gray could
create a truly herculean, if not impossible, undertaking. As a
practical matter, therefore, the behaviour of outsiders must
frequently be determined on the basis of something less adequate
than an assessment of the equities between the parties.

In the "gray" situations, I believe that the least inadequate
response for outsiders is to aim for some semblance of neutrality.
This means trying, as far as possible, to confine the scope of the
labour dispute to the primary parties. In the main, we do this by
avoiding acts of affirmative assistance to, or involvement with,
one side or the other. By way of example, I cite the position I
took in a "black and white" situation a number of years ago when I
joined a picket line of working people who were on strike against
a Toronto hotel. That act represented my direct involvement in the
dispute; it supported the union. If instead of joining the picket
line I had rented a room in the hotel, I would have become involved
to the extent of helping the hotel to carry on business; that would
have supported the employer. But, if I had done neither - if I had
neither joined the picket line nor patronized the hotel - I would
have been helping to confine the dispute to the endurance contest
between the primary parties. That, in my view, would have
represented the closest thing to neutrality that I could have
achieved under the circumstances.

A contrary view would essentially deny the possibility of any
semblance of neutrality in this kind of situation. On the basis of

3

such a view, if circumstances foisted choice upon us, it would not be possible to avoid favoritism. By going in, we would be supporting management; by staying out, we would be supporting the union. I think, therefore, that my analysis is fairer to the position of outside parties and more consonant with the realities of what happens in a labour dispute.

Since I regard the current library strike as a "gray" situation, I would prefer not to participate on one side or the other. Until and unless I became much more knowledgeable and convinced about the equities than I am now, I would prefer – even if asked – not to join the picket line, donate to the strike fund, or participate in any of the strikers' rallies. Similarly, I would prefer – even if asked – not to help the University conduct its normal business if that meant crossing such a picket line to do so.

I hasten to point out that the position I am developing here is not absolute. There are some circumstances in which the functions performed by an outsider would serve overriding interests. An obvious example would be one in which an ambulance driver or doctor was called across a picket line in order to treat a sick person. We know that, regardless of the pickets, many professors continued to report for work because of the obligations they had incurred to the welfare of their students. For my purposes here, it is not necessary to resolve how far these or many other interests would justify infringing such picket lines.

Suffice it to note that the interests to be served by my participation at convocation can, in no way, be described as overriding. For the students, convocation is at most a beautiful and enriching ceremony, symbolic of their achievements. Not a trivial interest, to be sure. But not pressing enough to warrant my compromising on the goal of avoiding such involvement with the parties.

For myself, the event represents a memorable occasion. It happens

4

to coincide with the 35th anniversary of my graduation from the University. I have very much looked forward to addressing the people who would be graduating from my faculty. I deeply regret the loss of such an experience. My sense of proportion, however, tells me that I cannot regard my interests in the occasion as pressing enough to warrant my compromising on the goal of avoiding such involvement with the parties.

On the basis of the foregoing, I regret having to advise you that I intend not to cross these picket lines in order to participate at convocation. After we talked the other day, I decided to give you this notice before the date you indicated, in the event that you wished to make other plans. In the absence of further word from you, I shall assume that you have made such other plans. You must realize how profoundly sorry I am – not only for what I am missing, of course, but also for whatever inconvenience this will cause to those who are planning the convocation ceremony. I am also deeply grateful to you and your colleagues on the governing council for having given me this wonderful honour. Please convey my best wishes to them and to the students who are graduating.

Best regards.

Sincerely,

A. Alan Borovoy
General Counsel

Index

Blakeney, Alan, 197, 305
Blaker, Rod, 224–226
Bliss, Michael, 153
Bloom, Allan, 328
Blum, Sid, 50, 53, 61, 62, 65, 75, 76–77, 319, 347
Borovoy, Alan, 9, 88, 103, 146, 235, 278, 292, 332, 335
Borovoy, Jack, 3
Borovoy, Rae, 3
Bourassa, Robert, 204, 214
Bourne, Robin, 220
Brown, Syd, 176–77
Bush, George H., 290
Bush, George W., 207, 290

C

Cadillac Fairview, 149
Callwood, June, 114, 125, 195, 207, 241, 284, 319
Camp, Dalton, 125, 207, 213, 312
Campbell, Kim, 283
Canadian Auto Workers (CAW) union, 320, 321
Canadian Bar Association, 216, 242, 307
Canadian Bill of Rights, 171, 172, 276, 278
Canadian Charter of Rights and Freedoms, 142, 149, 171, 173, 193–94, 233, 245, 249, 262, 265, 271, 278, 280, 301–8, 340
Canadian Civil Liberties Association (CCLA), 86, 98, 109–16, 119, 121, 125, 127–35, 139–42, 146, 148–51, 155, 156, 159–66, 170, 172, 174, 175, 177, 178, 180, 182, 183, 184, 186–89, 191, 193–200, 205–6, 208–9, 211–13, 215, 217–19, 221, 224, 226, 227, 229–30, 234–35, 238, 240–42, 245, 253, 254–55, 257, 259, 260–64, 266–70, 271, 273–92, 295–98, 301, 304–9, 311–115, 322, 334, 340, 341, 343–44

Canadian Constitution, 264, 269, 270
Canadian Human Rights Act, 135–36
Canadian Jewish Congress, 30, 32, 33, 51, 59, 93, 98, 109, 111, 127, 134, 137, 264, 323, 327
Community Relations Committee, 98, 100, 129, 321
Canadian Labour Congress (CLC), 110, 111–12, 321–23
Canadian Security Intelligence Service (CSIS), 233, 242–46, 312, 334–35, 341, 343
Canadian Security Intelligence Service Act, 239
Canadian Trotskyist movement, 121, 141, 235, 246, 343
Canadian Union of Public Employees (CUPE), 234
Castro, Fidel, 326
Categorically Incorrect, 248, 288, 312
Catzman, Fred, 99
CBC, 78, 100, 125, 133, 163, 203, 206, 241, 307
Censorship, 100–1, 148, 158, 161, 162, 166, 165, 312
China, 28–29
Chippewas, 114–15
Chrétien, Jean, 230–33, 306
Christie Pits, 9–10
Christie, Douglas, 131–33, 342
Chumir, Sheldon, xii, 347
Church of Scientology, 138–39
Chusid, Murray, 27, 34
Clairmont, Donald, 78–80
Clark, Dawn, xii, 347
Clément, Dominique, 311
Cohen, Maxwell, 134
Cohen, Mickey, 38
Cold War, 20, 23, 24, 25, 43, 103, 105, 336–37
Communism, 21, 23, 25, 35, 42, 43, 99, 151, 156–57, 234, 246, 320, 322, 323

T

Tarnopolsky, Walter, 219, 230, 304–05, 306
Taylor, John Ross, 135
Thadden, Von, 100
Toronto Argonauts, 19, 180
Toronto City Council, 109, 149, 180
Toronto Jewish Youth Council, 30, 31, 98
Toronto Police Commission, 120, 142, 148, 176, 180
Toronto Star, 65, 84, 96, 97, 144, 153, 259, 262, 266, 267, 275, 282, 287, 311, 335
Toronto Symphony Orchestra (TSO), 32–33
Tory, John, 60, 140, 197, 267–68
Treaty Council #3, 86, 89
Trowel, Doug, 219
Trudeau, Pierre, 186, 203, 204–5, 207, 211, 213–14, 219, 220, 224, 230, 240
Truman, Harry, 20, 26
Turner, John, 211, 213, 214

U

Uncivil Obedience, 260
United Church, 59, 95, 97, 195, 241, 267
United Jewish People's Order (UJPO), 30–32
University of New Brunswick, 122, 153
University of Ottawa, 155, 158–59, 226
University of Toronto, 24, 31, 33, 61, 71, 98, 103, 151, 169, 310, 331
University of Western Ontario, 154, 156
US Bill of Rights, 302, 304

V

Vanek, David, 104
Vietnam Mobilization Committee, 120, 121
Vietnam War, 121, 148, 169

W

Waffle faction, 234, 246
Wallace, Henry A., 20–21, 23–24, 26, 35, 319, 320
War Measures Act, 179, 205, 206, 209, 211, 213–15, 249, 308
Weinstein, Leon, 207
Welch, Joseph, 40
When Freedoms Collide, 144, 215, 274, 311
White, Bob, 318–19
Wilmington Public School, 93
Windsor *Star*, 63
Windsor, 57, 58, 59, 62, 63, 64, 65, 66, 117, 118
Wishart, Arthur, 175
Wolfe, Gordie, 38
World War II. *See* Second World War

Y

Yaqzan, Matan, 153—54, 167
Yaremko, John, 274
Yiddish, 24, 31, 42, 103–4, 268, 279, 280, 323
York Borough Council, 119
Young, Coleman, 118

Z

Zaccardelli, Giuliano, 234, 235
Zionism, 26–27, 129, 136, 322–23
Zundel, Ernst, 128–34, 307, 343